Ecology and Reclamation of
Devastated Land

Ecology and Reclamation of Devastated Land

Edited by

Russell J. Hutnik

The Pennsylvania State University

and

Grant Davis

Northeastern Forest Experiment Station
Forest Service, U.S. Department of Agriculture

VOLUME 1

GORDON AND BREACH
New York   Paris   London

Proceedings of a N.A.T.O. Advanced Study Institute on the Ecology and Revegetation of Drastically Disturbed Areas held at the Pennsylvania State University, University Park, Pennsylvania, August 3 to 16, 1969.

PREFACE

NATURAL CATACLYSMS have from time to time drastically altered the ecosystem. Plant and animal communities have been obliterated, creating an environment often hostile to reoccupation by living organisms.

Man has brought about a multifold increase in such land disturbance. He has buried forests, fields, and soil under huge piles of waste material. Most extensive has been the devastation resulting from surface mining. Probably even more offensive to people are the mountains of refuse produced by deep-mine and industrial operations. Such devastated areas are not only unsightly and unproductive, but often pollute both water and air and have a depressing effect on the local populace and communities.

Even while society is demanding ever-increasing supplies of energy and goods from the mining, processing, and manufacturing industries, there is a burgeoning public demand for protection of natural resources and reclamation of devastated lands. Unfortunately, technological progress in the extraction and conversion of minerals has far outstripped technological progress in the reclamation of lands disturbed by these processes.

The problem is world-wide in scope. Derelict landscapes and polluted air and streams are mute but persuasive evidence of the problem in the highly industrialized nations. As underdeveloped countries begin to exploit their natural resources, they too will be confronted by enormous tasks of land reclamation.

With these problems in mind, the International Symposium on Ecology and Revegetation of Drastically Disturbed Areas was planned and organized. It brought together scientists from many countries and many disciplines working on the common problem of disturbed areas. It provided an opportunity for the exchange of information and viewpoints, and it helped focus on similarities of the problems and of the solutions in various parts of the world. The goals of the symposium were to determine our present state of knowledge, define the most critical gaps in this knowledge, and plan future research to provide needed information.

The symposium opened with resumés of current and projected problems, research, and reclamation efforts concerning disturbed land in the various countries represented. These summaries, which are not included in the proceedings, contributed valuable background information and set the mood for the technical sessions which followed. Discussions following the presentation of formal papers were recorded and edited and are included in the proceedings. The papers are grouped into seven sections according to the principal subject.

The symposium was sponsored by the School of Forest Resources, College of Agriculture, The Pennsylvania State University and the Northeastern Forest Experiment Station, Forest Service, U.S. Department of Agriculture. The meeting was held at University Park, Pa., in the University's Conference Center from August 3 to 16, 1969. A total of 101 scientists from 14 countries participated.

Financial support was received from the North Atlantic Treaty Organization under its Advanced Study Institute Program and from a federal grant under Title I of the Higher Education Act of 1965 (administered by the Pennsylvania Department of Public Instruction). Without these funds, the wide participation of scientists from around the world would not have been possible.

We would like to express our appreciation to other agencies that contributed to the success of the symposium. Especially cooperative were Section 21 of the International Union of Forestry Research Organizations, the Pennsylvania Department of Mines and Mineral Industries, the National Coal Association, and the Mined-Lands Conservation Conference.

We would also like to express our sincere appreciation to those individuals who assisted during the program and in the preparation of the proceedings. Kenneth G. Reinhart and Donald N. Thompson performed an invaluable service in reviewing, editing, and preparing the papers included in the proceedings. Nellie B. Caldwell performed the tedious task of transcribing the tapes of the discussion following each presentation. Melvin B. Rockey, the Agriculture Conference Coordinator, handled the administrative details necessary in the preparation and conduction of a successful two-week meeting.

To the participants and session moderators we owe a debt of gratitude for making this symposium a stimulating and memorable occasion.

Russell J. Hutnik
Grant Davis

CONTENTS OF VOLUME 1

CONTENTS

PART II—HYDROLOGY AND POLLUTION

PART III—BIOLOGICAL CHANGES

PART IV—EFFECTS ON PLANTS

CONTENTS OF VOLUME 2

PART VII—ADVANCES IN RECLAMATION

APPENDIX

PART I

PHYSICAL AND CHEMICAL PROPERTIES

SOME CHARACTERISTICS OF SPOIL MATERIAL FROM KAOLIN CLAY STRIP MINING*

J. T. May, H. H. Johnson, H. F. Perkins, and R. A. McCreery

Professor of Forestry, School of Forest Resources, University of Georgia; Associate Professor, Abraham Baldwin Agricultural College, Tifton, Georgia; and Professor and Associate Professor of Agronomy, University of Georgia Agricultural Experiment Station, Athens.

Beds of relatively pure white kaolin occur in the Tuscaloosa formation in Georgia and the two Carolinas as irregular lenses from near the ground surface to depths of more than 60 m. Pockets of off-color kaolin and viscous clays may be intermixed.

The overburden or matrix surrounding the kaolin consists of two to seven strata of sands to clays, varying in thickness from about 0.3 to 6.0 m, with a mean thickness of 1.5 m. Physical and chemical characteristics within a stratum of overburden are relatively uniform, but wide variation exists in soil reaction and the concentration of plant nutrient elements between strata; differences are associated with mode of origin of the strata rather than depth. The pH, Ca and Mg values are generally low except in the presence of lime material. Generally, P and K are low in all strata. Manganese and Fe are most abundant in the upper strata.

Strip mining of kaolin clay has been under way since 1876. Strict specifications by industrial users on color and flow characteristics of kaolin necessitate selective mining and the stock-piling of various grades of clays with the result that mines have an extremely irregular landform, consisting of pits, stockpiles of clay, unmined overburden and spoil. The spoil is an unsorted mixture of all strata, including non-merchantable kaolin and viscous clays. There are extreme variations in particle-size distribution, concentration of nutrient elements, bulk density, infiltration capacity, internal drainage and erosion within small segments of the landscape. A sample of spoil may contain from 0 to 100% sand or 0 to 85% clay. The pH varies from about 4.5 to 8.0. Levels of available P and exchangeable K, Ca, and Mg range from about 2 to 160, 4 to 110,

*Journal Series Paper No. 581. Univ. of Ga. College of Agriculture Experiment Stations, College Station, Athens, Ga. Research supported by mining companies represented on the Kaolin Strip Mining Reclamation Research Advisory Committee and the Georgia Forest Research Council.

6 to 6000 and 2 to 600 ppm, respectively. Intense weathering of old spoils has resulted in lower values of pH and some nutrients than in the more recent spoils. Levels of elements that are considered toxic for plant growth have not been observed.

INTRODUCTION

A wedge-like series of unsorted and unconsolidated but crossbedded sands containing little gravel and much disseminated kaolinitic and micaceous clays constitutes the Upper Cretaceous series from central Georgia to central South Carolina. Cretaceous sediments were derived from the crystalline rocks by vigorous erosion from a youthful surface, and accumulated in coalescing deltas of coarse feldspathic sands. Kaolinite was formed by decomposition of the detrital feldspar in exposed parts of the deltas and, through low gradient erosion of the sands, collected in ponds formed as cut-off segments of the distributaries. Soft kaolin was precipitated slowly in fresh acidic water (Kesler, 1963). Wave erosion breached some ponds, admitting sea water in which kaolin was coagulated rapidly and became harder.

The crystalline rocks of the lower Piedmont include granite, quartz monzonite, diorite, gabbroic rocks, and a wide variety of felsic and mafic schists, gneisses, and pyroclastics. The Tuscaloosa formation, a part of the Cretaceous (Veatch, 1909), reflects rapid deposition without sorting of the clastic material. Most of the iron in the source rocks was taken into solution at the source in mildly acid ground and surface waters and was removed to the sea. However, yellow iron oxide stains and a small amount of bauxite have been formed in the kaolin lenses during the long period of weathering.

Tertiary series overlie the Upper Cretaceous series except near the Fall Line, where erosion has removed them as well as part of the Cretaceous beds. In central Georgia, Tertiary beds remain above the Cretaceous on the high ridges. The two series are separated by a gently undulatory unconformity that truncates the Cretaceous beds at a very low angle, and is essentially parallel with those of the Tertiary (Warren and Thompson, 1943). Geologic characteristics of the Tertiary beds (Eocene, Oligocene, and Miocene) overlying the Cretaceous along the Fall Line have been discussed by La Moreaux (1946), LeGrand and Furcron (1956), and LeGrand (1962).

Commercial mining of kaolin in central Georgia began about 1880. Beds of relatively pure kaolin occur as irregular lenses in the Tuscaloosa formation at elevations of from 300 to 400 ft above sea level. These beds gradually dip to the southeast at an average of 30 to 50 ft/mile. Kaolin lenses may be near the ground surface due to erosion of the Tertiary and Cretaceous formations; or they may occur at depths of 175 to 200 ft below the surface. Today, mining reaches deposits of any economic stripping depth whether the overburden is Tertiary, Cretaceous, or both (Murray, 1963).

This investigation deals with the characteristics of overburden and spoil overlying major kaolin deposits in Twiggs, Wilkinson, and Washington Counties, Ga.

METHODS

Field sampling

Stratigraphic horizons in the highwalls of the overburden above kaolin clay deposits were delineated and described. Soil samples were obtained from two columnar transects randomly located along the high wall in each of 10 different mines. The stratigraphy was described by measuring and recording the thickness and observable characteristics of each distinct stratum. Samples were taken from top to bottom of each highwall and located approximately in the center of each stratum. Fresh faces were exposed before sampling. All areas sampled were being actively mined or had been mined within the past five years. A total of 100 samples were collected from 19 highwalls.

Spoil material was sampled along line transects across the spoils of three mining areas. Bulk samples were taken from 17 sampling areas on one transect, at depths of 0 to 15, 15 to 30, and 30 to 61 cm. Samples from the 15- to 30-cm layer were obtained from other mining areas.

Laboratory analysis

Samples were air dried, ground, and passed through a 2-mm sieve prior to all chemical and physical analysis. The Bouyoucos (1936) hydrometer method of particle-size analysis was used in determination of sand, silt, and clay.

Values for pH were determined potentiometrically on a 1:1 soil:distilled water suspension. Phosphorus, K, Ca, Mg, Na, Zn, Fe, Mn, and Cu were extracted according to the procedures used in the Soil Testing Laboratory, Department of Agronomy, University of Georgia (Page, 1965). Phosphorus was determined colorimetrically; K and Na by atomic emission; and Ca, Mg, Zn, Fe, Mn, and Cu by atomic absorption.

The method of Richards (1949) was used in the determination of moisture desorption properties.

RESULTS AND DISCUSSION

Overburden above operable layers of kaolin is stratified in relatively uniform layers of sands, sandy loams, sandy clays, and clays. The spoil material is an unsorted, diverse mixture of all strata, including non-merchantable kaolin and viscous clays.

Physical properties of overburden

Overburden consists of both Tuscaloosa and Tertiary deposits of varying composition and thickness. Descriptions of well logs (La Moreaux, 1946) classify the overburden into strata of sands, clays, marl, lime, or mixtures of these.

Distinguishable strata ranged in thickness from less than 30 cm to 6 m, with a mean thickness of 1.5 m. Eight percent of the strata were over 2.4 m thick and 15% were less than 63 cm in thickness. The number of strata varied from 2 to 7. Depth to operable clay ranged from 4.2 to 15.0 m, and the depth is increasing each year as the near-surface deposits are worked out.

Textural classes ranged from sand to clay. Particle-size distribution ranged from 3 to 91% sand and 2 to 77% clay. Forty-one percent of the strata contained 60 to 79% sand (Table 1).

TABLE 1

Range of particle-size distribution in the overburden

Sand (2–0.05 mm)		Clay (<0.002 mm)	
Range %	% of Strata	Range %	% of Strata
>80	2	>80	0
60–79	41	60–79	10
40–59	37	40–59	27
20–39	11	20–39	57
0–19	9	0–19	6

Color was quite variable. Reds, yellows, and browns predominated. Calcareous strata were grayish to white. Mottles may occur in any strata below the surface.

Indurated material is limited to scattered manganese and iron concretions. Some marine fossils, soft calcareous rock, and soft partially lignified woody plants also occur.

Chemical properties of overburden

Acidity The pH ranged from 4.0 to 7.9, or from extremely acid to slightly alkaline. Seventy percent of the strata had pH values between 5.0 and 5.9. Only 2% had values above 7.4, and 13% were at 6 or above. Seventeen percent of the strata had values below 5. High pH values were not associated with the highest levels of Ca, Mg, Na, or K. One stratum with a pH of 5.2 had the following chemical properties: Ca – 2660 ppm; Mg – 640 ppm; Na – 3260 ppm; and K – 200 ppm. A stratum with a pH of 7.9 had contents of: Ca – 390 ppm; Mg – 10 ppm; Na – 88 ppm; and K of 6 ppm (Table 2).

Cations Cations of most interest in soil fertility are Ca, Mg, K, and Na. Each of these elements was extremely variable within highwalls and within mines (Table 2). Extractable Ca ranged from a trace to 3660 ppm. In 15% of the strata, representing nearly one-half of the highwalls, Ca was below 11 ppm. In 47% of the strata, representing 15 highwalls, Ca was below 100 ppm. In only 9% of the strata, representing one-fourth of the highwalls, was Ca above 1000 ppm.

Magnesium followed the same pattern as Ca, ranging from a trace to 640 ppm. Magnesium was low in 41% of the strata, with concentrations below 30 ppm. Concentrations were above 300 ppm in three strata and above 100 ppm in only 21% of the strata. More extractable Mg than Ca was found in 20% of the strata.

Sodium, although not an essential plant nutrient, was abundant in many of the strata. Concentrations ranged from a trace to 390 ppm, except for one sample which contained 3260 ppm. Concentrations were above 200 ppm for 23% of the strata and above 50 ppm for 77%. More Na than Ca was found in 51% of the strata.

Potassium was extremely low in nearly all strata, ranging from a trace to 200 ppm. Concentrations were above 100 ppm, or 0.256 meq/100 g, for only 3% of the strata and above 39 ppm for only 9%. Seventy-five percent of the samples had less than 21 ppm and 55% had 10 ppm or less.

TABLE 2

Ranges of pH and chemical concentrations (in ppm) of overburden

Location of overburden	pH	P	K	Ca	Mg	Na	Fe	Mn	Zn
Huber 1 A	4.3–6.4	4–57	4–50	135–915	10–156	18–390	T–16.0	T–80.0	0.6–2.6
Huber 1 B	5.2–7.9	1–160	6–70	390–1601	10–126	88–208	T–16.0	0.5–1.0	0.4–2.0
Huber 2 A	5.4–6.7	3–6	2–16	31–343	16–81	87–130	T–6.8	T–42.5	0.6–3.4
Huber 2 B	5.1–6.0	3–8	2–10	10–530	4–68	88–204	7–16.0	T–43.0	0.4–4.7
Georgia 1 A	4.0–5.9	2–10	4–20	16–1326	8–97	20–70	T–25.0	T–35.6	0.4–3.0
Georgia 1 B	4.2–4.7	1–5	12–18	31–391	87–170	19–22	16.0–25.0	1.0	0.4–0.8
Georgia 2 A	5.0–5.5	1–10	10–38	208–572	54–253	10–32	T–25.0	T–67.6	0.5–1.5
Georgia 2 B	4.3–6.5	4–160	16–50	551–1830	36–260	15–60	T–16.0	1.5–117.0	0.6–4.3
Freeport 1 A	5.1–5.6	3–15	2–22	10–52	10–23	104–143	T–15.0	T–17.5	0.5–1.4
Freeport 1 B	5.0–5.2	2–5	1–4	10–16	3–45	39–52	T–16.0	T–1.0	0.4–8.4
Freeport 2 A	4.8–5.1	1–7	2–12	10–16	10–65	39–215	T	T	0.5–5.6
Freeport 2 B	5.2–5.7	2–12	2–14	10–62	8–44	78–104	T–80.0	T–43.0	0.5–0.5
AIC 1 A	4.3–5.7	4–33	10–90	62–676	9–274	156–229	T–6.0	1.0–8.4	0.6–2.3
AIC 1 B	5.0–5.9	1–10	4–14	52–385	12–115	156–198	T–6.0	T	0.4–0.8
AIC 1 C	4.6–6.0	6–23	4–104	4–292	24–429	8–228	T–9.0	T–6.0	0.4–4.0
AIC 2 A	5.0–5.7	1–12	6–20	83–218	16–61	158–198	T–6.0	T–10.0	0.4–1.0
AIC 2 B	5.2–5.6	1–18	10–22	T–3660	12–68	158–177	T–12.0	T–20.4	0.4–1.0
Thiele 1 A	5.2–5.4	1–18	4–200	T–3660	T–640	177–3260	T–13.0	T–13.0	0.6–3.3
Thiele 1 B	5.3–5.8	6–27	4–178	73–3203	27–560	250–338	T–8.0	T–9.0	0.4–3.0

Other elements Available P ranged from 1 to 160 ppm. Only 8% of the strata had concentrations exceeding 21 ppm. Two samples in strata of lime-rock material had concentrations of 160 ppm. Five samples had concentrations ranging from 21 to 57 ppm. Forty-one percent of the strata had concentrations of 3 ppm or less.

Levels of extractable Fe, Mn and Zn were extremely variable. Iron ranged from a trace to 25 ppm, except for one sample which contained 80 ppm. Concentrations of 16 to 25 ppm were found at all depths but not in all strata. Fifty percent of the samples had only a trace of iron. Manganese was extremely low, except for seven samples with concentrations above 25 ppm; forty-nine percent of the strata had only traces. All concentrations above 10 ppm were in the top strata. Zinc was relatively low, ranging from 0.4 to 8.4 ppm. Eighty-two percent of the strata had concentrations of 2.0 ppm or less. Copper was found only in trace amounts.

Particle-size distribution and chemical properties are not correlated with distance below surface, except for Mn. High soil reaction values may occur at the top or bottom of highwalls. Concentrations of P, K, Ca, Mg, and Na are associated with unusual geologic formations. No direct relationship between soil acidity and the metallic ions existed. Some of the mildly alkaline samples have low concentrations of Ca, Mg, and Na. The stratum with the highest concentration of these cations is strongly acid.

Spoil material

Characteristics of the spoil bank are determined by the type of mining operation. Banks are a mixture of all strata in the overburden. Drag-line mining has left some high spoils with steep slopes, i.e. 15 to 30 m in height and 60° to 75° slope. Pan mining tends to leave the spoil in high banks, with steep to rolling slopes.

There is a wide diversity in particle-size distribution and elements within short distances and at all depths. The percentage of sand ranged from 4 to 75% and clay from 17 to 85%. Generally the surface of the spoil contains a much higher percentage of clay than the undisturbed sites. Thirty-five percent of the spoil samples contained more than 40% clay as compared to 21% of the undisturbed topsoil samples. Thirteen percent of the samples contained more than 60% clay; and 5% contained more than 80% clay. In the mining operation, the rug material, or low-grade clay directly above the merchantable clay, is placed on top of the spoil and is mixed with the spoil in later movements.

The infiltration capacity and the erodibility of spoil material are related to length and steepness of the slope, the sand-clay ratio, the diversity of

TABLE 3

Soil moisture characteristics of the spoil material[a]

Depth cm		Percent moisture for tensions of		
		0.3 bars	3.0 bars	15.0 bars
0–15	Range	6.1–40.6	5.1–33.6	2.0–15.4
	Mean	18.2	13.4	6.7
15–30	Range	5.7–40.6	3.9–33.5	3.0–25.7
	Mean	21.0	14.0	9.7
30–61	Range	7.7–32.2	4.0–24.6	2.9–25.5
	Mean	17.8	9.6	7.8

[a] Based on 51 samples from one mining area.

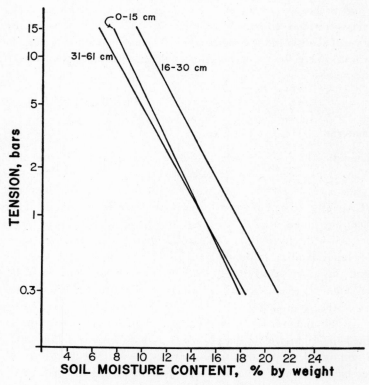

FIGURE 1   Soil-tension curve for different depths.

the sand-clay structure, and the extent of crusting and compaction in the surface layer.

The soil-moisture holding capacity of the spoil is extremely diverse for a single mining area (Table 3). For example, in the 0- to 15-cm layer, soil-moisture content at 0.3 bar ranges from 6 to 41%. However, there is little difference in the moisture desorption curves for the 0- to 15-cm layer and the 30- to 61-cm layer (Fig. 1).

Correlation coefficients for the percent moisture at the 0.3-bar tension as a function of percent clay plus fine silt were determined for each sampling depth (Fig. 2). Correlation coefficients were 0.944 for 0- to 15-cm depth; 0.625 for 15- to 30-cm depth, and 0.667 for 30- to 61-cm depth. The linear equations were $Y = 1.61 + 0.479 X$ for 0- to 15-cm depth; $Y = 7.46 + 0.275 X$ for 15- to 30-cm depth; and $Y = 4.40 + 0.280 X$ for 30- to 61-cm depth. Significant correlation resulted at each of the various sampling depths. Bartelli and Peters (1954) found that available soil moisture was highly correlated with the 1/3-bar moisture tension but not correlated with the 15-bar moisture tension and that available moisture was controlled primarily by the silt fraction.

In general, the range in concentrations of elements within the spoil is similar to the range within the combined strata of the overburden. A com-

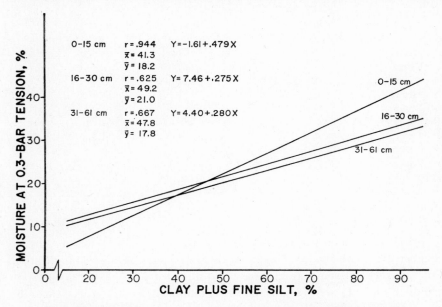

FIGURE 2　Moisture content at the 0.3-bar tension as function of clay plus fine silt for different depths.

TABLE 4

Variations in some physical and chemical characteristics of spoils with depth

Soil Characteristics	15 cm depth	15–30 cm depth			30–61 cm depth
	Mine 1	Mine 1	Mine 2	Mine 3	Mine 1
Sand (%)	7–75	4–75	–	–	12–72
Clay (%)	17–80	17–81	–	–	20–85
pH					
Range	4.6–5.5	4.6–5.4	5.2–6.3	5.0–8.0	4.7–5.5
Mean	5.1	5.1	5.5	6.8	5.1
Avail. P (ppm)					
Range	4–25	2–31	5–6	4–160	2–29
Mean	7	8	7	37	10
Exch. K (ppm)					
Range	4–22	4–32	2–10	8–34	4–32
Mean	10	10	7	19	12
Exch. Ca (ppm)					
Range	7–63	8–88	15–395	9–5960	6–82
Mean	29	37	65	1865	34
Exch. Mg (ppm)					
Range	8–87	8–88	1–13	10–99	4–46
Mean	39	40	4	50	20
Exch. Na (ppm)					
Range	7–41	3–29	7–39	15–50	9–24
Mean	16	10	14	29	15
Mn (ppm)					
Range	0.5–14.0	0.5–22.0	2.0–19.0	0.5–88.0	0.5–28.0
Mean	27	4.8	8.5	11.2	7.0
Fe (ppm)					
Range	10–35	5–40	5–20	5–60	5–40
Mean	17	14	14	17	15
Zn (ppm)					
Range	0.7–2.4	1.0–4.5	1.2–4.2	1.0–18.0	1.0–15.0
Mean	1.7	2.6	2.9	6.3	3.5

parison of data in Tables 2 and 4 reveals that the spoils have a slightly higher pH than found in some undisturbed strata. The high concentrations of K evident in some strata have been diluted due to mixing in the spoil. Sodium and Mg are lower in the spoils than in most strata of overburden. Calcium levels and pH are generally low except in the presence of Fuller's earth or calcareous spoil.

SUMMARY

This is the first part of a study to determine characteristics of kaolin spoil that may affect plant growth in the spoils. The results may not represent the entire range of characteristics within the kaolin mines, but they provide a basis for preliminary evaluation for revegetation prospects.

No elements were found in amounts considered toxic for plant growth. Rather, much of the overburden is deficient in some of the nutrients considered essential for plant growth. For example, if we assume that 200 ppm or approximately 1.0 meq/100 g represents a deficiency level for tree growth, 60% of the strata are Ca-deficient.

Studies are needed to determine the effects of diversity of spoil texture and structure on infiltration capacity, internal drainage, and erosion; and the effect of color on spoil temperature.

LITERATURE CITED

Bartelli, L. J., and D. B. Peters. 1954. Integrating soil moisture characteristics with classification units of some Illinois soils. *Soil Sci. Soc. Amer. Proc.* **23**, 149–151.

Bouyoucos, G. J. 1936. Directions for making mechanical analysis of soils by the hydrometer method. *Soil Sci.* **42**, 225–229.

Kesler, Thomas L. 1963. Environment and origin of the Cretaceous kaolin deposits of Georgia and South Carolina. *Ga. Mineral Newsletter* **XVI** (1–2), 1–11.

LeGrand, H. E. 1962. Geology and ground-water resources of the Macon area, Georgia. *Geol. Sur. Bull.* 72. Ga. Dept. of Mines, Mining and Geol. Atlanta, Ga.

LeGrand, H. E., and A. S. Furcron. 1956. Geology and ground-water resources of central-east Georgia. *Geol. Sur. Bull.* 64. Ga. Dept. of Mines, Mining and Geol. Atlanta, Ga.

La Moreaux, Philip E. 1946. Geology and ground-water resources of the Coastal Plain of east-central Georgia. *Geol. Sur. Bull.* 52. Ga. Dept. of Mines, Mining and Geol. Atlanta, Ga.

Murray, Haydn H. 1963. Mining and processing industrial kaolins. *Ga. Mineral Newsletter* **XVI** (1–2), 12–19.

Page, N. R. 1965. Procedures used by state soil-testing laboratories in the Southern Region of the United States. *Southern Cooperative Series Bull.* No. 102. South Carolina Agr. Exp. Sta., Clemson, S. C.

Richards, L. A. 1949. Methods of measuring soil moisture tension. *Soil Sci.* **68**, 95–112.

Veatch, Otto. 1909. Second report on the clay deposits of Georgia. *Ga. Geol. Survey Bull.* **18**, 82, 92–104.

Warren, W. C., and R. M. Thompson. 1943. Geologic map of the principal clay in Washington County, Georgia, U. S. Geo. Survey Prelim. Map.

DISCUSSION

CORNWELL: Kaolin mining tailings also occur around St. Austell in Cornwall, Great Britain, and some of them are composed of crushed pure silica sand. They are deficient in all the things that you have mentioned, as far as I know.

MAY: We have some of the same type of sands as that, but probably not as high a percentage.

CORNWELL: Most of the plants colonizing the Cornish kaolin tips are those species which vegetate the podzolised soils of that area. These include heather, bracken, and gorse; they form a thin cover on the tips.

TOXICITIES AND DEFICIENCIES IN MINE TAILINGS*

H. B. Peterson and Rex F. Nielson

Professor of Irrigation and Associate Professor of Agronomy
Utah State University, Logan, Utah

Tailings wastes from 15 operations have been studied in the laboratory, greenhouse, and in large containers in the field in an attempt to determine how to grow plants on these materials. Major emphasis has been on Cu tailings.

Great differences in properties have been found to exist among various mine and mill wastes. Tailings from Cu, Pb, Zn, and U mills have one or more adverse characteristics such as poor physical properties, toxic substances, nutrient deficiencies, high acidity or alkalinity, and salinity.

The oxidation of sulfides, such as iron pyrites in Cu wastes, has been found to lower the pH and increase the solubility of several of the heavy metals, such as Cu.

The concentrations of Cu, Fe, etc., were found to be much greater in the roots of plants grown on tailings than in the tops. It was difficult to distinguish the toxicity symptoms on plants because usually more than one element was in excess, such as Cu and Fe, while others were deficient.

The major problem associated with growing plants on Cu tailings is related to low pH. When the pH is in the neutral range, the level of water-soluble Cu is low. As the tailings become more acid, Cu can come into solution resulting in toxic levels to plants. On sites where heavy metals are in solution, it will be necessary to either leach or precipitate these elements and prevent the lowering of the pH.

INTRODUCTION

Waste accumulations from mine and milling operations often detract from the aesthetic appearance of our natural landscape in the West. Finely ground mill tailings also may contribute to air and water pollution prob-

* This work was supported by funds provided by the Bureau of Mines of the U. S. Department of Interior as authorized under the Solid Waste Disposal Act of 1965 and by the Utah Agricultural Experiment Station. The studies have been conducted in close cooperation with Mr. Karl Dean, who is also participating in this program.

lems under adverse climatic conditions. For these reasons, our research is being conducted to develop procedures for stabilizing and beautifying solid-waste accumulations by establishing and maintaining plant covers.

The major portion of this presentation is devoted to the deficiencies and toxicities encountered in attempting to determine how to establish the desired plant populations.

Samples from tailing wastes from different operations have been collected and studied in the greenhouse and laboratory, and some have been tested in large containers in the field. The major emphasis has been on materials from Cu mining operations, and unless otherwise indicated, the results are from trials with materials from Utah operations. The data presented were taken from the results of numerous, rather complicated experiments involving many treatments and plant varieties. Work on the evaluation of plant materials is reported in a companion paper.

NATURE OF TOXICITY PROBLEM

The Cu minerals in most areas are primarily chalcopyrite, bornite, chalcocite, and chorellite with a predominance of chalcopyrite. Although the composition is highly variable at any one mining operation, the following tabulation gives some indication as to the approximate non-Cu mineral composition of a Cu tailings waste.

Mineral	% by weight
Quartz	40
Orthoclase feldspar	30
Biotite	15
Pyrite	3
Clays, zircon, garnet, iron oxides, etc.	12

Sulfides, such as iron pyrite (FeS_2), are constituents in Cu and many other of the waste piles. When at or near the surface of a waste pile, they come in contact with moisture and with the oxygen of the air, and reactions such as the following are likely to take place:

$$FeS_2 + H_2O + 3\tfrac{1}{2}O_2 \longrightarrow FeSO_4 + \underline{H_2SO_4}$$

$$2FeSO_4 + H_2SO_4 + \tfrac{1}{2}O_2 \longrightarrow Fe_2(SO_4)_3 + H_2O$$

$$\text{Hydrolysis } Fe_2(SO_4)_3 + 6H_2O \longrightarrow 2Fe(OH)_3\downarrow + \underline{3H_2SO_4}$$

The sulfuric acid thus produced lowers the pH and increases the solubility of the compounds of Cu, Fe, Zn and other metals and minerals.

To ascertain what soluble toxic ions might be present, water extracts of samples from different locations were analyzed. Some of the data is included in Table 1. It is obvious that the higher concentrations of the metals are in the samples with the lowest pH values. There is also evidence that in one sample or another the B, Cu, Fe, Mn, and Pb concentrations would be, if not removed, excessive for plant growth. The salt content was variable but considerable in most samples.

TABLE 1

Analysis of water extracts of miscellaneous mine waste materials[a]

Sample Source and kind		Conductivity mmhos/cm	pH extract	Content in ppm of saturation extract					
				B	Cu	Fe	Mn	Zn	Pb
N. M.	Cu	9.5	2.2	10	>600	3000	24	21	<5
Mont.	Cu	3.2	5.2	0.4	195	0.6	154	2.4	<5
Mont.	Cu	2.1	7.6	0.2	<1	<0.5	0.6	0.2	<5
Utah	U	8.0	2.9	1.4	475	45	440	103	16
Utah	U	17.4	1.9	24	>600	>5000	1005	77	30
Col.	U	2.3	7.8	0.2	<1	1.0	<0.2	0.2	<5
Col.	U	3.4	7.8	0.4	<1	0.6	<0.2	0.4	<5
Col.	U	5.5	3.4	0.8	25	10	31	61	6
Col.	U	11.7	3.5	1.6	14	9	31	47	20
Col.	U	5.0	8.0	0.3	<1	<0.5	<0.2	0.2	<5
Ariz.	Cu	3.4	7.4	0.1	<1	<0.5	<0.2	0.1	<5
Ariz.	Cu	3.1	7.3	0.1	<1	<0.5	<0.2	0.2	<5
Utah	Cu	9.5	7.0	0.4	<1	0.6	<0.2	<0.6	<5

[a] Each material was wet to point of saturation and the water was then extracted from the solids by use of "suction" to obtain the extract. This was analyzed for total salt by determining the conductivity. Determination was made for the heavy metal content of the extract by Jarrell-Ash Direct Reading Spectrometer. Values printed italic emphasize relation of pH extremes and solubility of metals.

The acid in some of the wastes was applied during ore processing and was not generated by the oxidation of sulfides. It is apparent that lowering the pH must be prevented to minimize the solubility of heavy metals and to inhibit the pyrite-oxidizing organisms. In the case of added acidity, it may be only necessary to leach out the acid. Unfortunately, the ideal range for minimum solubility of the heavy metals is also the range of low solubility of P in a Ca–Na system.

Further evidence that pH is related to the amount of soluble toxic metals in the tailings is indicated in Table 2. Ten samples were taken from one waste pile composed of materials of different ages. In general, the older the material, the lower was the pH and the more salt and heavy metals in solution. This has been further substantiated by the results from multiple sampling and testing of the waste piles.

TABLE 2

Water-soluble metal content and salinity of Cu tailings

Sample[a] No.	pH[b]	Conduc- tivity mmhos/cm	Metal content in ppm on dry-wt basis			
			Cu	Fe	Mn	Zn
1	4.2	3.8	350	2	195	44
2	3.9	7.5	1400	35	390	130
3	2.5	15.0	5700	710	50	32
4	7.1	3.2	3	3	1	c
5	3.3	13.0	2300	360	420	140
6	2.2	11.0	900	875	20	11
7	2.6	3.8	260	20	3	2
8	4.3	3.2	170	8	60	13
9	2.8	10.5	850	30	15	9
10	2.4	12.5	1000	425	25	20

[a] Samples taken (0- to 10-in. depth) from 10 locations on a tailings pond of variable-aged materials in New Mexico.
[b] pH of a saturated paste.
[c] Less than 0.5.

With the exception of fresh Cu tailings from New Mexico (pH 8), crop growth has been better when the samples have been leached. Leaching removes the salts responsible for high osmotic pressures of the soil solution, some accumulated acid, and some soluble toxic materials, if present.

Throughout the study period, lime has been included among the treatments. There has been no general measurable benefit reflected by increased plant growth. This has been somewhat surprising, in view of the potential and active acidity in most of the samples. There are several probable reasons for these results. The period during which the plants have been growing is short enough so that little sulfide oxidation occurs. In addition, the water used in the greenhouse contains calcium and magnesium carbonates and bicarbonates equivalent to 0.32 tons/acre-ft of water. The leaching with this water, as well as irrigation, removed some of the acid and provided considerable lime equivalent. We have found, as would be expected, that when lime is applied before leaching less of the heavy metals are removed. Perhaps the addition of finely ground limestone could prevent slight pH decreases, but the lime may aggravate the P deficiencies that seem to persist. It is anticipated, however, that the addition of lime will be necessary when treating many of the wase piles in preparation for the establishment and maintenance of vegetation. This will be especially necessary if water applied does not contain lime and there is no residual lime in the waste material.

NUTRIENT DEFICIENCIES

With one exception, all of the waste materials thus far sampled have been very low in N and most were deficient in P. The single exception was a sample from a U pile where ammonium hydroxide had been used during processing.

The magnitude of the strong fertilizer interaction is indicated in the data of Table 3. There is also evidence that the P content is increased by adding phosphate fertilizer and even more by the addition of manure. The effects of leaching and fertilizing are illustrated by the data in Table 4. The amount of water necessary for the desired leaching is dependent on the amount of salt, acidity, and soluble toxic metals in the tailings and on the water capacity and moisture content. After some rather detailed studies, we have

TABLE 3

Yield and elemental contents of tall wheatgrass as influenced by fertilizer treatment

Treatment[a]	Yield g/pot	Metal content in ppm				P %
		Cu	Fe	Mn	Zn	
None	1.7	33	116	133	34	0.069
N	5.7	41	85	205	30	0.044
N + Soil	7.2	51	85	127	37	0.050
N + P + K	40.7	31	115	116	22	0.102
N + P	48.3	31	90	75	15	0.089
N + Manure	77.5	39	90	52	23	0.215

[a] N   = 100 lb/acre N as ammonium nitrate.
   Soil   = 5 tons/acre.
   P   = 45 lb/acre P_2O_5 as concentrated superphosphate.
   K   = 250 lb/acre K_2O as potassium sulfate.
   Manure = 10 tons/acre.

2*

TABLE 4

Effects of fertilizers and leaching on the germination, yield, and P content of tall wheatgrass

Leaching treatment in. water	Germ.[a] %	Yield g/pot	P content %	Metal content in ppm			
				Cu	Fe	Mn	Zn
N Fertilizer[b]							
0	83	1.0	0.042	27	100	234	125
1	100	1.6	0.039	25	80	272	103
2	99	2.0	0.034	23	65	270	115
3	96	2.0	0.020	20	73	260	88
N + P Fertilizer[b]							
0	83	3.2	0.125	20	80	165	78
1	100	14.0	0.098	20	80	148	70
2	99	14.5	0.089	18	63	120	53
3	96	16.1	0.098	18	65	130	63

[a] Germination percent given is the average of both fertilizer treatments.
[b] N = 100 lb/acre N as ammonium nitrate.
   P = 45 lb/acre P_2O_5 as concentrated superphosphate.

TABLE 5

Effect of various treatments on plant establishment and growth in selected U and Cu tailings[a]

Sample No.	Leached	N	P	K	Lime	Intermed. Wheatgrass	Sweet Clover
1	+	+	+	+	+	3	1
2	+	+	+	+	0	2	1
3	+	+	+	0	0	2	2
4	+	+	+	+	+	3	1
5	+	+	+	0	+	3	2
6	+	+	+	+	0	2	1
7	+	+	+	0	0	3	1
8	+	+	+	+	0	3	1
9	[b]	+	0	0	0	3	2
10	—	—	—	—	—	2	1
11	0	+	+	0	0	5	5
12	0	+	+	0	0	4	4

[a] Evaluations based on readings made at 43 and 76 days after planting according to the following system: 1 = None, 2 = Poor, 3 = Fair, 4 = Good, 5 = Excellent; + = Response, 0 = No response, — = Not readable.
[b] Not available.

concluded that a minimum leaching is one water-holding-capacity volume. Thus, if the material was dry and had a holding capacity of 1 ft, it would be necessary to apply at least 2 ft of water to effect the minimum desired leaching.

The summary ratings in Table 5 indicate the general response of plants to leaching, N, P, and K fertilizers, and lime. Sample 10 is unique in that only a very sparse growth of grass was produced. There is nothing in the results from analysis of the materials to indicate the reason for the failure.

SYMPTOMS

During the course of study, many unidentified deficiency and toxicity symptoms were observed and recorded on film. In early studies, some of the grasses often showed leaves with numerous probable deficiency and toxicity symptoms and the cause was not apparent. Corn was used at times as an indicator crop throughout the course of the study because it grew rapidly and symptoms of toxicity and deficiencies soon developed. Often the corn grew poorly and developed a reddish purple color on some of the leaves. This appeared to be evidence of a P deficiency, even though phosphate fertilizer had been applied. This coloration seldom, if ever, developed when some organic material was added. To provide more information about this problem, a study was initiated with treatments of various rates and combinations of N, P, and manure. The fertilizers were applied and mixed with the Cu tailings after leaching with 3 in. of water. In addition to corn, bush beans also were grown because we thought this crop would also be a good indicator of deficiencies and toxicities.

The corn developed normally for several weeks and then the leaves began to turn the characteristic reddish purple. The coloring developed first on plants with low levels of phosphate fertilizer and later on those receiving heavier rates. The plants growing in pots treated with manure never developed the reddish color, but did develop yellowing of the new growth with symptoms similar to Mn, or possibly Zn, deficiencies. Treatment of the leaves with various minor elements in the chelate form failed to correct the chlorosis.

The growth of beans was about in proportion to the amount of fertilizer applied. Those plants growing in pots treated with manure developed chlorosis and necrotic mottling of the lower leaves. At the time the pods were completely formed, the plants were harvested for chemical analyses. Part of the results are presented in Table 6. The data indicate that the reddish purple color of the corn leaves probably resulted from P deficiency and that the symptoms of chlorosis in corn could be caused by Mn deficiency in the tops.

TABLE 6

Elemental contents of corn and bush beans grown in soil and in Cu tailings as influenced by fertilizer treatments

Treatment	Plant parts	Metal content in ppm				P %
		Cu	Fe	Mn	Zn	
Corn						
Soil	Tops	11	53	20	32	0.14
Soil	Roots	55	1270	34	69	0.15
Tailings N 50 + Manure	Tops	16	21	13	46	0.16
Tailings N 50 + Manure	Roots	1138	1076	63	90	0.08
Tailings N 50 + P 45	Tops	21	30	15	36	0.06
Tailings N 50 + P 45	Roots	592	1416	193	56	0.05
Tailings N 100 + P 90	Tops	14	35	7	33	0.07
Tailings N 100 + P 90	Roots	540	1570	73	54	0.05
Tailings N 150 + P 135	Tops	12	38	13	32	0.08
Tailings N 150 + P 135	Roots	590	1610	90	66	0.07
Beans						
Soil	Tops	18	159	61	32	0.14
Soil	Roots	60	1340	63	117	0.17
Tailings N 50 + Manure	Tops	80	479	38	66	0.28
Tailings N 50 + Manure	Roots	198	2560	118	225	0.17
Tailings N 50 + Manure	Pods	16	44	44	34	0.31
Tailings N 50 + P 45	Tops	30	62	73	25	0.09
Tailings N 50 + P 45	Roots	550	1550	59	100	0.09
Tailings N 50 + P 45	Pods	24	53	20	30	0.20

Some rather elaborate experiments have been conducted in which varying amounts of the minor elements and P have been applied to the tailings materials in which plants have been grown. In none of these tests was it possible to eliminate the chlorosis developed when P and manure are used as fertilizers. In regular crop production, it is not uncommon for Mn deficiencies to develop when an abundance of Fe has been applied. Zinc deficiencies often are also noted when crops are being grown on areas where there has been abundant manure.

The adverse effects of high Cu and Fe on the root system probably greatly influence the absorption and translocation of other ions and make it very difficult to establish critical limits for the various plant nutrients as well as toxicants.

PARTICLE SEPARATION

In Cu production the tailings are carried by water to the waste ponds. Before depositing the solids, it is possible, by use of a cyclone separator, to divide the coarse or sand-like particles from the fines (slimes). Thus, by selective separation, it would be possible to place the most suitable sized material when preparing an active pond for retirement and stabilization with vegetation. The two fractions of a sample of Cu tailings from Utah were maintained separately. The materials were leached, dried, fertilized, and planted to alfalfa and intermediate wheatgrass. Growth on the sand fraction was less than on the fine fraction and less than on a mixture. The fine fraction was much more difficult to leach and very difficult to dry. It has, therefore, been concluded from this trial and observations made at several tailings ponds that there is no practical advantage in making particle-size separations of the solids. In fact, it would seem to be a distinct disadvantage to do so with Cu tailings as there is very little buffer capacity, water-holding capacity, and fertility in the coarse fractions.

CONCLUSIONS

1. Major differences exist among the various mine and mill wastes. Great differences exist between kinds of operations and also between different ages and exposures of materials from a given operation at one location.

2. Mill tailings from Cu, Pb, U, and other heavy metal operations have one or more of the following characteristics:

a. *Toxic substances.* The presence of specific toxic ions appears to be a probability in many if not all the tailings sampled. Excessive amounts of soluble Fe and Cu were encountered in the Cu tailings wastes and in many of the U wastes.

b. *Nutrient deficiencies.* All but one of the 13 tailings materials thus far evaluated have been very deficient in N; most were deficient in P and a few in K. In addition, there were either minor element deficiencies, toxicities, or imbalances in the samples.

c. *High acidity or alkalinity.* Low pH or acidity was a common problem in contrast to high alkalinity. The low pH appears to be caused by the treatment of ores with acid materials, or by the oxidation of sulfides in the tailings ponds, or by both. Active acidity induced by the addition of acid in the processing of ores appears more easily regulated by leaching than the active and total acidity resulting from the sulfides in the ores.

d. *High salinity.* Excessive concentrations of soluble salts are present in many of the mine waste materials. These salts accumulate from the ore body being processed, are in the water used for the processing, and are concentrated by recycling of the water. In most instances, provision must be made to leach at least a portion of the salt from the material before plants can be grown.

e. *Unfavorable physical properties.* Difficulties have been encountered with some of the physical properties of many of the materials. Some swell upon wetting and either crack or crust upon drying. Others form crusts of some soluble materials which inhibit plant growth. Structure in terms of that normally associated with soil is totally lacking.

Fractionation of the material seems to offer no solution to the problem. The fines (slimes) have been found to be relatively impervious to water, difficult to leach, and have, otherwise, poor physical properties. In contrast, the coarser materials or fractions of tailings have a low water capacity for plant growth and are very deficient in plant nutrients.

It is anticipated that these physical problems encountered in the greenhouse studies will be more severe in the field. They will also be further complicated by the unfavorable water relations and the damage by wind erosion. The latter problems are likely the most difficult of all that are encountered.

3. There is a considerable accumulation of data in the literature on deficiency levels for many elements and plants. There is very little data on limits toxic to various plants and practically no information on interacting toxicities. There is also considerable root damage caused by the metal toxicity. Thus, it is difficult to interpret the data from plant analysis in terms of plant damage resulting from the various elements found in tailings materials.

4. Several of the greenhouse tests were made with corn and beans. It is realized that it is unlikely these plants will be grown on the waste piles. They serve as good indicators that develop some of the symptoms from toxic substances in a very short period of time. Some of the same symptoms develop on grasses, but it takes a considerably greater period of time.

5. Each site must be studied separately to identify the adverse characteristics in preparation for treatment. Even though we made a rather careful analysis of the material, there was one waste sample in which we were unable to grow plants and to identify the cause for the failure.

6. There is considerable evidence that at most sites there are several adverse conditions; it is the interactions of these factors that militate against plant establishment and vegetative growth.

DISCUSSION

McDERMOTT: Have you tried to inoculate or create a normal situation of soil microorganisms?

PETERSON: We have added soil as an inoculant, and we have had companion studies on nitrification activities.

REPP: On Cu tailings in Germany, very special herbs and grasses have developed. Is there any natural vegetation coming in on these open Cu mining tailings which can be analyzed?

PETERSON: Almost none. Tamarisk does come in occasionally, and we have analyzed the roots and the tops of the plants from normal tamarisk and some that have invaded, but we have learned little from it. You must realize that these are harsh sites where precipitation and humidity are low, temperatures often high, and the natural vegetation around some of these areas is very sparse. We have quite adverse conditions for growing plants of any kind on these areas.

KNABE: You reported there was no result of liming, but did the pH increase after leaching? You must expect a liming effect at pH values of about 2.0.

PETERSON: We have some detailed studies on what results from leaching, and these are variable. If the pH is low, it is increased by the leaching with our waters. The amount of increase largely depends on the buffer capacity of these materials. Some of them have essentially no buffer capacity, and others are pretty well buffered. In one leaching I can remember we went from a pH of 2.9 to 5.6 with about 18 in. of water. Usually we attempt to leach only enough to remove the salt.

SOME PROPERTIES OF SPENT OIL-SHALE SIGNIFICANT TO PLANT GROWTH*

W. R. Schmehl and B. D. McCaslin †

Professor and Graduate Research Assistant, respectively, Department of Agronomy, Colorado State University, Fort Collins

Spent oil-shales from two pilot plant operations were analyzed for chemical and physical properties which affect plant growth. Plant-growth studies were then conducted on one of the spent shales in the greenhouse to determine treatments required to obtain normal plant growth.

Chemical analysis of the spent shales revealed that the materials were highly saline, highly alkaline, and low in available phosphorus and nitrogen. There was very little growth of tall wheatgrass (*Agropyron elongatum* L.) and Russian wild ryegrass (*Elymus junceus* L.) in untreated shale. When the shale was mixed with soil in varying amounts, growth on a 50–50 soil-to-spent-shale mixture was still less than 10% of that on normal soil. When excessive soluble salts were removed from the spent shale by leaching with a low-salt water, normal plant growth could be obtained after fertilization with nitrogen and phosphorus.

INTRODUCTION

Oil-shale resources in the United States cover more than 11 million acres of Colorado, Utah, and Wyoming, and the known petroleum reserve from this source is more than 60 times the proven reserve of crude liquid in the United States (U.S. Department of the Interior, 1968). There has been a continuing interest in the processing of shale for oil. With increasing needs

* Published with the approval of the Director of the Colorado Agricultural Experiment Station as Scientific Series Paper No. *1496*. Research supported by a grant from the Colony Development Company, Denver, Colo.

† At present, Graduate Research Assistant, University of Minnesota.

for petroleum in the United States, the use of oil-shale to supplement liquid resources becomes more likely as a major future development.

When the oil-shale industry does develop, large amounts of by-product "spent shale" will result. The disposition of spent shale without polluting the air and water will become a problem for the industry. One of the more feasible solutions to the problem is to vegetate the waste. Hence, there is need to investigate the chemical and physical properties of the spent shale important in plant growth. This paper presents the results of a preliminary study of the properties and growth of plants on spent shale from two retort processes.

MATERIALS AND METHODS

Oil-shale contains no oil as such, but an organic material called "kerogen" which is decomposed into shale oil and other products by heating. Since a good oil-shale yields only 25 to 35 gal of oil per ton of rock, from 80 to 90% of the weight of the original rock appears as spent shale (Stanfield et al., 1951).

The spent-shale materials used in this investigation were by-products from two pilot plant processes. One group of samples came from a retort operated by the Oil Shale Corporation using the Tosco II process (Lenhart, 1969). The second group of samples was by-product material from the U.S. Bureau of Mines gas combustion process (Matzick et al., 1966). Retorts for both processes were operated at about 500 C, but with variations in plant operation and charge material during the pilot plant phases of the shale-oil research. Oil-shale for both pilot plants came from the Piceance Creek Basin near Rifle, Colo.

Two shale-ash by-product materials also were analyzed. Shale ash is the resultant material after the ignition of spent shale at higher temperatures to utilize energy from carbon remaining in the spent shale. Both shale-ash samples came from the Oil Shale Corporation pilot plant near Denver.

The spent-shale and shale-ash samples were analyzed for fertility and salinity status in the Colorado State University Soil Testing Laboratory. Available nutrients were determined by the sodium bicarbonate procedure for P (Olsen et. al., 1954), the diethylenetriaminepentaacetic-acid procedure for Fe and Zn (Lindsay and Norvell, 1969), and by the ammonium acetate procedure for K (Chapman and Pratt, 1961). The other analytical procedures were similar to those used by the U.S. Department of Agriculture's Soil Salinity Laboratory (Richards, 1954).

Plant growth and germination studies were conducted in the greenhouse with Russian wild ryegrass (*Elymus junceus* L.) and Alkar tall wheatgrass (*Agropyron elongatum* L.). Temperatures were controlled to maintain optimum growing conditions, and plants were irrigated with low-salt tap or distilled water.

RESULTS AND DISCUSSION

Fertility and salinity analysis

The results of the spent-shale analyses are summarized in Table 1. All samples represent untreated by-product material from pilot plant operations during the last several years except for sample F. Samples A through E were taken soon after the pilot run; sample F was taken from a part of the tailings pile that had been exposed for about 10 years to atmospheric conditions near Rifle, Colo., where the average annual precipitation is 11 in.

Fertility tests developed for field soils indicate that all spent shales are deficient in available P and samples A and B are low in available K. Available Zn and Fe are adequate in the five spent shales tested. Thus, results show the need for P fertilization on all spent shales and possibly for K fertilization on two materials. Nitrogen deficiency also would be expected because the high retorting temperatures would destroy most N compounds. Plant-growth studies may indicate a need for other fertilizer nutrients.

Conductivity determinations (Table 1) show that all spent shales are too high in soluble salts for normal plant growth. When conductivity of the saturation extract is greater than 4 mmhos/cm, soluble salt content of a soil begins to have an adverse effect on germination and growth of most agricultural plants (Richards, 1954). The pH of the spent-shale samples also is high and probably should be lowered to obtain optimum plant growth.

The $CaCO_3$ equivalent given in Table 1 was determined by acid neutralization and includes all constituents that react with dilute sulfuric acid. This value is high for all samples and probably is largely residual dolomite and calcite from the oil-shale, but it also will include a small amount of nahcolite and trona that has decomposed into its oxides. The retorting temperature is below the decomposition temperature of calcite and most of the dolomite, but above the decomposition temperature of trona and

TABLE 1

Fertility and salinity analysis of six spent shale samples

Spent Shale Designation	Lab. No.	Retort Process	Conductivity[a] mmhos/cm 25 C	pH Saturation Paste	pH 1:5 Shale:Water	CaCO₃ Equiv. %	Available Nutrients			
							P ppm	K ppm	Zn ppm	Fe ppm
A	3766	Tosco II	16.0	9.7	9.9	40.0	8.5	27	–	–
B	7972	Tosco II	11.3	9.1	9.4	11.0	3.7	40	>10.0	>40
C	4216	Tosco II	26.0	8.9	9.3	31.2	6.7	135	8.4	>40
D	240	Gas Combustion	9.0	8.6	9.2	31.4	5.6	360	4.7	>40
E	241	Gas Combustion	22.0	8.7	9.0	31.2	3.6	>400	5.8	>40
F	243	Gas Combustion	12.0	8.7	9.0	30.8	3.6	>400	2.9	>40

[a] Conductivity of the solution removed from spent shale saturated with distilled water (Richards, 1954).

nahcolite (Matzick, 1966). The closeness of values for four of the six samples has no particular significance other than uniformity in the carbonate content of the charge material.

The soluble salt content of the "saturation extract" from the spent shales was analyzed to determine the kinds of ions and nutrient balances. Saturation extract refers to the aqueous solution removed from a shale-distilled water mixture at "saturation percentage" (Richards, 1954). Saturation percentage is the moisture content at which free water first begins to appear as water is added to the sample. The value is about twice field capacity moisture content. The salt content and pH of the saturation extract are closely related to plant growth (Richards, 1954).

Results of the analysis of the saturation extract from the spent-shale samples are given in Table 2. Soluble Na is the principal water-soluble cation for all samples except F. Sodium ranges from 24% of the total water-soluble cations in sample F to about 74% in sample E. As an approximate guide, plants will not grow satisfactorily where Na constitutes more than about 50% of the water-soluble cations in the saturation extract (Richards, 1954). The sodium adsorption ratio (SAR) of the saturation extract is a better guide for the effect of water-soluble Na. Generally, the SAR should be less than 10 to obtain normal plant growth (Richards,

TABLE 2

Water-soluble ions in the saturation extract removed from six spent shale samples

| Ion | Spent shale designation | | | | | |
| | A | B | C | D | E | F |
	Equivalents per million					
Ca^{++}	26.4	21.2	18.5	31.5	20.0	19.5
Mg^{++}	1.6	18.4	78.5	12.0	34.5	77.5
Na^+	124.0	113.1	195.8	37.0	156.6	30.5
K^+	1.4	0.7	2.6	7.0	16.6	9.0
$CO_3^=$	5.9	0.2	1.2	0.0	0.8	0.4
HCO_3^-	1.9	3.0	1.6	0.6	1.8	0.8
Cl^-	3.0	1.0	4.5	0.8	2.5	2.5
$SO_4^=$	137.5	139.3	266.3	99.3	191.8	123.5
SAR[a]	33.1	25.5	28.4	8.0	30.2	4.5

[a] SAR (Sodium Adsorption Ratio) $= \dfrac{Na}{\left(\dfrac{Ca + Mg}{2}\right)^{\frac{1}{2}}}$; Na, Ca, and Mg expressed in equivalents per million in saturation extract (Richards, 1954).

1954). The SAR values of samples D and F are less than 10, whereas those for the other spent shales are 25 and higher. Thus, not only are the spent shales too saline, but four of the samples are excessively high in water-soluble Na. The decomposition of nahcolite and trona is probably the principal source of the soluble Na. The analysis indicates that reclamation treatments to remove excessive salinity and Na will be required before normal plant growth can be expected. This is generally accomplished by applying leaching water to remove excessive salts and applying gypsum to reduce Na.

The Ca–Mg balance is another factor that must be considered. It is difficult to specify a limiting Ca–Mg ratio, but if Mg becomes excessively high, a Ca deficiency may be expected. This ratio is of the order of 0.24 for samples C and F, and problems of Ca nutrition might be expected under some conditions for plants with a high Ca requirement. Some decomposition of dolomite may occur during retorting with the recrystallization of calcite (Matzick, 1966). This may be the cause for the low Ca–Mg ratio in samples C and F.

The fertility and salinity analysis of two shale-ash samples is given in Table 3. The pH of the shale ash is two to three units higher than that for spent shale, and is so high that little if any plant growth can be expected without treatment to reduce the alkalinity. The high pH is caused apparently by conversion of dolomite and possibly some calcite to the oxides at the high ignition temperatures. As with the spent shales, both shale-ash samples are highly saline. Levels of available soil P and K are both adequate. The saturation extract from the shale-ash samples was not analyzed. Only spent-shale samples were studied in subsequent experiments because of the greater probability of these kinds of by-products in shale-oil processing.

TABLE 3

Fertility and salinity analysis of two shale-ash samples

Sample	Source	pH Paste	pH 1 : 5	Conductivity mmhos/cm 25 C	$CaCO_3$ Equiv.	Available nutrients	
						P ppm	K ppm
1	Reheated spent shale	12.1	12.0	11.0	38.0	20	355
2	Reheated spent shale	10.9	10.8	7.0	42.2	42	150

Physical properties of spent-shale samples

Some physical properties of the spent shales are given in Table 4. Samples A, B, and C are much finer grained than the other three samples. This is a reflection of variations in the preparation of the charge material introduced into the retort. Field moisture capacities indicate the spent shales have moisture holding properties adequate for good plant growth. Low cation exchange capacities for the samples show that the spent shales have only limited charged surfaces capable of holding exchangeable nutrient cations.

TABLE 4

Particle size, field moisture capacity, and cation exchange capacity of spent-shale samples

Sample Designation	Particle Size—% of Total			Field Moisture Capacity[a]	Cation Exchange Capacity, 2-mm Fraction
	>8 mm	8–2 mm	<2 mm	%	meq/100 g
A	0	20	80	18.5	7.6
B	0	11	89	22.2	5.6
C	0	11	89	20.4	6.0
D	29	23	48	22.1	7.8
E	43	33	24	20.5	8.0
F	31	25	43	16.8	8.6

[a] Total material for samples A, B, C; 2-mm fraction for samples D, E, and F.

In initial efforts to determine the amount of water required to remove salts from laboratory columns of spent shale from the Tosco II process, considerable difficulty was encountered in wetting the material. Under a 1-in. head, distilled water penetrated only to a depth of $1\frac{1}{2}$ in. in 5 days. Subsequent tests showed that neither calcium-sulfate-saturated water nor the use of wetting agents (Atlas Renex 30 or Tween 80) in the water was successful in obtaining sufficient water penetration to remove salts by leaching.

Other studies revealed that if the first water added was mixed mechanically with the spent shale and then air-dried, the spent shale could be wetted easily in subsequent treatments. An experiment conducted to determine the number of wet-dry cycles required to insure wetting indicated that only one wetting was required to promote the absorption of water. Resistance to wetting after the high-temperature ignition to remove kerogen apparently is temporary; once a monolayer of water is adsorbed, the spent shale is rewetted with ease, even after subsequent air drying. There was no wetting problem with the spent shales from the gas combustion process.

The results suggest that mechanical mixing or other treatment with water may be required with some spent shales to promote wetting. This should pose no major problem, however, and can probably be solved by treating the spent shale after retorting.

Plant growth studies with non-reclaimed shale

Emergence and plant growth studies were conducted in a glass-type greenhouse with spent shale C to which water was added the first time by mechanical mixing. Salts were not removed by leaching. Fertilizer was applied at rates of 50 ppm N, 22 ppm P, and 37 ppm K. The objective was to determine emergence and growth that could be obtained with minimum treatment of the spent shale.

Two Colorado soils, Nunn clay loam and Larimer sandy loam, were mixed with the spent shale in varying proportions. They were fertilized and placed in $\frac{1}{2}$-gal ice cream cartons, then planted to Russian wild ryegrass or Alkar tall wheatgrass. Russian wild ryegrass was selected because of known drought and salinity tolerance, and Alkar tall wheatgrass was planted because it has a very high salinity tolerance. Moisture was maintained at field moisture capacity (Table 4). The treatments were conducted in duplicate and plants were grown for a period of 7 weeks, beginning in July 1966. Air temperatures during the day, controlled by cooling fans, did not exceed 90 to 95 F. A cheesecloth shade on a wooden frame was suspended over the experiment to prevent excessively high surface temperatures in the spent shale.

Results of the greenhouse experiment (Table 5) show that emergence in 100% spent shale was delayed 6 days and percentage emergence was reduced to about 20% of that obtained with 100% soil. Results with soil-shale mixtures were intermediate. Reasonably good emergence was obtained with the 50-50 mixture.

Dry-matter production was affected more adversely by the spent shale than was emergence. Although the plants emergence in 50–50 soil-to-spent-shale mixtures, growth was very poor. The results demonstrate quite conclusively that reclamation will be required to reduce the toxic effects of soluble salts and high Na before plant growth can be maintained in the spent shale.

Wheatgrass was affected less by the adverse effects of the spent shale than was the ryegrass. Neither grass, however, grew satisfactorily on the non-reclaimed spent shale.

TABLE 5

Emergence and growth of two grasses in spent shale—soil mixtures in the greenhouse

Soil	Soil-to-Spent-shale[b] Ratio	Days to first emergence (both grasses)	Wheatgrass[a]		Ryegrass[a]	
			Emergence %	Dry matter Produced g/pot	Emergence %	Dry matter Produced g/pot
Nunn	100–00	3	100	10.5	100	5.9
Nunn	50–50	5	100	4.5	85	0.5
Nunn	25–75	8	88	0.8	78	0.1
Nunn	10–90	8	46	0.7	47	0.1
Larimer	100–00	3	100	9.5	100	5.9
Larimer	50–50	6	86	1.9	78	0.2
Larimer	25–75	8	78	0.6	33	<0.1
Larimer	10–90	8	65	0.3	28	<0.1
Spent shale	0–100	9	18	0.1	29	<0.1

[a] Highly significant F test for treatment effects for both emergence and dry matter production.

[b] Spent shale C.

Reclamation to remove soluble salts

Since the chemical analysis and plant-growth studies indicated the need to remove excess salts, an experiment was conducted to determine if salts could be removed by leaching with low-salt water.

Spent shale sample C, pretreated to insure wetting, was placed in plastic tubes of $1\frac{3}{4}$-in. inside diam. The shale was packed to give a uniform bulk density of 74 lb/ft³ in columns of 6, 12, 18, 24, 30, and 36 in. The water saturation capacity of the shale in the column was 100 ml (2.5 in.) per 6 in. of column. Distilled water was added to each column under a constant 1-in. head. The leachate was collected and successive 100 ml samples (2.5 in. of water) were removed for measurement of conductivity, pH, and SAR.

Conductivity measurements, summarized in Fig. 1, show that the soluble salts were removed rapidly. Conductivity of the leachate was below 4 mmhos/cm after passing 5 in. of water through the 6-in. column and after 10 in. of water through the 36-in. column.

Although the conductivity of the leachate in all columns was less than 4 mmhos/cm after collecting 10 in. of water, leaching was continued until from 15 to 20 in. were collected. The amount varied with column length.

When leaching was discontinued, columns were separated into 6-in. segments, distilled water was added to saturation percentage, and the saturation extract was removed and analyzed for total soluble salt. Soluble salt remaining in the shale after leaching, expressed as conductivity of the saturation extract, is given in Table 6. The results show that the soluble

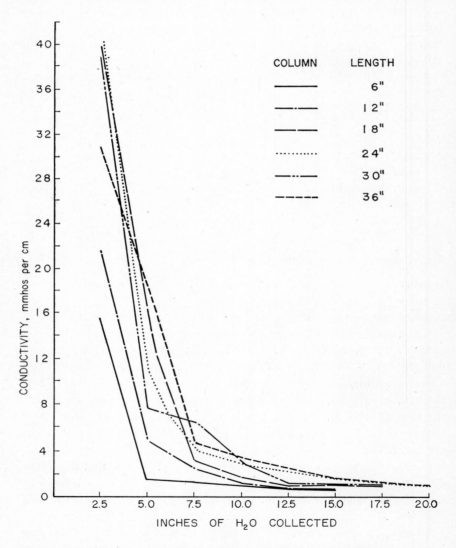

FIGURE 1   The conductivity of aqueous leachates collected from spent shale columns.

salts could be reduced below the tolerance limit of 4 mmhos/cm by leaching with water. Salts remaining in the column were lowest at the top and highest at the bottom of the column as indicated by comparing the average conductivity for the whole column with the conductivity from the bottom 6 in.

About 62% of the soluble salt must be removed from spent shale C to reduce the conductivity of the saturation extract below 4 mmhos/cm. The relative amount of salt removed by passing 2.5 in. of water per 6-in. depth was calculated for the six columns.

The results (Table 7) show that about 75% of the salt was removed in the 6-in. column to 82% or more for the 30- and 36-in. columns. Salt removal is slightly more efficient for the longer columns because water is

TABLE 6

Soluble salts remaining in spent shale C after leaching in columns with distilled water

Column length in.	Leachate in.	Conductivity of the saturation extract mmhos/cm, 25 C	
		Average for column	Conductivity of column, bottom 6 in.
6	15	1.33	1.33
12	15	1.50	1.78
18	$17^1/_2$	1.83	2.53
24	20	1.45	1.92
30	20	1.50	2.08
36	20	1.77	2.09

TABLE 7

Soluble salts removed by passing 2.5 in. of water per 6 in. depth through spent shale C placed in columns

Length of column in.	Leachate in.	Salt removed % of total present
6	2.5	75.0
12	5.0	77.9
18	7.5	78.5
24	10.0	83.0
30	12.5	83.2
36	15.0	81.9

in contact with the salt in the shale for a longer time. In extrapolating the results to field conditions, it must be recognized that the bulk density was 74 lb/ft³ and that a low-salt water was used. More leaching water might be required if a high-salt water were used or if the bulk density were increased.

The pH of successive leachates increased from 7.3 to about 9.1, then decreased to about pH 8.7. No great difficulty would be expected with this pH, but it is a borderline value and further research is needed to determine possible effects of the pH of spent shale on plant growth.

Analysis of the spent shale after removal of soluble salts showed that the SAR after leaching with distilled water ranged from 9 to 12, which is equivalent to about 10 to 12% exchangeable Na on the exchange complex. This is high for normal crop-plant growth and indicates the possible need for gypsum as an amendment if the spent shale is leached with a low-Ca water.

In a second experiment, gypsum was added to the surface of the spent shale column to determine the influence of additional soluble Ca on the rate of water movement through the spent shale. The application of gypsum had little effect on the rate of movement of water through the column at any stage of reclamation. Thus, the exchangeable-Na level of the spent shale appeared to have little or no effect on water movement. This normally is a problem in high-Na soils containing swelling clays. X-ray examination of spent shale C, however, revealed no swelling clay. Therefore, the lack of a dispersive effect of the high level of exchangeable Na probably resulted from the combined effect of the absence of swelling clay and the low cation exchange capacity of the spent shale (Table 4).

Greenhouse experiment

An experiment was conducted in a fiberglass house in ½-gal containers with spent shale C reclaimed by leaching with low-salt tap water until the conductivity of the leachate was about 2 mmhos/cm. Nitrogen, P, and K fertilizers were applied singly or in combination at rates of 100, 200, and 100 ppm N, P, and K, respectively. Two additional treatments were applied at the NPK fertilizer level: (1) micronutrients Cu, Mn, B, Zn, and Fe; and (2) a quartz-sand mulch was placed in the surface to moderate surface soil temperatures. Two treatments with unleached spent shale and one field soil were included for controls. All treatments were conducted in triplicate. Alkar tall wheatgrass was planted February 21 and harvested April 1, 1969.

Yield results summarized in the first data column of Table 8 were highly significant for treatment effects. There were no significant differences among the three NPK treatments on the reclaimed spent shale (see footnote "a" to Table 8); therefore, the three NPK treatments were averaged. Plant

TABLE 8

Yield of tall wheatgrass on spent shale C after reclamation and fertilization, and salinity and fertility analysis after cropping

Treat-ment	Yield [c] g/pot	SAR	Conducti-vity mmhos/cm 25 C	pH Paste	Available nutrients				
					NO$_3$-N ppm	P ppm	K ppm	Zn ppm	Fe ppm
Spent shale, leached									
Check	0.08	2.1	6.0	8.1	0.1	6.2	39	7.5	42.5
N	0.15	1.9	8.0	8.1	37.7	5.4	39	6.7	37.8
P	0.07	1.8	5.0	8.1	0.1	64.7	37	8.1	36.8
NP	3.41	1.2	8.0	8.0	5.0	66.9	12	8.0	33.4
NPK [a]	3.33	1.6	7.3	8.0	4.9	66.9	21	7.5	34.7
Spent shale, unleached									
Check	nil	28.2	26.0	8.2	6.2	6.7	135	8.4	57.5
NPK [b]	0.10	27.5	27.5	8.3	42.2	61.3	290	8.8	57.5
Nunn soil									
NPK	3.20	<1.0	2.2	7.7	50.7	14.5	275	0.9	5.4

[a] Average of 3 treatments—NPK, NPK plus micronutrients, NPK plus micronutrients with quartz-sand mulch.

[b] Average for NPK plus micronutrients, and NPK plus micronutrients with quartz-sand mulch.

[c] Highly significant F test for treatment effects.

growth for the averaged NPK treatments was as good in the spent shale as in the field soil similarly fertilized. Growth was very poor on the leached material for the check, N, or P treatments, but there was a 40-fold yield increase over the check on the NP combinations. Plant growth was equally poor on the unleached material even though fertilized with NPK.

Deficiencies in both N and P were so marked that satisfactory plant growth could not be obtained without the combination. No additional benefit was obtained by the further addition of K fertilizer. The extreme N deficiency was predictable, but the P deficiency was more intense than indicated by the fertility analysis (Table 8). The soil test indicates available Zn and Fe were adequate, and no response to these nutrients was observed.

The quartz-sand mulch had no influence on the yield for the leached spent shale. Thermocouples placed in the containers at about $\frac{1}{2}$-in. depth showed no difference between temperatures for the mulched and unmulched treatments. The combined effects of a lower light intensity during February and March and the diffuse light in the fiberglass greenhouse may have reduced the influence of the dark color on the surface temperature in the spent shale.

The spent shale was analyzed after cropping for fertility and salinity status. The results given in Table 8 show that the fertilizer treatment increased NO_3—N, available P, and K, but had little influence on available Zn or Fe. Although the level of available K was increased by K fertilization, there was no yield response because the original supply was adequate for optimum plant growth.

Reclamation by leaching with tap water reduced the conductivity from about 26 to an average of 6.8 mmhos/cm and reduced the SAR from 28 to about 2 (Table 8). The latter SAR value is below the SAR of 9 to 12 obtained when the shale was reclaimed with distilled water in the column study previously discussed. The tap water, with a conductivity of 53 micromhos/cm and an SAR of less than unity was more effective in lowering the SAR of the spent shale than was the salt-free water used in the column study.

The conductivity of the saturation extract removed after cropping was several times greater than the conductivity of the leachate after reclamation for cropping. There may have been channeling during the pre-leaching or the spent shale may not have been entirely wetted. Either effect would result in the failure to remove all salt from the spent shale. However, tall wheatgrass was selected as the test crop because it has high salt tolerance. This may explain, in part, the good growth in the spent shale which was still quite saline.

The reclamation (leaching) treatment reduced the available K from 135 to 39 ppm K (Table 8). Cropping without the application of K fertilizer further reduced available K to 12 ppm, a level generally considered deficient. The application of K, however, did not increase the yield of tall wheatgrass in this experiment. The results suggest that available K may become deficient with continued cropping unless K fertilizer is added. The spent shale does contain mineral sources of K, such as feldspar and mica (Stanfield et al., 1951), but the release of available K from these minerals will be slow. Nor can much exchangeable K be retained by the spent shale because the cation exchange capacity is only about 6 meq/100 g (Table 4).

Other factors in need of investigation

The dark color of the spent shale may cause lethal temperatures for germinating seeds. Unshaded spent shale in a glass house reached 140 to 150 F at about ½-in. depth. A light-colored surface mulch may be required through the germination period until the surface is shaded by plants. The kind and amount of mulch feasible under field conditions needs investigation. Talus or soil from the local area is a possible source of surface mulch.

Bulk density of the spent shale will be increased by mechanical operations during piling. The resulting compaction may be sufficient to retard air and water movement to such an extent that salt removal and root growth will be restricted greatly. If the spent shale in the pile is compacted in such a manner, several feet of loose material should be left on the surface to establish plant growth. Investigations are needed to determine the depth of loose material required for continued plant growth, and the need to install tile drains or other mechanisms to remove saline drainage water from the top several feet of loose spent shale without removing soluble salts from the bulk of the pile of spent shale.

In most areas where oil-shale deposits are found, rainfall is low. Irrigation water will be required for reclamation and to establish plant growth. Continuous use of supplemental water may be required in some areas to maintain sufficient vegetative growth to control wind and water erosion of the spent shale. The need for supplemental water will vary with the plant species, and research is needed to determine the species best adapted to vegetation of spent shales in low-rainfall areas.

SUMMARY

Spent oil-shales from two pilot plant operations were analyzed for chemical and physical properties that relate to plant growth. Plant-growth studies were then conducted on one of the materials in the greenhouse to determine treatments required to obtain normal plant growth.

1. Chemical analysis of spent shale from the processing of oil-shale revealed the material was highly saline, highly alkaline, and low in available P and N.

2. Growth of wheatgrass and Russian wild ryegrass in the greenhouse in untreated spent shale was almost nil. When the spent shale was mixed with soil, growth still was far below the level that would be practical in the field, even with a mixture of equal weights of soil and spent shale.

3. Soluble salts could be leached readily from spent shale in columns packed to a bulk density of 74 lb/ft^3.

4. When one of the spent-shale materials was reclaimed by leaching with low-salt water to remove excess salts, good growth of tall wheatgrass was obtained if both N and P fertilizers were applied. There was no yield response to K nor to micronutrients for the first crop after reclamation.

LITERATURE CITED

Chapman, H. D., and P. F. Pratt. 1961. *Methods of analysis for soils, plants, and waters.* Univ. of California, Riverside, 309 p.

Lenhart, A. F. 1969. The Tosco process—economic sensitivity to variables of production. *Proc. Am. Pet. Inst., Div. Refining.* Chicago, May, 1969. p. 907–925.

Lindsay, W. L., and W. A. Norvell. 1969. Development of a DPTA micronutrient soil test. *Agronomy Abstracts, Amer. Soc. Agron.* p. 84.

Matzick, A., R. O. Dannenberg, J. R. Ruark, J. E. Phillips, J. D. Lankford, and B. Guthrie. 1966. Development of Bureau of Mines gas-combustion oil-shale retorting process. U. S. Dep. Interior, *Bur. Mines Bull.* **635**, 199 p.

Olsen, S. R., C. V. Cole, F. S. Watanabe, and L. A. Dean. 1954. Estimation of available phosphorus in soils by extraction with sodium bicarbonate. *U. S. Dep. Agr. Circ.* **939**. 19 p.

Richards, L. A. (ed.). 1954. Diagnosis and improvement of saline and alkali soils. *U. S. Dep. Agr. Handbook* **60**, 160 p.

Stanfield, K. C., J. C. Frost, W. S. McAuley, and H. N. Smith. 1951. Properties of Colorado oil shale. *U. S. Dep. Interior, Bur. Mines Report of Investigation* **4825**. 27 p.

U. S. Department of the Interior. 1968. Prospects for oil shale development—Colorado, Utah, and Wyoming. U. S. Dep. Interior. 134 p.

DISCUSSION

MORGAN: What is this oil used for that you extract from the shale?

SCHMEHL: Oil is derived from the shale by the thermal decomposition of an organic material called kerogen. The kind of oil that is recovered will depend upon the process that is used. Some processes will give more volatile materials as well as liquid oil, whereas other processes may give a solid, tar-like material. The extracted material will be used to produce the various oils similar to those obtained from liquid petroleum.

CORNWELL: Was the kerogen completely destroyed by heating? Was there any nitrogenous residue from the kerogen?

SCHMEHL: Only about 75% of the organic material is converted to oil and gas. Analyses by Stanfield et al. (1951) show that about 38% of the N remains in the spent shale. An average spent shale may contain 3 to 4% organic residue and 0.15 to 0.19% N.

H. PETERSON: Because of the many problems of pollution and of revegetation of spoils as identified by Schmehl, we are hoping that an in-place distillation process will work.

REPP: What is the toxic substance in this shale?

SCHMEHL: It appeared to be largely salt toxicity in the materials that we tested, but other toxic materials may appear with further testing.

GOOD: Since you have been considering leaching these shales after the oil has been removed, has consideration been given to the leach water?

SCHMEHL: Yes, this has been discussed. The general thinking is that the main part of the pile might be stored in a canyon and only the top 3 to 4 ft would be leached to remove salts. The bulk of the salts would remain in the pile. Thus salts removed in the drainage water would contribute very little to stream pollution.

THIRGOOD: Are you trying to establish vegetation on wastes in areas which were not vegetated before mining?

SCHMEHL: Not as a part of this project. However, vegetation is very sparse in many of the areas. The amount of vegetation will vary greatly because of differences in elevation, rainfall, and soils. The areas are important, however, as range for stock and wildlife and as a part of the watershed for irrigation and municipal water supplies.

EDAPHOLOGICAL PROBLEMS ASSOCIATED WITH DEPOSITS OF PULVERIZED FUEL ASH

W. N. Townsend and D. R. Hodgson

School of Agricultural Sciences, Leeds University, England

Pulverized Fuel Ash (PFA) is the fine ash remaining after pulverized coal has been burnt at temperatures around 1500 C. Apart from a small content of unburnt carbon, it is entirely inorganic. Its empirical composition is: silica and alumina (ca. 75%), Fe oxides (ca. 10%), alkaline earth elements (ca. 6%), alkali metals (ca. 5%), S (ca. 1%), and traces of most other naturally occurring elements. It is essentially sterile.

Physically the ash consists mainly of glassy spheroidal particles with a relatively narrow size range, mostly within the coarse silt fraction.

The edaphological problems fall into three categories: (1) the adequacy of plant nutrients, (2) the presence of directly toxic factors, and (3) the physical nature of the deposits.

In terms of major nutrients, the ash is amply supplied with K but is low in available P; it contains no N. The micronutrient status is adequate.

In contact with water, appreciable hydrolysis of the mineral fraction occurs which leads to excessive salinity; pH values as high as 11 often develop. The hydrolysis also produces contents of water-soluble B as high as 60 to 80 ppm. Until these levels can be reduced, either by treatment or by natural weathering, the establishment of higher plants is not possible.

When allowed to settle in the mass, PFA exhibits a pozzolanic activity and becomes progressively harder and less permeable to air and moisture. Root development is severely restricted and, unless this tendency to set is reduced, plant establishment is severely curtailed. On the other hand, if PFA deposits dry out before particle aggregation can occur, severe wind erosion problems arise.

INTRODUCTION

The majority of modern electricity-generating stations in the U.K. burn coal which is pulverized so that 80% passes a 200-mesh sieve. It is then fluidized in a hot air stream and passed through a burner where

45

it is combusted with additional air giving temperatures of the order of 1500 C.

During the combustion up to about 97% of the C is oxidized, although older, less-efficient furnaces oxidize only 90%. The mineral impurities and mineral ash in the coal are consequently ignited at the furnace temperature before being carried from the combustion chambers. While a small proportion falls to the bottom of the furnace as clinker, the bulk has to be separated from the flue gasses as a finely comminuted ash. The separation is effected by both mechanical and electrostatic precipitators. The pulverized fuel ash (PFA) may be collected dry or "conditioned" (moistened slightly to reduce possible dust nuisance), and removed for disposal by truck. Otherwise it may be converted into an aqueous slurry and transported via pipeline to a suitable disposal site, either a lagoon formed by specially constructed earth banks or a disused gravel or clay pit, where the ash particles settle out in layers similar to a sedimentary deltaic deposit. Adequate supplies of water are necessary for this method of disposal, and this may involve constructing reservoirs and recirculating the pumping water. Occasionally several small lagoons adjacent to a power station are filled and emptied in rotation. The moisture content of drained lagooned ash varies widely, ranging from 20 to 40%.

Disposal schemes for the 2000-MW coal-burning power stations producing 3/4 to 1 million tons of PFA per year are designed so that economies in land use can be achieved by raising the ash to considerable heights above ground level. For example, one method consists of successive lifts of bunds to raise lagoon upon lagoon, creating layers each 15 to 20 ft thick, progressively diminishing in area, and having a flat top buttressed by steeply sloping sides. The bunds, built of earth, shale, or compacted PFA faced with waste colliery shale, comprise a high proportion of the total volume of the hill. Another proposed method involves mounding the conditioned ash to heights up to 165 ft using a conveyer belt system. "The resulting land form becomes almost geological rather than engineering in extent, and geological shapes, strata, dipped plains, escarpments are necessary to achieve a general structural accord with the landscape" (Weddle, 1968).

In physical terms, PFA consists predominantly of discrete, white or colorless, glassy, spherical particles with a small proportion of black particles, mainly magnetite. Quartz, mullite, and hematite are also present, usually in trace quantities. The glassy spheres may be solid or may contain bubbles in varying numbers. Some are filled with gas occlusions and give the appearance under the microscope of a whitish sponge while others contain only a few small bubbles. About 2 to 3% of the ash consists of thin-walled glass bubbles, or cenospheres, which float on the surface of water and are commonly known as "floaters."

The size distribution of particles is comparable with that of a "fine sand" or "silt." Particle-size analyses of PFA using the International scale are presented in Table 1. In each sample, particles in the size range 0.2 mm to 0.002 mm predominate.

TABLE 1

Particle-size analysis of PFA (percent by weight)

Sample	Coarse sand 2.0–0.2 mm	Fine sand 0.2–0.02 mm	Silt 0.02–0.002 mm	Clay <0.002 mm
A	3	51	45	1
B	1	31	64	4
C	1	40	58	1
D	<1	26	70	4

The chemical composition is complex and variable, but there is a qualitative similarity between samples, even those from different coal sources. A typical analysis will include:

	%	RANGE
SiO_2	48	40 to 60
Al_2O_3	26	20 to 40
Fe_2O_3	10	6 to 16
CaO	4	2 to 10
MgO	2	1 to 4
SO_3	1	0.5 to 2
$Na_2O + K_2O$	4.5	2 to 6

Traces of most other naturally occurring elements are also included. A small proportion of the ash is water-soluble, and gives an alkaline solution containing principally Ca and sulphate together with Mg, Na, K, silicate, and bicarbonate ions.

PFA also possesses pozzolanic properties, i.e. it reacts with lime in the presence of water to form a cementitious material. It also has self-hardening propensities when subjected to compaction; the latter may be related to the calcium sulphate content or, according to Simons and Jeffrey (1960), to the formation of *ettringite* ($3\,CaO \cdot Al_2O_3 \cdot CaSO_4 \cdot 31\,H_2O$).

PFA AS A MEDIUM FOR PLANT GROWTH

The slow natural colonization of ash sites suggests that conditions adverse to plant growth exist in the ash; pot and plot experiments confirm that a number of factors may, either singly or collectively, militate against the establishment and growth of higher plants. The factors are associated with (1) the adequacy of plant nutrients, (2) the presence of directly toxic factors, and (3) the physical nature of ash deposits.

Plant-nutrient status of PFA

Cope (1961) examined the plant-nutrient status of a wide range of PFA samples. Table 2 records the mean values quoted (with the range in parentheses), together with average values for "available" nutrient levels in fertile mineral soils.

TABLE 2

Available macronutrient content of PFA and a fertile soil in % (Cope, 1961)

Nutrient	PFA		Soil Available
	Total	Available	
N	0.035	—	0.180[a]
P_2O_5	0.114	0.033 (0.013 to 0.054)	0.022
K_2O	2.68	0.042 (0.008 to 0.115)	0.027
Ca	4.69	0.990 (0.28 to 1.87)	0.080
Mg	0.71	0.150 (0.008 to 0.516)	0.024
Fe	6.09	0.057 (0.001 to 0.229)	0.013
S	0.48	0.390 (0.07 to 0.55)	0.060

[a] Total; not available.

These figures show an almost total lack of N, which, together with the sterile nature of the ash and complete lack of organic matter, means that biological development and modification will be exceedingly slow under natural conditions.

The phosphate status on the other hand appears by comparative standards to be adequate, but experiments on a variety of test plants show substantial yield increases following fertilization with water-soluble phosphate. This suggests that the citrate-soluble phosphate test used to determine availability is not appropriate for this particular material.

Potassium levels are almost invariably high, and nil or negative responses to added K are the rule. The available Ca, Mg, and S contents are also higher in ash than in soil.

The status of the important micronutrients in the ash is given in Table 3. With the exception of Zn, the ash is adequately supplied with essential trace elements, so well that the possibility of toxic excesses may exist. This point is discussed more fully below.

TABLE 3

Available micronutrient content of PFA and a fertile soil in ppm
(Cope, 1961)

Nutrient	PFA			Soil Available
	Total	Available		
Mn	848	99	(12 to 347)	4.8
B	236	43	(3 to 150)	2.5
Zn	283	2.1	(0 to 4.0)	2.5
Cu	248	25	(10 to 50)	2.5
Mo	42	5.4	(0.7 to 12.8)	0.2

According to Swaine (1962), As, Cr, Ni, and Pb are harmful in a direct sense. PFA contains these elements, together with traces of practically all other naturally occurring elements (Table 4).

TABLE 4

Content of available trace elements in PFA and soil in ppm

Element	PFA	Soil	Element	PFA	Soil
Ag	1	1	Pb	10	10
Al	144	58	Se	— [a]	2
Co	8.5	1.6	Sn	10	10
Cr	22	1.7	Ti	15	10
Ni	60	2.7	V	6	1.3

[a] Not detected

Toxicity factors of PFA

Plants grown in PFA, even when adequately supplied with moisture and nutrients, show relatively poor growth and frequently exhibit leaf symptoms suggesting nutrient disorders. It has been amply demonstrated that fresh precipitator ash is more injurious to plants than lagooned ash, and that as weathering proceeds in the lagoons the ash becomes less harmful. Hodgson (1961) and Cope (1961) have shown that the toxicity of ash may involve: (1) abnormal pH levels, (2) high non-specific soluble-salt concentrations, and (3) toxicity of high concentrations of water-soluble B.

Alkalinity of PFA   On contact with water the soluble components of the ash are dissolved, and the solution becomes highly alkaline. Figure 1 shows this development with time in a closed system of ash and water, and Fig. 2 indicates the changing composition of the solution. Figure 3 shows the changes in solution composition during the progressive leaching of an ash sample.

Alkalinities of the order pH 11 to 12 are not uncommon with fresh ash, but lagooned ash, which in effect has been subjected to a preliminary water-extraction process, more often develops a pH value of around 9 which gradually decreases but rarely drops as low as 8. However, high pH *per se* does not appear to be a primary toxicity factor, although there may be indirect effects on plant growth if nutrient availability is affected. Natural weathering tends to reduce pH values, but these stabilize at a

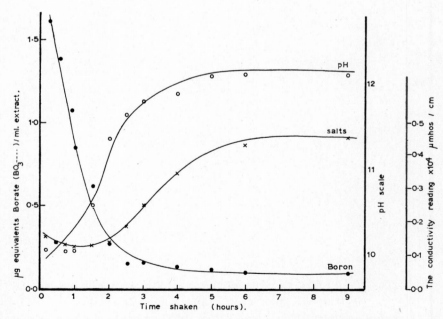

FIGURE 1   Changes of pH values, soluble-salt contents, and water-soluble B levels with time in an ash : water (30 : 70) slurry.

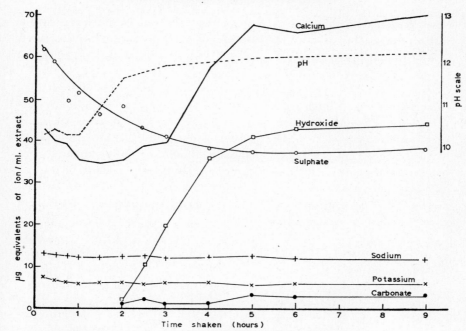

FIGURE 2 Changes in the composition of the solution phase with time in an ash : water (30 : 70) slurry.

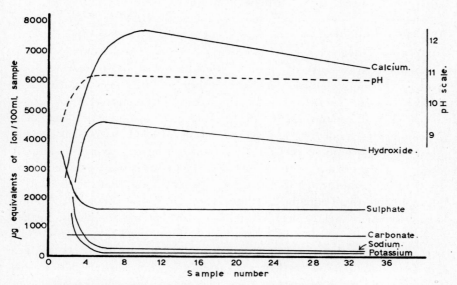

FIGURE 3 Progressive changes in the composition of 50 ml samples of an ash leachate with a percolation rate of 50 ml/hour.

4*

level greater than that of productive agricultural soils. Nevertheless, fresh ash will invariably produce far more severe phytotoxicities than weathered ash of similar pH.

Soluble-salt effects   Associated with the high pH values of fresh ash-water mixtures are high electrical conductivities which reflect the water-soluble salt contents. Soil conductivities exceeding 4.0 millimhos will cause crop yield reductions (U.S. Department of Agriculture, 1954). Since values measured on fresh ash samples range from about 8 to 13 millimhos/cm, inhibition of plant growth can be expected. However, this form of toxicity is not of long duration; the considerable reduction in soluble-salt content during the lagooning process, and 2 or 3 years weathering in the field usually reduces it to a harmless level.

Boron toxicity   Even after pH values and soluble-salt contents of ash samples have been reduced to acceptable levels, there remains a further toxic factor. Tables 3 and 4 show several elements with a greater availability in PFA than in soil; Al, B, Cr, Cu, Mn, Mo, Ni, Ti, and V can be suspected of having an adverse effect on plants. Hodgson (1961) demonstrated that the toxicity effects were centered around the B content of the ash. With the exception of Al, which interferes with P uptake by plants, the other elements appear to have a negligible influence on crop growth.

Analyses of power station ashes for water-soluble B have given values that range from 3 to 250 ppm with a mean value of about 60 ppm (Cope, 1961). The ratio of total to "available" B varies in ash from 1.8 to 4.5. Thus, there is a reserve of insoluble B which is believed to be present as part of the molecular structure of a borosilicate glass. Similar materials, known as glass frits, are applied to agricultural soils to correct B deficiency; their effectiveness depends on the slow release of soluble B (Wear and Wilson, 1954). Something of a similar nature probably occurs in PFA, the slow decomposition of the glassy particles giving rise to a long-term B toxicity in the material. Jones and Lewis (1960), in laboratory experiments with PFA, demonstrated that leaching can reduce the available B content from 46 ppm to an equilibrium value of 20. Therefore, although lagooning and subsequent weathering may remove some of the soluble B, further quantities will be released as weathering continues.

According to Eaton (1944), 5 ppm B in a culture solution will produce toxicity symptoms on the leaves of a sensitive plant such as barley; this characteristic has been used to assess the toxicity status of PFA (Hodgson and Townsend, 1973).

The physical factors

The ash profile of lagooned sites is characteristically that of a sedimentary deposit and exhibits distinct stratification. The strata often display different characteristics even though their particulate composition is essentially similar. The most important differences in the field are associated with hardness and wetness. There is no systematic variation down the profile; hard and compact layers, from 1 mm to several cm thick, occur randomly, strongly influencing root development and the drainage characteristics of the profile.

The greater hardness is a consequence of more compact packing of the individual particles during sedimentation. Table 5 gives bulk densities and permeabilities of samples from strata differing in hardness.

TABLE 5

Bulk density and permeability of PFA of differing degrees of hardness

Sample No.	Hardness in Empirical Units	Bulk Density g/cm^3	Permeability 10^{-5} cm/sec
1	1.4	0.99	24.8
2	18	0.91	81.6
3	35	1.13	4.55
4	240	1.73	0.013

The greater hardness of the more tightly packed samples is primarily due to increased pozzolanic cementation resulting from the larger number of particle contacts; the actual hardness would not be expected to correlate closely with bulk density. The variation in permeability between layers is very marked. In terms of soil air-water relationships favorable for deep root development, the values for Samples 1 and 2 would be adequate, but the permeability of Sample 3 would be considered too slow; the last sample is so nearly impermeable that leaching is negligible.

These impermeable layers within the profile impede drainage and cause lateral movement of water through the less compacted layers. The importance of packing to water relationships can be illustrated as follows: Cubically packed spheres of uniform size have a pore space of 47.8%; the same spheres rhombohedrally packed have only 26% pore space. The effect of compaction on individual pore size is also important. According to the calculations of Slichter (1898) for uniform spheres 50 μ in diameter, the radii of the circles at the narrowest and widest parts of the pore space of closely packed spheres would be 2.8 μ and 7.2 μ respectively. These dimensions are well below those of typical roots, and root penetration would be prevented. The roots of plants established on highly weathered ash often develop horizontally on reaching some particularly compacted horizon. On tipped ash sites, this sedimentation phenomenon is not present. However, sub-surface hardening, as a result of pozzolanic action, does take place and unnatural drainage problems can be produced.

Another physical problem of ash deposits is surface erosion. The nature of the ash particles and the intrinsic difficulty of creating stable aggregates render ash surfaces particularly susceptible to wind and water erosion. Wind erosion is perhaps more important. Wind tunnel tests, using open-ended trays of dry ash exposed to a non-turbulent air stream, showed that the cenospheres are especially erodible, with a threshold wind velocity of less than 12 mph compared with 20 to 30 mph for dry bulk ash (Cope, 1961). These threshold velocities can be compared with 15 mph for a post-glacial aeolian sand. Wind erosion is to some extent reduced by the "capping" of surfaces after rainfall, but considerable dust nuisance can arise should the surface "cap" be broken.

CONCLUSION

PFA is not an appropriate material for the establishment of vegetation without either prolonged exposure to natural weathering or considerable artificial treatment. Measures that can be taken to ameliorate the adverse conditions are described by Hodgson and Townsend (1973). They include: reduction of surface erodibility through creation of a crumb structure; treatments to reduce toxicities and the tendency for compaction; and cropping and fertilizing programs.

LITERATURE CITED

Berger, K. C. 1949. Boron in soils and crops. *Adv. in Agron.* **1**, 321–348.

Cope, F. 1961. The agronomic value of power station waste ash. *Ph. D. Thesis*. Univ. of Leeds.

Eaton, F. M. 1944. Deficiency, toxicity, and accumulation of boron in plants. *J. of Agric. Research* **69**, 237–277.

Hodgson, D. R. 1961. Investigations into the reclamation of land covered with pulverized fuel ash. *Ph. D. Thesis*. Univ. of Leeds.

Hodgson, D. R., and W. N. Townsend. 1973. The amelioration and revegetation of pulverized fuel ash, this symposium.

Jones, L. H., and A. V. Lewis. 1960. Weathering of fly-ash. *Nature* (London) **185**, 404–405.

Simons, H. F., and J. W. Jeffrey. 1960. An x-ray study of pulverized fuel ash. *J. Appl. Chem.* **10**, 328–336.

Slichter, C. S. 1898. *U. S. Geol. Survey, 19th Annual Report*, Part 2, 301–384.

Swaine, D. J. 1962. The trace element content of fertilizers. *Tech. Comm.* **52**. Commonwealth Bureau of Soils. Harpenden.

U. S. Department of Agriculture. 1954. Saline and alkali soils. *Agr. Handbook* No. **60**. Regional Salinity Lab.

Wear, J. I., and C. H. Wilson. 1954. Boron materials of low solubility and their use for plant growth. *Soil Sci. Soc. Amer. Proc.* **18**, 425–428.

Weddle, A. E. 1968. Techniques No. 3. The disposal of pulverized fuel ash. *Inst. of Landscape Architects J.* No. **84**, 30–32.

DISCUSSION

SCHMEHL: Is the increase in Ca and hydroxyl ions due to hydrolysis of calcium silicate minerals?

HODGSON: Yes.

HEIDE: Mr. Hodgson spoke of the high content of soluble salts in the fuel ash. Is there not a danger that the greater content of soluble salts will influence the ground water in a large area? I think the highest permissible content of sulfates for water is 250 mg/liter, and in parts of the Rhine brown coal region in Germany contents have increased to more than 1000 mg/liter. Isn't there a danger that the ash surface may sink if soluble salts are leached out of a deposit?

HODGSON: There is no record in England of ash subsidence caused by the leaching of soluble salts from a deposit. One must be careful of course, not to site an ash lagoon over a coal mine. There is no record of high sulfate contents in the ground water as a result of ash disposal but this and other elements which might be toxic are closely checked by the Water Boards.

PLASS: Do you find great variations in chemical composition or pH of power fuel ashes?

HODGSON: Yes, the pH of pulverized fuel ash in the United Kingdom may vary from as low as 7 to as high as 11 or 12. However, the first washings from pulverized fuel ash are sometimes acid, with a pH of 4 to 5, due to the condensation of sulfur dioxide and trioxide on the particles; thereafter it gradually increases. There is tremendous variation in B content, the main cause of toxicity. Ash from S. Wales coals has a very low B content; ash from Midlands coals may have a B content of 250 ppm.

GOODMAN: How does the particle size of the coal affect the burning properties and therefore the availability of B and other elements?

HODGSON: I don't know how the particle size affects the burning of the coal, but one would imagine that the finer the grinding, the more effective the burning. Since most of the soluble B in PFA is in the finer particles, this creates great difficulties for the agronomist by increasing the availability of this element to plants.

ONOSODE: You said the lagooned ash, when leveled out, has a hard surface and isn't blown off by the wind. Might not the hard surface retard percolation, so that the ash may have to be cultivated before the land can be used? Have you investigated the effect of cultivation on the rate of decline of pH towards the equilibrium level?

HODGSON: We have not measured the effect of constant cultivation on the rate of decline in pH. Although a hard surface controls wind erosion, it can reduce rates of percolation of rain water.

TOXICITY OF ACID COAL-MINE SPOILS TO PLANTS

William A. Berg* and Willis G. Vogel

Research Soil Scientist and Range Scientist, Northeastern Forest Experiment Station, Forest Service, U. S. Department of Agriculture, Berea, Kentucky

Toxicity of extremely acid coal-mine spoils to plants is caused primarily by excess soluble Mn and other metals, most probably Al. Manganese toxicity, expressed by chlorosis on the margins of legume leaves, was observed on herbaceous legumes, shrub lespedezas, and black locust grown from seed in extremely acid spoils in the greenhouse and in the field. Spoil pH was useful in predicting Mn toxicity to the legumes, but water-soluble Mn extracted from the spoils was not. Symptoms of Al toxicity were expressed by stubby roots without laterals. One year after extremely acid spoils were mulched with hardwood chips, the pH of the top 30 cm of spoil was raised while total soluble salts and water-soluble Al were reduced.

INTRODUCTION

Revegetating extremely acid spoils is a major problem in some areas surface-mined for coal in the eastern and central United States. Observations and studies indicate that excess Mn and other metals, most probably Al, which come into solution in increasing amounts as acidity increases, are major causes of spoil toxicity to plants on extremely acid spoils. Also, a study indicates that mulch has an effect in reducing toxic conditions.

Spoils used in our studies were collected from surface coal-mining operations in eastern Kentucky. The spoils, from geological formations of Pennsylvanian age, consisted mainly of shales and siltstones, but some included sandstone fragments and waste coal. In the mining process the

---

* At present Assistant Professor of Agronomy, Colorado State University, Fort Collins, Colorado.

shales and siltstones usually are well shattered, and some weather rapidly into soil-size particles. The spoils have a range in pH from below 3 to 8, and many are extremely acid (below pH 4.5).

MANGANESE TOXICITY

Manganese toxicity to legumes grown in acid soils is well documented (Hewitt, 1946; Morris, 1948; Foy, 1964; Jackson, 1967). Manganese toxicity to certain small-seeded legumes is readily recognized by the characteristic chlorotic margins that it causes on the leaflets (Hewitt, 1946; Morris and Pierre, 1949; Ouellette and Dessureaux, 1958; Foy, 1964). We found this characteristic pattern on legumes grown in acid spoils in field and greenhouse studies and in nutrient solutions containing excess Mn (Fig. 1).

Water-extractable Mn might provide a satisfactory method for predicting occurrence of Mn toxicity on legumes grown in acid soils (Morris, 1948). To investigate this, we grew six species of legumes in the greenhouse on 46 different spoils (Berg and Vogel, 1968). The spoils had a range in pH from 3.0 to 7.1, but most were in the 4.0 to 5.5 pH range. Chlorosis on leaf margins of legumes grown on the spoils varied from none to severe.

FIGURE 1 Manganese toxicity symptoms on four species of lespedeza grown in acid spoil are shown in the top row; normal leaves are in the bottom row. The distinct marginal chlorosis is typical of Mn toxicity on Korean lespedeza (left), sericea lespedeza (right center), and shrub lespedeza (right). On Kobe lespedeza (left center), the chlorosis gradually becomes obvious at the margins.

The legume species also varied in susceptibility. Seedlings of Korean (*Lespedeza stipulacea*), sericea (*L. cuneata*), and bicolor lespedeza (*L. bicolor*) developed chlorosis on many more spoils than did seedlings of Kobe lespedeza (*L. striata*), birdsfoot trefoil (*Lotus corniculatus*), or black locust (*Robinia pseudoacacia*).

Water-soluble Mn was determined on the spoils, but it was not useful in predicting the occurrence of Mn toxicity to the legumes. For example, Korean lespedeza had Mn toxicity symptoms when grown on various spoils containing as little as 1 to as much as 50 ppm of water-soluble Mn, but showed no symptoms when grown on other spoils with as much as 30 ppm of water-soluble Mn.

However, the data (Table 1) indicated that spoil pH can be used as a rough guide for predicting Mn toxicity on legumes seeded in spoils. Korean and bicolor lespedeza developed symptoms of Mn toxicity when grown in most spoils with pH below 5, and occasionally in spoils with pH in the 5.0 to 5.4 range. Sericea lespedeza in the seedling stage usually had Mn toxicity symptoms when grown in spoils with a pH of 5 or lower. The more tolerant species, Kobe lespedeza, birdsfoot trefoil, and black locust, seldom developed Mn toxicity symptoms on spoils with a pH above 4.4.

TABLE 1

Number of spoils in given pH ranges producing Mn toxicity symptoms on legumes

Species	Number of spoils in pH range ...			
	4.0 to 4.4 (11)[a]	4.5 to 4.9 (12)[a]	5.0 to 5.4 (11)[a]	Over 5.4 (4)[a]
Bicolor lespedeza	11	11	4	0
Korean lespedeza	10	8	3	0
Sericea lespedeza	11	8	0	0
Kobe lespedeza	8	2	0	0
Birdsfoot trefoil	5	1	0	0
Black locust	5	1	0	0

[a] Number of spoils in grouping.

OTHER METAL TOXICITIES

Stubby roots and the absence of lateral roots are the classical symptoms of Al toxicity (Ligon and Pierre, 1934; Rorison, 1958). However, toxicity caused by excess Cu and other heavy metals may have similar effects on roots (Bradshaw et al., 1965; Struckmeyer et al., 1969).

In one of our studies with acid spoils, soybeans (*Glycine max*) and cane (*Sorghum vulgare*) were used as test species. When grown in spoils with a pH of 4.0 to 4.5, the top growth was poor, and stunting of the main root and lack of laterals was obvious (Fig. 2). We have also observed similar growth characteristics on roots of cereal species and herbaceous legumes grown on extremely acid spoils.

The limited root development of grasses grown on extremely acid spoils indicates that there is also a toxic effect on these species with fine fibrous roots. In an effort to characterize this decreased root growth under acid conditions, we investigated the shoot/root ratios by weight on three grass species grown in N- and P-fertilized spoils ranging in reaction from extremely acid to near neutral. These studies failed to show a significant difference in shoot/root ratios over the range of pH's, but some species were more tolerant of the acid conditions than others (Vogel and Berg, 1968). Additional studies are needed, using nutrient solutions to determine if the growth differences among the grass species are due to differences in tolerance to soluble metals.

We have noted the characteristic stubby roots and lack of lateral roots on black locust and caragana (*Caragana arborescens*) grown in extremely acid spoil. We have inspected the roots of a few other hardwood species and pines planted in extremely acid spoils for the characteristic toxicity symptoms. We noted no gross differences that could be attributed to toxicity. It is probable that stubby roots and lack of laterals are observed only in cases of severe toxicity and that lesser degrees of toxicity are difficult to detect. Additional studies supplemented by microscopic study of root cross-sections (Wind, 1957; Fleming and Foy, 1968; Struckmeyer et al., 1969) would be of interest. The recent work by Beyer and Hutnik (1969) indicated that two species of birch (*Betula*) were more tolerant of soluble Al than two species of pine (*Pinus*), but that the pines were more tolerant of low pH than were the birches.

The cause of the toxicity that results in restricted root growth on extremely acid spoils cannot be affirmed from our information. However, we assume that soluble Al is the most likely cause. Concentrations of soluble Al that could be toxic to plants are found in spoils that have a pH in the range of 5.5 and below. The increase in exchangeable Al in spoils as acidity increases is shown in Fig. 3. The information from the studies of Beyer and Hutnik (1969) and Berg and Vogel (1968) are in fair agreement (Fig. 3). The low amounts of exchangeable Al reported by Barnhisel and Massey (1969) in some extremely acid spoils were believed to be due to non-equilibrium conditions in freshly crushed samples.

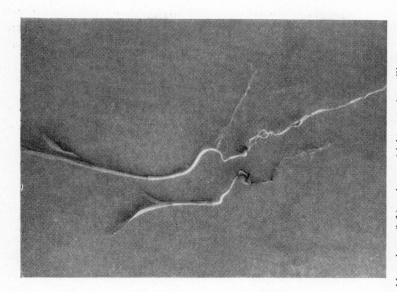

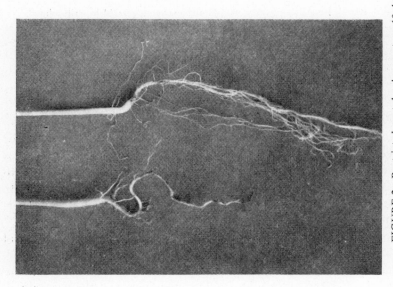

FIGURE 2 Restricted root development on 10-day-old soybean (left) and cane (right center) seedlings grown in extremely acid spoil (pH 3.9). The soybean (left center) and cane (right) seedlings grown in a less acid spoil (pH 6.0) have good root elongation and branching.

Concentrations of soluble Fe, Cu, Zn, and Ni that could be toxic to plants also exist in some extremely acid spoils (Cummins et al., 1965; Barnhisel and Massey, 1969). Such concentrations are most likely to occur on extremely acid spoils where plant-toxic concentrations of Al and Mn would also be present. Research is needed to determine the level at which these elements may become toxic to plants in various spoils.

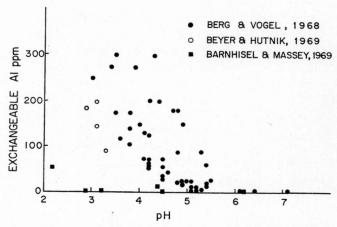

FIGURE 3   Relationship between pH and exchangeable Al in strip-mine spoils from eastern United States.

LEACHING OF ACID SPOILS

When dealing with toxicities on extremely acid soils and spoils, we can take two approaches to overcome the toxicity. One method is to look for tolerance to the acid conditions among and within plant species. This has proved to be a fruitful field as evidenced by many publications on the subject (Morris and Pierre, 1949; Ouellette and Dessureaux, 1958; Foy et al., 1965; Stolen, 1965; Bradshaw et al., 1965; Fleming and Foy, 1968; Morrison and Armson, 1968).

The other method of dealing with toxicities caused by extremely acid conditions is to treat the soils or spoils. Liming is the traditional method, and some liming has been done on spoils (Grandt and Lang, 1958; Einspahr et al., 1955). The quantity of lime required, and the necessity to mix the lime into the spoil, limit the feasibility of liming spoils on the steep slopes of the Appalachian Mountains.

Tyner and Smith (1945) and Struthers (1965) have stressed the importance of leaching to ameliorate toxic conditions in acid spoils. In studies on salty soils, Fanning and Carter (1963) have shown that surface mulching will promote salt leaching by natural precipitation. So we investigated mulching as a method of increasing leaching efficiency and thus reducing the level of soluble salts and water-soluble Al in acid spoils.

This study was done in eastern Kentucky, where the mean annual precipitation is about 114 cm. Field plots were established on nearly level benches in areas that had been strip-mined 3 years previously. On each plot, two 1- by 1-m holes were dug to a depth of 60 cm in the spoils; the holes were 2 m apart. The spoil was screened to remove coarse particles larger than 1.3 cm. Some extra spoil also had to be obtained from a third hole. During and after screening, the spoil for each plot was mixed. After mixing, the spoil was put back into the original two holes by alternately placing one shovelful in one hole and then a shovelful in the other hole. Each hole was edged with boards so that 7.5 cm of board extended above the ground surface. A mulch treatment of hardwood chips (from a commercial sawmill) was applied to the spoil on one of each pair of refilled holes, to a depth of 7.5 cm.

The plots were established in September 1964 and were sampled in August 1965. By then, the fill had sunk several cm in each hole. Each plot was sampled at the 0- to 5-cm, 5- to 15-cm, 15- to 30-cm, 30- to 45-cm, and 45- to 60-cm depths. Sampling was done in a 60- by 60-cm area near the center of each hole, the 60- by 60-cm area being divided into 30- by 30-cm quarters; samples were taken at each depth from each quarter. The samples were air-dried.

Initially, chemical determinations were made on the whole spoil, but there was considerable variability in soluble-salt content; so the spoils were sieved through a 10-mesh (2 mm) screen, and the fines were used for the chemical determinations. The fines made up 30 to 40% of the spoil and were medium-textured. Conductivity was determined on a 2 to 1 distilled water to spoil ratio, after mixing and equilibrating for 1 hr. pH was determined from the supernatant liquid after the conductivity measurement was made. Water-soluble Al was extracted by shaking 50 g of spoil in 100 ml of distilled water for 30 minutes. After filtration, Al was determined by the aluminon method (McLean, 1965).

Within each depth on each plot, statistical comparisons between mulched and unmulched treatments were made by using a t-test.

No statistically significant differences were found in pH among the mulch treatments. However, the pH of the 0- to 5-cm layer of the extremely acid spoils (Plots 1, 2, and 3) was consistently higher in the mulched spoils than in the unmulched spoils (Table 2).

TABLE 2

pH of spoils as affected by mulch treatment[a]

Depth cm	Plot 1		Plot 2		Plot 3		Plot 4	
	No mulch	Mulch	No mulch	Mulch	No mulch	Mulch	No mulch	Mulch
0 to 5	2.6	2.8	2.5	2.9	3.4	3.7	4.9	4.7
5 to 15	2.6	2.9	2.5	2.8	3.6	3.7	4.9	4.9
15 to 30	2.5	2.7	2.5	2.7	3.5	3.7	5.0	4.8
30 to 45	2.5	2.7	2.5	2.6	3.7	3.6	4.9	4.9
45 to 60	2.5	2.4	2.5	2.5	3.7	3.6	5.0	4.9

[a] Each pH value is the mean of four samples. There were no significant differences between mulched and unmulched treatments within a given plot.

As predicted, the mulch substantially reduced the salt content near the surface on the extremely acid spoils (Table 3). Here it should be noted that conductivity is not a precise indication of salt concentration under extremely acid conditions. However, it is an approximation and should be adequate for comparison purposes as long as comparisons are made with the same spoil.

TABLE 3

Conductivity of spoils as affected by mulch treatment[a] *(mmhos/cm)*

Depth cm	Plot 1		Plot 2		Plot 3		Plot 4	
	No mulch	Mulch	No mulch	Mulch	No mulch	Mulch	No mulch	Mulch
0 to 5	1.90	0.53[b]	2.80	0.56[b]	0.71	0.20[b]	0.077	0.051[c]
5 to 15	1.12	0.64[b]	1.48	0.57[b]	0.41	0.18[c]	0.061	0.035[c]
15 to 30	1.28	0.73[d]	1.90	0.85[b]	0.53	0.22[c]	0.044	0.042[c]
30 to 45	1.55	0.89[b]	2.18	1.07[b]	0.42	0.29[c]	0.053	0.046[c]
45 to 60	1.57	2.90[c]	2.85	2.30[c]	0.41	0.32[c]	0.062	0.046[c]

[a] Each value is the mean of four samples.
[b] Significantly different from no mulch treatment at 0.01 probability level.
[c] Not significantly different from no mulch treatment at 0.05 probability level.
[d] Significantly different from no mulch treatment at 0.05 probability level.

Water-soluble Al near the spoil surface usually decreased with the mulch treatment (Table 4). Some large differences in water-soluble Al between mulch and no-mulch treatments were not significantly different because of the large range in water-soluble Al within treatments. For example, in Plot 2, 0- to 5-cm depth, there was a range of 30 to 192 ppm Al in unmulched spoils and a range of 3.2 to 6.0 ppm Al in mulched spoils. Little water-soluble Al was present in the spoils on Plot 4 because of the relatively low acidity.

The reduction in water-soluble Al under mulched conditions could mean the difference between plant survival and death on sites that are marginal in Al toxicity. However, mulching spoils on steep slopes is probably no more feasible than liming. Yet the study shows that treatments that reduce surface evaporation and promote leaching will tend to decrease toxic conditions in spoils. This principle might apply to spoils with interspersed toxic and nontoxic areas. Vegetation should be established on the nontoxic areas because it can reduce surface evaporation on the adjacent toxic areas by reducing wind velocities, providing some shade, and maybe eventually providing a mulch.

TABLE 4

Water-soluble Al extracted from spoils as affected by mulch treatment[a] (*in ppm*)

Depth cm	Plot 1		Plot 2		Plot 3		Plot 4	
	No mulch	Mulch	No mulch	Mulch	No mulch	Mulch	No mulch	Mulch
0 to 5	56	22[c]	111	4[c]	7.5	4.4[c]	0.3	0.1[c]
5 to 15	22	13[c]	42	4[b]	7.0	6.1[c]	0.2	0.1[c]
15 to 30	53	5[d]	132	9[b]	13.6	5.3[c]	0.1	0.1[c]
30 to 45	20	99[b]	89	122[c]	9.8	10.1[c]	0.1	0.2[c]
45 to 60	21	97[d]	189	86[b]	6.7	7.8[c]	0.1	0.2[c]

[a] Each value is the mean of four samples.
[b] Significantly different from no mulch treatment at 0.01 probability level.
[c] Not significantly different from no mulch treatment at 0.05 probability level.
[d] Significantly different from no mulch treatment at 0.05 probability level.

LITERATURE CITED

Barnhisel, R. I., and H. F. Massey. 1969. Chemical, mineralogical and physical properties of eastern Kentucky acid-forming coal mine spoils. *Soil Sci.* **108**, 367–372.

Berg, W. A., and W. G. Vogel. 1968. Manganese toxicity of legumes seeded in Kentucky strip-mine spoils. U. S. Dep. Agr., Forest Service, Northeastern Forest Exp. Sta. Paper NE-119. 12 p.

Beyer, L. E., and R. J. Hutnik. 1969. Acid and aluminium toxicity as related to strip-mine spoil banks in western Pennsylvania. Pennsylvania State Univ. Spec. Res. Rep. SR-72, 79 p.

Bradshaw, A. D., T. S. McNeilly, and R. P. G. Gregory. 1965. Industrialization, evolution and the development of heavy metal tolerance in plants. In: G. T. Goodman, R. W. Edwards, and J. M. Lambert (Ed.). *Ecology and the industrial society.* Blackwell Sci. Publ., Oxford. p. 327–343.

Cummins, D. G., W. T. Plass, and C. E. Gentry. 1965. Chemical and physical properties of spoil banks in eastern Kentucky coal fields. U. S. Dep. Agr., Forest Service, Central States Forest Exp. Sta. Res. Paper CS-17, 11 p.

Einspahr, D. W., A. L. McComb, F. F. Riecken, and W. D. Shrader. 1955. Coal spoil-bank materials as a medium for plant growth. *Proc. Iowa Acad. Sci.* **62**, 329–344.

Fanning, C. D., and D. L. Carter. 1963. The effectiveness of a cotton burr mulch and a ridge-furrow system in reclaiming saline soils by rainfall. *Soil Sci. Soc. Amer. Proc.* **27**, 703–706.

Fleming, A. L., and C. D. Foy. 1968. Root structure reflects differential aluminum tolerance in wheat varieties. *Agron. J.* **60**, 172–176.

Foy, C. D. 1964. Toxic factors in acid soils of the southeastern United States as related to the response of alfalfa to lime. U. S. Dep. Agr., *Agr. Res. Serv. Production Res. Rep.* **80**. 26 p.

Foy, C. D., W. H. Armiger, L. W. Briggle, and D. A. Reid. 1965. Differential aluminum tolerance of wheat and barley varieties in acid soils. *Agron. J.* **57**, 413–417.

Grandt, A. F., and A. L. Lang. 1958. Reclaiming Illinois strip coal land with legumes and grasses. *Bull.* **620**. 64 pp. Ill. Agr. Exp. Sta., Urbana.

Hewitt, E. J. 1946. The resolution of the factors in soil acidity: some effects of manganese toxicity. *Long Aston Res. Ann. Rep.* p. 50–61.

Jackson, W. A. 1967. Physiological effects of soil acidity. In: *Soil acidity and liming.* Amer. Soc. Agron. Madison, Wis. p. 43–124.

Ligon, W. S., and W. H. Pierre. 1934. Soluble aluminum studies: II. Minimum concentrations of aluminum found to be toxic to corn, sorghum, and barley in culture solutions. *Soil Sci.* **34**, 307–322.

McLean, E. O. 1965. Aluminum. In: C. A. Black (Ed.). *Agronomy 9, Methods of Soil Analysis,* Part 2. Amer. Soc. Agron. Madison, Wis. p. 978–998.

Morris, H. D. 1948. The soluble manganese content of acid soils and its relation to the growth and manganese content of sweet clover and lespedeza. *Soil Sci. Soc. Amer. Proc.* **13**, 362–371.

Morris, H. D., and W. H. Pierre. 1949. Minimum concentrations of manganese necessary for injury to various legumes in culture solutions. *Agron. J.* **41**, 107–112.

Morrison, I. K.,and K. A. Armson. 1968. Influence of manganese on growth of jack pine and black spruce seedlings. *Forestry Chron.* **44**(8), 32–35.

Ouellette, G. J., and L. Dessureaux. 1958. Chemical composition of alfalfa as related to degree of tolerance to manganese and aluminum. *Can. J. Plant Sci.* **38**, 206–214.

Rorison, I. J. 1958. The effect of aluminum on legume nutrition. In: *Nutrition of the legumes.* Butterworths Sci. Publ., London. p. 43–61.

Stolen, O. 1965. Investigations on the tolerance of barley varieties to high hydrogen-ion concentrations in soil. *Royal Veterinary and Agr. Coll. Yearbook* 1965. Copenhagen. p. 81–104.

Struckmeyer, B. E., L. A. Peterson, and F. Hsi-Mei-Tai. 1969. Effects of copper on the composition and anatomy of tobacco. *Agron. J.* **61**, 932–936.

Struthers, P. H. 1965. Rapid spoil weathering and soil genesis. *Proc. Coal Mine Spoil Reclamation Symposium.* Pennsylvania State Univ., p. 86–90.

Tyner, E. H., and R. M. Smith. 1945. The reclamation of the strip-mined coal lands of West Virginia with forage species. *Soil Sci. Soc. Amer. Proc.* **10**, 429–436.

Vogel, W. G., and W. A. Berg. 1968. Grasses and legumes for cover on acid strip-mine spoils. *J. Soil Water Cons.* **23**, 89–91.

Wind, G. P. 1957. Root growth in acid soils. *Neth. J. Agric. Sci.* **15**, 259–266.

DISCUSSION

HEALD: What are the ages of these spoils?

BERG: All the spoils were exposed three years or less.

HILL: With Al and Mn, solubility depends on the pH. Would liming help the Al and Mn toxicity situation?

BERG: Yes, if you apply lime you get away from the toxicity symptoms I described. We would first like to find species that are adapted to these more acid conditions because it is expensive to lime steep mountain slopes.

CARUCCIO: Did you establish the increase in concentration of both Al and Mn with decrease in pH?

BERG: Yes, this is a general relationship that we find. However, water-soluble Mn was determined in these spoils, and we tried to correlate this with the degree of chlorosis, but there was no apparent relationship. I think the factor that makes this so complicated is that if we have high water-soluble Mn we also have high water-soluble Ca and Mg.

CARUCCIO: Do you think the oxidation state of the metals will be affecting the solubility?

BERG: Yes, particularly with Mn, we note that black locust and sericea lespedeza in the greenhouse will tend to outgrow this chlorosis. I think what's happening is that as these plants get a little larger their water use increases, the spoils dry out, and the Mn oxidizes and is less available to the plants.

BAUER: I was astonished to find that you had good germination without organic fertilizing. Is that normal? As far as I know, clover doesn't grow without organic fertilizing such as humus.

BERG: We have no trouble with germination on these. These legumes were all inoculated with the proper *Rhizobium*.

BAUER: Is there any humus in this spoil?

BERG: The spoils do not contain organic matter as we know it in our soils, although they do contain a certain percentage of carbon.

BAUER: These experiments apparently involved only first-year seedlings. Do you have any further experiments with older plants?

BERG: Yes, we have done a lot of field work on many of these same species.

BAUER: And they grow without any humus fertilizing?

BERG: Yes.

CRESSWELL: I presume that the acidity was largely due to the oxidation of pyrites? Did you find any relationship between Fe content and Mn toxicity?

BERG: We did not determine Fe on these spoils, and so I cannot comment on that.

BENGTSON: Do your experiments or observations indicate at what spoil pH level Mn toxicity might become apparent in seedlings of southern pines, such as Virginia or loblolly pine?

BERG: We have no information on the pines. The only species we observed these Mn toxicities on were the small-seeded legumes. In the greenhouse we have also found it on one species of grass and on buckwheat.

AHARRAH: In one of the plots that we were working with, we found 18-year-old red pine to be definitely chlorotic; and although we have had no opportunity to make either soil or needle analysis, I believe it was either Al or Mn toxicity. It appears very similar to the Mn toxicity in red pine as described by some of the Canadian workers. The needles are very short, yellowed, and bunched at the ends of the twigs.

FUNK: Did you have any opportunity to make any foliar analysis of the Mn-tolerant and Mn-susceptible plants?

BERG: Yes, we determined Mn on all these plants. It isn't a good linear relationship, but Mn toxicity symptoms were associated with higher Mn content in these plants. The species that were more susceptible to Mn toxicity tended to have the toxicity at lower levels of Mn.

HIGH SURFACE TEMPERATURES ON STRIP-MINE SPOILS

Daniel J. Deely and F. Yates Borden

Former graduate assistant and Associate Professor of Forestry, School of Forest Resources, The Pennsylvania State University, University Park, Pennsylvania

Surface temperatures of strip-mine spoil materials ranging from bituminous coal to light sandstone were measured with an infrared thermometer between June 4 and July 8, 1968. During this period, temperatures exceeded 50 C at least once on all the spoils measured. When the surface layer was dry (at least 3 to 7 days after rain), when solar radiation was intense, and when air temperatures ranged from 30 to 35 C, maximum temperatures on level spoil surfaces consistently reached 50 to 55 C on the lightest materials, and 65 to 70 C on the darkest materials. The average temperature difference observed between the lightest and the darkest spoil materials was approximately 15 C.

Spoil materials that underwent the largest decreases in surface moisture content experienced the greatest rises in surface temperature during a sequence of sunny days following rain. Maximum surface temperatures generally increased at an average rate of from 2 to 4 C per day for the first 6 to 10 days after rain.

The maximum amplitude of the diurnal variation in surface temperature was roughly 50 to 60 C on the darkest materials of lowest thermal conductivity, and 35 to 45 C on the lightest spoil materials of highest thermal conductivity.

The surface temperature measurements recorded on strip-mine spoils indicated that heat injury to planted seedlings is a very real possibility on all commonly occurring bituminous spoil materials. The potential threat of high temperature injury is especially serious on black bituminous coal and black organic shales, but far less severe on light mineral shales and light sandstones.

INTRODUCTION

Seedlings growing on bituminous strip-mine spoils in central Pennsylvania are subject to many hazards. Among these are the high temperatures of the surface of the spoils. To assess the severity of the high temperatures, a study was made in the summer of 1968. The specific objectives were to measure the absolute values or obtain good estimates of extreme surface

69

temperatures on bituminous strip-mine spoils in central Pennsylvania during periods of intense insolation and to specify the conditions under which high surface temperatures occur.

A very limited amount of information concerning the surface microclimate of bituminous strip-mine spoils in Pennsylvania is available from previous studies. Accurate maximum surface-temperature measurements are conspicuously lacking in the literature on bituminous strip-mine spoil research. Largely because of this lack of adequate information concerning surface microclimate, the lethal potential of high temperature may not be fully appreciated by those connected with the revegetation effort.

Ashley (1950) measured a surface temperature of 57 C (135 F) on a sunny day in September, 1949 on a spoil bank in central Pennsylvania when the air temperature was only 31 C (88 F).

Horn (1968) established seedling test plots in 1966 and again in 1967 on a variety of spoil materials from the Brookville and Lower Kittanning coal cycles near Kylertown in Clearfield County, Pa. The study area and spoil materials used by Horn are the same as those reported in our study. He demonstrated a correspondence between the occurrence of high temperatures and drought during June and July of 1966, and seedling mortality rates among several of the 18 species of conifers, hardwoods, and shrubs he used in his planting trials. Mortality was much less during 1967 when precipitation was greater and more frequent and temperatures were lower. Using thermo-sticks, he found that the temperature of the spoil surface exceeded 52 C at least once during 1966 but did not reach that temperature at any time during the summer of 1967.

More detailed studies of surface temperature have been carried out on deep-mine wastes. Richardson (1958) studied the surface microclimate of black shale pit heaps at Ouston, County Durham, England (52°N latitude) during the summer of 1953. Temperatures were measured with constantan-manganin thermocouples. He reported that "on 16 successive days the temperature was above 45 C for periods ranging between 3 and 6 hours." The highest surface temperature occurred on a 30°S slope on July 23, reaching a value of 57 C (135 F) for a period of about 1 hr.

Schramm (1956) measured summertime surface temperatures on black anthracite coal sludge and breaker refuse from deep mining in Pennsylvania with both mercury-in-glass and thermistor thermometers. He obtained measurements which illustrate the steepness of summer temperature gradients, and the effects of color, texture, depth of dry layer, and angle of incidence on the magnitude of surface temperatures developed. On a sunny July 5 at 11:05 AM true solar time, 12 days after the most recent rain,

Schramm, using a thermistor, recorded a temperature of 67 C near the surface of dry, horizontal anthracite coal refuse.

These results are comparable to those obtained by a large number of independent investigators from all over the world who have shown the regular occurrence of high summer surface temperatures on bare, sunlit, organic, and inorganic naturally occurring materials.

Baker (1929) presented a table of maximum summer surface soil temperatures recorded by 13 different investigators from Russia, Germany, Canada, USA, and the tropics. Values ranged from a low of 50 C (122 F) measured by Tubuef on a gravel slide above 10,000 ft elevation in Yosemite National Park, to a high of 84 C (183 F) measured by Schimper at the surface of a sand soil in the tropics. Even in temperate regions, surface temperatures approach 80 C. Rudolf (1939) recorded a maximum surface temperature of 79 C in an opening in a young red pine plantation in Michigan (44°N latitude) during a severe drought in 1936. At one location, the temperature exceeded 54 C for $8\frac{1}{2}$ consecutive hours.

Vaartaja (1954) measured temperatures of exposed natural surfaces on dry pine heaths and on wet spruce sites in Finland (60°N latitude). The surface temperature of dry peat was 61 C when that of moist peat 3 ft away was only 31 C. The very rapid response of surface temperature to the prevailing energy balance was shown by a sharp drop in the surface temperature of burnt humus on a 10°SW slope from 69 C to 36 C within a period of 5 minutes after a thick cloud moved in front of the sun.

Day (1963) measured surface temperatures on decayed wood, sandy loam, F and H humus, and A_h horizon seedbeds common on clearcut areas in the spruce-fir subalpine forests of Alberta, Canada (55°N latitude) at an elevation of 5500 ft. He found that "during a hot dry period in 1960 temperatures exceeded 50 C for periods of several hours on all commonly occurring seedbeds, and reached 75 C for short periods on particularly heat-prone materials." His comprehensive review of the literature indicated that "heat injury may become serious for most coniferous species when surface temperatures in the 50 C to 60 C (122 F to 140 F) range are reached for periods of a few minutes up to several hours."

TEMPERATURE MEASUREMENTS

Surface temperatures are difficult to measure accurately with contact measuring instruments. Temperature gradients above and below the surface are greatest at those times when surface temperatures are highest.

No contact measuring instrument is capable of indicating any temperature other than its own. Any solid object placed in contact with the surface is subject to the same physical influences that operate on the surface layer itself. The temperature-measuring device receives short-wave global solar radiation from the sun and sky, receives long-wave solar radiation from the atmosphere and surrounding soil, emits long-wave radiation to the soil beneath and the sky above, gains or loses heat by convection to or from the surrounding air, and gains or loses heat by conduction to or from the soil surface. The temperature at which the instrument stabilizes will be determined by its own peculiar energy balance, and this temperature may or may not be equal to the surface temperature of the material for which the temperature is to be measured.

Remote measurement of surface temperature by means of an instrument which records the intensity of long-wave thermal infrared emission from the surface is probably the most accurate means of surface-temperature measurement currently available. In this study, such an instrument, a Model IT-3 Type S Infrared Radiation Thermometer manufactured by the Barnes Engineering Company of Stamford, Conn., was used. Hereafter, the instrument will be referred to simply as the IRT. The conical field of view of the IRT was 2° so that an area of about 1 in.^{2} was sensed from a perpendicular distance of 30 in. To the IRT was connected a 10-in. Beckman integrating strip-chart recorder. The recorder not only allowed continuous records to be kept, but by use of the integrator, the fluctuations of instantaneous reading could be smoothed. Power for these components was supplied by a Terado Model 50–160 117-v a-c portable power supply. The complete unit was by no means manually portable but could be easily handled in a station wagon or similar vehicle. In order to reduce transportation shock, the complete unit was carried on a piece of plywood underlain by a 4-in. layer of foam material.

Surface-temperature measurements were made on overburden associated with the Brookville and Lower Kittanning coal seams on land near Kylertown, Pa.

Twenty-two permanent surface-temperature measurement plots were established within one half mile of one another in such a way as to represent a variety of spoil rock types and colors. All sites were nearly horizontal and capable of being approached by a vehicle from the northern side to avoid shading.

The rock type, the geologic unit, the slope in degrees, the aspect, and the official Munsell soil-color chart designations were recorded for each site. Three rain gauges, partly filled with motor oil to prevent evaporation,

were set up at selected points within the confines of the study ⸺
each of six measurement sites representing a variety of geologic m⸺
and colors, a calibrated maximum-minimum mercury thermometer was
placed in a small wooden shelter facing north 1 ft above the spoil surface.
These thermometers were read at the end of each measurement day as well
as simultaneously with each IRT surface-temperature measurement.

The daily maximum mercury thermometer readings were revised in
accordance with information supplied by simultaneous IRT and mercury-
thermometer measurements to provide estimates of the highest summer
maximum surface temperatures on each material.

The in-place surface bulk densities and moisture contents of all 22
measurement sites were measured with a Nuclear Chicago moisture-density
gage 1 day following a heavy rain and again 6 days later. Percent cloud
cover and cloud type in the northern and southern halves of the sky were
recorded at the time of each surface temperature measurement.

A rough indication of wind speed at the time of each IRT measurement
was provided by a 4-ft long piece of plastic flagging held 4.5 ft above the
surface. The calibration of the angle of the wind ribbon from the vertical
was made with the actual wind speed at 4.5 ft as measured with a thermopile
anemometer.

Spot measurements of surface temperature were made continuously
from 11 AM until 3 PM true solar time with the IRT on all sunny and
partly sunny days between June 4 and July 8, 1968. Records could be taken
for six to eight sites per hour.

RESULTS

The rock type, Munsell color designation, slope, aspect, and highest surface temperature recorded between June 4 and July 8 with the IRT and
estimated from maximum-recording mercury thermometers are listed for
the more frequently visited sites in Table 1.

Surface temperatures in excess of 50 C were either measured directly
or were strongly suspected of having occurred at some time during the
period of observation on all of the essentially horizontal measurement plots
used in this study. Surface temperatures of 50 C or above were found to
occur on dark organic and mineral shale with low surface moisture contents
as soon as 1 day following a heavy rain. Temperatures of this magnitude
generally did not occur on light siltstone and light sandstone until at least

TABLE 1

Highest surface temperatures recorded and estimated on bituminous spoil measurement plots between June 4 and July 8, 1968

Rock Type	Munsell Color Designations		Slope deg	Aspect bearing	Times Site Visited no.	Maximum Temp.	
	Common Name	Hue Value/Chroma				IRT Meas. C	Est. from Hg Ther. C
Bituminous coal	Black	N 2/	0	—	22	64.8	69.0
Mineral shale	V.D. grayish-brown V.D. gray D. gray D. yellowish-brown	10YR 3/2 N 3/ N 4.5/ 10YR 4/4	4.5	N39W	5	55.6	61.5
Silty and sandy mineral shale	Olive D. yellowish-brown V.D. gray	5Y 5/3 10YR 4/4 N 3/	3.5	N30W	21	55.7	62.0
Organic shale and bituminous coal chips	Black V.D. gray D. gray	N 2/ N 3/ N 4/	7.0	N55W	15	58.6	69.5
Sandy mineral shale	Gray Lt. olive-gray V.D. gray Yellowish-brown	5Y 5/1 5Y 5.5/1 N 3/ 10YR 5/6	2.5	N56W	13	56.9	65.5
Sandstone	Yellowish-brown D. brown Olive	10YR 5/7 7.5YR 4/4 5Y 5/3	8.0	N79W	22	55.4	58.0
Organic shale	V.D. gray	N 3/	6.0	due S	12	59.4	61.0

Rock type	Color	Munsell					
Sandy mineral shale	Gray	5Y 5/1					
	Olive-brown	2.5Y 4/4					
Mineral shale	D. reddish-gray	10R 3/1	1.5	N45W	12	56.5	64.0
	Dusky red	10R 3/2					
	D. reddish-brown	5YR 3/2					
Fine sandstone	Yellowish-brown	10YR 5/4	3.5	S30E	12	41.7	50.0
Sandy mineral shale	Lt. olive-brown	2.5Y 5/4					
	Brown	7.5YR 4/4					
Organic shale	Black	N 2/	3.5	S5E	12	59.1	63.5
	V.D. brown	10YR 2/2					

3 days after rain unless the surface moisture content of the particular site was exceptionally low. Dark materials registered temperatures in the 50 C + range even on days when the air temperatures 1 ft above the spoil surface were below 25 C. High temperatures were not reached in light materials unless the air temperatures at 1 ft were at least in the vicinity of 32 C. Surface temperatures on dark materials were 25 C above air temperatures at a height of 1 ft by the second day after rain, and were as high as 35 C above air temperatures on the seventh day after precipitation. The temperature difference between the surface layer and the air over light materials varied from about 10 C the day after a rain to about 20 C after the surface layer had become dry.

Temperature differences between the lightest and the darkest spoil materials on any given day were generally between 10 C and 20 C.

The highest air temperature recorded 1 ft above the spoil surface was 36.7 C over bituminous coal. Horn (1968) reported air temperatures as high as 45 C during July of 1966 at the same height above the surface and on the same study area used in this research. The results of the present study indicate that air temperatures as high as 45 C could very well be accompanied by surface temperatures near 65 C on light sandstone and light mineral shale, and by temperatures in the vicinity of 80 C on dark organic shale and bituminous coal.

Bare-surface temperatures should ideally be expected to increase gradually throughout the morning and early afternoon. Surface temperatures were found to either increase very slightly or to remain virtually unchanged from noon until 2:30 PM. The maximum surface temperature on a given material on a given day was also more dependent on the vagaries of wind and clouds than on any ideal time-dependent progression, and was found to occur unpredictably at any time between 10 AM and 3 PM.

With air temperatures of 30 C or higher, surface temperatures above 50 C were continuously maintained on the darkest materials from 11 AM to 3 PM by the third day following rain. After 7 days without rain, surface temperatures were found to stay at 60 C or above throughout the same 4-hr period. The temperature for the same duration on the lightest materials was much less than for black organic shale and bituminous coal. Three days after rain, surface temperatures between 40 and 45 C were steadily maintained from 11 AM to 3 PM on light siltstone and sandstone. Surface temperatures were between 45 and 50 C for the same duration after 7 days without rain. Surface temperatures above 50 C were found to be of relatively short duration on light materials when air temperatures were no higher than 35 C (95 F).

The surface temperature measurements recorded on strip-mine spoils in the course of this investigation indicate that heat injury to planted or volunteer seedlings is a very real possibility on all commonly occurring bituminous spoil materials. The potential threat of high-temperature injury is especially serious on black bituminous coal and black shales, but far less severe on light shales and sandstones.

LITERATURE CITED

Ashley, R. H. 1950. The invasion and development of natural vegetation on spoil banks in central Pennsylvania. *M. F. Thesis.* Pennsylvania State Coll. 88 p.

Baker, F. S. 1929. Effect of excessively high temperatures on coniferous reproduction *J. Forest.* **29**, 949–975.

Day, R. J. 1963. Spruce seedling mortality caused by adverse summer microclimate in the Rocky Mountains. Can. Dep. Forest., Forest. Res. Branch Publ. 1003. 35 p.

Horn, M. L. 1968. The revegetation of highly acid spoil banks in the bituminous coal region of central Pennsylvania. *M. S. Thesis.* Pennsylvania State Univ. 69 p.

Richardson, J. A. 1958. The effect of temperature on the growth of plants on pit heaps. *J. Ecol.* **46**, 537–546.

Rudolf, P. O. 1939. Why forest plantations fail. *J. Forest.* **37**, 377–383.

Schramm, J. R. 1966. Plant colonization studies on black wastes from anthracite mining in Pennsylvania. Amer. Phil. Soc., Philadelphia, Pa. 194 p.

Vaartaja, O. 1954. Temperature and evaporation at and near ground level on certain forest sites. *Can. J. Bot.* **32**, 760–783.

DISCUSSION

AHARRAH: I have wondered if the difference in temperature between the root and the surface area might have more to do with this than just surface temperature. Have you measured temperatures, let us say, two inches below the surface?

BORDEN: We didn't, but differences of the magnitude of 50 C have been observed between the surface and a few centimeters underneath. This kind of gradient under some conditions may be more of a problem in seedling survival than a high surface temperature per se. In early spring, root temperatures may be near freezing and the tops in 40–50 C environment. It is well-documented that temperature environments of the magnitude of 50 C are lethal if the plant tissue gets this hot.

CHADWICK: Can your type of infrared detector measure subsurface temperatures? Also, what difference would you obtain if you used thermistor apparatus instead?

BORDEN: One cannot easily use an infrared thermometer to measure subsurface temperatures. Any contact device, as long as it does not substantially modify the medium in which it is put, will be satisfactory for measuring temperature. So, for subsurface temperature measurements, small thermocouples, thermistors, etc., are completely adequate. They are inadequate to measure the surface temperature because of the points I mentioned in the paper.

GOOD: How much does an infrared thermometer cost? At what distance can you obtain a reading?

BORDEN: The cost is roughly $ 2000 to $ 2500. Ours is a Barnes instrument, but others may be less costly and just as suitable. Measurement may be made at any distance, but one must remember that the field of view increases in proportion to the square of the distance. The cone is two degrees for the instrument we used; so at 30 inches the field is about a square inch.

RAY BROWN: Barnes has a new hand-held model for about $ 1000 which does essentially the same thing that your model does.

BORDEN: We anticipated that these things could be miniaturized. A recorder may still be necessary if the instrument is fundamentally the same. It is too hard to get a good reading from the dial, and since the internal reference cell is 50 C, measurements near and above 50 C cannot be made satisfactorily without a recorder.

NEUMANN: Did you measure the temperatures in the shadow of plants?

BORDEN: Temperature gradients and rates of change have been frequently reported in the literature for completely insolated to fully shaded conditions. Differences of the magnitude of 35 C have been frequently found. The rate of change of temperature from shaded to sunlight and vice versa caused, for example, by moving clouds is also dramatic. A change of 30 C in five minutes is not unusual. We measured increases of 8 C in 60 seconds and like decreases in 30 seconds caused by cumulus clouds.

KNABE: Dr. Schramm reported that high temperatures were the main cause for plants dying on anthracite spoils. Is this your opinion, too; or do you think that other factors might be involved?

BORDEN: Schramm gives pictorial evidence of seedling mortality because of high temperatures on coal sludge which is not at all like the spoil we dealt with. It is our opinion that lethal temperatures occur not only on the dark materials similar to those studied by Schramm but on almost all kinds of materials of disturbed land.

In some cases high temperature alone causes death to plants; for example, heat girdling of stems at the surface of the growing matrix. In other cases, death may be caused by a heat-related phenomenon such as steep gradients or the combination of temperature effect and drought.

METHODS OF ASSESSMENT OF ACID COLLIERY SPOIL AS A MEDIUM FOR PLANT GROWTH

M. J. Chadwick

Senior Lecturer, Department of Biology, University of York, Heslington, York, United Kingdom

Some properties of coal spoil are considered in relation to the chemical activity of some of the components of the spoil (detrital fraction, iron pyrites, ankerite, and amorphous material content) and their interactions during the spoil weathering process. A system is outlined that attempts to integrate these interactions by making use of the ratio between the total exchangeable acidity and the cation exchange capacity on the one hand and the acid-extractable cations (being the potential source of acid-neutralizing ions) on the other. The results of controlled weathering investigations are used to evaluate elements of the proposed system which is then discussed in the light of simpler methods of chemical analysis of the substrate, bioassay results, comparative tests of plant growth on a range of spoils, and correlations between plant occurrence and the level of certain spoil factors in the field.

INTRODUCTION

Although physical factors play a part in preventing successful plant establishment and growth, it is generally held that substrate nutritional factors (nutrient deficiencies and toxicities and extreme soil reaction) are most frequently the cause of vegetational failure on acid colliery spoil (Knabe, 1965). It is therefore necessary to assess realistically the nutritional status of spoil before attempting reclamation and revegetation. Conventional methods of soil analysis are often employed in attempting this assessment, although many are inappropriate for use on spoil. Colliery spoil is not the well-buffered medium represented by most humid soils; methods based upon an extracting solution coming into rapid equilibrium with the solid phase are often inapplicable. Furthermore the presence of large quantities of salts render invalid many of the assumptions upon which normal methods of soil analysis are based. Neither is it meaningful to divide spoil into a "chemically inactive" fraction (>2 mm diameter) and a "chemically active" fraction ($\leqq 2$ mm) as is usually done prior to soil chemical analysis. Soft shale and mudstone material break down rapidly and even large particles are potentially chemically active and may rapidly become so.

This paper outlines some of the methods being developed for the assessment of colliery spoil, and in particular for unburnt spoil, by a team in the Department of Biology, University of York, United Kingdom. The mineral composition of spoil, spoil chemistry, and the weathering sequences exhibited by spoil under controlled conditions are the bases for the work.

COLLIERY SPOIL COMPOSITION

Coal seams are generally associated with mudstones, shales, siltstones, sandstones and seat earths, or combinations of any of these. When the coal is mined, this material forms the waste that constitutes the coal tip. Apart from the carbonaceous material that is slow to weather and produces little in the way of nutrients for plant growth, most of the debris (>90%) is represented by quartz and the clay minerals of the mudstones and shales. The clay minerals are present in varying proportions of the illite and kaolinite types. Also present as part of this detrital fraction are very small amounts of amorphous ferric and aluminum hydroxides, mainly as molecular films blocking exchange sites on the clay minerals. In addition, the debris contains the minerals ankerite, pyrite and siderite which together form about 5% of the total. The exact amounts and proportions depend upon the original environmental conditions of deposition.

The chemical reactions associated with FeS_2 breakdown in the tip determine some of the features of subsequent spoil composition and have been described as follows (Stumm, 1965):

$$FeS_2 + 3\tfrac{1}{2}O_2 + H_2O \longrightarrow 2SO_4^{-2} + 2H^+ + Fe^{+2}$$

$$Fe^{+2} + \tfrac{1}{4}O_2 + H^+ \rightleftharpoons Fe^{+3} + \tfrac{1}{2}H_2O$$

$$Fe^{+3} + 3H_2O \longrightarrow Fe(OH)_3 + 3H^+$$

These equations do not indicate the mechanisms of reaction or the intermediate products that may be formed, and it has been suggested that they may give rise to an oversimplification of the system of pyritic oxidation

(Shumate, Smith, and Brant, 1969). However, the equations do indicate the final products of the reactions, and it will be seen that abundant H^+ ions are produced. The carbonate mineral ankerite is potentially capable of neutralizing this acidity, and in so doing, large quantities of soluble salts, chiefly sulfates, are produced (Chadwick, Cornwell, and Palmer, 1969). The minerals gypsum and jarosite are formed as the tip material weathers in this way.

EXCHANGEABLE ACIDITY IN UNBURNT COLLIERY SPOIL

It is for the reasons outlined above that the percentage base-saturation values, sometimes calculated by workers more familiar with soil materials than spoil, may be extremely misleading when taken as an indication of the nutrient status of the substrate. Percentage base-saturation values make use of two of the following three measurements: cation exchange capacity,

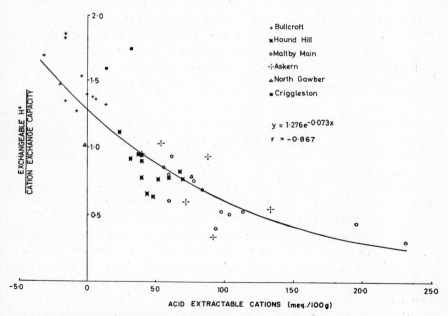

FIGURE 1 The relationship between the exchangeable acidity: total cation exchange capacity ratio and acid-extractable cations for unburnt spoil samples from the field sites.

6*

exchangeable metal ions, and exchangeable hydrogen ions (Knabe, 1965). However, in view of the high soluble salt content that may be present in spoil, it is more appropriate to estimate the total acid-extractable cations (Jackson, 1958) as a measure of the net neutralizing capacity of the spoil and compare this with the degree of saturation of the ion exchange sites with acidic ions (H^+ and Al^{+3}). Figure 1 shows that when this is done for spoil from six tip sites in the Yorkshire Coalfield a consistent relationship emerges. It also indicates that in some spoil no net neutralizing capacity is available. Field observation, as well as experience with trial and large-scale attempts at vegetational establishment and growth, indicate that these sites are particularly difficult reclamation sites.

It will be seen from Fig. 1 that values of the saturation ratio exceed unity for three of the spoil materials. This may be due to the inclusion of acidic ions not adsorbed on exchange sites. The amorphous aluminium hydroxides, already referred to, may also be a significant source of acidic cations in the pyritic spoil. When films of this amorphous material are removed from the exchange sites on the clay minerals, by treatment with hot thio-sulfate and excess dilute sodium hydroxide, a substantial increase in the cation exchange capacity results. This effect is illustrated by the Maltby Main spoil sample (the fraction passing through a 100-mesh screen, at a pH of 3.5) which had a cation exchange capacity of 12.3 meq/100 g before treatment and 20.9 after treatment; comparable values for the Hound Hill spoil sample were 12.8 and 19.1 meq/100 g. This effect has been investigated in much greater detail by Palmer (unpublished work).

SATURATION EXTRACTS

Extreme acidity is closely connected with the high degree of toxicity to plants shown by much colliery spoil. In any assessment of the potential of acid spoil for supporting plant growth, we must obtain some index of this toxicity. Once the points already made concerning spoil have been accepted, it is clear that toxicities cannot be estimated by the normal soil procedure of allowing an extractant to come into equilibrium with a ≤ 2 mm sample followed by subsequent determination of quantities of available ions in the solution. In place of this, a saturation extract, frequently used in determinations on saline and alkali soils (Richards, 1954), has been adopted using a sample of the ≤ 1-cm fraction of spoil. A determination of water-soluble elements in this extract provides an appraisal of the effect of spoil solution on plant growth. Table 1 illustrates the unsatisfactory nature of extractants like 1 N ammonium acetate in assessing "available" cations.

In two spoils (Bullcroft and Woolley) the values obtained for a single cation greatly exceed the measured total cation exchange capacity. Table 2 gives the results of an alternative method of assessment using saturation extracts. The values quoted in both tables are means obtained from 12 random samples on each of the five sites.

Using the spoil saturation extracts, a comparison has been made with a similar extract obtained from a moderately fertile brown earth soil termed "moorland". Table 3 gives the spoil values expressed as ratios with the corresponding moorland soil extract values. The latter values are used as common denominators. Particularly high proportions of Fe, Al, and Mn are evident in some of the spoils.

TABLE 1

Composition of 1 N ammonium acetate (pH 7.0) extracts of five spoils

Site	Cations as meq/100 g of spoil				Cation Exchange Capacity
	Na	K	Mg	Ca	(meq/100 g spoil)
Bullcroft	0.034	0.899	2.50	20.38	13.22
Hound Hill	0.007	0.230	1.40	1.46	10.88
Maltby Main	0.054	0.221	3.59	4.84	10.64
Mitchells Main[a]	0.108	0.162	1.41	3.48	13.55
Woolley[b]	0.126	0.418	0.16	17.78	14.78

[a] Some burnt material.
[b] All burnt material.

BIOASSAY METHODS

In view of the unsatisfactory nature of some of the methods of chemical analysis of spoil, and in order to assess whether the results obtained from such analyses are realistic, barley (*Hordeum vulgare*, var. Proctor), *Agrostis tenuis*, and Brussels sprouts (*Brassica oleracea gemmifera*) have been used in bioassay experiments. These plants were grown in the $\leq$1-cm fraction of spoil and also in spoil diluted in varying proportions with acid-washed sand. A modified Long-Ashton culture solution was employed to supply a complete range of nutrients at a relatively constant level to each spoil dilution treatment. The five spoils listed in the tables were used.

TABLE 2

Composition of saturation extracts of five spoils

Site	Specific Conductivity 10^{-3} mhos	Cations as meq/100 g spoil					Elements in spoil in ppm			
		Na	K	Ca	Mg	Al	Mn	Cu	Zn	Fe
Bullcroft	5.55	0.003	0.001	0.86	0.68	13.00	8.20	3.17	2.45	123.7
Hound Hill	0.33	0.016	0.013	0.03	0.02	—[c]	0.55	0.05	0.15	—[c]
Maltby Main	1.52	0.031	0.009	0.23	0.12	0.20	2.75	0.18	0.25	0.36
Mitchells Main[a]	2.32	0.019	0.005	0.38	0.25	0.15	2.20	0.20	0.25	0.28
Woolley[b]	1.46	0.023	0.006	0.57	0.02	1.00	0.27	0.24	0.16	—[c]

[a] Some burnt material.
[b] All burnt material.
[c] Trace.

TABLE 3

Levels of nutrients in saturation extracts of five spoils compared with soil

Site	Nutrient levels as a ratio of those in a moorland soil								
	Na	K	Ca	Mg	Al[a]	Mn	Cu	Zn	Fe[a]
Bullcroft	0.70	0.09	24.85	57.83	120.00	31.36	16.06	21.59	125.00
Hound Hill	0.95	0.88	0.73	1.99	—	2.08	0.27	1.35	—
Maltby Main	1.89	0.63	6.54	10.30	0.20	11.11	0.92	2.20	0.36
Mitchells Main	1.11	0.33	11.06	21.02	0.15	0.85	1.04	2.24	0.28
Woolley	1.38	0.38	16.38	1.44	1.00	1.23	1.20	1.38	—

[a] The soil had only trace levels of Al and Fe.

Being the most resistant species to a number of ions that are toxic in all but small amounts, *A. tenuis* proved the most useful as a bioassay plant on toxic spoil material; however, a refinement of the technique may render some of the more sensitive species valuable. Chemical analyses of the shoots of *A. tenuis*, grown in undiluted spoil, revealed a relationship between nutrient uptake (as indicated by shoot composition) and the composition of saturation extracts for each spoil sample. The order of the content of shoots of *A. tenuis* grown on undiluted spoil is given below for four elements:

Mn: Maltby Main > Mitchells Main > Hound Hill > Woolley
Mg: Mitchells Main > Maltby Main > Woolley and Hound Hill
K: Hound Hill > Maltby Main > Woolley > Mitchells Main
Ca: Woolley, Mitchells Main, and Maltby Main > > Hound Hill

The results agree exactly with the ranking of amounts from these spoils as estimated by saturation extracts (Table 2).

PLANT PERFORMANCE

It may be useful to measure plant performance on spoil and use this as a method of integrating various spoil factors. This may be done by following comparatively their performance on a number of spoil materials. This approach has been adopted at York, not only to obtain comparisons of spoils but also to allow naturally occurring populations of *A. tenuis* to be assessed (Harding, 1970).

Figure 2 shows the growth of a population of *A. tenuis*, over an 8-week period, on $\leq$ 1-cm fractions of three spoil materials and the moorland soil. The spoil was kept moist with water, but no nutrients were added. It will be seen that the result agrees well with the saturation extract determinations and with the bioassay results.

PLANT OCCURRENCE AND THE DISTRIBUTION OF SPOIL CHEMICAL FACTORS ON TIPS

When the relationship between the exchangeable acidity : total cation exchange capacity ratio and the acid-extractable cations is considered, and when to this is added results from saturation extracts, bioassay determinations, and plant performance on a range of spoils, it becomes evident

that considerable agreement on the assessment of spoil has been obtained
The example of spoil from Bullcroft can be used to illustrate this.

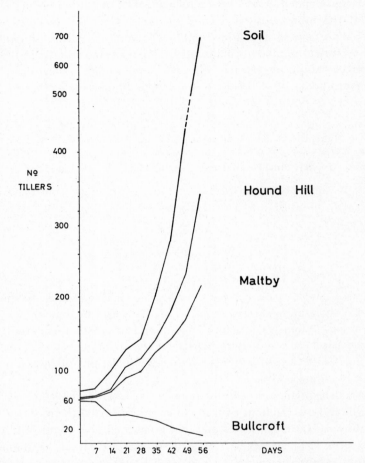

FIGURE 2 The performance (number of tillers) of a population of
Agrostis tenuis on soil and on three spoil materials.

Most of the samples of spoil from Bullcroft have not only an excess of
acidic ions, which include those not adsorbed upon exchange sites, but also
no net neutralizing capacity in the spoil. This produces a very toxic spoil
(Tables 2 and 3). Bioassay plants do not grow on this undiluted spoil
sufficiently well to provide suitable material for analysis. However, tiller
number decreases rather than increases when *A. tenuis* is grown on well-
watered spoil not supplied with additional nutrients. Experience gained

from establishing vegetation on this tip, and from field trials, indicates that it is one of the most toxic spoils encountered in the Yorkshire Coalfield. Only a patchy establishment of vegetation has ever been achieved.

Field investigations on the Bullcroft tip have been carried out to ascertain whether or not the patchy distribution of vegetation is related to observable chemical variability in the spoil itself. This was done by taking a number of paired random samples of spoil. When the sample of spoil was taken the presence or absence of vegetation was recorded. If vegetation was present at the original sampling location, the second sample of the pair was taken from the nearest point on the tip without vegetation; if vegetation was absent, the nearest point with vegetation was also sampled. Each spoil sample was used to obtain a saturation extract, the composition of which was determined. Table 4 gives the results of these determinations

TABLE 4

Spoil factors and the distribution of vegetation on Bullcroft

Vegetation	Spoil pH	ppm in saturation extract		
		K	Al	Fe
Present	3.82[a]	2.83[b]	14.5[c]	5.1[b]
Absent	2.86[a]	0.85[b]	28.5[c]	19.1[b]

[a] Significantly different at less than the 0.001 probability level.
[b] Significantly different at less than the 0.01 probability level.
[c] Significantly different at less than the 0.05 probability level.

for the four spoil factors for which significant differences between bare and vegetated areas were obtained. It will be seen that higher spoil pH and water-soluble K values were found in vegetated spoil, but significantly lower values of water-soluble Fe and Al. Results from field trials suggest that it is unlikely that the vegetation is the cause rather than the effect of these differences. It is of extreme interest that these spoil factors are the ones that apparently determine vegetational success and also that there is a close correlation between spoil pH and the amounts of K and Al released from the spoil. These elements are located in the alumino-silicate minerals of the detrital component of spoil. This detrital component also contains amorphous oxyhydroxides of Fe and Al, and it appears that, in the acid medium that results from pyritic oxidation, decomposition may be rapid enough to result in a substrate of such a degree of toxicity that plant establishment and growth is prohibited. Factors that determine the precise rate of release and to what extent these conditions vary in weathering spoil are the subject of current weathering studies (Palmer, unpublished work). The rate of release of Al is apparently affected much more by the concentration of total dissolved salts and by the clay mineral composition than by the acidity of the medium.

DISCUSSION

It is concluded from these studies that an understanding of spoil chemistry and spoil-weathering sequences is essential in order to devise realistic methods of assessing spoil as a substrate for plant growth. Existing information indicates that the more conventional methods of soil analysis, though frequently used on spoils, are not really appropriate. Field evidence suggests that the products of pyritic oxidation, which in turn affect the stability of the detrital components of spoil, largely influence the success of plant establishment and growth on the medium. The outlined procedures offer some relatively rapid and reliable methods of spoil assessment. Undoubtedly these will be improved, and others will become available as our knowledge of spoil-weathering sequences is expanded.

ACKNOWLEDGEMENTS

My colleagues, Mr. M. E. Palmer and Mr. C. P. Harding, have generously agreed to quotation being made from work in progress in writing this paper. Thanks are also due to the West Riding County Council for supporting some of this work.

LITERATURE CITED

Chadwick, M. J., S. M. Cornwell, and M. E. Palmer. 1969. Exchangeable acidity in unburnt colliery spoil. *Nature* (London) **222**, 161.

Harding, C. P. 1970. Plant available nutrients in colliery spoil and their relation to ecotypic differentiation within populations of *Agrostis tenuis* L. Ph. D. Thesis. Univ. of York.

Jackson, M. L. 1958. *Soil chemical analysis*. Constable, London. 498 p.

Knabe, W. 1965. Observations on world-wide efforts to reclaim industrial waste land. In: G. T. Goodman, R. W. Edwards, and J. M. Lambert (Ed.). *Ecology and the industrial society*. Blackwell, Oxford, p. 263–296.

Richards, L. A. 1954. Diagnosis and improvement of saline and alkali soils. U. S. Dep. Agr., Washington, D. C. 160 p.

Shumate, K. S., E. E. Smith, and R. A. Brant. 1969. A model for pyritic systems. *Symp. on Pollution Control in Fuel Combustion Processing and Mining*, Amer. Chem. Soc., p. 50–58.

Stumm, W. 1965. Oxygenation of ferrous iron properties of aqueous iron as related to mine drainage pollution. *Symp. on Acid Mine Drainage Research*, Ohio River Valley Water Sanitation Commission, p. 51–63.

DISCUSSION

THIRGOOD: Did you not find great variability on individual pit heaps in your chemical analysis?

CHADWICK: Yes, they are variable. We never take less than 12 samples from each tip, and we always calculate standard errors in order to discern whether there is really some significant difference.

SCHMEHL: Have you tried to characterize the various spoils by determining the equivalence between carbonates and sulfides as a means to predict whether or not it will become strongly acid?

CHADWICK: No, we haven't.

CRESSWELL: I wonder if you would clarify the bio-technique employed. You mentioned you used a nutrient medium and determined the specific metal content. Was this nutrient medium deficient in specific ions, or was it a complete nutrient media?

CHADWICK: No, it was a complete nutrient medium. We used this because we wanted to be able to grow the plants on a whole range of spoils. There are some spoils on which we can grow these plants if we just add water. But, if we want to keep plants alive on some of the more acid spoils, we have to add a fairly low level nutrient medium. This was a common factor throughout all the spoils. I realize there are pitfalls involved in this, but we were looking for relationships between the chemical analysis of the spoil material and that of the shoots of plants growing on the spoil.

HEALD: In your last slide, you showed 14 ppm Al. Isn't this still a very toxic level, and yet you had plant growth?

CHADWICK: Yes, I am surprised, but I should add that this is Al as ppm of spoil. Some of the literature quotes *Agrostis tenuis*, the plant we were using, as tolerating up to 60 ppm of Al.

BERG: We have found on our spoils that if you sampled under individual plants, or small stands of plants, you are likely to come up with a lower pH or more soluble Al or Mn than these plants can tolerate in the greenhouse. This indicates that the plant in the field is starting in a microsite that can't be completely sampled.

EVALUATION OF P AND K SOIL
FERTILITY TESTS
ON COAL-MINE SPOILS*

William A. Berg †

Research Soil Scientist, Northeastern Forest Experiment Station, Forest Service, U. S. Department of Agriculture, Berea, Kentucky

Commonly used soil tests for available nutrients may not produce valid results when used on mine spoils, so greenhouse studies of plant growth on spoils were used to evaluate the ability of common soil tests to determine plant-available P and K in Southern Appalachian coal-mine spoils.

Phosphorus extracted by the Bray #1 method was significantly correlated with grass-growth response to added P on N-fertilized spoils. Phosphorus extracted with 0.05 N HCl + 0.025 N H_2SO_4 or with 0.15 N H_2SO_4 was not significantly correlated with grass-growth response to added P.

Potassium-extracting solutions of 1 N ammonium acetate, 0.15 N H_2SO_4, and 0.05 N HCl + 0.025 N H_2SO_4 gave similar results on the spoils. By agronomic standards, K in the spoils ranged from moderately low to high; however, there was no yield response to K in the greenhouse studies.

INTRODUCTION

Where vegetation is to be established on coal-mine spoils, it is important to determine the status of available plant nutrients in the spoil, so the proper species and fertilizers can be used. Laboratory tests for nutrients, like those used on agricultural soils, are relatively quick and cheap; but the commonly used tests for determining available nutrients in soils may not

---

* Research supported in part by the Federal Water Pollution Control Administration, U. S. Department of the Interior.

† At present Assistant Professor of Agronomy, Colorado State University, Fort Collins, Colorado.

produce valid results when applied to mine spoils. So, using greenhouse studies of plant growth to indicate nutrient availability, we evaluated several of these soil tests for estimating plant-available P and K in Southern Appalachian coal-mine spoils. Also, we studied the influence of coarse spoil fragments on test results.

METHODS AND MATERIALS

Spoil materials

In the Central and Southern Appalachians, coal is surface mined from formations of Pennsylvanian age composed largely of shales and siltstones. The shales and siltstones are shattered in the mining, some weathering rapidly to produce spoil materials that usually contain 15 to 45% soil-size material. Sandstone fragments and waste coal sometimes make up part of the spoils.

Fifty-two of the 63 spoils used in this study were collected from surface coal mining operations in eastern Kentucky; the remaining spoils came from similar operations in adjoining states. The spoils were collected from 39 stripping operations and represent 21 different coal seams. Spoils were selected that appeared to be typical of extensive spoil areas; they were tested for pH in the field and were not collected if extremely acid (pH below 4.5).

The spoils were sieved in the field through a screen with 1.3-cm-square mesh, and the material not passing through the mesh was discarded. The discarded material ranged from an estimated 20 to 50% of the spoil volume.

Greenhouse studies

A requirement of a valid fertility test is that the amount of a given nutrient extracted from the growth medium by the test be highly correlated with plant growth on the medium. If the correlation is high, then the quantity of the nutrient extracted from a medium by the test can be described in terms of relative availability to plants (i.e. inadequate or adequate). If the correlation is low, the soil test is meaningless.

The plant-growth information reported here is from three separate greenhouse studies. The first study was conducted on 17 spoils in January and February of 1966; the test species was K-31 tall fescue (*Festuca arundinacea*). The second study was conducted on 15 spoils in May and June of

1966; the test species was weeping lovegrass (*Eragrostis curvula*). The third study was conducted on 31 spoils in September and October of 1967; the test species was K-31 tall fescue. In all the studies, 1800 g of spoil, including coarse fragments up to 1.3 cm in diameter, were weighed out for each pot, the fertilizer treatment was applied, and the spoil was placed in polyethylene sacks lining 2-liter paper cartons. After the pots were seeded, they were watered with distilled water as needed. Plants were harvested 60 days after planting, oven dried at 70 C, and weighed to the nearest 0.1 g.

In the first two studies, N, P, and K were applied alone and in all combinations on each of the 32 spoils. One pot of each spoil was not fertilized. Nitrogen was applied in solution as ammonium nitrate at the rate of 50 ppm N; P was applied in suspension as monocalcium phosphate at the rate of 21 ppm P; and K was applied in solution as potassium chloride at the rate of 41 ppm K. The spoil for each pot was spread out on a polyethylene sheet and the appropriate fertilizer solution distributed over the spoil surface with a pipette. The spoil and fertilizer were mixed together and replaced in the pot. Only one replication of fertility treatments was applied on each spoil.

In the third study, only four fertility treatments were used: check, N, P, and the combination of N + P applied at the same rates as in the first two studies. There were two replications on each spoil.

In order to combine the results of the three greenhouse studies for correlating yield of N-fertilized grass with soil P tests, percentage yield was calculated on each of the 63 spoils by using grass yields of the N-only treatment (numerator) and the N + P treatment (denominator) as follows (Soil Test Work Group, 1956):

$$\text{percentage yield} = \frac{\text{yield without P fertilizer}}{\text{yield with P fertilizer}} \times 100$$

Soil tests

Three different P-extracting solutions were evaluated. The solutions were: 0.03 N HCl + 0.025 N NH$_4$F, commonly referred to as the Bray # 1 (Olsen and Dean, 1965); 0.05 N HCl + 0.025 N H$_2$SO$_4$ (Olsen and Dean, 1965); and 0.15 N H$_2$SO$_4$ (Page et al., 1965). The Bray # 1 is the soil test used by state soil test laboratories in Kentucky, Ohio, and several other midwestern states. The 0.05 N HCl + 0.025 N H$_2$SO$_4$ method was developed for use on the acid soils of the southeastern United States and is used in the state soil test laboratories of Virginia and West Virginia. The 0.15 N H$_2$SO$_4$ method of extraction was used in the Kentucky state soil test laboratory until 1967. In the initial spoil test work on P, the usual laboratory procedure was modified to use 20-g test samples of the same particle-sized spoil as used in the pot studies (fragments up to 1.3 cm in diameter included). All soil P tests were run twice, and the average was used in the analyses.

The three extracting solutions used for estimating plant-available K were: 1.0 N ammonium acetate (Pratt, 1965), 0.05 N HCl + 0.025 N H_2SO_4 (Page et al., 1965), and 0.15 N H_2SO_4 (Page et al., 1965). The 1.0 N ammonium acetate is a commonly used soil test for K and is often used in laboratories where P is determined by the Bray method. The 0.05 N HCl + 0.025 N H_2SO_4 extracting solution for K is usually used in those laboratories where plant-available P is determined by the use of this extractant. The 0.15 N H_2SO_4 was used in Kentucky for extracting K and has been shown to give results similar to 1 N ammonium acetate for extractable K (Sutton and Seay, 1958). All K soil tests were made on spoil samples that had coarse fragments greater than 2 mm in diameter sieved out.

Spoil pH was determined with a pH meter on a 2 to 1 distilled water to spoil mixture that was stirred, allowed to settle 30 minutes, and stirred again before the electrodes were immersed into the supernatant liquid.

RESULTS AND DISCUSSION

Response to N, P, and K

In addition to their use for evaluating the validity of the P and K soil tests, the greenhouse fertility trials are important for determining which of the elements are limiting to grass growth and for interpreting the test results for practical application in the field.

Grass yields on spoils in this study ranged from very low to low where no fertilizer was added. Adding P alone had little influence on grass yields. Nitrogen fertilization alone increased yield many fold on some spoils and little or none on others. The combination of N and P produced fair to good yields on all spoils. There was no yield response to K added alone or in combination with N and P. Thus, native K was adequate for grass growth in all the spoils. The range in grass-yield response to addition of N and P on the 63 spoils is illustrated by yields on 8 selected spoils in Fig. 1.

Nitrogen is limiting for grass growth in all of these spoils in Fig. 1, but plant-available P ranges from extremely deficient to adequate. These findings are in agreement with studies on coal-mine spoils of Pennsylvanian age in West Virginia (Tyner and Smith, 1945) and Iowa (Einspahr et al., 1955), where N and sometimes P were shown to be the limiting fertility elements in growth of non-leguminous herbaceous species.

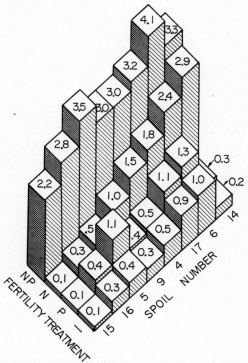

FIGURE 1   Fescue yields in g per pot on eight spoils as influenced by addition of N and P.

Phosphorus

A highly significant correlation was found between percentage yield on N-fertilized spoils and Bray # 1 extractable P in the spoils (Fig. 2). Fifty-five percent of the variance in the grass yields can be related to differences in plant-available P in the spoils as estimated by the Bray # 1 extraction. Although not strictly comparable with variances derived from soil tests of other soil populations, this variance is similar to that (49%) reported for the Bray # 1 extraction on 74 soils by the Soil Test Work Group (1956), but is considerably less than the 80% variance mentioned by Mattingly and Talibudeen (1967) in other soil test studies. Subsequent to the work reported here, we found that the amounts of added N and P used in this study were too low for optimum plant growth on a few of the spoils, a factor that may have reduced the correlation in this study.

However, the correlation appears to be good enough so that meaningful interpretations can be made of Bray # 1 extractable P in spoils—namely, that spoils testing less than 4 ppm P usually are very deficient in plant-available P, and that spoils testing over 8 ppm P have adequate P for growth of a herbaceous ground cover. In spoils testing in the range of 4 to 8 ppm extractable P, grass showed a variable response to P, and probably the best interpretation of the data is that about one-half of the spoils testing in this range are very deficient in plant-available P.

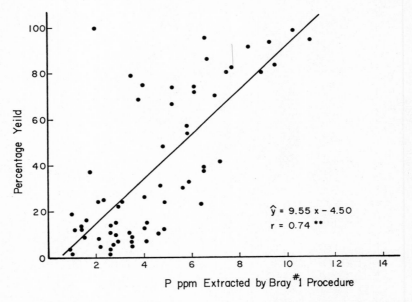

FIGURE 2   Percentage yield of grass on 63 N-fertilized spoils as related to Bray # 1 extractable P.

Of interest was the one spoil that tested very low in P by the Bray # 1 extraction, but produced excellent grass yields without the addition of P (upper left hand point on Fig. 2). Four more samples of this spoil were tested for Bray # 1 extractable P. Three of these samples also tested very low, but the fourth sample tested 23 ppm P, which is high even by agronomic standards (Olsen and Dean, 1965). It appears that the source of plant-available P in this particular spoil may be in discrete particles, and that these particles supply adequate P in the pot tests (1800 g), but the particles were so few that they were seldom a part of the laboratory test samples (20 g).

The correlation between percentage yield on N-fertilized spoils and P extracted with 0.05 N HCl + 0.025 N H_2SO_4 was low (Fig. 3). Because the 0.05 N HCl + 0.025 N H_2SO_4 extracting solution was developed for use on acid soils, the results were plotted so as to distinguish those 37 spoils with pH less than 6.0 from the 26 spoils with pH 6.0 and higher (Fig. 3). No relationship between percentage yield and P extracted by 0.05 N HCl + 0.025 N H_2SO_4 is evident even from the acid spoils.

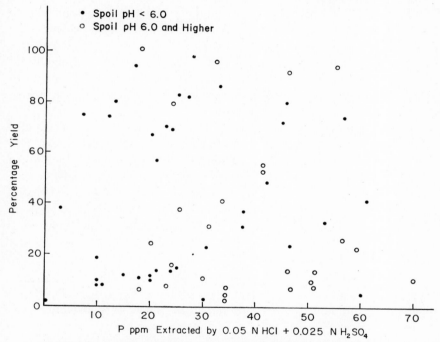

FIGURE 3 Percentage yield of grass on 63 N-fertilized spoils as related to 0.05 N HCl + 0.025 N H_2SO_4 extractable P.

The 0.15 N H_2SO_4 extracting solution was used only on the 17 spoils in the first greenhouse experiments. The correlation between percentage yield on the N-fertilized spoils and P extracted by 0.15 N H_2SO_4 was low. Thus, it appears that extracting solutions of 0.05 N HCl + 0.025 N H_2SO_4 or 0.15 N H_2SO_4 do not give meaningful results when used to estimate plant-available P in spoils of Pennsylvanian age.

To further investigate the characteristics of the three extracting solutions on spoils, the relative amounts of P extracted were compared. There was

7*

no significant correlation between relative amounts of P extracted by 0.05 N HCl + 0.025 N H_2SO_4 and the Bray # 1 procedure on all 63 spoils. On the 17 spoils in the first study where 0.15 N H_2SO_4 was also used as a P extractant, the correlation was highly significant between P extracted by 0.05 N HCl + 0.025 N H_2SO_4 and P extracted by 0.15 N H_2SO_4 (r = 0.92), but the correlation between P extracted by these extractants and P extracted by the Bray # 1 method was low.

Coarse fragments

In routine soil test procedures, soil samples are usually lightly crushed and screened, and coarse fragments (material over 2 mm diameter) are discarded. Because coarse fragments may make up 50 to 90 percent of a spoil's weight, discarding the coarse fragments might have a significant influence on soil test results and interpretations. Therefore, the third greenhouse study was also used to investigate the influence of coarse fragments in spoils on Bray # 1 P test results.

In the P test work reported above, 20-g spoil samples, which included coarse fragments up to 1.3 cm in diameter, were used in the P tests. This size sample was convenient for use in our research laboratory as no grinding or sieving was involved. However, state and commercial soil testing laboratories are set up to quickly process large numbers of samples. Usually, their soil samples are run through crushing rollers, and chemical analyses are made on 1 to 2 g of the material that passes through a 2-mm sieve. Thus, the use of larger samples that include coarse fragments does not fit into routine soil testing procedures.

In the coarse-fragment study, a 4-kg sample of each spoil was quartered by using a sample splitter. One of the samples was tested for P without further preparation. On the second sample, all coarse fragments larger than 2 mm in diameter (54 to 77% of the samples by weight) were screened out, and P was determined on the fines.

A third sample was put through the usual preparation for soil test samples received at the Kentucky State Soil Testing Laboratory. This consisted of crushing in a mortar with a motorized pestle*, then tipping the sample onto a vibrating 2-mm screen. Normally, the material passing through the screen is used in the soil tests and the coarse fragments discarded. In this study both the fines and the coarse fragments were saved,

---

* Nasco, Fort Atkinson, Wisconsin. Mention of a particular product or company name is for the information of the reader and should not be taken as endorsement by the Forest Service or the U. S. Department of Agriculture.

and Bray # 1 extractable P was determined on each. The coarse fragments made up 30 to 48% of the crushed samples.

The correlation between extractable P and percentage yield of fescue grown on N-fertilized spoils was not significantly different among the different sample preparations (Table 1). An explanation for this is that

TABLE 1

Effect of spoil particle size on correlation of Bray # 1 extractable P and percentage yield of N-fertilized fescue on 31 spoils

Particle size	Sample preparation	Sample weight	Std. deviation between duplicate samples	Correlation coefficient
		g	ppm P	
<1.3 cm	None	20	0.60	0.61[a]
<2.0 mm	Sieved out >2 mm particles	2	0.41	0.62[a]
<2.0 mm	Crushed, then sieved out >2 mm particles	2	0.37	0.61[a]

[a] Statistically significant at 0.01 probability level.

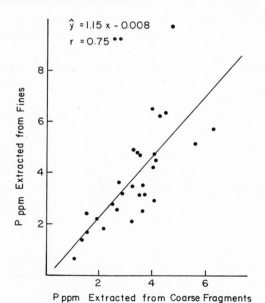

FIGURE 4 Relationship between Bray # 1 extractable P in coarse fragments (2–13 mm diameter) and fines (less than 2 mm diameter) from 29 spoils.

coarse fragments yield P to the extracting solution in approximately the same amounts as the fines (Fig. 4).

Thus, this study indicates that routine sample preparation procedures (where samples are crushed and sieved, then material passing 2-mm sieve openings is used in analysis) do not have to be modified when using the Bray # 1 P extraction on spoils containing coarse fragments from relatively soft Pennsylvanian shales.

Potassium

There were no grass-yield responses to added K on the 32 spoils in the greenhouse studies where K was added alone or in combination with N and P. The herbage produced in the greenhouse pots would be equal to forage production of 6000 to 8000 kg/ha (approximately 3 to 4 tons/acre); thus K would probably not be limiting under field conditions where the management objective is growth of a herbaceous cover crop for site protection.

Soil tests for K on the spoils ranged from moderately low to high. However, these interpretations are based on agronomic cropping of soils and not on the basis of a cover crop that is not to be harvested. The three extracting solutions used to estimate plant-available K in the spoils gave values that were in general agreement (Table 2).

TABLE 2

Correlation coefficients for K removed by three different extracting solutions from 63 spoils

Extracting solution	Correlation coefficient
1 N ammonium acetate vs. 0.15 N H_2SO_4	0.81[a]
1 N ammonium acetate vs. 0.05 N HCl + 0.025 N H_2SO_4	0.83[a]
0.15 N H_2SO_4 vs. 0.05 N HCl + 0.025 N H_2SO_4	0.92[a]

[a] Statistically significant at 0.01 probability level.

CONCLUSIONS

The Bray # 1 soil test for P gives meaningful results on spoils derived from relatively soft Pennsylvanian shales. The other P-extracting solutions give results that are of no value and could be misleading. The high content of coarse fragments (composed largely of shale) in these spoils had no evident influence on the relation between plant yields and P extracted by the Bray procedure.

The greenhouse studies indicated that K was not limiting for cover crop growth on these spoils. The soil test results indicated that K ranged from moderately low to high; which, interpreted on an agronomic basis, suggests that K might become deficient on some spoils if the vegetation is frequently harvested and removed. The three soil tests for K gave values that were in general agreement with one another.

Results of soil fertility tests and test interpretations should be used with caution until the relation between soil tests and plant growth on spoils or other non-soil material has been determined.

LITERATURE CITED

Einspahr, D. W., A. L. McComb, F. F. Riecken, and W. D. Shrader. 1955. Coal spoil bank materials as a medium for plant growth. *Proc. Iowa Acad. Sci.* **62**, 329–344.

Mattingly, G. E. G., and O. Talibudeen. 1967. Progress in the chemistry of fertilizer and soil phosphorus. In: M. Grayson and E. Griffith (ed.). *Topics in Phosphorus Chemistry*, Vol. 4. Interscience Publ. New York., p. 157–290.

Olsen, S. R., and L. A. Dean. 1965. Phosphorus. In: C. A. Black (ed.). Agronomy 9, *Methods of Soil Analysis*, Part 2. Amer. Soc. Agron. Madison, Wis., p. 1035–1049.

Page, N. R., G. W. Thomas, H. F. Perkins, and R. D. Rouse. 1965. Procedures used by state soil-testing laboratories in the southern region of the United States. *Southern Coop. Ser. Bull.* 102. South Carolina Agr. Exp. Sta. 49 p.

Pratt, P. F. 1965. Potassium. In: C. A. Black (ed.). Agronomy 9, *Methods of Soil Analysis*, Part 2. Amer. Soc. Agron. Madison, Wis., p. 1022–1030.

Soil Test Work Group. 1956. Soil tests compared with field, greenhouse and laboratory results. *North Carolina Agr. Exp. Sta. Tech. Bull. 121.* 36 p.

Sutton, P., and W. A. Seay. 1958. Relationship between the potassium removed by millet and red clover and the potassium extracted by 4 chemical methods from 6 Kentucky soils. *Soil Sci. Soc. Amer. Proc.* **22**, 110–115.

Tyner, E. H., and R. M. Smith. 1945. The reclamation of the stripmined coal lands of West Virginia with forage species. *Soil Sci. Soc. Amer. Proc.* **10**, 429–436.

DISCUSSION

GOODMAN: Were you able to try successive leachings of your P extractant to obtain an index of the supplying power of the various shales?

BERG: No, we did not, nor did we try successive croppings.

JACOBY: Did you try to correlate your K and other extractants with pH?

BERG: Yes, we had some data on over 200 spoils on K. In general, there is a trend for soil test available K to decrease with pH on these spoils.

CORNWELL: It is excellent that quantitative data are being obtained to show element availability from geological materials. In soils, available P is assumed to be related to the fine fraction. Such a system does not apply to spoil banks composed of freshly exposed geological materials.

BERG: In soils, the situation is that the coarse fragments usually will be rocks, and thus the P available from the larger particles is small.

SPOIL TYPE LITHOLOGY AND FOLIAR COMPOSITION OF *BETULA POPULIFOLIA**

Susan M. Cornwell and Earl L. Stone

Lecturer, Department of Landscape Architecture, Sheffield University, England, and Pack Professor of Forest Soils, Agronomy Department, Cornell University, Ithaca, New York

Spoil dumps derived from deep- or strip-mining in the Southern Field of the Pennsylvania Anthracite region were classified into five types on the basis of mineralogy and petrology. To assess availability of plant nutrients or possible toxic elements, leaves of gray birch, *Betula populifolia*—which colonizes all types—were sampled in a standard manner on 10 randomly selected locations of each type. Eleven elements were determined.

Foliar concentrations of all elements except Cu differed significantly among spoil types, indicating that the strictly lithological classification was meaningful in terms of plant nutrient uptake. Differences in N and P resulted from rock composition and weathering rate and were nutritionally important. Gray birch accumulated Zn to >400 ppm and Mn to >1500 ppm on all types but without evidence of Zn or Mn toxicity. Rather, species diversity was high on the types with highest uptake of Zn and Mn.

Because concentrations within locations differed markedly according to leaf position, collection date (after August 15) and year, caution should be taken in attempting to set absolute limits of deficiency or toxicity.

INTRODUCTION

The anthracite coal deposits of eastern Pennsylvania lie within folds of the Ridge and Valley Province of the Appalachian Mountains; they form four separate fields. The anthracite is extracted by both deep- and strip-mining methods, which together produce vast complexes of spoil banks and pits within the mined valleys. The ability of these mining wastes to support plant growth was studied at a site near Tamaqua, in the Southern Field.

---

* Agronomy Paper No. 862, Cornell University.

105

Of importance in revegetation of all such materials is the availability of nutrients for plant growth and the possible occurrence of toxic concentrations of elements as the raw rock dumps weather. Standard procedures of soil analysis have several limitations for this purpose. As an alternative therefore, we examined the foliar composition of gray birch (*Betula populifolia* Marsh.) as a means of assessing element availability. This birch is a hardy pioneer species and the only tree to freely colonize all spoils, even the most inhospitable.

Foliar analysis has great promise for characterizing the chemical environment of rock wastes and other unfamiliar substrates, even though it appears to have been little used so far. It does, however, involve several assumptions, among them the following: (1) leaf concentration may be taken as an index of relative uptake despite variations in growth rate; (2) concentrations in late summer are relatively stable as compared with the rapid increases or decreases earlier in the season (Mitchell, 1936) and later withdrawal of some elements prior to leaf fall; (3) a deep-rooted perennial integrates the elements made available in the whole of the rooting volume over a certain period of time, in contrast to conventional results from soil analysis.

MATERIALS AND METHODS

The Tamaqua study site was about 6 miles long and $\frac{1}{2}$ to 1 mile wide. It consisted of a chaotic assortment of strip-mine banks, rock dumps from the breakers (coal-processing plants), silt basins (settling areas for fine coal and shale suspended in the breaker waters), and small patches of unmined land ("placeland"). As a foundation for all subsequent work, the spoils were classified into five types on the basis of their dominant mineralogy and petrology (Cornwell, 1966). This classification is similar to that reported by Czapowskyj and McQuilkin (1966). Briefly, these five types were:

Type I – black shales; pyritic and highly acid, with reactions as low as pH 2.8.

Type II – gray shales; weakly calcareous.

Type III – sandstone spoils; mainly coarse-grained, buff-colored sandstones.

Type IV – "oxidized-surface" spoils; various rock types derived from strata immediately underlying the unconsolidated valley deposits; all fragment surfaces with bright orange to brown surfaces presumably resulting from oxidation *in situ* before stripping.

Type V – surficials; unconsolidated valley deposits—gravels, alluvium, and colluvium.

"Placeland" inclusions are labelled Type VI in all tables and figures. These undisturbed soils were normally thin, rather sandy, and podzolized.

The sampling scheme consisted first of dividing the study area into mutually-exclusive topographic units, 1 to 5 acres in size, on aerial photos. The units were homogeneous in composition and easily located in the field. Units were then drawn at random until a total of 10 per spoil had been sampled. This sampling procedure was first used in a survey of vegetation colonizing the area (Cornwell, 1966), and the birch leaf samples were collected from the same units. Hence, 10 units of each spoil were characterized both in terms of plant cover and nutrient status. Leaf samples were also collected from three undisturbed placeland areas to provide comparative data.

At each unit, the 10 largest trees around a random point were sampled by taking leaves from five long shoots of the current year (i.e. ignoring spur shoot foliage) from each tree. The branches sampled were all fully exposed to overhead light. The leaves were divided into two groups according to their position on the shoot, and hence maturity: (a) younger, on the distal half of the current shoots, and (b) older, on the proximal half. Damaged leaves and those from heavily fruiting branches were not collected. Thus in total, each spoil type was represented by leaf samples of two ages from five branches on each of 100 trees. Our primary sample was taken between August 15 and 26 because of the expected constancy of plant nutrient concentration at that time (Mitchell, 1936; Lutz and Chandler, 1946).

In addition, comparable samples were later collected from three of the original units on each spoil type, using the same sample points, to demonstrate the effect of sampling date on foliage composition; these collections were made on September 29th and 30th, i.e. a month or more after Mitchell's "plateau" in element concentrations. All samples were promptly air dried in the field and subsequently at 70 C. Nitrogen was determined by Kjeldahl, P colorimetrically, and K by flame photometry. Calcium, Mg, Na, Zn, Mn, Al, Fe, B and Cu were determined by an emission spectrograph.

The effects of spoil type, leaf age and sampling date on foliage concentration of each element were examined by analysis of variance, and mean differences at the first sampling by Duncan's multiple range test (Steel and Torrie, 1960).

RESULTS

Table 1 summarizes the elemental composition of gray birch foliage, each figure representing the unweighted mean of the combined distal and proximal leaf values. For comparison, it also indicates species diversity, expressed

TABLE 1

Mean elemental concentrations* (distal and proximal positions combined) of Betula populifolia foliage according to substrate, and as related to species diversity

Spoil Type	No. of Samples	Mean No. Plant Species Per Unit†	Element										
			N %	P %	K %	Ca %	Mg %	Na ppm	Zn ppm	Mn %	Al‡ ppm	Cu ppm	B ppm
I Acid black shale	10	4.7a	2.47c	0.18a	0.80bc	0.90c	0.32b	22a	247a	0.116a	363a	8.0bc	29a
II Gray shale	10	16.2c	1.68a	0.21b	0.71ab	0.85bc	0.30b	32abc	347b	0.261bc	348a	7.0abc	38bc
III Buff sandstone	10	10.0b	1.51a	0.17a	0.73ab	0.68a	0.28b	23a	340b	0.244b	293a	6.5ab	40c
IV Oxidized surface	10	21.8d	1.88ab	0.22b	0.65a	0.67a	0.29b	40bc	361b	0.310b	748b	6.1a	35bc
V Surficial	7	13.5bc	2.34bc	0.21b	0.74ab	0.70a	0.21a	44c	384b	0.325c	688b	8.5c	34b
VI Placeland	3	—	2.41bc	0.17a	0.91c	0.74ab	0.13	30ab	369b	0.122a	371ab	6.2ab	39bc

* Comparable values with same superscript letter do not differ at the 5% level. Solid underline indicates maximum value for each element; dash underline indicates minimum value for each element.

† From Cornwell (1966).

‡ Values greatly affected by dust contamination (see text).

as the average number of higher plant species per unit for each spoil type. Also shown are the significant differences among spoils for all elements, examined by Duncan's multiple range test. The range (ratio of minimum : maximum) in mean concentrations over all spoil types and undisturbed soils ranged from about 1 : 1.3 or 1.4 for several elements to about 1 : 2.7 for Mn.

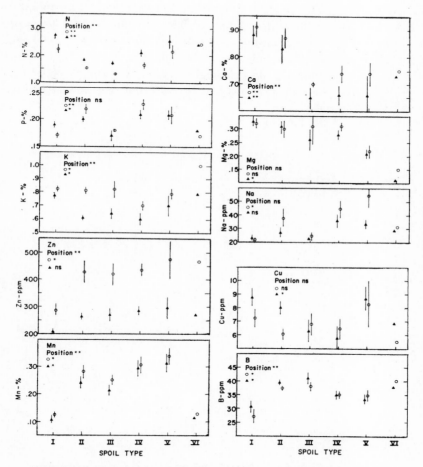

FIGURE 1 Elemental concentration in gray birch foliage from two positions, proximal, "older" foliage (circles) and distal, "younger" foliage (triangles) on current year's shoots of *Betula populifolia* according to spoil type. Collected Aug. 15–26. Vertical line indicates ±1 standard error (I to IV, *n* = 10; V, *n* = 7; VI, *n* = 3). Significance of position (shown adjacent to word "position") and of spoil type within position (shown adjacent to circle and triangle) by separate analyses of variance.

Hence, toxic or nutritional factors significant for plant growth should be looked for within limits of this magnitude.

Foliar Fe data have not been presented in view of Wallihan's (1966) evidence that dust contamination can make Fe determinations of unwashed leaves meaningless. Obviously, the same could apply to Al, which has been shown to exceed Fe in the Tamaqua spoils (Cornwell, 1966). Comparison of the apparent concentrations of Fe and Al in both distal and proximal leaves yields a linear correlation of 0.98 with an approximate slope of 1.88 Al : 1 Fe. This relationship holds true over the range 100 to 1100 ppm, thus beginning well above the probable minimum requirement (Stone, 1968). Aluminum values from proximal leaves are invariably higher than from distal, but the two positions tend to vary together and fit a single

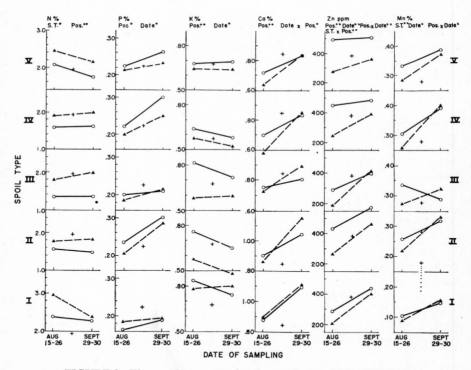

FIGURE 2 Elemental concentration in *Betula populifolia* foliage from two shoot positions (solid line = distal, broken line = proximal) at two sampling dates (Aug. 15–26, or Sept. 29–30, 1965) according to spoil type (*n* = 3). Overall means for each element marked by cross. Variables significant in analysis of variance are indicated. See Table 2 for summer rainfall.

regression. Thus, differences in Al shown in Table 1 are attributable simply to variable amounts of dust contamination and no conclusions should be drawn from them.

Figure 1 demonstrates the effect of leaf position (relative maturity) on element concentrations and on the occurrence of significant differences among spoil types. Figure 2 compares foliar concentrations at the two sampling dates. Rainfall patterns in 1965 (Table 2) may well have delayed or prevented development of the stable element concentrations of late August reported by Mitchell (1936). Concentrations of several elements had altered significantly by the end of September. Only slight shoot growth would normally have occurred after the August sampling; moreover, there was little evidence of element "dilution" through continued expan-

TABLE 2

Comparative foliar concentrations in % of dry weight in Betula populifolia *and* Populus grandidentata *sampled comparably at the same locations in two successive years with contrasting rainfall patterns.* (*Prox = leaves from proximal half of current year's shoots; dist = distal leaves*)

Species, spoil type, and year	Leaf position and composition							
	N		P		K		Ca	
	Prox	Dist	Prox	Dist	Prox	Dist	Prox	Dist
Betula populifolia								
Spoil Type II								
1964	1.76	2.28	0.41	0.37	0.91	0.76	1.05	1.13
1965	1.50	2.04	0.25	0.24	0.94	0.62	0.74	0.74
Spoil Type IV								
1964	1.45	2.00	0.41	0.26	0.70	0.96	0.92	0.95
1965	1.40	1.90	0.24	0.20	0.88	0.60	0.54	0.47
Populus grandidentata								
Spoil Type II								
1964	2.05	2.06	0.26	0.25	1.07	0.77	2.34	2.67
1965	1.42	1.50	0.20	0.17	0.32	0.37	1.67	1.67
Spoil Type IV								
1964	1.88	2.11	0.23	0.25	1.05	0.85	1.00	0.98
1965	1.51	1.48	0.19	0.21	0.49	0.37	0.72	0.90

Monthly Rainfall in Inches					
Year	June	July	Aug.	Sept.	Sum
1964	5.4	2.5	1.6	3.5	13.0
1965	1.0	2.7	6.1	3.4	13.2

al foliage, or of concentration due to dry-matter losses from
ives. Hence, the changes must have reflected element leaching,
or accumulation.

compares the foliar concentrations of major elements in gray
birch and bigtooth aspen, at a single location on each of two spoil types,
sampled in two successive years characterized by contrasting rainfall
patterns. In 1964 a severe mid-summer drought following favorable spring
moisture appears to have limited shoot extension and resulted in accumulation of elements in the foliage. In 1965, however, a severe June-July drought
restricted early growth and perhaps nutrient uptake as well; heavy rains
prior to the late August sampling favored shoot regrowth and may also
have leached foliage. In spite of limited samples, the general agreement
between species reinforces the seasonal difference.

DISCUSSION

Foliar concentrations characterize the availability of elements only to the
extent that they are absorbed and transported by the plant. Nevertheless,
foliage composition of gray birch reflected very great differences in the
relative availability of elements among spoil types despite the great influence
of leaf maturity and season. Such differences must have been largely due
to spoil mineralogy and weathering rate, because there was no reason for
assuming that atmospheric contributions differed appreciably among the
spoils.

Nitrogen

Nitrogen deficiency in raw rock spoils was expected and had in fact already
been reported by several investigators (e.g. Schramm, 1966; Hedrick and
Wilson, 1956). All the Tamaqua spoils except the buff sandstones (III),
however, appeared to supply moderate N levels to established birch. On the
sandstones, deficiency was manifested by the lowest foliar contents (Table 1),
small yellowish leaves, sparse crowns, slow height growth, and narrow
annual rings. In marked contrast, birch on the acid black shales (1) contained as much or more N than on undisturbed soils of the region; growth
was excellent, and leaves were large, glossy, and dark green. We have already
postulated that the surprisingly high N levels in the black shales were
derived from N fixed within the clays and released by sulfate weathering
(Cornwell and Stone, 1968). Nitrogen in the surficial (V) spoils (in effect,

deep subsoils) was probably derived from traces of organic matter from the surface zone buried during stripping operations, as well as from fixed ammonia in the clays.

In the August sample, distal leaves averaged about 0.35 to 0.55% more N than proximal (Fig. 1) and the difference was maintained with time (Fig. 2).

Phosphorus

At the first sampling, spoils fell into two distinct groups on the basis of foliar P content with the gray shale (II), oxidized surface (IV), and surficial (V) spoils containing significantly more than the black shales and buff sandstones (Table 1). Differences between these two groups widened appreciably during the following month (Fig. 2), although relative leaf maturity within sampling date had no consistent effect.

Phosphorus availability must be a major chemical factor determining plant colonization, and it may be significant that those spoils allowing greatest P uptake by birch also supported a significantly more diverse vegetation than the other materials (Table 1). Certainly, low levels of available P in the black shales must have been a factor restricting their colonization, and in fact, field trials using birch seedlings on these spoils showed greater survival on P-treated plots than on untreated controls. The high solubility of Al and large quantities of precipitated Fe in these spoils (Cornwell and Stone, 1968) may well have caused the low P availability.

Potassium

Mean foliar K concentrations from all the spoil types were lower than those from undisturbed soils (VI) (Table 1). Mean values, however, obscure the large concentration differences obtained among spoil types for the younger (distal) foliage—a disadvantage, as these differences may well be the best measure of current K availability in the spoils. With one exception, distal leaves were consistently lower in K than proximal at both sampling dates (Fig. 2), so that there was no indication of the translocation from older to younger leaves which characterizes K deficiency in many other species. Rainfall leaching might well have affected the less mature distal foliage to a greater extent than the proximal, but should have acted similarly over all spoil types.

Of the spoils proper, the black shales surprisingly supplied most available K (Table 1). This was almost certainly due to continuing release from clay minerals in the intensely acid weathering environment of these materials. Active sulfate generation also occurred in the gray shales, however, but resulted in the liberation of large quantities of soluble Ca and Mg, as well as K, which may have reduced K uptake. Foliar contents on the surficials were also high; these materials (deep subsoils) contained much more silt and clay than the other raw spoils, and could therefore be expected to supply adequate K to birch. But interpretations of K availability, and spoil "supplying power" based on the present data are necessarily equivocal, particularly in view of possible foliage leaching by August rains (Table 2).

Sodium

Although the foliar concentrations of Na differed significantly among the spoil types, the absolute amounts were small, and at most equivalent to less than 2% of the K content. Hence, Na apparently had little significance for plant nutrition in the Tamaqua spoils.

Calcium and magnesium

Foliar Ca and Mg concentrations differed significantly among spoil types (Table 1) but apparently independently from each other, and from K (Fig. 1). At the first sampling, Ca was appreciably higher in the more mature proximal foliage; but leaves in both positions continued to accumulate the element, and by late September distal leaf concentrations equalled or exceeded the proximal (Fig. 2). On the other hand, Mg content was not affected significantly by either leaf position or sampling date.

Ranking of the spoils according to foliar contents of the two elements did not follow any pattern predictable from initial considerations of spoil reaction and mineralogy. Birch foliage from the intensely acid black shales (I) (pH 2.7 to 3.4) contained the highest concentrations of Ca and Mg, slightly but not significantly more than from the weakly calcareous gray shales (II) where reactions of the <2 mm fraction varied between 4.3 and 7.0. Both spoil types were pyritic, and the sulfate generated liberated quantities of soluble Ca and Mg from calcareous minerals and cements.

Evidence for this release was supplied by the abundant secondary gypsum ($CaSO_4 \cdot 2H_2O$), precipitated in the black shales as surface films, and as crystals at depths of about a meter or so, and by surface coatings of epsomite ($MgSO_4 \cdot 7H_2O$) which developed on gray shales weathered under greenhouse conditions.

The sandstone and oxidized-surface spoils contained few basic minerals, and their accessibility was limited by low pyrite contents and by resistance of the major rock components to frost shattering. As a result, Ca availability was lowest in these spoils. In contrast, Mg availability was lowest in the surficial spoils and undisturbed soils; both materials supplied significantly less Mg than all the raw rock spoils (Table 1). This presumably reflects preferential loss of Mg over Ca in the early stages of soil weathering, leading to the depletion of Mg reserves in acid soils and subsoils suggested by these data. As there were no deficiency symptoms in birch growing on placeland, adequate Mg supplies could be expected from the raw spoils.

Manganese and Zinc

These two elements displayed some similarity in occurrence and behavior. *Betula* is a known Zn accumulator (Gerloff et al., 1966; Stone, 1968) and probably should be regarded similarly with respect to Mn. Like Ca, both Zn and Mn accumulated steadily in the leaves throughout the growing season, and to amounts far beyond any requirement for cell functioning. At the first sampling, the more mature proximal leaves contained significantly more of both elements than the younger distal leaves (Fig. 1); by the second sampling, however, these differences were much reduced (Fig. 2). Presumably, the greater increases of Ca, Zn, and Mn in the distal leaves were consequences of greater transpiration by the peripheral foliage.

Surprisingly, foliar levels of Zn and Mn were lowest in the black shales. This result was contrary to a number of reports that toxic levels of these elements—and of Al—develop in pyrite-bearing materials actively generating sulfates (e.g. Knudsen and Struthers, 1953; Massey and Johnson, 1965; Cummins, Plass, and Gentry 1965). These spoils however, contained abundant secondary iron minerals—as surface films of melanterite $(FeSO_4 \cdot 7H_2O)$ and as coatings of limonite- and hematite-like minerals. Antagonism between Fe and Mn has been widely reported (e.g. Morris and Pierre, 1947), and it is plausible to assume that Mn uptake from these acid materials was inhibited by high concentrations of soluble Fe. Comparisons between pyritic black shale and sandstone spoils elsewhere in the Anthracite Region, however, indicated only 2 ppm or less of Mn extractable by Morgan's solution from the shales, as compared with 12 to 22 ppm from sandstones; parallel values after extraction with boiling 1 N HCl were 10 to 22 ppm vs. 46 to 215 ppm. Hence, lower soluble Mn rather than Fe antagonism probably accounted for the low foliar contents

8*

on the black shale spoils. Obviously, spoil reaction does not provide a sure basis for predicting amounts of plant available Mn.

Foliar Mn levels from unmined placeland were similar to those from the black shales, and both materials supplied less than half the amounts available from the other spoil types. In contrast, foliar Zn concentrations were similar over all spoils (except the black shales) and unmined placeland as well (Table 1).

The mean values for Zn and Mn in Figs. 1 and 2 were generally higher than reported for other species of *Betula* (Gerloff, Moore and Curtis, 1966; Stone, 1968), but were substantially less than the maxima obtained at the first sampling from individual sites within spoil types, as indicated below:

Spoil Type	Mn ppm	Zn ppm
I	2010	396
II	4160	731
III	4030	594
IV	4560	572
V	4540	726
VI (Placeland)	1320	511

Despite these high concentrations, there was no evidence of toxicity to birch or other established species. Indeed, the oxidized surface (IV) and surficial (V) spoils, on which gray birch attained its highest mean concentrations of both Zn and Mn, supported the greatest number of plant species. The general similarity in foliar Zn levels from most spoils and undisturbed soil suggested that solubility of this element in spoils was not excessive. Soluble Mn, however, was clearly abundant in all spoils except the black shales, and may well have been among the factors preventing colonization of many native species not yet found on these spoils. Gray birch and numerous other species tolerate foliar Mn concentrations of at least 5000 ppm (Bennett, 1945), but many species are far more sensitive to excess.

Aluminum

As already indicated, the apparent foliar concentrations of Al presented in Table 1 are specious, but are included for their cautionary value. The mere ability to determine Fe and Al in foliage does little to insure meaningful results. Large differences in soluble Al within and among these spoil types are known (Cornwell, 1966; Cornwell and Stone, 1968), but any real effects on plant uptake have been obscured.

Boron and Copper

Boron uptake varied significantly with spoil type, though not in accordance with reaction or clay content. All concentrations were within the range displayed by naturally growing birch and many other deciduous tree species (Stone, 1968); hence, availability from all substrates seemed adequate and far from toxic.

Foliar Cu concentrations likewise differed significantly among spoil types, although variation within spoils was relatively high (Fig. 1), possibly reflecting analytical error at these low concentrations. Most of the individual Cu values fell within the lower part of the normal ranges found in birches and many other tree species. The mean concentration from the oxidized-surface spoils, however, was only 6.1 ppm, and proximal foliage from two locations on this spoil type contained only 2.0 ppm. Although these low values suggested the likelihood of Cu deficiency, no recognizable symptoms were seen and there was no plant response to added Cu in exploratory greenhouse trials. The effects of insufficient Cu are sometimes obscure, and can, moreover, be intensified by increased availability of N and P; fertilization of plants on this spoil type might readily induce Cu deficiency.

CONCLUSIONS

In sum, the large and significant differences among spoil types in elemental contents of gray birch bore out the original lithological classification. But so far as composition of this species revealed, element availability in the spoils did not differ greatly from that in undisturbed soils of the region, although the indicated differences in N, K, and Mn were probably large enough to be highly important for some plant species. With the possible exception of P, however, no direct relationship emerged between birch leaf composition and the number of species successfully colonizing a spoil type (Table 1).

It became obvious that foliar concentrations of any one element could be affected both by availability of other elements in the substrate, and particularly, by restrictions in growth imposed by any cause; increasing N availability to birch on the sandstone spoils, for example, might have revealed greater limitations in available K and P than were evident from our results.

Foliar contents of birch can provide indices of the nutritional suitability of the spoils for other plant species, and at a more general level, can indicate nutritional or toxic restraints which could be encountered by colonizing or planted vegetation. But species idiosyncracies must be allowed for; birch is, for example, a Zn (and possibly Mn) accumulator, and also, as a deep-rooted species, would likely encounter very different conditions than plants growing in the weathered surface layers of the rock dumps.

In short, choice of an adapted and ubiquitous species, control or measurement of sample variables such as leaf maturity or contamination, and acquisition of comparative data from different substrates are all important if interpretations of, and predictions from, foliar data are to be meaningful.

In the Tamaqua materials, the large variations in foliar contents due to leaf maturity and year make it impossible to set limits of toxicity and deficiency at the present time. Nevertheless, foliar contents are probably superior to conventional soil analyses as indices of element availability from spoil materials. Availability is controlled not by storage and release from a relatively stable reserve, or an organic matter cycle, as in natural soils, but by rate of solution from fresh mineral surfaces or freshly-exposed subsoil particles. Hence, elemental availability cannot be predicted from tried and tested parameters such as pH, because relationships between the two are unknown for spoil bank materials.

ACKNOWLEDGEMENTS

The first author wishes to acknowledge the generous assistance of a Department of Scientific and Industrial Research, NATO, "Studentship" for much of the time during which this work was carried out. She also wishes to thank Dr. Miroslaw Czapowskyj for an introduction to the Anthracite Region.

LITERATURE CITED

Bennett, J. P. 1945. Iron in leaves. *Soil Sci.* **60**, 91–104.

Cornwell, S. M. 1966. Anthracite mining spoils as media for plant growth. *PhD Thesis*, Cornell Univ.

Cornwell, S. M., and E. L. Stone. 1968. Availability of nitrogen to plants in acid coal mine spoils. *Nature* **217**, 768–9.

Cummins, D. G., W. T. Plass, and C. E. Gentry. 1965. Chemical and physical properties of spoil banks in the eastern Kentucky coal fields. U. S. Dep. Agr., Forest Service Res. Pap. CS-17.

Czapowskyj, M. M., and W. E. McQuilkin. 1966. Survival and early growth of planted forest trees on strip-mine spoils in the Anthracite Region. U. S. Dep. Agr., Forest Service Res. paper NE-46, 29 p.

Gerloff, G. C., D. D. Moore, and J. T. Curtis. 1966. Selective absorption of mineral elements by native plants of Wisconsin. *Plant and Soil* **25**, 393–405.

Hedrick, H. G., and H. A. Wilson. 1956. The rate of carbon dioxide production in a strip mine spoil. *Proc. W. Va. Acad. Sci.* **28**, 11–15.

Hiatt, A. J., and J. L. Ragland. 1963. Manganese toxicity of Burley tobacco. *J. Agron.* **55**, 47–49.

Knudsen, L. L., and P. H. Struthers. 1953. Strip mine reclamation research in Ohio. *Ohio J. Sci.* **53**, 351–355.

Lutz, H. J., and R. F. Chandler. 1946. *Forest soils*. Wiley and Sons, Inc. N. Y. 514 p.

Massey, H. F., and G. C. Johnson. 1965. Solution compositions of certain coal mine spoil-bank materials as related to soil pH. Paper presented at Ann. Mtg. Amer. Soc. Agron., Columbus, Ohio.

Mitchell, H. L. 1936. Trends in nitrogen, phosphorus, potassium and calcium content of the leaves of some forest trees during the growing season. *Black Rock Forest Paper* **1**, 30–44.

Morris, H. D., and W. H. Pierre. 1947. The effect of calcium, phosphorus and iron on the tolerance of Lespedeza to manganese toxicity in culture solutions. *Proc. Soil Sci. Soc. Amer.* **12**, 382–386.

Oullette, G. J. 1951. Iron/manganese interrelationships in plant nutrition. *Sci. Agr.* **31**, 277–285.

Schramm, J. R. 1966. Plant colonization studies on black wastes from anthracite mining in Pennsylvania. Trans. Amer. Phil. Soc. New Series, Part 1, 56.

Steel, R. G. D., and J. H. Torrie. 1960. *Principles and procedures of statistics*. McGraw-Hill. N. Y. 481 p.

Stone, E. L. 1968. Micronutrient nutrition of forest trees: A review. In: *Forest fertilization: theory and practice*. Nat. Fertilizer Develop. Cent., Tennessee Valley Authority, Muscle Shoals, Ala. p. 132–175.

Wallihan, E. F. 1966. Iron. In: *Diagnostic criteria for plants and soils*. Univ. Calif. Div. Agr. Sci. p. 203–212.

Young, H. E., and V. P. Guinn. 1966. Chemical elements in complete mature trees of seven species in Maine. *TAPPI* **49**, 190–197.

DISCUSSION

SCHMEHL: Would you please give the pH of these various materials?

CORNWELL: Yes, the pH of these materials was: acid black shales, 2.7 to 3.4; gray shales, 4.3 to 7.0; buff sandstones, 3.5 to 4.7; oxidized-surface spoils, 3.9 to 5.2 and surficials, 4.1 to 5.0. However, such pH levels cannot be used to predict availability to gray birch of such elements as Mn, Al, Ca, K, or Mg.

SCHMEHL: These are plant data. You did not make any determinations of soluble Al in the soil?

STONE: We have 1 N HCl extracted values, and the black shales are not all that different from some of the other spoil types.

HEALD: Was any account taken of the fact that the trees were obviously of different sizes, which would produce different size leaves, etc.?

CORNWELL: I tried to choose all the largest trees around a random sampling point. After that no account was taken of variation in leaf size.

STONE: There is probably more variation within plants due to leaf position and to nutrition of the tree than there is between tree sizes. This can be seen in gray birch.

GOODMAN: Did you find any evidence of withdrawal of elements in the September samples? Perhaps on some of the shales there was K deficiency which might show up as a more acute withdrawal than on other shales.

CORNWELL: There was only a hint of K withdrawal at the second sampling. There was no sign of K withdrawal from older to younger leaves through the season in birch, as I believe characterizes K deficiency in other species. Elements had accumulated by the September date, particularly Ca, Mn, and Zn, and the differences obtained between proximal and distal leaves had more or less disappeared by the second sampling date because of accumulation.

REPP: I think it is a very good idea to use one plant species as a tool for determining the differences in chemistry of the site and to locate the source of toxic materials, but I think one has to take some precautions. First of all, there is a basic difference between nutrients which the plant is using for growth and the excess salts in the toxic substances which are not used but which are accumulated in the plant during the course of transpiration. So, I would suggest taking only the oldest leaves for this analysis, because these would have the maximum possible accumulation for that species, and you would eliminate the influence of age.

CORNWELL: Yes, but I think the differences in element levels that we found between proximal and distal leaves were large enough to justify taking the two leaf groups at the earlier sampling date. I agree, we needed many more samples at the later date to demonstrate element changes right at the end of the growing season. But the information supplied earlier in the season was useful for birch. Use of one species is open to question, and we must emphasize that these element levels are for this species only. We have other data for bigtooth aspen which also occurred on these spoils. This tree was less widespread than gray birch, so we couldn't use it as a comparative species over all spoil types.

PREDICTING MINED-LAND SOIL

Rodney R. Krause

Field Representative, National Coal Association, Washington, D. C.

The key to achieving a predictable growing medium lies in identifying which combination of overburden strata is best suited for the survival and growth of vegetation. The approach involves the analysis of weathered in-place overburden materials and their handling in the mining and grading process.

INTRODUCTION

The problem of reclaiming strip-mined land varies widely in the United States, according to the topography, climate, types of materials found in the overburden, and machines used to move the overburden. By the time revegetation begins, the nature of the mined land is already established in the mining process.

The manner in which the overburden is handled may create reclamation problems which last for years, or which are costly to cure. In short, the typical overburden above a coal seam consists of various layers of earth and rock. Some of these—not necessarily the top-most layer—may be good for growing vegetation. Others may be definitely hostile. If we consider the layers of overburden like a deck of cards, it is easy to see that picking up a heterogeneous section of overburden and spilling it at another location is like shuffling the deck. Nobody knows what will come out on top. This makes reclamation somewhat of a gamble.

Any gambler with a little larceny in his heart knows he could do better if he could stack the deck and control which cards were in the hand dealt him. I propose a way to mark the cards, if not stack the deck, of reclamation.

As a necessary first practice, we have learned to successfully revegetate the majority of our mined lands. However, certain of the multi-overburden types within five southeastern Ohio counties, where I gained my experience and with which this paper is concerned, presented difficulties of revegetation due to the presence of S-bearing materials, their physical nature, and the manner in which the materials were handled in the mining process by both draglines and shovels.

Predicting mined-land soils requires an understanding of the nature of the overburden, operating characteristics of the machines, and methods of mining. Mined land is generally described as a mixed-up mass of rock and earth materials. Where a consistent mixture of mined-land soil material exists it is the product of the overburden and the type of machine which moved it, and indicates that, for the most part, neither the strata over the coal nor the operating cycle of the mining machine changed.

One of the variables of the overburden is the influence of time and the weathering process. A number of workers have reported the changes occurring in overburden materials over periods of years. However, as Knabe (1965) pointed out, these samples indicate only the progress of the weathering and leaching processes. He added that the factors which determine when mined-land soil materials reach a state of equilibrium depend on the amount of S present and the exchange capacity of the material. I would include also the physical size of soil particles.

For practical purposes, seldom if ever do we know the depth or concentration of the various materials which make up mined-land soils, let alone the amounts of S or exchange capacity of the materials. Assuming that there are levels where these different materials stabilize and we can learn approximately what those levels are and how long it takes to reach them, then we might prescribe vegetation better suited to the capability of the mined land.

METHODS AND RESULTS

Our first attempts to improve the growing medium, physically and chemically, began with the bulldozer in grading operations and later evolved to classifying and diagramming portions of exposed highwalls as to which combinations of strata offered the best prospects for plant survival and growth. We did this by measuring how trees thrived on various materials of the overburden, which were deposited in such depth in the spoil as to be clearly identifiable as the growing medium, and then relating this material to its original position in the highwall by color, structure, and thickness.

Figures 1 and 2 are diagrams indicating the desired materials of the overburden, and where feasible, the types of topography desired. Figure 3 illustrates one operating cycle, developed with mine management for a 35-cubic-yard dragline, which resulted in an improved growing medium. The method changed handling of the bench-cut material from one point in the cycle to another, without reducing the operating efficiency of the machine. It did not require setting aside or storing so-called topsoil.

Our diagrams indicated which overburden materials and kind of topography are most desirable. This give mine management and machine operators an objective in coordinating the various phases of the mining

DRAGLINE OPERATION

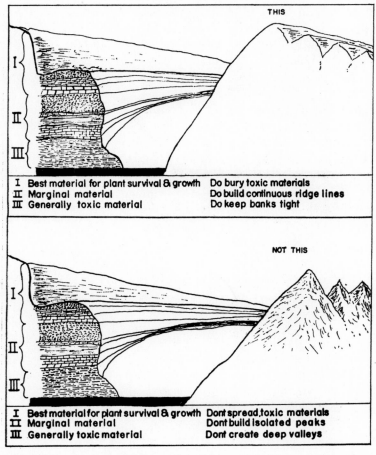

FIGURE 1   Typical desirable and undesirable methods of depositing overburden in a dragline operation.

operation. These men are the best qualified to deal with the digging characteristics and limitations of both the overburden and the machines used to
move it. By this approach a satisfactory growing medium has been empiri-
cally achieved, and for practical purposes, this may be sufficient.

In 1966, we started a study concerning a theoretical soil and the theoretical performance of a 220-cubic-yard dragline, more than six times as
large as the dragline then in use. (Three years later, both the soil and machine
are reality.) It was obvious the capability and opportunity to deposit
favorable or unfavorable materials in high concentration would be greatly

SHOVEL OPERATION

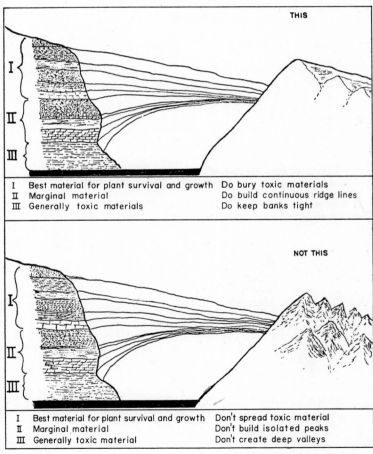

FIGURE 2   Typical desirable and undesirable methods of depositing
overburden in a shovel operation.

increased. Therefore, the success of reclamation would depend more than ever on the depth of materials deposited and their physical and chemical nature, especially after undergoing the weathering process.

The objective was to determine before mining, which combinations of overburden materials offer the best potential for survival and growth after known periods of weathering. Procedures involved selecting highwalls of various ages typical of the major overburden types of the field, sampling the strata for chemical analyses, measuring their thickness, and describing

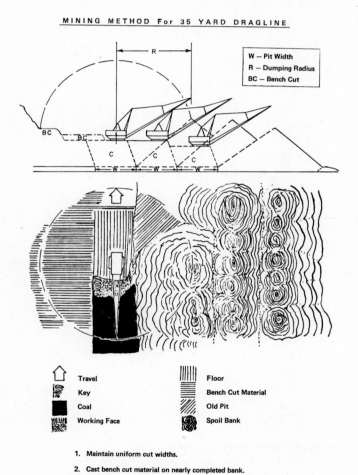

MINING METHOD For 35 YARD DRAGLINE

W — Pit Width
R — Dumping Radius
BC — Bench Cut

Travel		Floor
Key		Bench Cut Material
Coal		Old Pit
Working Face		Spoil Bank

1. Maintain uniform cut widths.

2. Cast bench cut material on nearly completed bank.

3. Maintain continuous ridge lines.

FIGURE 3   A mining method for a 35-cubic-yard dragline which results in an improved growing medium.

the material in terms of structure and color. The results for one 5-year-old highwall, considered a problem wall, are illustrated in Fig. 4. Table 1 lists results of trace element tests for portions of the same wall.

The analysis gives us a quick way to determine the best combinations in terms of quality and quantity. As Fig. 4 indicates, they dovetail closely with the combinations indicated by the empirically-developed diagrams. From this overburden material we also learned that material previously believed to be highly acid, and classified generally toxic on our diagrams, was not—at least not after weathering 5 years in the wall.

OHIO POWER HIGHWALL STUDY
East Pit Highwall

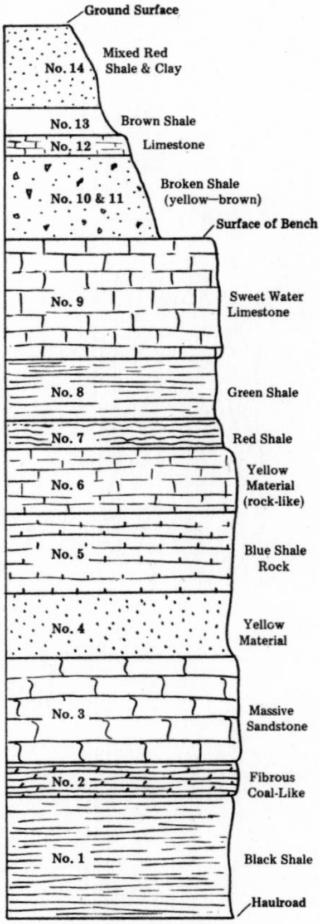

			POUNDS PER ACRE			
	Thickness (feet)	ph	Fe (ferric)	Sulfates	Soluble Salts	Toxic Aluminum
No. 14 — Mixed Red Shale & Clay	4	5.3	.4	40	320	.42
No. 13 — Brown Shale	1.5	7.7	.2	22	420	0
No. 12 — Limestone	1	8.1	.3	30	100	0
No. 10 & 11 — Broken Shale (yellow–brown)	4	8.2	.1	25	360	0
No. 9 — Sweet Water Limestone	6					
No. 8 — Green Shale	3	8.1	.3	91	800	0
No. 7 — Red Shale	1.5	7.8	.5	82	940	0
No. 6 — Yellow Material (rock-like)	3	8.0	.5	61	520	0
No. 5 — Blue Shale Rock	4	8.2	.3	61	660	0
No. 4 — Yellow Material	3	3.8	22.5	106	3,200	.72
No. 3 — Massive Sandstone	5	3.4	23.5	289	5,000	.66
No. 2 — Fibrous Coal-Like	1.66	3.1	25.0	310	5,500	.54
No. 1 — Black Shale	6	8.4	1.3	61	1,200	0

Source: Farm Clinic of U.S.

FIGURE 4   Analysis of the East Pit Highwall, a problem wall 5 years old. Ohio Power Highwall Study.

TABLE 1

Chemical analyses of the East Pit Highwall.
Ohio Power Highwall Study, 1967.

(Source: The Farm Clinic, West Lafayette, Ind.)

Sample No.	Organic Matter %	pH	Total Sol. Salts	Nitrogen NO3	Nitrogen NH3	P2O5	K2O	Ca	Mg	Ferric Fe	Ferrous Fe	Mn	B	Cu	Zn	SO4	Al (Toxic)	Mo (Toxic) ppb
										lb/acre								
4	0.9	3.8	3200	10.8	42	1.1	91	1365	270+	22.5	0.2	3.0	0.34	0.8	0.65	106	0.72	12
6	0.8	8.0	520	9.2	46	4.4	112	3500	270+	0.5	0.1	4.5	0.36	1.0	0.13	61	0	62
10	0.9	8.2	360	12.7	43	4.2	40	3450	270+	0.3	0.1	0.6	0.40	0.8	0.11	25	0	75
12	0.8	8.1	180	8.5	47	2.6	44	3640	270+	0.4	0.3	0.5	0.39	0.5	0.09	30	0	50
13	1.0	7.7	420	9.7	45	6.1	82	3250	270+	0.3	0.2	1.4	0.42	0.8	0.16	22	0	58
14	0.8	5.3	320	8.1	49	1.5	52	3080	114	0.5	0.4	4.5	0.37	2.1	0.50	40	0.42	25

Interpretation

	Organic Matter %	pH	Total Sol. Salts	NO3	NH3	P2O5	K2O	Ca	Mg	Ferric Fe	Ferrous Fe	Mn	B	Cu	Zn	SO4	Al	Mo
Low	—	—	—	<20	<30	<5	<80	<500	<100	—	—	<1	<0.32	<1	<1	—	—	<25
Medium	—	—	—	20–40	30–50	5–20	80–150	500 to 1000	100–180	—	—	1–4	0.32 to 0.37	1–4	1–4	—	—	25–50
Satisfactory	—	—	—	>40	>50	>20	>150	>1000	>180	—	—	>4	>0.38	>4	>4	—	—	>50
Excessive or toxic	—	—	—	—	—	—	—	—	—	—	—	>20	>0.45	—	—	—	>1	—

How long do in-place materials of the highwall need to weather before they approach a static condition? Although the analysis of weathered in-place materials is only an approximation of the weathering that occurs on mined land, it does yield quantitative data as to thickness of materials that will be handled. Figures 4 and 5 also indicate that where similar materials occur in highwalls of 5 and 10 years weathering respectively, they are reasonably close in chemical characteristics.

Einspahr et al. (1955) reported that most Pennsylvanian era shales from fresh highwalls in Iowa reached maximum acidity within 6 months, and

OHIO POWER HIGHWALL STUDY
4250 - W Dragline Area

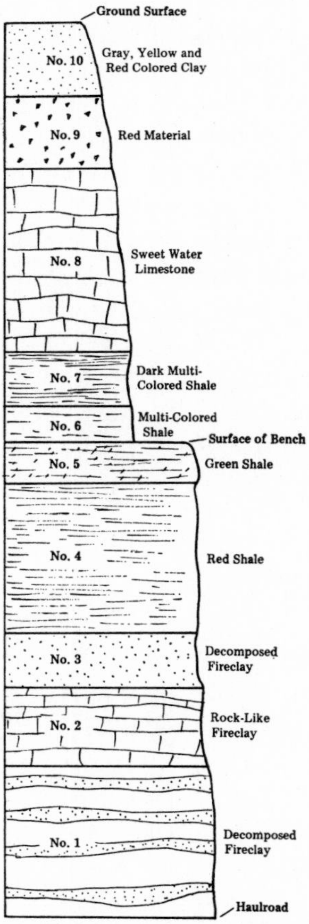

	Thickness (feet)	ph	POUNDS PER ACRE Fe (ferric)	Sulfates	Soluble Salts	Toxic Aluminum
No. 10 — Gray, Yellow and Red Colored Clay	4	8.2	.3	52	360	0
No. 9 — Red Material	4	8.0	.4	46	440	0
No. 8 — Sweet Water Limestone	10					
No. 7 — Dark Multi-Colored Shale	3	8.4	.4	91	520	0
No. 6 — Multi-Colored Shale	2	8.5	.3	61	500	0
No. 5 — Green Shale	2	8.7	5.4	58	900	0
No. 4 — Red Shale	8	8.5	.7	46	600	0
No. 3 — Decomposed Fireclay	3	7.0	.3	232	2,840	.06
No. 2 — Rock-Like Fireclay	4	6.5	.3	234	2,700	.24
No. 1 — Decomposed Fireclay	8	4.4	8.9	256	4,200	.42

Source: Farm Clinic of U.S.

FIGURE 5   Analysis of the highwall in the 4250-W Dragline Area, a problem wall 10 years old. Ohio Power Highwall Study.

did not change significantly over a 2-year weathering period. Additional analyses of similar materials occurring in highwalls of various ages may provide more information as to how old weathered highwalls should be to provide usable data.

Another point that might be clarified is how thick the desired materials will be when deposited. That will depend on the thickness of those materials in the wall, the capacity of the bucket or dipper being used, and may vary from 2 to 10 ft. From the standpoint of reclamation and improvement of the growing medium, it is well to consider that with a dragline, the material first loaded in the bucket comes out last. On the other hand, with a shovel the material last loaded in the dipper comes out last.

While rows of banks on mined land give the impression of continuous ridges, they are at one time in their construction single peaks or cones ultimately joined so as to utilize all available space for depositing overburden. The desired materials will generally be deposited during the final stages of construction, representing only a small portion of the bank volume and of the total time required to build the bank. For example, assuming 100% operating efficiency, a 35-cubic-yard dragline on a 60-sec cycle is capable of moving 2100 yd^3/hr. If only 1 hr of a full shift is used to dig the premium material, a growing medium of 2100 yd^3 would cover an area about 97 ft square to a depth of 6 ft. The rest of the time the operator could mine as he pleased.

When it is time for grading, we already have a good idea of what our growing medium is made of and what it looks like. We can tell the bull-dozer operator to watch for the desired material, which can be identified by structure and color, and spread it over as much of the area as possible.

SUMMARY AND CONCLUSIONS

In summary, we know that, while reclamation may be a small part of the total mining operation, it is a significant part. We also know that a great deal more information is needed about the physical and chemical nature of overburden materials and the influence of the weathering process. We accept the fact that it is entirely possible that few if any of the layers of the overburden may offer an acceptable growing medium; however, we are interested in knowing the best that is available.

We know that the time required to build the growing medium is a small fraction of the time required to create the total bank; further, that how the overburden is handled before or after that point is of no consequence.

Before mining operations, we can use artificially-weathered core-drill samples as the basis for prediction. However, exposed highwalls offer a more sure method of identifying a problem overburden, enabling us to concentrate on how to care for it. To be successful soil prophets we must understand the nature of overburdens, the mining machines and methods used, the weathering process, and the techniques of grading. Manipulating these factors lets us produce a predictably consistent and beneficial growing medium. When we can predict the nature and behavior of the soil, we know what vegetation we can plant with assurance it will live. We can know in advance the productive capacity of the land after mining, so we don't grade and plant land for hayfields, for example, when it will best grow trees.

This sort of knowledge is fundamental to intelligent management of any land.

ACKNOWLEDGEMENTS

Success in achieving a predictable mined-land growing medium makes use of diverse talents.

The author is especially indebted to Ronald V. Crews, Mines Manager, Central Ohio Coal Company, for an on-the-job training course in strip mine operations; to Walter D. Smith, Reclamation Supervisor, Ohio Power Company, for his assistance in this project; and to Marshall Allman, Consulting Soils Analyst, Farm Clinic of U. S., for helpful suggestions and interpretation of overburden analysis.

LITERATURE CITED

Einspahr, D. W., A. L. McComb, F. F. Riecken, and W. D. Shrader. 1955. Coal spoil-bank materials as a medium for plant growth. *Proc. of the Iowa Acad. Sci.* **62**, 329–344.
Knabe, Wilhelm. 1965. Observations on world-wide efforts to reclaim industrial waste land. p. 264–296. In: G. T. Goodman, R. W. Edwards, and J. M. Lambert (ed.) *Ecology and the industrial society*. Blackwell Sci. Pub., Oxford.

DISCUSSION

PLASS: Please comment on the economics of this type of mining. Could it be used on small operations, as well as large ones such as you described?

KRAUSE: This can be answered only for a given set of circumstances: a known overburden, a specific type of machine. The principal is always applicable. Our biggest problem is that the principal function of mining is to get at the coal. Aside from stability, for which they put the large heavy rocks down the face, placement of the overburden doesn't matter to the miner. This has been mostly our fault for not indicating which materials were best suited for vegetation.

DOWNING: The fact that reclamation is a significant part of the mining operation, has been very much recognized in England. The 1958 opencast coal act has two equally important aims for the National Coal Board, the sole operators of opencast mining: first, the working of coal; second, the restoration of land. In the words of the act—the land was to be restored so as to be reasonably fit for agriculture. Your profile diagram significantly mentioned neither topsoil nor subsoil. Could you explain this?

KRAUSE: In the true sense we do not have topsoil. I call it the upper horizon. The particular area that I was speaking of is unglaciated hill country of southeastern Ohio. It has been pretty well farmed to death.

RITS: What is the average cost of the type of reclamation work you propose?

KRAUSE: It varies. I can recall spending $ 30 an acre and $ 3000 an acre for grading only—it depended on whether the material would support the type of vegetation we were aiming for. For grading, seeding, and planting, we were pretty close to the bonding rate of Ohio, which is around $ 300.

RITS: What is the difference in cost between the normal way of reclaiming this land and the way you are proposing?

KRAUSE: The difference is not significant. It is more a problem of coordination. For example, in this overburden material they had to change the drilling cycle. That is, a change in the mining process placed better material for vegetation at the surface.

PART II

HYDROLOGY AND POLLUTION

MOISTURE AND DENSITY RELATIONS ON GRADED STRIP-MINE SPOILS

Willie R. Curtis

Hydrologist, Northeastern Forest Experiment Station,
Forest Service, U. S. Department of Agriculture, Berea, Kentucky

Past research indicates that compaction during spoil-bank leveling results in less infiltration and decreased tree growth where ridges had been. This paper reports the first-year results of a study to determine the disposition of subsurface moisture on leveled spoil banks in western Kentucky and to determine whether the moisture conditions can be changed through scarification and vegetative treatments. A significant difference was noted in density and available moisture between former ridge and valley locations. The lowest moisture values were noted in the surface foot. Surface scarification apparently has not affected moisture or density.

INTRODUCTION

Spoil-bank leveling to some degree is required by many state reclamation laws. Any compaction, or other changes in the spoil surface resulting from the leveling operation, are accepted because leveling—or grading, as it is often called—is considered by some to be synonymous with good reclamation. But comparisons between leveled and unleveled spoils indicate that leveling results in reduced tree growth, lower infiltration rates, and changes in the availability of nutrients. Also, there is evidence that trees may grow faster on the fill portion of graded spoils than on the cut portion, where a ridge had been.

In addition to spoil grading, the type of vegetation used in reclamation may affect the distribution of soil moisture at various depths. For example a grass-legume cover may rapidly deplete moisture in the surface foot of spoil, while trees may have little effect on spoil moisture for several years. Also, vegetation may gradually improve infiltration rates by depositing litter and forming an organic layer on the surface.

This paper reports first-year results of a study to determine the disposition of rainfall as subsurface moisture on graded spoil banks and to determine opportunities for improving the moisture regime of spoil through scarification and vegetative treatments. The study is somewhat limited because only one spoil type is being sampled and only one method of grading was used.

A definite need exists for well-documented data on the disposition of moisture in spoil materials. This information could be of wide interest not only for revegetation, but for hydrologic reasons as well. Observations on native soils have little application to spoil conditions. Spoil-moisture investigations have been neglected in the past in large part because of the physical problems associated with taking measurements below the surface. Today—with portable drilling equipment, nuclear sensing devices, and improved materials for access tubes—the opportunities for conducting meaningful moisture studies in spoils are much improved. Nevertheless, a considerable effort must be expended to modify procedures used in native soils to adapt them to spoil conditions.

PAST WORK

The differences in moisture content of graded and ungraded spoil banks have been attributed in large part to differences in rates of infiltration and percolation. The lower rates on graded spoils are thought to be due in large part to puddling, or crusting over, of the smoothed surface and to greater density and reduced pore space caused by the compaction of spoils during the grading operation. Several studies, carried out independently by different investigators, have disclosed a large difference in water infiltration rates between graded and ungraded spoils.

Coleman (1951) measured infiltration rates in Pennsylvania ranging from 65 to 297 in./hr on spoils derived from dark, thin-bedded carbonaceous shales, and ranging from 0 to 17 in./hr on spoils derived from yellow, thick-bedded shales and sandstones.

Merz and Finn (1951) measured an average infiltration rate of 17 in./hr on graded spoil banks and 178 in./hr on ungraded banks in Ohio.

In Illinois, Grandt and Lang (1958) noted a significantly higher rate of infiltration on undisturbed spoil ridges than on level areas and strike-off tops. Infiltration on graded spoil was 0.9 in./hr as compared to 5.2 in./hr on ungraded ridges. The sites were bare of vegetation.

Limstrom (1960) found infiltration rates up to seven times greater on ungraded banks than on adjacent graded banks in Ohio. The rates were 4.0 and 0.6 in./hr, respectively.

Thurn (1953) found percolation rates in graded spoils from 0.2 to 1.5 in./hr in the 0- to 3-in. layer and from 0.1 to 0.6 in./hr in the 9- to 12-in. layer.

Vegetation influences infiltration and percolation rates on both graded and ungraded spoils. On ungraded silty clay banks in Illinois, Grandt (1952) reported field percolation rates of 9.3 in./hr on barren areas and 13.6 in./hr on areas of the same texture that had been covered with vegetation for several years. On graded sections of the same sites, the rates were only 0.9 in./hr on the barren part and 1.5 in./hr on the part covered with grasses and legumes. Thurn (1953), reporting on the same study, found percolation rates to vary from 0.1 to 1.5 in./hr, according to the amount of vegetation present.

Grandt and Lang (1958) found infiltration rates to range from 0.9 to 5.2 in./hr on bare graded and ungraded banks respectively and to range from 1.4 to 27.9 in./hr on graded and ungraded vegetated banks, respectively.

There have been several studies conducted on spoil materials, but it is interesting to note that they have been confined in large part to infiltration rather than to spoil moisture relations. Though the two are related, moisture storage capacity and the amount of moisture potentially available to plants may be of greater importance than the infiltration rate.

METHODS

The study was installed in area stripping in the Western Kentucky Coal Field near Drakesboro. In area stripping operations, the overburden is usually deposited in long, roughly parallel ridges or banks. Banks may vary in height from only a few feet to as much as 100 ft, and may vary in slope from almost level to as steep as 75%. When newly formed, these banks are a mass of boulders, stones, and soil material.

A 4-acre tract was selected that before grading included three spoil ridges and three valleys (Fig. 1). The area measured 400 ft parallel to the ridges and 450 ft perpendicular to the ridges. The tract was graded to level or gently rolling topography during January 1968.

The tract was subdivided into four blocks 100 ft wide, running at right angles to the ridge lines. Two of these blocks were scarified and two were not. Scarification consisted of traversing the plots with a road grader equipped with ripper teeth that were set approximately 18 in. apart and penetrated 8 to 10 in.

Each of the four blocks was divided into six equal parts or plots. Three of these plots were planted to trees only, and three were planted to trees plus a grass and legume mixture (Fig. 1).

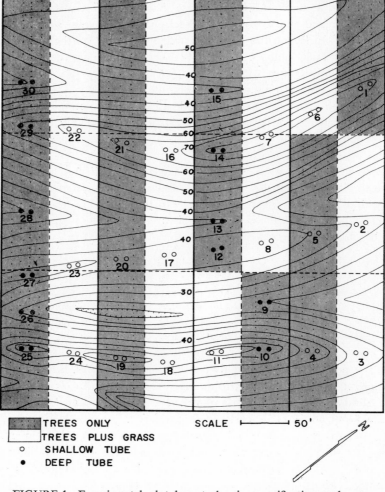

FIGURE 1 Experimental plot layout showing scarification and vegetation treatments and access-tube locations. Contour lines represent topography before grading (elevations are in ft).

Access tubes were installed in pairs at a uniform distance apart along the entire length of each of the three ridge lines. The ridge lines were selected as the point of measurement because this is where compaction probably would be the greatest. Of the 48 access-tube measuring sites thus established, 36 are 3 ft deep, and 12 are 17 ft deep. In addition, 12 deep tubes were established where valleys were before grading. All the deep tubes were located in subplots that were unscarified and planted to trees only, and the tubes were placed so that a set of ridge tubes and a set of valley tubes could be paired.

Nuclear methods are being used to determine moisture content and density of the spoil material. Measurements are being taken at the surface near each access tube and at 1-ft depth intervals within each tube. Moisture and density determinations are being made four times a year as follows:

(1) During maximum recharge (about March 1).
(2) During the growing season (about May 15).
(3) During a summer dry period (any time after July 15 following a 14-day rain-free period).
(4) At the end of the growing season. This is also the beginning of the recharge period (about October 31).

RESULTS

The experiment is designed so that an approved method of statistical analysis can be used to evaluate results and significance. The first year's study of moisture and density conditions is reported.

Between the time of scarification (March 1968) and the first full set of moisture and density readings (11 July 1968) there were approximately 15 in. of precipitation at the study site.

We expected scarification to result in a less dense surface layer, but, by the time our first data were collected, any differences in surface density due to scarification were obliterated. Evidently the first few rainstorms caused enough settling of the spoil to cancel the effects of scarification.

A significant reduction in surface density did occur between 11 July 1968 and 20 March 1969 within both the scarified and unscarified plots (Table 1). Still, no difference was found between scarification treatments.

The reduction in density noted on 20 March 1969 has been attributed to frost action during the winter. It may be noted that the greatest reduction in mean density over the period occurred in the unscarified plots,

TABLE 1
Density of strip-mine spoil surface on ridge locations

Unscarified			Scarified		
Tube no.[a]	7/11/68 lb/ft^3	3/20/69 lb/ft^3	Tube no.[a]	7/11/68 lb/ft^3	3/20/69 lb/ft^3
7	99.0	85.1	1	103.3	95.6
8	101.3	84.9	2	85.3	84.0
10	102.3	88.7	3	80.0	84.3
11	82.0	92.2	4	78.8	78.5
12	90.9	88.5	5	84.2	85.4
14	101.7	84.1	6	106.6	87.2
22	107.3	95.3	16	101.3	88.2
23	95.8	84.2	17	108.5	85.6
24	97.8	85.1	18	101.3	90.6
25	86.8	77.0	19	108.3	100.5
27	103.9	81.9	20	86.9	81 6
29	120.4	92.7	21	99.5	81.5
Average	99.1	86.7	Average	95.3	86.9

[a] See Fig. 1 for tube location.

TABLE 2
Average spoil density of ridges and valleys by depth on 11 July 1968

Depth ft	Ridge lb/ft^3	Valley lb/ft^3
0	101.0	102.2
1	79.9	60.6
2	85.9	63.1
3	84.1	65.6
4	84.5	62.3
5	80.7	66.2
6	83.5	63.2
7	84.3	55.7
8	86.6	58.5
9	81.4	50.9
10	77.2	56.5
11	78.6	62.1
12	77.6	65.1
13	82.9	74.3
14	84.5	81.7

and that, after one winter, surface densities are almost identical within the two treatments. Thus it appears that, in areas where frost action is encountered, mechanical scarification of the surface is unnecessary except perhaps for seedbed preparation at other times of the year.

The 11 July 1968 data indicated a significant difference between ridge and valley subsurface densities at each foot from the 1-ft to the 9-ft depth (Table 2). Densities in the valleys are about 20 lb/ft³ less than on the ridges. No significant differences were noted from the 9- to 16-ft depths. This may be attributable to the presence of voids and large boulders that caused a wide variation in density among tubes.

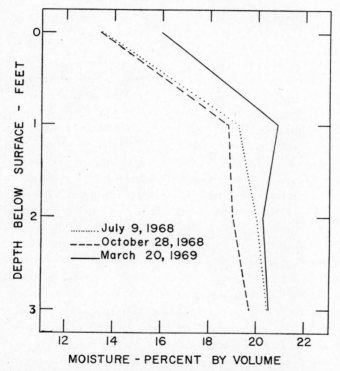

FIGURE 2   Spoil moisture by depth on three sampling dates, based on averages for 24 tubes.

It is assumed that ridges become compacted in two ways. First, the weight of the stacked spoil results in compaction; and second, during the grading operations bulldozers work on the ridges pushing material from ridge peaks into the valleys. This equipment undoubtedly causes compaction.

Moisture did not differ by scarification treatment, but a highly significant difference was observed in the amount of moisture at various depths. On all three sampling dates (9 July and 28 October 1968 and 20 March 1969) we observed an increasing moisture content with depth (Fig. 2). A small amount of moisture was lost from 9 July to 28 October 1968 and a significant amount was gained from 28 October 1968 to 20 March 1969. Thus, moisture conditions at the beginning of the 1969 growing season were favorable for plant establishment and growth.

In the study area, vegetation has had little or no influence on moisture to date. The first seeding in April 1968 failed almost entirely, and the 1969's vegetation density is such that we can assume it has had no effect on moisture content yet.

DISCUSSION

The first-year results of this experiment show definite differences in compaction from ridge to valley locations on graded spoil banks. At the same time, any differences in surface density due to grading or surface treatment are of short duration. Valleys are about 20 lb/ft³ less dense than ridges, except for the surface layers, which have the same density.

Moisture, when expressed as percent by volume, is the same on ridges and valleys. Generally, the surface few inches exhibit a moisture deficiency. Within a few months following grading, there should be sufficient moisture at 1-ft depth and below. Of course, this would depend on rainfall.

First-year results do not indicate water-logging to be a problem. In fact, it is possible that a drought condition exists within the surface few inches of spoil. The generally dark color, complete exposure to the sun and wind, and high rock content contribute to a droughty condition. This points up the need for seeding spoil banks at times when surface moisture is available. That moisture at depth does not appear to be limiting, may partly explain why some species of plants do well while others fail completely. Species having a tendency toward deep rooting might be able to get moisture while shallow rooted species die from lack of it.

As has been stated, there were no differences in moisture when expressed as percent by volume. But, because valleys are approximately 20% less dense than ridges, a significant difference does exist in moisture content expressed as the ratio of weight of water over dry density. Might this mean more water potentially available to plants? We need more information on the moisture constants (field capacity and wilting point) of various spoils in order to determine moisture availability.

LITERATURE CITED

Coleman, G. B. 1951. A study of water infiltration in the spoil banks in Central Pennsylvania. *J. Forest.* **49**, 574.

Grandt, Alten F. 1952. The potentialities of revegetating and utilizing agronomic species on strip-mined areas in Illinois. Ill. Agr. Exp. Sta. and Ill. Coal Strippers Assn. *5th Year Progr. Report*: 56 p., illus.

Grandt, A. F., and A. L. Lang. 1958. Reclaiming Illinois strip coal land with grasses and legumes. *Univ. Ill. Agr. Exp. Sta. Bull.* 628. 64 p.

Limstrom, G. A. 1960. Forestation of strip-mined land in the Central States. *U. S. Dep. Agr. Handbook* 166. 74 p.

Merz, R. W., and R. F. Finn. 1951. Differences in infiltration rates on graded and ungraded strip-mined lands. U. S. Dep. Agr., Forest Serv., Central States Forest Exp. Sta. Note 65. 2 p.

Thurn, Edward A. 1953. The potentialities of revegating and utilizing agronomic species on strip mined areas in Illinois. Ill. Agr. Exetp. Sta. and Ill. Coal Strippers Assn. *6th Year Progr. Report*: 48 p.

DISCUSSION

CARUCCIO: How did you measure the density at depth?

CURTIS: With a Nuclear Chicago depth density sampler, with a Cs source.

CARUCCIO: Isn't this a function of the C content?

CURTIS: Yes, coal would influence the density but I showed actual figures here for ease of presentation. I am interested primarily in differences; and I am assuming that if there is C at one spot today it will be there next month, and that differences with time will show up.

CARUCCIO: Might other stratification be due to the stratification of lithologic types rather than the density differences?

CURTIS: I would say that in area type stripping there would be no stratification as such. This spoil is about 100 ft deep. It was solid rock before, and it has been thoroughly mixed in the initial stacking process and also in the grading or leveling process. Larger boulders may predominate in the areas that were originally valleys. As the tops of the ridge are pushed off, larger rocks roll into the valleys. Our density measurements tend to substantiate this.

NEUMANN: I think that mositure of soil should be investigated during the night because Dr. Dunger and I found that extremely hydrophilic animals live on spoil banks. Because of low density of spoil material, it is possible for water vapor to move from the depth to the surface during the night when temperatures of the surface becomes less than those at depth.

CURTIS: With nuclear methods we cannot determine accurately enough the microclimatic moisture contents to which Mr. Neumann is referring. Diurnal moisture fluctuations of spoil moisture should be studied; however, refined techniques must be used.

MEDVICK: I expect you are familiar with Dr. Chapman's work on compaction and vegetation response. Chapman emphasized the effects of compaction relative to the amount of clay as a result of tractor grading on coal spoils. Would you comment on this?

CURTIS: I did not try to identify the spoil material. The only thing I did was take density measurements in it. Some of my density measurements might have been taken in the middle of a large piece of rock, so we haven't gone further into the type of work that Chapman did. Clay content will have an effect.

FUNK: Some previous work has also indicated that perhaps compaction effects might be more serious if the grading was done in the winter when spoil moisture content was high. When was the grading done?

CURTIS: Grading was done in January. Moisture content was fairly high. The spoil was about a year old before the grading. Grading equipment affected only the surface foot. Although I show significant differences in density from ridge to valley, much of this density was a result of the stacking. This material was stacked for a year before it was graded. And at the same time, the less dense materials in the valleys resulted from the equipment pushing the material in so that there was less compaction in the valley-type situation than on the ridges.

EFFECTS OF STRIP MINING
ON THE HYDROLOGY
OF SMALL MOUNTAIN WATERSHEDS
IN APPALACHIA

Willie R. Curtis

Hydrologist, Northeastern Forest Experiment Station,
Forest Service, U. S. Department of Agriculture, Berea, Kentucky

The effects of strip mining on the water resources of small mountain watersheds are being investigated in eastern Kentucky. Six subdrainages have been instrumented to record pre-mining conditions, changes during active mining operations, and the rate of recovery after mining. Stream turbidity and peak flows increase during mining, but on one subdrainage, turbidity returned to near pre-mining condition within about 6 months after mining. Storm runoff durations apparently do not change. Sulfate and magnesium in the streamflow have increased since mining.

INTRODUCTION

Strip mining for coal in the Appalachian Region can have a pronounced effect on the hydrology of a watershed. How long does erosion and sedimentation continue? What happens to streamflow and stream chemistry? How long after mining will it take the watershed to recover? After the first 2 years of a study to evaluate the effects of strip mining on the water resources of two small Appalachian watersheds, we can begin to answer some of these questions. Even though the observations are from individual watersheds, the basic knowledge gained should apply to much of the coal-producing mountain land in Appalachia.

Little research has been done on the hydrologic implications of strip mining. Public pressures against the unsightly areas created by mining have put the emphasis on revegetation. At the same time, the public, the mine operators, and the land managers have tended to believe that once

10 Hutnik/D (1440)

the mined area is revegetated, *all* runoff and erosion problems are auto-matically solved. On the contrary, successful revegetation may not be possible until runoff and erosion have been controlled.

Knowledge of the influence of strip mining on the water resource is basic to the development of improved mining methods and standards to prevent accelerated erosion and related watershed deterioration. The know-ledge is basic for rehabilitation of strip-mined areas, and for improving water yield and quality from strip-mined mountain watersheds.

PRESENT KNOWLEDGE

The effects of strip mining may be classified broadly according to stream discharge, erosion and sedimentation, and stream chemistry.

Stream discharge

Strip mining affects stream discharge. The importance of the effect will undoubtedly vary according to the physical condition of the area during and after mining.

One of the first attempts to evaluate the hydrological impact of strip mining was the Beaver Creek study in southeastern Kentucky (Musser, 1963; Collier, et al., 1964; Collier, et al., 1966). In this study, three water-sheds, one without mining and two with mining, were gaged. The authors reported that the mined watersheds were more variable than the control and tended toward higher storm flows and lower base flows. But because data on runoff characteristics of the watersheds for the period before mining were not available, and because of the relatively short period of record, the results were somewhat inconclusive.

Medvick (1965), Truax (1965), Corbett (1965), and Agnew (1966)—all reporting on the same investigation made during the unusually dry summer of 1964—found an apparent increase in base flow due to increased deten-tion storage in the watershed. In the mining, the geologic strata of the overburden are shattered and generally mixed. The result is a substantial increase in the depth of unconsolidated materials, sometimes by as much as 100 ft in area stripping. These stripped lands may have a greatly increased storage potential. This effect would be much less in contour stripping where only small percentages of the area are disturbed and where spoil is piled on steep slopes.

Erosion and sedimentation

In general, three major sources of sediment in strip-mined areas have been recognized (Striffler and May, 1965). These are spoil slides, haul roads, and the mined area itself.

A survey of strip mining in eastern Kentucky indicated that about 12% of the outslope area had failed (Plass, 1966 and 1967a, b, c, d, and e). Such bank failures often cause considerable damage to the land and adjacent property. Large masses of spoil moving down the slope carry trees and debris great distances. Slides frequently enter and block stream channels.

Road erosion is a universal problem in the Appalachian coal fields. In general, roads are put in as cheaply as possible by operators inexperienced in good road-building design or practices. Most roads are extremely steep and are either poorly drained or lack drainage altogether. The usual practice is to maintain roads daily, shut down during a storm, and regrade the road after the storm. Upon completion of mining, most haul roads are abandoned, and little or no attempt is made to bed them down. Such roads deteriorate rapidly and are an important source of sediment (Weigle, 1965).

The strip-mine area is also an important source of sediment, even though erosion tends to vary considerably among operations. With the exception of the Beaver Creek studies, little measurement of erosion has been reported. In a partially stripped watershed, an average erosion rate of 5.9 tons/acre per year was observed. In comparison, the unmined watershed had an average rate of erosion of 0.7 tons/acre per year. Ninety-seven percent of the erosion in the partially stripped watershed was attributed to the strip-mined area, which then covered only 6.4% of the area.

Stream chemistry

The chemical breakdown of freshly exposed pyrites causes toxicity in spoils and acid pollution in streams; this pollution is damaging to aquatic flora and fauna. In 1964 about 5000 miles of stream and 14,000 acres of surface impoundments in the Appalachians had already been affected adversely by acid mine drainage (Kinney, 1964). A more recent survey of mine pollution in Appalachia indicated that the water quality of 194 of 318 sampling sites was measurably influenced by mine drainage; water at 30 sites contained free mineral acid (Biesecker and George, 1966).

Other surveys have provided information on the extent and nature of mine-drainage pollution (Barnes, Stuart, and Fisher, 1964; Hopkins,

10*

1965). Braley (1954) suggested that the acid-producing potential of out-crop strip mines is less than that of underground mines, because the coal and associated strata have been subjected to weathering. Yet the effects of strip-mines must not be overlooked.

In the Beaver Creek studies, mining disturbance increased total dissolved solids in runoff by 13 times for the period 1957–61. Sulfate was the most prominent compound released. Concentrations of Al, Fe, Mn, Ca, Mg, Na, and K also increased. Acidity increased from 0 to 1.0 ppm, and pH decreased from 6.8 to 4.0. Dissolved solids were found to decrease slightly from 1960 through 1964. This was probably due to chemical erosion and removal of the more readily available minerals

Parsons (1956) suggested that salts from spoil banks reach the stream by the concentration of soluble salts at the soil surface through evaporation and the subsequent solution and transportation to the steam by overland flow during a storm. Collier et al. (1966) suggested that salts are dissolved in the groundwater as it percolates through the spoil and seeps into the stream. A lysimeter study in Ohio showed large volumes of dissolved solids being leached from the spoil and carried in the percolate (Struthers, 1964). The effect of acid water seeping from ponds through spoil banks is not known.

Negruckij (1959) reported generally adverse effects of mine waters dis-charged on the forest area below. On the other hand, the Beaver Creek studies indicated a growth-rate increase for sample tress below the mines. This increased growth was attributed to increased levels of minerals neces-sary for growth.

It has been widely reported that mine drainage waters generally create an unfavorable environment for aquatic organisms because of increased acidity, the presence of specific ions in quantities toxic to aquatic life, the precipitation of ferric sulfate on stream bottoms, and the choking of streams with sediment. This literature was reviewed by Parsons (1957) and Riley (1960) and will not be repeated here.

Methods of controlling stream pollution from strip mines have been recommended but have not been thoroughly tested (Braley, 1954). In general, these include the following: (1) Identification and segregation of pyritic materials during reclamation. This should be an effective measure and is being incorporated into strip-mine regulations in many states. However, it is a difficult measure for mine operators to fulfill and it is seldom fully met. (2) Maintaining the pit free of water at all times, both during and after mining, to retard oxidation of pyritic materials. This has generally been accomplished, but often at the expense of increased erosion. (3) Backfilling the pit after mining to cover the exposed coal seam. This is also a general practice although it rarely results in coverage of all pyritic materials and, on orphan banks where a vegetative cover has become established, may do more harm than good. (4) Grading the surface to permit complete runoff of surface water. This is a controversial practice. Braley (1954) recommends exclusion of surface water to reduce oxidation of pyrites and to decrease acid production and stream pollution. On the other hand, Struthers (1964) recommends grading to increase infiltration to hasten the leaching process in order to secure a more favorable vegetation cover.

OUR STUDIES

Two watersheds, Leatherwood Creek and Bear Branch, in Breathitt County, Ky., were selected for study. The watershed areas are 2.4 and 2.2 sq. miles respectively. Three subdrainages within each watershed have been instrumented. These subdrainages vary from 172 to 380 acres, and the expected land disturbance ranges from 10 to 60%.

The watersheds range in elevation from 800 to 1500 ft. Average stream slope is 4%, and average slope of the land surface is about 30%. Three minable coal beds outcrop at approximate elevations of 1350 ft, 1380 ft, and 1420 ft.

Precipitation, streamflow, sediment yield, and water chemistry are being measured. The United States Geological Survey began recording streamflow from Bear Branch in December 1954 and has maintained a recording rain gage near the mouth of the watershed since October 1960. Average annual precipitation for 1962 through 1966 was 43 in. at the Bear Branch gage. Weirs were installed in the three subdrainages in Bear Branch in April 1968. Stream gaging on Leatherwood Creek began in March 1966, and the substations were installed and instrumented in September 1967.

The stream-gaging stations consist of broad-crested concrete weirs equipped with automatic water-level recorders. Weirs on the main streams were poured in place. Weirs on the subdrainages were constructed of concrete blocks.

Water samples are collected weekly at each weir for chemical analysis and determination of sediment content. When the weirs fill with sediment, the volume is measured, and the weir is cleaned.

Biologists from Eastern Kentucky University at Richmond are cooperating in a study of stream-bottom fauna; streams will be sampled four times a year during mining and during a recovery period. We want to find out what species of fish and insects are present, what happens to their populations during mining, and how long it takes the populations to recover after mining.

RESULTS

Preliminary results and trends observed over the past 2 years are reported in this paper. The data have not been analyzed statistically; however, the results are readily apparent, and statistical tests were deemed unnecessary.

The results are given in terms of three subdrainages of the Leatherwood Creek watershed (Table 1). Results and trends discussed for these subdrainages are typical of the results from the other subdrainages.

TABLE 1

Size and mining of three subdrainages of the Leatherwood Creek watershed

Subdrainage	Total area acres	Dates of mining		Area disturbed %
		Beginning	Ending	
A	380	1 Aug. 1968	Continuing	45
B	174	1 July 1968	17 Nov. 1968	40
C	283	15 Aug. 1967	10 Dec. 1967	10

Stream discharge

The study has some limitations because of the lack of an adequate pretreatment period of streamflow measurement. However, as the first subdrainage was mined, the adjacent ones were yet undisturbed. This allows comparisons of streamflow records for determining gross changes resulting from contour strip mining.

After adjusting for differences in drainage area, we found little difference in stream discharge between unmined subdrainages; differences during nonstorm periods were particularly small.

About one-half the perimeter of subdrainage C was stripped between August and December 1967. Total disturbance amounts to only 10% of the drainage area. Even so, some influences have shown up. When the records from the mined and an adjacent unmined watershed are compared, a number of peaks appear on the hydrograph from the mined area, but not on the other. These peaks are caused by drainage of pits during mining.

Contour strip mining results in one or more cuts around a mountainside that interupt the natural movement of water down the slope. The water that collects in the pit along the highwall must be removed periodically during the mining operation.

Storm-runoff peaks appear to have changed after strip mining. If we assume that, before mining, subdrainage C reacted to rainfall in the same way as A and B, then storm peaks increased (Fig. 1). At the same time, the duration of storm discharge does not appear to have changed. Neither has base flow.

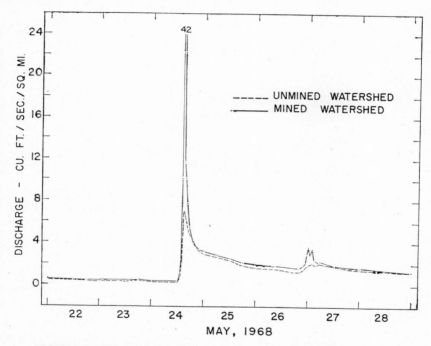

FIGURE 1 The effect of strip mining on storm runoff peaks. One inch of precipitation produced these peaks.

Sediment

Recently disturbed soil material is usually very susceptible to erosion. This is especially true when the material is piled in loose heaps with steep slopes, as in spoil banks.

In most cases, sediment sampling began before any surface disturbance. It must be pointed out that interval sampling may not represent actual maximum sediment concentrations.

All watersheds showed increases in suspended solids during the active mining periods. However, mining in subdrainage C ended in December 1967, and the suspended-solid content soon returned to near pre-mining

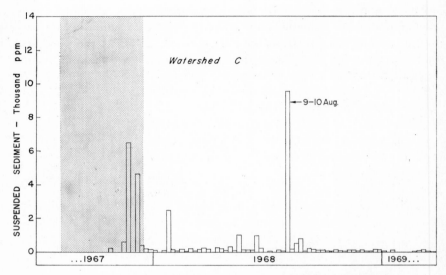

FIGURE 2   Suspended sediment content in the stream flowing from strip-mined subdrainage C. The shaded section represents the period of active mining operations.

TABLE 2

Sediment trapped in and removed from weirs

	Subdrainage		
Date	A	B	C
	ft³/sq. mile of watershed		
5-14-68	374	1,165	626
6-4-68	222	450	464
7-25-68	0	2,303	1,203
9-4-68	1,413	13,455	2,223
9-30-68	546	2,608	0
10-22-68	350	0	0
1-28-69	925	7,304	0
4-29-69	2,099	6,426	0
6-18-69	354	7,996	0
Total	6,283	41,707	4,516

levels, except for severe storm conditions (Fig. 2). One such storm occurred on 9–10 Aug. 1968 when over 3 in. of rain fell on the area. That same storm produced very little sediment from subdrainage A, which was not mined at that time. But, later in 1968, while subdrainage A was being mined, suspended sediments reached over 46,000 ppm.

Subdrainage B has produced the greatest amounts of suspended sediments. Mining was completed in subdrainage B in mid-November 1968; yet, sediment production remains high.

In addition to soil loss as suspended particles, much sediment has been trapped in the weir basins. As weirs were cleaned, the volumes of trapped sediment were determined (Table 2).

The values in Table 2 can be used for comparative purposes only, because all sediment was not trapped. No sediment has been removed from the weir on subdrainage C since cleanup of that produced by the large storm of 9–10 Aug. 1968.

In subdrainage A, which is still being mined, a number of spoil slides occurred that extended all the way to the valley bottom. These slides blocked the channel and are causing deposition of sediment. A check dam was constructed above the weir to trap sediment. On 1 June 1969 this dam was full with an estimated 400 ft^3 of sediment.

Chemistry

In our experimental areas, acid-forming elements are not predominant. Thus stream acidity has not changed greatly after mining.

We have run tests on samples collected weekly for Ca, Mg, Mn, Fe, Cu, Zn, sulfate, pH, specific conductance, turbidity, and total alkalinity. A number of changes have been observed. In subdrainage C, sulfate increased—but not until about July 1968, 6 months after the completion of mining. Subdrainage B began showing significant increases in sulfate in December 1969, approximately 7 months after mining began in the subdrainage (Fig. 3). This further substantiates the lag in sulfate production.

Magnesium began to increase at the onset of mining activities (Fig. 3). There has been a slow but steady increase in Mg content in the flow from C, from 1968 to mid-1969.

Calcium has shown some change after mining, but, like a number of the other elements, not enough data are available on which to base a decision. Some elements for which tests were run have not been detected either before or after mining.

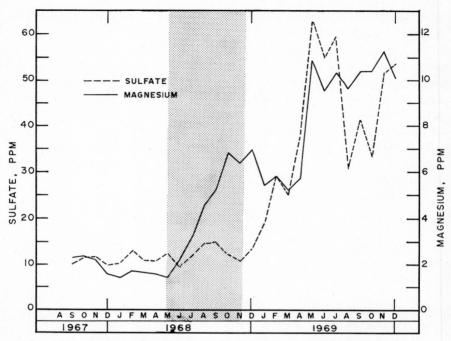

FIGURE 3 Sulfate and magnesium content in streamflow from sub-drainage B. The shaded section represents the period of mining operations.

DISCUSSION

In watershed experiments, so much depends upon climatic variation—as well as on natural variation in geologic, edaphic, and vegetative characteristics—that to report more than general trends with only 1 or 2 years of data would be presumptuous. Also, stripping around the contour takes several weeks—and multiple-seam operations may take months or even years—depending upon the operator, weather, geology, coal market, thickness of overburden, etc.

As this study continues, the preliminary results presented in this paper will either be substantiated or refuted.

The study has not provided for adequate measurement of soil loss; however, relative measurements have been made. More work is recommended and planned along this line.

The Beaver Creek study discussed earlier showed a tendency toward higher storm flows and lower base flows from a watershed with 10% of the area disturbed. Our study also indicated increased storm runoff peaks; however, base flows do not appear to have changed.

The apparent lag in chemical changes in the streamflow is reasonable, because time is essential for chemical weathering to take place, and some elements are more soluble than others. Also, some time is necessary for elements in solution to reach stream channels. More information will be collected in this phase as other already instrumented watersheds are mined.

The scope of this study includes determination of changes in the water resource after strip mining, but not the evaluation of these changes— whether harmful or beneficial.

LITERATURE CITED

Agnew, Allen F. 1966. A quarter to zero—surface mining supplies. *Mining Congr. J.* **52**(10), 29, 32–34, 38–40.

Barnes, Ivan, W. T. Stuart, and D. W. Fisher. 1964. Field investigations of mine waters in the northern anthracite field, Pennsylvania. U. S. Dep. Interior, Geol. Surv. Prof. Paper 473-B. 8 p.

Biesecker, J. E., and J. R. George. 1966. Stream acidity in Appalachia as related to coal mine drainage, 1965. U. S. Dep. Interior, Geol. Surv. Cir. 526. 27 p.

Braley, S. A. 1954. *Summary report of Commonwealth of Pennsylvania Industrial Fellowship.* Mellon Inst. Ind. Res., 1 to 7. 279 p.

Collier, Charles R., et al. 1964. Influences of strip-mining on the hydrological environment of parts of Beaver Creek Basin, Kentucky. 1955–59. U. S. Dep. Interior, Geol. Surv. Prof. Paper 427-B. 85 p.

Collier, Charles R., et al. 1966. Influences of strip-mining on the hydrological environment of parts of Beaver Creek Basin, Kentucky, 1959–64. U. S. Dep. Interior, Geol. Surv. Prof. Paper 427-C, (Unpublished preliminary draft). 76 p.

Corbett, Don M. 1965. Water supplied by coal surface mines, Pike County, Indiana. Indiana Univ. Water Resources Res. Center, Rep. Invest. 1. 67 p.

Hopkins, T. C. 1965. Western Maryland mine drainage survey. Maryland Dep. Water Resources, Water Quality Div. Vol. 1, 259 p; Vol. II, 251 p; Vol. III, 203 p.

Kinney, E. C. 1964. Extent of acid mine pollution in the United States affecting fish and wildlife. U. S. Dep. Interior, Fish Wildlife Service, Bur. of Sport Fisheries Cir. 191. 27 p.

Medvick, Charles. 1965. Why reforest surface mined areas? *Mining Congr. J.* **51**(6), 86–89.

Musser, John J. 1963. Description of physical environment and of strip-mining operations in parts of Beaver Creek Basin, Kentucky. U. S. Dep. Interior, Geol. Surv. Prof. Paper 427-A. 25 p.

Negruckij, S. F. 1959. The danger of mine waters to forest. Lesn Hoz 12(11). 79 p.

Parsons, J. D. 1956. The effects of acid strip-mine pollution on the ecology of a central Missouri stream. *Ph. D. Thesis.* Univ. Missouri. 185 p.

Parsons, J. D. 1957. Literature pertaining to formation of acid mine wastes and their effects on the chemistry and fauna of streams. *Trans. Ill. Acad. Sci.* **50**, 49–59.

Plass, William T. 1966. Land disturbances from strip-mining in eastern Kentucky. 1. Upper Cumberland coal reserve district. U. S. Dep. Agr., Forest Service, Northeastern Forest Exp. Sta. Res. Note NE-52. 7 p.

Plass, William T. 1967a. Land disturbances from strip-mining in eastern Kentucky. 2. Princess Coal Reserve District. U. S. Dep. Agr., Forest Service, Northeastern Forest Exp. Sta. Res. Note NE-55. 8 p.

Plass, William T. 1967b. Land disturbances from strip-mining in eastern Kentucky. 3. Licking River Coal Reserve District. U. S. Dep. Agr., Forest Service, Northeastern Forest Exp. Sta. Res. Note NE-68. 6 p.

Plass, William T. 1967c. Land disturbances from strip-mining in eastern Kentucky. 4. Big Sandy Coal Reserve District. U. S. Dep. Agr., Forest Service, Northeastern Forest Exp. Sta. Res. Note NE-69. 7 p.

Plass, William T. 1967d. Land disturbances from strip-mining in eastern Kentucky. 5. Hazard Coal Reserve District. U. S. Dep. Agr., Forest Service, Northeastern Forest Exp. Sta. Res. Note NE-71. 7 p.

Plass, William T. 1967e. Land disturbances from strip-mining in eastern Kentucky. 6. Southwestern Coal Reserve District. U. S. Dep. Agr., Forest Service, Northeastern Forest Exp. Sta. Res. Note NE-72. 8 p.

Riley, C. V. 1960. The ecology of water areas associated with coal strip-mine lands in Ohio. *Ohio J. Sci.* **60**, 106–121.

Striffler, W. D., and R. F. May. 1965. The forest restoration of strip-mined areas. *Proc. Soc. Amer. Forest. Ann. Meeting.* p. 105–108.

Struthers, P. H. 1964. The chemical weathering of strip-mine spoil. *Ohio J. Sci.* **64**(2), 125–131.

Truax, Chester N., Jr. 1965. Water storage potential of surface mined lands. *Mining Congr. J.* **51**(11), 40–41, 45–46.

Weigle, Weldon K. 1965. Road erosion and spoil-bank stability. *Proc. Coal Mine Spoil Reclamation Symposium*, Pennsylvania State Univ., p. 82–85.

DISCUSSION

PETSCH: In Westphalia we have an area with dams on several small rivers. We have trouble with sediment in these dams. Do you also have this problem?

CURTIS: I have only measured sediment on small streams draining 300 acres or less. I have not measured sediment in the larger streams; but through observations, it is easy to see that it is there.

HEALD: Was the chemical analysis run on filtered samples?

CURTIS: Yes, for many tests we use atomic absorption, and this requires filtration.

CRESSWELL: I wondered if you considered estimating diatom populations in your streams. A scientist in my department has been doing this and has found that there is very close correlation with the runoff from the gold mine dumps and the pollutibility of the water.

CURTIS: I have only a preliminary summary of the first three observations on the stream fauna. If our cooperators are not presently studying the diatoms, we should perhaps recommend it.

KRAUSE: What reclamation measures, if any, were made? Also, were there any special measures made to control rainfall or ground water on the surface of these areas?

CURTIS: These watersheds are presently being stripped and reclaimed under existing Kentucky laws. We deviated slightly from one requirement in order to study sediment. We allowed the operator to refrain from installing small check dams that are required by law. We wanted all the sediment to have a chance to get to our measuring site.

HYDROLOGY OF A WATERSHED CONTAINING FLOOD-CONTROL RESERVOIRS AND COAL SURFACE-MINING ACTIVITY, SOUTHWESTERN INDIANA

Allen F. Agnew* and Don M. Corbett

Director and Research Associate, Water Resources Research Center, Indiana University, Bloomington, Indiana

The effect of man's activities that have disturbed land areas can be both beneficial and deleterious. One of the important areas for study concerns the quality and quantity of water produced during the process of surface mining, which results in (1) groundwater contained in the piles of cast overburden, (2) water in last-cut lakes and ponds in the disturbed area, and (3) affected water in the streams.

Our hydrologic studies in Indiana show that surface mining for coal can (1) provide additional supplies of ground water, (2) aid in flood control, and (3) alter the water quality in some areas. Current mining practices in conformance with Indiana law are controlling the latter problem—acid mine-drainage—which is caused mainly by old mine-waste piles, compacted areas such as haul roads, and underground mines.

The Busseron Creek watershed, a Public Law 566 Project of the U. S. Soil Conservation Service, contains sites for 26 reservoirs, of which 23 are for flood control only. In this watershed of 237 sq miles, surface mining for coal has already disturbed one site and at least two others are scheduled for mining.

During flushouts—periods of high runoff caused by sudden and intense storms—acid mine-drainage is a problem in this watershed; normally runoff from unmined areas and non-acid mined areas provides sufficient dilution. Proper management of releases of water impounded by the mining process can materially remedy this problem.

---

* At present, Director, State of Washington Water Research Center, Washington State University, Pullman, Washington.

THE PROBLEM AND HYROLOGY

We, who are participating in this symposium, recognize the importance of reclaiming land that is disturbed by man. Other elements of our society also desire clean streams, restored scenery, and land that is again productive, and they need answers to the questions of how this can be accomplished and at what cost. Answering these questions is not easy; it requires an out-of-the-ordinary blending of scientific and engineering knowledge and social and economic inputs.

In order to achieve these goals, the mining industry, state and federal regulatory and reclamation agencies, and university researchers have been working on the problem for many years.

Recent reports that have surveyed the situation in the U.S. (Hill, 1968; Kinney, 1964; Lorenz, 1962; Ohio River Valley Water Sanitation Commission, 1965 and 1968; U.S. Department of Agriculture, 1968; U.S. Department of the Interior, 1967) have been very helpful in providing an assessment of the present status, and in recommending additional facets that need to be studied. According to the U.S. Department of the Interior (1967), the research needs in surface-mine reclamation are:

A. Fundamental research:
   1. Acid formation.
   2. Nutrient deficiency.
   3. Bacterial action.
   4. Groundwater hydrology.
   5. Classification of waste or spoil-bank materials.

B. Applied research:
   1. Improved mining equipment and procedures.
   2. Slope stabilization.
   3. Erosion control.
   4. Prevention of acid-water production.

One part of this many-faceted problem is hydrology. Although hydrology is basic to all other phases of reclamation, it has not received the attention it deserves. Therefore, its many roles as related to surface mining and the need for additional answers will be emphasized.

Surface mining changes the natural or pre-existing hydrology of an area by affecting both the quantity and the quality of the water. These changes can be positive or negative. In the positive category are (1) increased groundwater contained in the piles of disturbed or cast-overburden material, and (2) water newly available in last-cut lakes and in ponds in the irregular mined surface. However, if the quality of the water in these two situations is poor, then the negative aspects cancel the positive ones.

These impoundments have a positive effect when the water is of good quality and can be regulated to offset acid flows in streams. On the other hand, when acid waters are impounded, a slug caused by flushouts, due either to sudden intense storms or to man-caused "dumping", can have a detrimental effect on streams.

Another positive effect of the surface-mining process is that the ridges of cast-overburden material can act as a flood retardant if they are aligned across the drainage-ways. On the other hand, they must be properly engineered or they can fail and thus result in "dumping" or flushing.

Our research in Indiana has dealt with two areas; one of these, the Busseron Creek watershed has been described elsewhere (Corbett and Agnew, 1968) and is discussed further in this paper; the other area, in Pike County some 50 miles to the south, has been described elsewhere (Corbett, 1965, 1968 and 1969).

PHYSICAL FEATURES

The Busseron Creek watershed, tributary to the Wabash River south of Terre Haute, Ind., consists of 237 sq miles (Fig. 1). Within the watershed, 26 reservoirs are being constructed by the U.S. Soil Conservation Service, 23 for the sole purpose of flood control (Fig. 2); 12 have been completed. The watershed of one proposed reservoir has already been mined out, and at least two others are in areas scheduled for mining in the future.

The gently rolling land surface is covered with soil derived from a thin veneer of windblown silt and sand, which lies on a small thickness of glacial drift. This in turn rests on the nearly flat bedrock containing coal and associated shale, sandstone, and some limestone.

Because of the relatively subdued topography, damage from sediment has not been serious. However, acid waters were known to exist in certain parts of the watershed.

The climate is temperate-continental with a mean annual temperature of 55 F, and extremes ranging from −24 to 111 F. Mean annual precipitation is 37 inches, ranging from a minimum of 26.2 to a maximum of 46.8 inches.

Evaporation, adjusted to open-water bodies, averages 30 inches annually, with a departure of about 4 inches for a minimum or a maximum year. (These determinations were made by applying appropriate correction to the U.S. Weather Bureau observations at Evansville, Lafayette, and Dubois 80 miles to the south, 80 miles to the north, and 60 miles to the southeast respectively.)

The watershed was instrumented to obtain accurate and representative samples of the water quantity and quality at different times of the year and in response to unusual as well as normal physical events, both natural

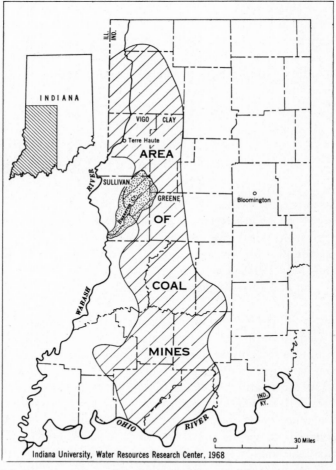

FIGURE 1   Map of southwestern Indiana showing area of coal mines and Busseron Creek watershed.

and man-made. The U.S. Geological Survey, in cooperation with the U.S. Soil Conservation Service, installed five recording stream gages as part of the project to supplement the one gage that existed near the mouth of the watershed (Fig. 2). Two years of accurate streamflow data were thus acquired during the study period, 1966–68, and data are still being accumulated. Furthermore, estimates of streamflow were made on numerous occasions at five additional sites and on a few occasions at more than 100 other locations.

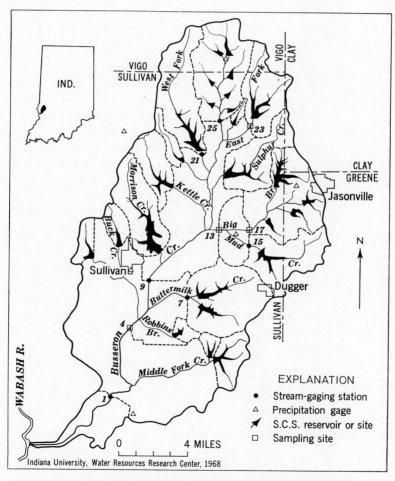

FIGURE 2   Map of Busseron Creek watershed showing tributary watersheds, Soil Conservation Service reservoir sites, and hydrologic data stations.

11*

Approximately 450 water samples were taken at different stages of stream height and volume of discharge and at different times of the year in cooperation with the U.S. Federal Water Pollution Control Administration. That agency and the Indiana State Board of Health performed the chemical analyses as part of their pollution investigation programs.

WATER DEVELOPMENT AND POTENTIAL GROUNDWATER STORAGE

Cast overburden of coal surface mines in southwestern Indiana has created massive man-made aquifers capable of storing large volumes of groundwater resulting from precipitation. The cast overburden materially reduces peak discharges of streams within the watershed when storms are of sufficient magnitude and intensity to cause flooding. We observed that the groundwater contributed by this material not only fills the last cut resulting from the termination of surface mining to half or two-thirds of its capacity, forming sizeable lakes, but also the cast overburden retains a large part of the precipitation in its voids and releases it to the lakes, replenishing supplies lost by evaporation, seepage, and outflow. Consequently, the water levels of these lakes show little seasonal variation.

The water-storage potential of this cast-overburden material can be likened to a mixed sand, silt, and clay aquifer. Such an aquifer contains 30% or more of void space, and specific yields of 30 to 40% of the voids are probable. The specific yield depends upon particle-size distribution and upon the hydraulic gradient within the cast overburden toward the stream or lake. In the absence of specific quantitative data, it seems reasonable to assume that the specific yield of the cast-overburden material should be at least 15%.

The seven completed Soil Conservation Service single-purpose reservoirs in the Busseron Creek watershed have a combined storage of 1808 acre-ft. Because their total water-surface area is 229 acres at flood-pool elevation, an average depth of slightly less than 8 ft is required to provide the 1808 acre-ft of storage.

The approximate total area of last-cut lakes needed in the Busseron Creek watershed to produce this amount of water is 60 acres, if the lakes average 30 ft in depth. Furthermore, recharge from surrounding groundwater contained in the cast-overburden material could replenish these lakes so that they would not be as susceptible to evaporation losses and changes in water level as are the Soil Conservation Service reservoirs.

Another factor of considerable economic importance is that some of these seven reservoirs were built over coal reserves that could be surface mined. There is a good possibility that mining will be carried out in the future, in which case we understand that the mining companies will be required to provide water storage equivalent to that destroyed in the mining process. We believe that such storage can be provided by normal processes of surface mining at considerably less cost than is entailed in the normal construction of a surface dam and reservoir.

SURFACE-MINING EFFECTS ON WATER QUANTITY AND QUALITY

Surface mining for coal has been carried out in the Busseron Creek watershed since 1927 (Fig. 3). Acid mine-drainage in the watershed, however, was given little or no consideration until recently, when surface-mining activity in the Mud Creek tributary watershed was about to be discontinued. During a 2-year period (May 21, 1963–July 7, 1965), the Indiana State Board of Health made analyses of 13 water samples collected during five visits to the area, and identified the Big Branch-Mud Creek tributary watersheds as acid-producing areas. There was some indication that the Buttermilk Creek tributary watershed farther south might be an offender, and Sulphur Creek to the north had been suspected because of its name.

On October 24, 1963, the junior author and Damon H. McFadden of Ayrshire Collieries Corporation inspected 14 sites in the Busseron Creek watershed, including both surface-mined and unmined areas. Surface-mined watersheds showed a water yield of as much as 60,000 gal/day, whereas adjoining undisturbed watersheds, although much larger in area, were dry and the channels were parched. This field observation attains even greater significance when it is recalled that the 1963 drought was then at its worst. During the preceding 57 days, only 0.32 inch of precipitation had been recorded at the nearby Jasonville State Park weather station.

On November 23, 1965, a field inspection of the watershed was made by representatives of the Indiana State Board of Health, the Indiana Department of Natural Resources, the U.S. Soil Conservation Service, the U.S. Federal Water Pollution Control Administration, the U.S. Geological Survey, and the Indiana University Water Resources Research Center. Samples were collected at 13 sites and analyzed for pH, conductivity, acidity, alkalinity, total hardness, sulfate, total Fe, Mn, and chloride. On the basis of pH, acidity, and sulfate, the offending tributary watersheds were identified as Mud Creek, Sulphur Creek, and Buttermilk Creek. Because of deficient precipitation, flows were generally low for this time of the year.

In the next few months the U.S. Geological Survey, with the financial cooperation of the U.S. Soil Conservation Service, constructed five additional stream gaging stations; these have since been maintained by the U.S. Geological Survey and the Indiana Department of Natural Resources.

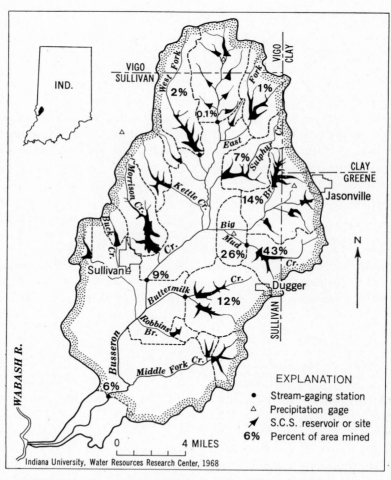

FIGURE 3   Map of Busseron Creek watershed showing percentage of tributary watersheds surface mined for coal.

In the succeeding year, water samples were collected by the authors, in cooperation with federal, state, and mining company personnel, at the 6 gages and at an additional 29 sites where the streamflow was measured or estimated. Analyses were made of 68 water samples from these 35 sites by the Federal Water Pollution Control Administration and the Indiana State Board of Health during a 9-month period (November 23, 1965–August 1, 1966).

FLUSHOUTS

A flushout is a hydrologic event in which the precipitation falling on a watershed is sufficient in quantity and intensity to cause storm runoff; this can change drastically the quality of the water in the streams. Flushouts are most effective when caused by intense rains occurring during sustained periods of low flow and droughts.

During the 2-year reporting period, results of analyses of several hundred water samples collected by the Federal Water Pollution Control Administration in southwestern Indiana were studied and evaluated, and three flushout periods were discussed in detail (Corbett and Agnew, 1968). Significant data are given below:

April 26–27, 1966—13 water samples collected at 10 sites, before and during periods of lowland flooding; flow determinations made at time of sampling.

November 10–17, 1966—26 water samples collected at 11 regular sampling sites (including 6 recording stream gages) during the first significant rise in streamflow following a 50-day dry period that had recorded only local showers.

April 30–May 5, 1967—50 water samples collected at the same 11 regular sampling sites during a rise that had been immediately preceded by larger rises on April 30 and April 21.

Water analyses included determinations for temperature, pH, conductivity, acidity, alkalinity, total hardness, sulfate, Ca, Mg, total Fe, Mn, and chloride (Corbett and Agnew, 1968).

Using pH, acidity, alkalinity, and sulfate as an index of the acid mine-drainage problem, we determined that all acid mine water in the watershed was coming from the Big Branch-Mud Creek, Sulphur Creek, and Buttermilk Creek tributary watersheds (Table 1).

Mainstream Stations No. 9, 4, and 1 (Fig. 2) show successively down-stream the general improvement that is expected when water from unmined areas and non-acidic mined areas dilutes the poor quality waters. Station 9 integrates two of the aforementioned mined streams (excluding Butter-milk Creek) and the three unmined tributaries; Station 4, which is 3 miles farther downstream, receives waters from Buttermilk Creek and from two more unmined tributaries; and Station 1, which is 4 miles farther downstream, gathers the waters from another unmined tributary and gives the integrated effect of the drainage from 228 sq miles of the total of 237 sq miles in the watershed.

TABLE 1

Water-quality data from surface-mined and non-mined watersheds

Watershed or Station	Area Surface Mined %	pH	Acidity mg/l	Alkalinity mg/l	Sulfate mg/l
Surface-mined (median values of three flushouts)					
Big Branch-Mud Creek	26.2	5.4	158	10	1400
Sulphur Creek	6.0	4.1	182	0	650
Buttermilk Creek	11.6	6.4	42	36	1395
Non-mined (median values of three flushouts)					
Upper Busseron	0.1	7.3	0	108	42
East Fork	0.9	7.1	0	135	130
West Fork	2.0	7.0	6	158	250
Combinations (flushout of June 24, 1968)					
Station 9	9.0	6.7	43	42	560
Station 4	7.7	6.9	27	52	500
Station 1	6.0	6.8	19	67	520

The best documented illustration of the flushout effect in the Busseron watershed is the flushout of June 24, 1968, when a torrential rainstorm swept across Mud Creek tributary watershed and dropped 1.04 inches of rain in 15 minutes at the Minnehaha rain gage near the lower end of the Mud Creek watershed (Fig. 3).

The junior author and an Indiana University microbiologist were nearby and arrived at the U.S. Geological Survey stream gage on Mud Creek near its mouth at 1420 hours, Central Standard Time. Ten water samples were collected in the next 90 minutes, during a preliminary crest and the main crest which followed at 1520 hours (Fig. 4). The final water sample was collected at 1710 hours when the flood recession was beginning to taper off.

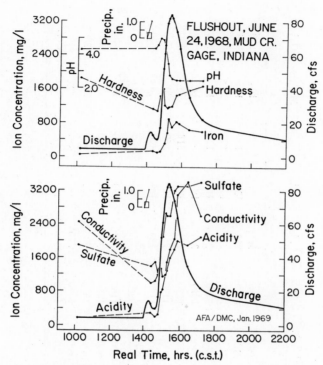

FIGURE 4   Effects of flushout of June 24, 1968 on water quantity and quality at Mud Creek stream gage, Busseron Creek watershed.

Significant trends in acidity, sulfate, and conductivity are shown in Table 2 and Fig. 4; these parameters increased in concentration during the rising discharge (although conductivity dropped just before the crest) and then continued to increase as the discharge was decreasing. (The final drop in conductivity is unexplained and may be due to a sampling or analytical error.)

Hardness and total Fe increased during the rise in discharge, but experienced a drop during the peak discharge. Hardness then continued to increase during the discharge recession, whereas Fe increased briefly and then gradually decreased during this period of recession.

We expected the pH to decrease abruptly as the peak discharge was attained, and to continue at a low level throughout the period of decreasing

TABLE 2

Chemical quality of water samples obtained during flushout of June 24, 1968, at Mud Creek stream gage, Busseron Creek watershed

Real time C.S.T.	Conductivity[a]	pH	Alka-linity[b]	Hot Acidity[b]	Total Hardness[c]	Ca[d]	Mg[d]	Total Fe[d]	Mn[d]	SO$_4$[e]	Discharge (cfs)
1010	2450	4.3	0	180	1840	362	228	45	19	1900	4.6
1420	1000	4.4	0	310	1130	233	134	137	13	1400	13.0
1435	1050	4.6	1	210	1080	227	125	104	14	1300	10.0
1445	1200	5.0	3	270	1330	263	164	126	15	1200	17.0
1455	1350	4.9	10	790	1610	321	197	—	18	1900	52.0
1500	1150	4.6	2	850	1220	251	144	318	25	2100	61.0
1510	1200	3.5	0	1200	1140	257	120	560	20	2660	79.0
1515	1500	2.8	0	1300	1170	289	109	890	16	2600	82.0
1520	Peak Discharge—No water sample collected										84.0
1525	1800	2.6	0	1600	1180	321	93	700	15	2600	82.0
1540	2050	2.5	0	1800	1450	364	131	830	21	3200	74.0
1550	3100	2.5	0	2000	1470	375	131	780	26	3300	64.0
1625	3400	2.5	0	1900	1570	396	142	647	26	3300	35.0
1710	2600	2.5	0	2100	1670	396	153	592	21	3400	22.0

[a] Micromhos per cm at 25 C.
[b] Potentiometric titration, mg/l
[c] Calculated only from Ca and Mg, mg/l.
[d] Atomic absorption spectrophotometer, mg/l.
[e] Turbidimetric by precipitation as BaSO$_4$, mg/l.

discharge. The latter occurred, but the decrease in pH occurred earlier than expected.

Obviously, if only one water sample had been taken during this flush-out, projection of its analytical results for a much longer period such as a month or a year would have given data that would likely be highly un-representative of the stream's true character. Although the concentrations of ions in this acidic stream exceeded acceptable water-quality standards before the flushout, the flushout aggravated the problem by causing increases of 1150% in acidity, 1300% in total Fe, and 180% in sulfate.

CONCLUSIONS

The foregoing discussion represents an attempt to enunciate further the thesis that a physical hydrologic event, known as a flushout, has a major effect on the chemical quality of the water in a watershed. Where surface mining for coal is carried out in Indiana in conformance with present state laws and regulations, acid mine-drainage can be held to a minimum except for the short-term and drastic effect of a flushout.

The acid waters in Indiana are due mainly to drainages from old waste piles, compacted areas, and underground mines; these accumulate on slopes and in valleys and then are moved downstream as a slug. Accordingly, field demonstration projects should be undertaken to test the effect of regulated releases of impounded poor quality water in some lakes and good quality water in most lakes and reservoirs on the chemical quality of the stream during all parts of the water year.

This, of course, requires the monitoring of water quality during normal high flow, normal low flow, and the "abnormal" events known as flush-outs. The examples described herein have documented the wide range in concentration of ions under these conditions of greatly different stream discharge, and reinforce our conclusion that calculated loads of acid or other chemical-quality parameters are likely to be highly unrepresentative if based on only a limited number of samples.

LITERATURE CITED

Biesecker, J. E., and J. R. George. 1966. Stream quality in Appalachia as related to coal-mine drainage, 1965. U. S. Dep. Interior, Geol. Surv., Circ. 526, 27 p.

Corbett, Don M. 1965. Runoff contributions to streams from cast overburden of surface-mining operations for coal, Pike County, Indiana. Indiana Univ. Water Resources Res. Center, Rept. Inv. 1, 67 p.

Corbett, Don M. 1968. Ground-water hydrology pertaining to surface mining for coal—southwestern Indiana, p. 164–189. In: *Second Symposium on Coal Mine Drainage*, Pittsburgh, Pa., May 14–15, 1968. Monroeville, Pa., Bituminous Coal Research, Inc.

Corbett, Don M. 1969. Acid mine drainage problem of the Patoka River Watershed, Indiana. Indiana Univ. Water Resources Res. Center, Rept. Inv. 4, 173 p.

Corbett, Don M., and A. F. Agnew. 1968. Hydrology of Busseron Creek Watershed, Indiana. Indiana Univ. Water Resources Res. Center, Rept. Inv. 2, 186 p.

Hill, Ronald D. 1968. Mine drainage treatment; state of the art and research needs. U. S. Dep. Interior, Fed. Water Polln. Control Adm. Rept., 99 p.

Kinney, Edward C. 1964. Extent of acid mine pollution in the United States affecting fish and wildlife. U. S. Dep. Interior, Fish and Wildlife Service Circ. 191, 27 p.

Lorenz, Walter C. 1962. Progress in controlling acid mine water, a literature review. U. S. Dep. Interior, Bur. Mines Circ. 8080, 40 p.

Ohio River Valley Water Sanitation Commission, Coal Industry Advisory Committee. 1965. *Symposium on Acid Mine Drainage Research*, Mellon Institute, May 20–21, 1965, Pittsburgh, Pennsylvania. Monroeville, Pa., Bituminous Coal Research, Inc., 23 papers and 232 p.

Ohio River Valley Water Sanitation Commission, Coal Industry Advisory Committee. 1968. *Second Symposium on Coal Mine Drainage Resarch*, Mellon Institute, May 14–15, 1968, Pittsburgh, Pennsylvania. Monroeville, Pa., Bituminous Coal Research, Inc., 27 papers and 406 p.

U. S. Department of Agriculture. 1968. Restoring surface-mined land. U. S. Dep. Agric., Misc. Publ. 1082, 18 p.

U. S. Department of the Interior. 1967. Surface mining and our environment. U. S. Dep. Interior Spec. Rep., 124 p.

DISCUSSION

CORNWELL: Did you say that disturbed land spoil banks contribute more to the ground water supplies? These surfaces become heavily crusted and I am surprised that infiltration is increased.

AGNEW: I believe your assumption that the surface of this material gets crusted over is not completely valid. Remember, we are working with slopes, with different positions on the slopes, and with the constant changing of this slope as it ages. I am speaking, by the way, of undisturbed and uncompacted surfaces of cast-overburden material resulting from surface mining. Now if we run equipment on it to level it off, then we do get compaction, and I would agree with you. So as a hydrologist, I would like to leave it more alone than the regulations of some of our states will permit. But we feel that infiltration, both on the slopes and down in the valleys, will continue even though it may be slowed down considerably because of the transport and deposition of sediment. Although preliminary studies suggest this, unfortunately we don't have enough information yet—we need to acquire this kind of physical information in the field.

CORNWELL: We have no information on the opencast sites. In the deep-mine colliery tips, the so-called water table appears to consist of a surface skin only. The great bulk of the tip appears to be dry.

AGNEW: I think that the waste piles from the deep mines contain a considerable amount of clay and shale which, together with combustion of the material, causes the piles to be coated over, so I agree with you there. However, in the surface-mining process we handle these different materials selectively and isolate them, so as a result we don't have this kind of problem of sealing of the surface, unless equipment moves on it.

SURFACE MINING DISTURBANCE AND WATER QUALITY IN EASTERN KENTUCKY

W. David Striffler

Associate Professor of Watershed Management
Colorado State University, Fort Collins, Colorado *

Surface mining for coal in the eastern Kentucky coal fields has disturbed thousands of acres of mountain land. Land mined in this manner is frequently considered to be a major source of acid pollution. Observations, however, indicated that this is not true in many instances and that acid pollution varies considerably from place to place and depends more on factors other than acreages disturbed.

A survey of water quality was conducted in eastern Kentucky during the summer of 1966. A total of 180 sampling points, including all fourth-order and larger watersheds, were measured. Field measurements included stream discharge, water temperature, dissolved oxygen, pH, oxidation-reduction potential and specific conductance. Laboratory determinations included Al, Ca, Mg, total Fe, Mn, and sulfates.

Results indicated that, under the conditions of the survey, very little acid pollution occurs in the major rivers and streams, although localized pollution may be very severe. Small, severely disturbed first-order watersheds were the primary sources of acid pollution. However, their effect was rapidly diminished as dilution by other branches in the drainage net occurred. Acid pollution also varied according to the nature of the geologic material exposed on a particular coal seam and the presence of other neutralizing materials in the watershed. In summary, although acid pollution is a very serious problem on small, severely disturbed watersheds, it is not important on the larger watersheds or major rivers during low-flow conditions in eastern Kentucky.

INTRODUCTION

Strip mining for coal in eastern Kentucky is a relatively recent development. Since its beginnings in the early 1950's until the present time, it has

---

* The study reported in this paper was made while the author was a Hydrologist for the Northeastern Forest Experiment Station, Forest Service, U. S. Department of Agriculture at Berea, Ky.

grown into an important industry and a major method of mining coal. As the industry has grown, so has the technology of mining coal and the problems associated with surface mining. Early surface mining operations utilized comparatively light equipment and created light disturbances on the steep mountain slopes of eastern Kentucky. However, the size of equipment and consequently the degree of disturbance increased greatly up to 1966 when state regulations limiting the disturbed area went into effect. As of October 1964, approximately 17,800 ha had been disturbed by surface mining in eastern Kentucky (Plass, 1967a, b, c, d, e). Since then an estimated 1600 ha have been mined annually (Boccardy and Spaulding, 1968).

The rapid expansion of surface mining has created many problems. Prior to the enactment of the 1966 Kentucky Strip-Mine Law, surface mining was completely uncontrolled and the extent and nature of disturbance was limited only by the size of the individual operator's equipment. Although reclamation of mined areas was required, the severity of the disturbance frequently precluded effective restoration by vegetative means. As a result, uncontrolled erosion of the mined area caused thousands of tons of sediment and debris to move into the rivers and streams of eastern Kentucky.

Associated with sediment pollution is the pollution of streams by acid drainage. Although most commonly associated with drainage from underground mines, acid pollution may also result from surface mining. Freshly exposed geologic material containing pyrites or other sulfur-bearing compounds rapidly weather to release sulfuric acid and toxic quantities of other elements.

Two mechanisms for pollution from surface mines have been observed. One is the seepage of water into and through the spoil and eventually into a stream. In this instance, the percolate becomes enriched as it passes through the spoil. The other mechanism is the dissolving of salts on the spoil surface by rainfall and surface runoff and the transportation of the salts to the stream by a surface route. In this instance, salts are concentrated at the spoil surface by evaporation and readily dissolved during a storm.

Because of the rapidly increasing area disturbed by surface mining in eastern Kentucky, it was anticipated that uncontrolled drainage from surface mines might have a severe effect on the water resources of eastern Kentucky. It was further anticipated that the extent of acid pollution in the region or in any individual watershed would be determined to some extent by the area or proportion of the watershed disturbed by mining.

A survey of water quality in eastern Kentucky was conducted during the summer of 1966 for the express purpose of determining the extent of mine-water pollution in the region's waterways, and if possible, to determine some of the watershed characteristics which exert an influence on the degree of acid pollution in the region.

THE EASTERN KENTUCKY COAL FIELDS

The eastern Kentucky coal fields occupy the eastern one-third of the state, an area of about 27,000 km² (Fig. 1). The area, representing the central portion of the Appalachian coal region, has been an important source of coal for many years. Since 1923, approximately 10% of the Appalachian

FIGURE 1   Generalized geologic map of the Eastern Coal Field Region, Kentucky. (Based on state geologic map by W. R. Wilson.)

coal production has come from eastern Kentucky (U.S. Bureau of Mines, 1964). In 1963, about one-third of the region's production came from surface mines.

Geologically, the major portion of the area is part of the Appalachian Plateau which extends from New York to Alabama (Fenneman, 1946). In eastern Kentucky, the Appalachian Plateau has been subdivided into three regions: the Kanawha Plateau in the central and northeastern portions; the Cumberland Plateau along the western margin, and the Cumberland Mountains in the southeastern portion. The Kanawha Plateau region is characterized by a deeply dissected topography with narrow, steep-

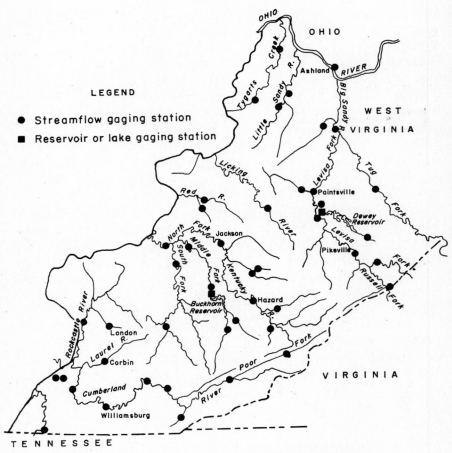

FIGURE 2   Major river systems in eastern Kentucky.

sided valleys and narrow, irregular ridges. Valley bottoms are generally numerous with occasional narrow floodplains.

The Cumberland Plateau region to the west is typically a broad upland with moderate relief. It is primarily a hilly, rolling upland as compared to the rugged mountain topography of the Kanawha Plateau.

The Cumberland Mountain section is characterized by two parallel ridges, Pine Mountain and Cumberland Mountain, ranging in elevation from 2000 to 4000 ft. Structurally, these mountains are part of the Cumberland Mountain over-thrust block.

About 90% of the eastern Kentucky coal fields is underlain by shale, sandstone, and coal of Pennsylvanian Age (Fig. 1). However, Mississippian formations of limestone and shales are found along the western margin of the area and Devonian and Mississippian Age shales and limestones occur along the Pine Mountain fault line.

The eastern Kentucky coal field region is drained by four major river systems (Fig. 2). In the south, the Cumberland River drains the area between Pine and Cumberland Mountains, with the river passing through a gap in the mountains at Pineville and continuing west to the Ohio River. Major tributaries include the Rockcastle and Laurel Rivers which enter from the north near the southwestern corner of the region.

The large Kentucky River system drains the southcentral portion of the region with three main branches originating in the heart of the coal country. A fourth tributary, the Red River, flows westward and enters the Kentucky just outside the coal region.

The east side of the coal region is drained by the Big Sandy River and its major tributaries including Tug Fork and Levisa Fork. The Big Sandy and Tug Fork are the state boundary with West Virginia; Levisa Fork drains from within the state.

The Licking River flows to the northwest from the center of the coal region. However, it has few tributaries and represents only a small portion of the coal region.

Two other smaller rivers drain the northern portion of the region. These are Tygarts Creek and the Little Sandy River. Both flow generally northward and enter the Ohio River, the northern boundary of the coal region.

SURVEY METHODS

During the summer of 1966, water quality for the entire eastern Kentucky coal field region was studied. In order to adequately cover the region and obtain a representative sampling of all major drainages, sample water-

12*

sheds were selected on the basis of their drainage networks. All fourth-order watersheds were selected for sampling. In addition, most basins representing combinations of fourth-order watersheds (i.e., fifth order or larger) were also sampled as well as a small number of second- and third-order watersheds with known areas of mining disturbance. Where possible, sampling points were selected to coincide with U.S. Geological Survey gaging stations. In all, a total of 188 stations were measured.

Sampling stations were marked on U.S. Geological Survey 7.5-min quadrangle maps, and each site was visited by a field crew which conducted a set series of field measurements and collected a water sample for laboratory analysis. Field measurements included stream discharge, pH, oxidation-reduction potential (Eh), dissolved oxygen (DO), specific conductance, and stream temperature. Stream discharge was determined by standard current meter procedures. Eh and pH were determined with a battery-powered electric pH meter; dissolved oxygen, with a YSI semipermeable membrane probe and meter*; and specific conductance, with a conductance meter and platinum cell.

Water samples in the laboratory were analyzed for Al, Ca, Mg, total Fe, Mn and sulfate. In addition pH and Eh measurements were repeated in the laboratory although not reported in this paper. Calcium, Mg, Fe and Mn were determined using an atomic absorption spectrophotometer. Aluminum was measured using a colorimetric procedure, and sulfate, using a turbidity procedure.

Watershed areas were determined from topographic maps. However, where sampling stations coincided with U.S. Geological Survey gaging stations, both watershed areas and stream discharge for the date of sampling were taken from published reports (U.S. Geological Survey, 1967). Areas of disturbance by mining were abstracted from data by Plass (1966, 1967a, b, c, d, e) and Striffler (1965).

WATER QUALITY

Numerous investigations have been made of water quality in relation to coal mine drainage. Kinney (1964) studied the extent of acid-mine pollution with respect to fish and wildlife resources. He estimated a total of 580 miles of streams seriously polluted by acid mine drainage in Kentucky. Collier et al. (1964) studied the the effects of strip mining on water quality on

---

* Yellow Springs Industries Model 51 Oxygen Meter.

several small watersheds in eastern Kentucky. Biesecker and George (1966) reported on a 1965 survey of water quality in Appalachia as related to coal-mine drainage. Among the several problems which they suggested for future regional surveys were: (1) the significance of mine drainage upon stream quality during low-flow conditions; (2) types of hydrologic environments that produce sudden flushes of mine water to streams which normally contain relatively little mine water; and (3) the geologic and hydrologic factors contributing to high alkalinity of affected streams within isolated parts of the region.

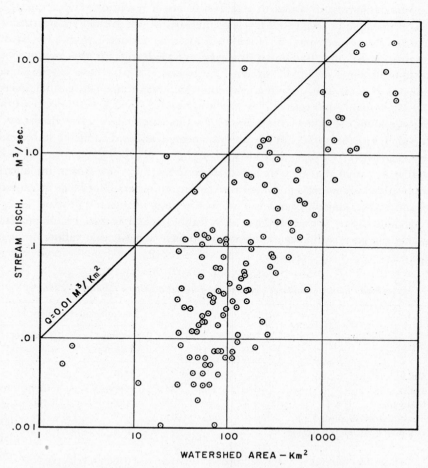

FIGURE 3   Stream discharge vs. watershed area in eastern Kentucky, summer, 1966.

This survey was conducted during a period of unusually low stream flow. Average stream discharge during the study period was less than 0.1 m³/km²/sec (Fig. 3). Although a few streams were sampled after storms, most sampling was done during very low-flow conditions and represents groundwater recession flows. For purposes of the survey this condition seemed ideal, since acid mine drainage entering a stream would be less likely to be neutralized by dilution and hence its effect should persist for a greater distance downstream. Consequently, this survey should provide data on maximum pollution levels for the streams of the region.

In reporting water-quality conditions for a region, it is necessary to have standards from which to establish levels of pollution. Unfortunately, it is impossible to set precise levels of the various water-quality parameters, which if exceeded may be attributed to mine drainage. Similarly, it is impossible to state that mine drainage is responsible for the presence of certain elements in all the streams. Fortunately, we do have a few guide lines as to indicators of mine pollution and maximum permissible levels of water-quality parameters for public water supplies. U.S. Public Health Service (1962) standards for some of the elements measured in this study, together with the number of our samples meeting and exceeding the standards are reported in Table 1.

It is apparent that the streams of eastern Kentucky are within the maximum permissible levels in some respects but not others. Sulfate as measured in this study, ranged from 3.5 to about 650 ppm. Of the 179 primary sampling points, only 9 exceeded the U.S. Public Health Service recommended maximum permissible levels of 250 ppm which suggests that sulfate derived

TABLE 1

Water quality standards and measured levels in eastern Kentucky, 1966

Parameter	Standard	Number of Samples	
		Meeting Standards	Exceeding Standards
Sulfate (SO_4)	250	170	9
Total iron	0.03	59	120
Manganese	0.05	79	100
Total dissolved solids[a]	500	164	15
Dissolved oxygen (minimum)[b]	5.0	157	22

[a] Total dissolved solids may be roughly approximated from specific conductance (TDS = 0.655 C).

[b] This level suggested by California Water Quality Control Board, 1963.

from mine drainage is not a great problem. However, Biesecker and George (1966), in a survey of water quality for the entire Appalachian region, reported maximum levels of sulfate of 20 ppm for streams draining watersheds unaffected by mine drainage. They suggested that sulfate is a key indicator of mine drainage; if concentrations exceed 20 ppm, the stream can be considered to have a mine-drainage influence. If this is an accurate indication level, then approximately half of the streams sampled in this study are influenced by mine drainage. Of the 179 main sampling points, 81 had sulfate concentrations greater than 20 ppm and 98 had less. Even though mine drainage influences the streams, it is not a serious influence, at least with respect to sulfate concentration.

Probably the most severe consequence of mine drainage pollution is the injection of free mineral acid into the stream system. Although free acidity was not measured in this study, pH as an indicator of acidity was measured. The pH measurements ranged from 3.3 to 8.6. Of the 179 primary sampling points, only 18 had pH values on the acid side of the pH range (less than 7.0). The distribution of samples by pH ranges was:

pH Range	No. of Samples
3.0–3.9	1
4.0–4.9	5
5.0–5.9	1
6.0–6.9	11
7.0–7.9	148
8.0–8.9	13

The majority of streams in eastern Kentucky are slightly alkaline in reaction. Those few streams with acid reactions, particularly those with pH values less than 6.0, may be traced directly to a mine influence. Unfortunately, pH is not a good indicator for mine-drainage pollution, although it does indicate when pollution levels become severe enough to seriously damage the stream ecosystem. One of the problems with pH measurement as an indicator of mine drainage is that mine-drainage water may be highly alkaline due to minerals associated with particular geologic formations. Differences may occur in relatively short distances. Big Run, for example, carries discharge from underground mines of the Hazard No. 7 Coal Seam and has a pH of about 8.1 while the adjacent watershed, carrying drainage from strip mines and underground mines on the Hazard No. 9 Seam, has a pH of 2.8. These two coal seams are separated vertically by about 100 feet of strata.

TABLE 2

Median water quality observations by basins, 1966

Basin	No. of Samples	Specific Conductance μmhos	pH	Dissolved Oxygen ppm	Al ppm	Ca ppm	Mg ppm	Total		
								Fe ppm	Mn ppm	SO$_4$ ppm
Cumberland R.	44	281	7.5	6.2	0.07	24.0	9.6	0.9	0.06	67.0
Kentucky R.	62	240	7.4	7.0	0.05	43.0	8.2	0.9	0.2	26.0
Licking R.	11	190	7.4	6.5	0.04	24.8	5.6	0.9	0.1	22.5
Tygarts Cr.	11	210	7.4	7.0	0.04	27.9	4.6	0.3	0	14.0
Little Sandy Cr.	17	240	7.4	6.5	0.04	26.1	5.8	0.3	0	16.0
Big Sandy R.	35	245	7.5	7.0	0.05	19.2	5.0	0.9	0	19,0

Manganese appears to be a sensitive indicator of acid pollution. Manganese levels ranged from 15 ppm down to no observable quantities. Of the 179 primary sampling points, 100 had Mn levels exceeding the maximum permissible. However, many of these (28 samples) were reported at 0.1 ppm which is very close to the permissible level. Only 12 samples exceeded 1 ppm of Mn. Manganese thus appears to be a problem element with respect to water supply in eastern Kentucky streams during low-flow conditions.

Iron and Al are both related to the pH or acidity level of the stream. Streams with low pH values may release considerable quantities of these two elements. This is also true of the other cations (Ca, Mg and Mn). In this study, total Fe ranged from 0 to 14 ppm with 120 stations exceeding the recommended maximum permissible level of 0.3 ppm. Aluminum ranged from 0 to 45 ppm, Ca from 5 to 400 ppm, and Mg from 0.9 to 82 ppm.

Dissolved O_2 levels may be related to mine drainage since O_2 is used in the oxidation of pyritic materials (FeS_2). However, O_2 in a stream is subject to depletion by many other forces and represents a rather complex part of the pollution picture. Minimum levels of 5.0 ppm have been suggested (California Water Quality Control Board, 1963). In this study, dissolved O_2 levels ranged from 0.5 to 15.0 ppm with no apparent relationship to mine pollution. Of the primary sampling stations, 22 fell below the suggested minimum level of 5.0 ppm.

Observed water quality was comparatively uniform among the major river basins of eastern Kentucky. Median values for the various basins show remarkable agreement for some parameters (Table 2). Total Fe ranged from 0.3 to 0.9 for the major basins, pH from 7.4 to 7.5, and total

TABLE 3

Areal extent of mining disturbance in eastern Kentucky, October 1964 (after Plass)

Coal Reserve District	River Basin[a]	Disturbed Area % of Total
Upper Cumberland	Cumberland above Pineville	2.6
Southwestern	Lower Cumberland	0.7
Hazard	Kentucky River	1.0
Licking River	Licking River	0.1
Princess	Tygarts and Little Sandy	0.6
Big Sandy	Big Sandy River	0.8

[a] River basins do not coincide exactly with coal reserve district.

dissolved solids from 190 to 281. Sulfate concentrations were greatest for the Cumberland and Kentucky basins, with median values of 67 and 26 ppm respectively. Both basins are known to have extensive areas of strip mining and underground mining activity (Table 3). Basins with relatively high values for specific conductance, Al, Ca, Mg, and Mn do have a mine drainage influence although the influence is generally rather mild.

INFLUENCE OF STRIP MINING

One of the objectives of this study was to relate water quality to strip-mining disturbances. In studying the data, it is apparent that strip mining does have an influence on water quality but that the relationship is rather inconsistent and the specific conditions of each mined area are more important than the areal extent of the disturbances. Considerations which have a direct influence on the water quality include geologic material (chemical oxidation products), physical spoil properties (determine internal drainage), degree of drainage control on the surface, and the extent of natural or planted revegetation.

It is possible to relate water quality to strip-mining disturbance in a general way. Plass, in his survey of strip mining in eastern Kentucky, reported results by coal reserve districts, which generally correspond to the major drainage basins of the region (Fig. 4). Areas of strip mining, presented as percentages of each region, are given in Table 3.

As mentioned, the Cumberland River with a greater proportion of its watershed area mined, has the highest median sulfate, Mg, Al, and specific conductance. The Kentucky River with the next greatest proportion of areal disturbance over the watershed has the highest median values of Ca and Mn and high values of Mg and sulfate. On the other hand the Licking River, with the least mining disturbance, has relatively low values of the various parameters. It is not possible to attribute these differences to strip-mining disturbance alone since the frequency of underground mines is without doubt correlated with the extent of strip mining. In addition, geologic variations between basins may also account for some of the differences.

Water quality is more closely correlated with strip-mine disturbance within watersheds of fourth-order or smaller streams. In this instance, differences due to geology are minimized since geology within is more uniform. In addition, differences due to variations in the nature of the

TABLE 4

Water quality of severely disturbed small watersheds

Station	Drainage Area km²	Disturbed Area % of total	Temp. C	Eh mv	Specific Conductance μmhos	Dissolved oxygen ppm	pH	Al ppm	Ca ppm	Mg ppm	Total Fe ppm	Mn ppm	SO₄ ppm
STFK	12.6	6.2	28	140	130	8.0	7.0	0.25	15	4	0.3	0.1	19
BHWD	2.2		25	250	320	6.5	4.2	1.15	19	9	0.3	4.3	112
BRUN	2.4		30	330	650	6.5	3.4	10.10	43	21	1.5	5.3	335
PTBR	1.1	33.8	22	150	410	7.0	6.3	0.00	38	23	0.0	1.1	200
LTFK	29.3		30		1400	7.5	5.0	1.00	334	119	2.4	15.8	675
CLFK	1.8	33.0	27		1300	7.0	7.3	0.04	334	107	5.2	0.6	690
BGFK	1.1		29		840	7.5	8.2	0.14	198	48	1.5	0.1	372
YOFK	2.7	18.3	30		3000	8.0	2.7	74.40	281	224	88.8	74.4	2100
KEFK	1.8		29		1100	7.5	3.5	22.60	367	76	3.9	56.0	1225

disturbance may also be minimized since frequently a single operator may be operating in the basin and applying a more or less uniform mining and reclamation technology. Examples are given in Table 4 of severely disturbed watersheds and the resultant effect on water quality. It is obvious that severe pollution can result from mining disturbance. Fortunately, severely polluted streams are limited to comparatively small watersheds and the effect is rapidly diminished downstream. The pollution load is diluted increasingly as water from undisturbed tributaries merges with the main stream. Nevertheless, significant deterioration of the water supply may result from even moderate levels of pollution.

FIGURE 4   Coal reserve districts of eastern Kentucky.

CONCLUSIONS

The quality of water carried in the streams and rivers of eastern Kentucky during the summer low-flow period in 1966 was influenced by mine drainage. Although the water quality parameters of many streams do not exceed maximum permissible levels, the measured values begin to approach these levels and the situation could become more serious without corrective measures. During the sampling period, over half the streams measured exceeded maximum permissible levels of Fe and Mn indicating that a serious deterioration already occurs during low-flow conditions. In addition, sulfate concentrations exceeded normal levels but only rarely exceeded the maximum permissible levels. Sulfate appears to be a rather sensitive indicator of mine drainage if normal levels can be determined.

Analysis of pollution loads below severely affected reaches of streams indicates rapid dilution and a corresponding decrease in pollution loads. However, a general deterioration of the water, which may persist for considerable distances downstream, occurs.

The degree of pollution is related to some extent to the amount of mining activity occurring within the basin. This is particularly true within small basins where more uniform geologic and mined-area conditions exist. However, the pollution load of any small watershed appears to be more directly related to drainage conditions within the mined area than to the area of mining disturbance. This suggests that proper control of drainage from mined areas may be the solution to controlling or limiting mine-drainage pollution from strip-mined areas.

LITERATURE CITED

Biesecker, J. E., and J. R. George. 1966. Stream quality in Appalachia as related to coal-mine drainages, 1965. U. S. Dep. Interior, Geol. Surv. Circ. 526. 22 p.

Boccardy, J. A., and W. M. Spaulding, Jr. 1968. Effects of surface mining on fish and wildlife in Appalachia. U. S. Dep. Interior, Bur. of Sport Fisheries and Wildlife. Resource Publ. 65. 20 p.

California Water Quality Control Board. 1963. *Water quality criteria*. California Water Control Board Publ. No. 3-A. 548 p.

Collier, C. P. et al. 1964. Influences of strip-mining on the hydrologic environment of parts of Beaver Creek Basin, Ky., 1955–1959. U. S. Dep. Interior, Geol. Surv. Prof. Paper 427-B. 85 p.

Fenneman, N. M. 1938. *Physiography of eastern United States*. McGraw-Hill, New York. 714 p.

Kinney, E. C. 1964. Extent of acid mine pollution in the United States affecting fish and wildlife. U. S. Dep. Interior, Bur. of Sport Fisheries and Wildlife Circ. 191. 27 p.

Plass, W. T. 1966. Land disturbance from strip-mining in Eastern Kentucky. 1. Upper Cumberland Coal Reserve District. U. S. Dep. Agr., Forest Service, Northeastern Forest Exp. Sta. Res. Note NE-52. 7 p.

Plass, W. T. 1967a. Land disturbance from strip-mining in Eastern Kentucky. 2. Princess Coal Reserve District. U. S. Dep. Agr., Forest Service, Northeastern Forest Exp. Sta. Res. Note NE-55. 8 p.

Plass, W. T. 1967b. Land disturbance from strip-mining in Eastern Kentucky. 3. Licking River Coal Reserve District. U. S. Dep. Agr., Forest Service, Northeastern Forest Exp. Sta. Res. Note NE-68. 6 p.

Plass, W. T. 1967c. Land disturbance from strip-mining in Eastern Kentucky. 4. Big Sandy Coal Reserve District. U. S. Dep. Agr., Forest Service, Northeastern Forest Exp. Sta. Res. Note NE-69. 7 p.

Plass, W. T. 1967d. Land disturbance from strip-mining in Eastern Kentucky. 5. Hazard Coal Reserve District. U. S. Dep. Agr., Forest Service, Northeastern Forest Exp. Sta. Res. Note NE-71. 7 p.

Plass, W. T. 1967e. Land disturbance from strip-mining in Eastern Kentucky. 6. Southwestern Coal Reserve District. U. S. Dep. Agr., Forest Service, Northeastern Forest Exp. Sta. Res. Note NE-72. 8 p.

Price, W. E., D. S. Mull, and Chabot Kilburn. 1962. Reconnaissance of ground-water resources in the Eastern Kentucky Coal Field Region, Ky. U. S. Dep. Interior, Geol. Surv. Water Supply Paper 1607. 56 p.

Striffler, W. D. 1965. The selection of experimental watersheds and methods in disturbed forest areas. *IASH Symp. of Budapest* Publ. No. 66. p. 464–473.

U. S. Bureau of Mines. 1964. 1963 *Minerals Yearbook*. Vol. 2. Fuels. U. S. Dep. Interior, Bur. of Mines. 533 p.

U. S. Geological Survey. 1967. Water resource data for Kentucky. Part 1. Surface water records. 1966. U. S. Dep. Interior, Geol. Surv. 160 p.

DISCUSSION

GOODMAN: It is possible to use the water quality criteria as an index of the toxicity of the spoil bank?

STRIFFLER: The primary problem is that we are not able to differentiate between deep-mine drainage and pollution from surface sources. If it were certain that no underground mining was present I think this would be worth testing.

CARUCCIO: In establishing the effect of mine drainage, might it not have been a good idea to measure water-quality parameters in the areas unaffected by mining to obtain background concentrations rather than public health requirements? For example, in my work the sulfate concentration in an undisturbed area is about 85 mg/liter and in no way reflects the result of mining.

STRIFFLER: Yes, this is what Biesecker and George (1966) did in their survey. They worked watersheds in which they knew they had no disturbance. However, their surveys were conducted during the winter— during high-flow conditions and they anticipated greater concentrations during low-flow conditions. This is essentially what we found.

HILL: I disagree with your sampling periods. First, you mentioned that the drainage from strip mines occurs during wet periods, then you turn around and sample in dry periods. I think you were perhaps sampling the underground-mine discharges and missed completely the surface-mine contributors. At Elkins, W. Va., where we have been sampling in a concentrated effort for over 4 years, such a pattern is definitely the case. Also, deep mines tend to flush out in the early spring when the first high flows come, and you may entirely miss the maximum concentration or load factor of pollution. The dilution may be greater, but the actual total pollution load is greater during early spring. Another point on the sulfate, a survey by our group indicated that the 20 mg/liter value for unpolluted areas is probably a conservative number. A recent report by the FWQA states that the sulfate concentration of unpolluted streams is less than 20 mg/liter. Thus anything above that level indicates mine pollution. A third point, on your TDS, we found that the ratio of conductivity to TDS was close to 1 : 1.

STRIFFLER: We considered all these points which you have raised. Your first point is that we do get flushes of acid from strip-mined areas during storms. We too have measured this. However, we have not observed a flushing of underground-mined areas during the spring. Our water held fairly constant in the few auger holes and sources which we have observed. I suspect this could be a geologic difference or difference in infiltration above the mined area. I agree with your point that we may not have sampled maximum concentrations during the low-flow period. This has occurred to us.

CORNWELL: Mr. Gordon Glover of the National Coal Board is coming to the opinion that soluble Mn in mine drainages is the best indicator of acid conditions.

STRIFFLER: I would say that after sulfate, Mn would probably be the next best indicator we have.

CORNWELL: Does pH differ in the solution on the surface of the tip and in the toe drainage? I ask this because the Pennsylvania tips contain large concentrations of secondary sulfates deposited within the spoil profile, indicating much sulfate neutralization.

STRIFFLER: Actually we have observed both. In a situation where water was actually ponded on the strip above the spoil bank, its pH was essentially the same as that of the drainage at the toe of the spoil. At the other extreme, we have observed a decrease in pH of water going through the spoil.

CHARACTERIZATION OF STRIP-MINE DRAINAGE BY PYRITE GRAIN SIZE AND CHEMICAL QUALITY OF EXISTING GROUNDWATER*

Frank T. Caruccio

Associate Professor of Geology, Department of Geology, University of South Carolina, Columbia, S.C.

The acidity of mine drainage from strip mines in the bituminous coal field of Pennsylvania is largely determined by three interrelated factors. These are the oxidation rate of the pyrite found in the coal and the associated strata, the presence of a catalyst (iron bacteria), and the neutralizing capacity of the existing groundwater. The first factor is dependent upon the pyrite granularity and the last two factors are a function of the chemical composition of the mine strata. All these, in turn, are indicative of a particular sedimentary paleo-environment which can be used to delineate three stratigraphic horizons within the Allegheny Group of the Carboniferous. Significantly, mines located in each horizon produce a mine drainage with a characteristic chemical composition.

By evaluating the distribution of the grain size of the pyrite in the mine strata and analyzing the chemical composition of the existing groundwaters, it is possible to outline, and consequently predict, areas which will yield (1) highly acid-high sulfate mine drainages, (2) moderately acid-moderate sulfate mine drainages, (3) neutral mine drainages containing negligible amounts of sulfate (reflecting the stability of pyrite in these areas) and (4) neutral mine drainages containing moderate amounts of sulfate (indicative of acid mine drainages that were neutralized by high alkaline waters).

PREFACE

The first part of this paper was presented before the Second Symposium on Coal Mine Drainage Research held at the Mellon Institute, Pittsburgh,

---

* The writer expresses his appreciation to Dr. R. Parizek, Department of Geology and Geophysics, the Pennsylvania State University, who supervised the first part of this study and gave many valuable suggestions; and to the Coal Research Board of the Commonwealth of Pennsylvania who financed this study.

Pennsylvania on May 14, 1968. Consequently it appears in the proceedings of that symposium and may be obtained from the Bituminous Coal Research Inc., 350 Hochberg Road, Pittsburgh, Pa., 15146.

New findings have been made since that time and the logical presentation of these new results is contingent upon the background contained in the paper mentioned above. I realized that, because of the international nature of the present symposium, many of the participants may not have access to the above mentioned publication and therefore elected to incorporate a portion of the paper into the present article in order to provide the necessary background. This represents, in part, a duplication in publication and I solicit the indulgence of those participants who find the first part of this article redundant.

INTRODUCTION

Background of the acid mine drainage problem

Since the opening of the first coal mine in Pennsylvania in 1761, coal mining has become one of the main industries in the state. As the coal is mined, the iron disulfides, occurring either as marcasite or pyrite in the unmined coal and in the undisturbed strata associated with the coal, are exposed to the atmosphere and are readily decomposed. During this decomposition, compounds are formed by a complex series of chemical reactions and appear as yellow and white crusts along certain horizons on the surfaces of the rocks and coals. These compounds easily dissolve in water to produce acid and associated hydrous iron complexes.

Acid mine drainage commonly has a pH in the range of 2, contains an acidity ranging from 4 to 20 mg/liter (as H^+), has an abundance of Fe, usually 50–500 mg/liter as ferrous iron, and a high sulfate content, in the range of 500–10,000 mg/liter (as $SO_4^=$).

It has been generally acknowledged that the oxidation of pyrite in the presence of water and air to a soluble hydrated iron sulfate, and the subsequent dissolution and hydrolysis of the oxidized form in water, is responsible for the generation of acid and the concentration of iron and sulfate found in acid waters (Clark, 1965).

The hydrolysis of the hydrous iron sulfate is in accord with equation (1).

$$FeSO_4 \cdot XH_2O + 2HOH \rightleftharpoons Fe(OH)_2 + SO_4^- + 2H^+ + XH_2O \qquad (1)$$

The ferrous iron generated in the reaction described by equation (1) can be oxidized to the ferric state with the generation of additional acidity, as in equation (2).

$$Fe(OH)_2 + HOH \rightleftharpoons Fe(OH)_3 + H^+ \tag{2}$$

Stumm and Lee (1961) estimated that, "fifty percent of the acidity in acid mine drainage arises from the oxygenation of ferrous iron; the remainder arises from the oxygenation of sulfide or polysulfide." The ferrous and ferric hydroxides associated with equations (1) and (2) impart the red color that is characteristic of acid mine drainage. The precipitated iron hydroxide is the "yellowboy" often observed in streams.

From the previous discussion it follows that the amount of acidity produced is dependent in part upon the amount of iron disulfide available for decomposition. If the acidity produced does not exceed the natural alkalinity, assuming the presence of calcium carbonate, then the drainage will not be acid. The threshold value beyond which the drainage will be acid is fixed by the natural alkalinity found in an area, which is more or less determined by the solubility of calcium carbonate and hence can be viewed as a constant (in the sense of a maximum value). On the other hand, acidity is dependent upon the amount of pyrite and marcasite and, in a general way, areas of high S content should be the areas with a greater acid potential.

For the time being the word "sulfur" will be used to indicate the gross value of the S content of the sample, bearing in mind that the majority of this value is composed of pyrite, marcasite, or both. Unless a specific comparison is made, "pyrite" will be used in this report to mean iron disulfide, regardless of its form.

Geological control of the occurrence of acid mine drainage

The occurrence of sulfurous materials in the stratigraphic section of western Pennsylvania has been outlined in a general way by Williams (1960) and Williams and Keith (1963). Williams (1960) documented a transgression of paleo-environments, based on fossil evidence, in the Allegheny group of the Pennsylvanian age rocks (Fig. 1). In the basal portion of the Allegheny of western Pennsylvania, the rocks contain fossils indigenous to a marine-brackish water paleo-environment. In the upper portion of the group, the rocks show evidence of having been deposited in a continental-freshwater paleo-environment. In a vertical succession, the lower "marine" rocks, in general, grade upward into the upper "continental" rocks. Additional

13*

work by Ferm and Williams (1960) has shown that the basal "brackish" rocks also exhibit a lateral transgression, becoming more "marine" in the western portion of Pennsylvania.

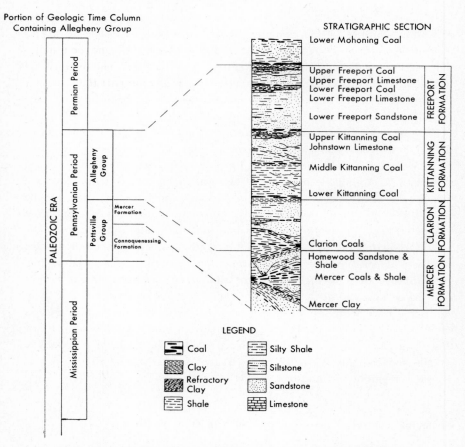

FIGURE 1   Stratigraphic nomenclature and generalized section of the Allegheny Group in western Pennsylvania (Williams, 1960).

The rocks deposited in a marine paleo-environment in the Pennsylvanian age commonly contain bitumens which are preserved only under reducing conditions, whereas the rocks of continental origin show evidence of being deposited in an oxidizing paleo-environment. Because the formation and deposition of iron disulfide is favored by reducing environments, the lithologies of the basal portion of the Allegheny group in the eastern portion of the bituminous coal field should be higher in S (as pyrite) than the rocks in the top portion of the group. Further, the S content in the basal section should increase as the paleo-environment becomes progressively more marine toward the western part of the bituminous area.

Mansfield and Spackman (1965) traced the variations in the petrography and composition of the Lower Kittanning, Lower Clarion and Upper Freeport seams across the bituminous coal field of Pennsylvania. They found the coals to become more sulfurous as the environment of deposition became more marine.

Williams and Keith (1963) statistically related the distribution of sulfur in coals to the occurrence of marine roof rocks. By comparing the Lower Kittanning coal to the Upper Freeport coal, they showed that the coals capped by marine roof rocks had a greater S content than the coals capped by continental roof rocks.

On the premise that the amount of acidity varies directly with the pyrite content, the drainages of mines extracting coals associated with strata of a marine paleo-environment (the lower portion of the Allegheny group) should be more acidic than those of mines associated with strata of a non-marine paleo-environment (the upper portion of the Group).

A water sample containing mine drainage is considered "acid" in this study if the potential free acidity exceeds the alkalinity. The potential free acidity (as mg of H^+ per liter) is determined by boiling the sample for 2 min (thereby driving off the carbon-dioxide acidity and completing the oxidation of the Fe), cooling to room temperature, and titrating the sample with a 0.0248 N sodium hydroxide solution to pH 7.0; the alkalinity (as mg of HCO_3^- per liter) is determined by titrating the raw sample with a 0.01639 N sulfuric acid solution to pH 4.5 (Rainwater and Thatcher, 1960).

Acid mine drainage pollution is defined in this study as any water sample whose potential free acidity exceeds the alkalinity and whose sulfate content (as $SO_4^=$) exceeds 250 mg/liter.

Objectives of the study

The two chemical parameters affecting water quality of direct concern in this study were the alkalinity, as generated by calcium carbonate, and the acidity, as generated by the decomposition of the iron disulfides. These parameters are strongly influenced by, and related to, the chemical composition of the rocks in contact with the water. Accordingly, the study was designed to compare two areas of strip mining, one area underlain by rocks of the "marine-brackish water" Lower and Middle Kittanning formations, against an area underlain by the "freshwater" Freeport strata, to determine their compositional variations. The former was expected to produce acid water, while the latter was expected to produce non-acid water, and accordingly, water-quality variations could be ascribed to the rock types and the groundwater interactions.

While the mechanisms for the generation of alkalinity from calcium carbonate were rather well known, the mechanisms of acid generation under varying field conditions and the factors influencing acid production were not fully understood. For this reason, an evaluation of factors responsible for the production of acid mine drainage was necessary to gain an understanding of the mechanism of acid formation.

METHOD OF STUDY AND DATA PROCUREMENT

Introduction

The approach to achieving the above objectives was divided into two phases. In the first phase, distributions of various formations were mapped for the two areas, and rock samples were collected and analyzed for total S content. Based on these values, a number of rock samples were selected for leaching studies that related the acid potential of the rock to its S content. Consequently, the areas from which the rocks were collected could be assigned a "rank" of probable acidities.

In the second phase of the study, water samples were collected and analyzed for ions indicative of certain chemical reactions. From these water samples a comparison could be made between the water quality of the virgin (unaffected by mining) areas and the strip-mined areas.

Two areas of study were selected to the north and south of Clearfield, Pa. The northern area, hereafter referred to as "the Clearfield area", is underlain mostly by strata of the "marine-brackish water" Kittanning formations. Strip mines in this area produce acid mine drainage. The other area, hereafter referred to as "the Glen Richey area", is underlain mostly by "freshwater" Freeport strata and contains strip mines that produce non-acid waters.

The geology can be described generally as consisting of cyclic sequences of shale, siltstone, sandstone, limestone, and clay. These are the predominant rock types in the Allegheny group. The coals, underclays, and limestones constitute a minor part of the total thickness. The most persistent beds are the major coal zones and the associated underclays, whereas the most variable are the sandstones (Dutcher et al., 1959).

Stratigraphic data collection

Samples of the various rock types were taken from sections in strip-mine highwalls or fresh exposures representative of dissimilar paleo-environments as designated by the geologic maps. When possible, the rocks were sampled from the walls of active mines so as to obtain unweathered samples. In abandoned mines, the weathered surface of the exposure was picked away until a fresh surface was exposed.

To ensure representative analysis of field samples, the rocks were crushed, sieved, and riffled into two portions. One portion, about 300 g, was used for leaching studies while the other portion, about 5–10 g, was pulverized by a ball mill and mortar and pestle in preparation for total S analyses. Samples used in the leaching study were analyzed for total S, pyritic S, and calcium carbonate content. In the leaching tests, partial neutralization could occur due to the calcareous matter in some of the rocks and must be considered. The smaller samples were analyzed only for total S contents by the Leco (Laboratory Equipment Company) automatic S titrator.

The purpose of the leaching studies was to evaluate the acid potential of rocks with varying composition using a technique described by Hanna and Brant (1962). The technique involved placing a sieved portion of the crushed rock sample into an inert chamber whereby a continuous flow of humidified air passed over the sample. Periodically, the sample was flushed and the effluent analyzed for various components indicative of certain chemical reactions. The components analyzed were the acidity, pH, alkalinity, Ca, and sulfate ion concentrations. Placing the sample in an oxidizing environment and periodically flushing the sample simulated field conditions of normal atmospheric oxidation with occasional flushings by rainfall.

The effects of variables such as the availability of water and oxygen, the size of the sample particle, the amount of pyrite present, and the crystallography of the disulfide, the flushing interval, the temperature and the presence of the iron bacteria were either standardized or controlled in order to make a valid comparison of the results (Caruccio and Parizek, 1967).

In order to accurately compare the samples, acidities produced were adjusted to a common base. The curves presented in the following section represent cumulative milligrams of H ion produced per 100 g of sample for a given period of time (Caruccio, 1968).

Water chemistry

A major concern in this study was the rock-water quality interactions, in particular, the effect of the aquifer composition on the water quality. In the leaching study, the composition of the rock was known and the quality of the effluent determined. Conversely, the analyses of the water samples collected in the field had to be related to rock compositions. If the reactions of concern in this study could be identified by certain chemical parameters, the presence of these chemical parameters in the water sample could be related to the rock strata.

The reactions affecting water quality, as concerned in this study, were the formation of acidity and alkalinity, with the consequence of neutralization should the two mix.

Alkalinity is defined as, "the capacity of a water containing a compound with or without hydrolysis, for neutralization of strong acid to pH 4.5," (Rainwater and Thatcher, 1960). Carbonate and bicarbonate are the predominant components of natural alkalinity and result from the action of carbon dioxide dissolved in water (carbonic acid) upon basic materials in the strata (principally calcium carbonate).

The acidity in acid mine drainage is assumed to develop principally from the hydrolysis of the oxidation products of pyrite. From equation (1) it can be seen that the sulfate content is generally related to the acidity. Because the acidity generated is a function of the oxidation state of the Fe, it may be possible to have a sample whose acidity content increases with time as the Fe is gradually oxidized [equation (2)]. The sulfate content, however, remains constant assuming no significant dilution has taken place.

The sulfate anion is the tracer of acid mine drainage and can be used to approximate what the acidity must have been before neutralization took place. This is done by analyzing the sulfate and acidity content of acid mine drainage from various sources, and plotting concentrations of sulfate against acidity. An assumption is made that all of the sulfate in the sample arises from the oxidation of pyrite. From the plot of various acid mine drainage compositions, a range of acidity can be interpolated for a particular value of sulfate concentration. This expected range of acidity is compared to the titratable acidity of a sample suspected of being neutralized (Caruccio, in press).

Although many workers consider pH and acidity synonymous or homologous, a sharp distinction is made in this study between the two. The potential free acidity is the capacity of water containing non-volatile compounds for neutralizing a base and does not include the component due to dissolved carbon dioxide in the form of carbonic acid (driven off during the boiling of the sample). The pH, on the other hand, represents the concentration of the hydrogen ions in a solution at the instant of measurement and represents the state of the environment at the time of the measurement, which is a critical factor in this study. The iron bacteria, which catalyze the oxidation reactions, thrive in a low pH environment. A water sample may have no free acidity, but due to a high dissolved carbon dioxide content, may have a pH low enough to be conducive to bacterial existence.

The ionic strength, to a great extent, determines the electrical properties of the solution and within rather wide limits can be used as an indicator of the dissolved solids content. Resistivity measurements were also used to confirm ionic strengths measured by conventional wet methods and to rapidly reconnoiter an area for water-quality expectations.

Water-sample temperatures were required for pH and resistivity measurements as these were partially temperature-dependent and had to be adjusted accordingly. Temperature readings were also used to indicate the depth of circulation of the water discharges. Generally, the deeper the circulation, the colder the water temperature.

Water samples were collected from homes, springs, streams, and mine pools in 16-oz screw-cap plastic bottles. In homes where the pump or well was inaccessible, water samples were taken from the household spigots, in which cases pH measurements were eliminated.

Water samples were labelled by a code designating the area and source from which the water sample was collected as follows:

C—the Clearfield study area;
R—the Glen Richey study area;
CL-near Clarion, Pa.;
GR-a strip mine near Grove City, Pa.;
HR-a strip mine near Harlansburg, Pa.;
SL-a strip mine near Slippery Rock, Pa.; and
K—the Krebs mine.

The following letters indicate the source sampled and are joined to the letters above:

H—private water supply from a home;
T—stream; and
M—mine drainage or a pool in a mine.

A number following the letters locates the exact sampling point by a corresponding number on a field map showing the locations of water sampling points.

DATA AND INTERPRETATIONS

Stratigraphic data and interpretations

Distribution of total sulfur The stratigraphic profiles of mine highwalls and roadcuts from both areas showed the lithologic variations, the sampling intervals, and the S content of the rock taken at the sampling interval (Caruccio and Parizek, 1967). Before a comparison could be made between the S content of the study areas, the source of variation due to sampling, riffling, and analyzing had to be ascertained.

It was found that a significant error is introduced when rocks and coals containing megascopic pyrite grains are riffled; this precludes valid comparisons of S contents between samples. Further, a significant lateral

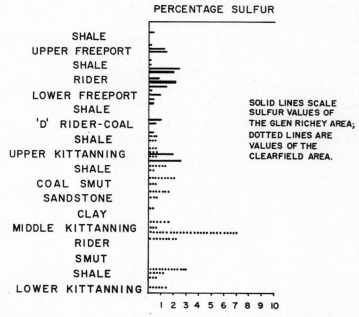

FIGURE 2   Graphic representation of total S contents of the Clearfield and Glen Richey areas.

variation in S content exists along the strata and presents a sampling problem. This also serves to reduce the validity of comparing S contents between two areas (Caruccio, 1968). Nevertheless, total S contents plotted according to the spatial distribution of the various strata show significant overlaps and suggest that the ranges of S contents of the two areas are comparable (Fig. 2). Thus, the original contention that a difference in the S content between the Clearfield and Glen Richey area accounts for the acid and non-acid drainages, is rejected.

Leaching studies   Three separate leaching studies were performed in an attempt to relate the acid potential of a rock to its S content and to evaluate the factors affecting the amount of acid generated. A total of 30 different samples, including coal, binder (silicious coal), and shale, were subjected to leaching.

The *first leaching study* was performed to determine the optimum leaching interval and grain size of the sample and the ranges of acidities that could be expected. The samples were crushed to pass a 4-mm sieve.

The results showed that in general, the higher the S content, the greater the acidity produced. All samples showed an initial surge of acid development with a subsequent slackening with time. This is attributed to an initial high acidity generated by the oxidation products that had developed prior to the first flushing with water. Thereafter, the time interval was too short to allow for development of a high concentration of oxidation products, but did permit a gradual oxidation to take place with a steady increase in acidity (Caruccio, 1968).

All samples in subsequent leaching tests were sieved and the 1- to 2-mm fraction (passed a #10 sieve and caught by a #18 sieve) was used in the leaching chamber. This size was noted to retain a minimum amount of liquid when the sample was drained. The time interval between flushings was the same as used in the first leaching study.

A *second leaching study* attempted to relate the acid potential of various rocks to their S contents. The sieved sample was riffled to obtain two 5-g portions. One portion was used to make pellets for microscopic examinations and the other was analyzed for total S, pyritic S, and calcium carbonate. The samples used in, and the results of, the second leaching study are shown in Fig. 3.

The data prior to the 20th day show many anomalies. For example, coal sample CM-10-9 (2.82% pyritic S) yielded less acid than coal sample RM-9-2 (1.25% pyritic S). Similar anomalies can be found with the shales. The most obvious explanation for the anomalous acidities was the difference in

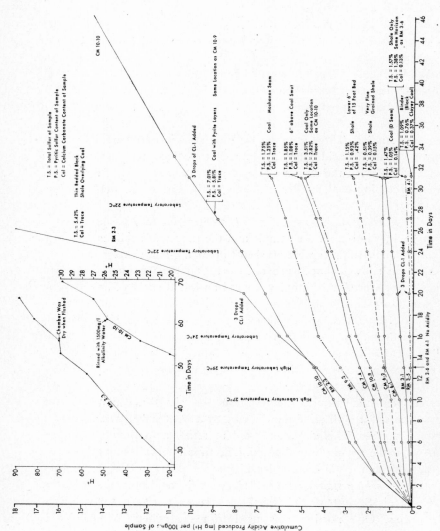

FIGURE 3 Acid-production trends of the leaching experiment using distilled water.

weatherability of the various samples. In all pellets, the only form of the iron disulfide found was pyrite; marcasite was not detected. Thus, the anomalous acidities of the leaching study cannot be explained by the crystallographic state of the iron disulfide. Nor can the trace amounts of calcium carbonate present be used to explain the differences in acidities.

RM- 9/2

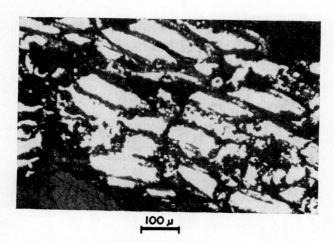

100 μ

CM – 10/9

FIGURE 4   Photomicrographs of samples RM-9-2 and CM-10-9.

Photomicrographs showed significant variations in grain size among the samples with different acidities (Fig. 4). On the average, coals containing pyrite grains measuring less than $10\,\mu$ in diameter yielded 2-1/2 times more acid than coals containing pyrite grains measuring greater than $150\,\mu$.

Twenty days after the trends of acid generation were established, the effect of bacteria (the Thiobacilli and the Ferrobacilli) on acid generation

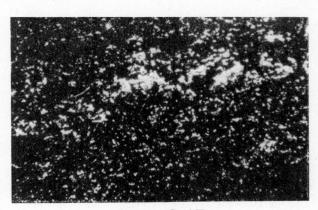

RM-2/3

⊢100μ⊣

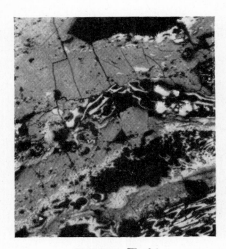

RM-3/1

RM-3/5

FIGURE 5　Photomicrographs of samples RM-2-3, RM-3-1 and RM-3-5.

was tested by adding three drops of acid mine drainage (sample #CL-1) to RM-2-3, RM-3-1, and RM-3-5. There was a dramatic surge of acid generation for sample RM-2-3. Prior to the addition of the bacteria, the acidity generated by RM-2-3 ranged from 3.65 to 5.00 mg/liter and released sulfate concentrations on the order of 2000 mg/liter. After the addition of the bacteria, the acidity concentration in the leachate soared to about 19 mg/liter and on one day yielded 74.9 mg/liter acidity (based on leaching 29 g of sample with 100 ml of water). Sulfate concentrations were around 34,000 mg/liter. However, RM-3-1 and RM-3-5 were not affected. Perhaps the presence of calcium carbonate in the sample or the larger grain size had a nullifying affect (Fig. 5).

Leachate from the samples presumably containing the bacteria commonly had a deep red color and stained the glassware with iron compounds. Effluents from the other samples commonly were clear or slightly milky and turned deep red only when the sample was heated or permitted to stand for weeks. This suggests that the bacteria do indeed oxidize their environmental components, thereby releasing additional acidity.

In Fig. 6, all rock samples used in the leaching study are plotted according to the sulfate and acidity yields for each flushing interval. There is a tendency for all values of acidities generated by binders to cluster about the lower part of the axis, that is, the low values. This suggests that binders produce less acid than coals and shales. A linear trend is apparent and expresses the previously described relationship of the sulfate ion to the acidity. The effect of bacteria is readily apparent. All values with a "b" subscript are from samples that were innoculated with bacteria.

The *third leaching study* was designed to determine how the acid potential of the rocks would be affected by flushing the samples with water that was in contact with limestone at the partial pressure of carbon dioxide found in the atmosphere. This leachant is hereafter referred to as "limestone water." For this test, samples of rocks indigenous to an area high in calcium carbonate content (GRC-2) were included in the leaching study.

In general, the limestone water did not appear to affect the generation of acid (Figs. 7 and 8). If neutralization had taken place, the points in Fig. 8 should cluster in a high sulfate, low acidity range. If acid waters had not been created (indicating an inhibitory action), then the points should cluster in a low sulfate, low acidity range. Instead, the points from the second and third leaching studies intermingle at all ranges. Note in Fig. 7 that sample GRC-2 rinsed with distilled water gave identical acidities as sample GRC-2 rinsed with limestone water.

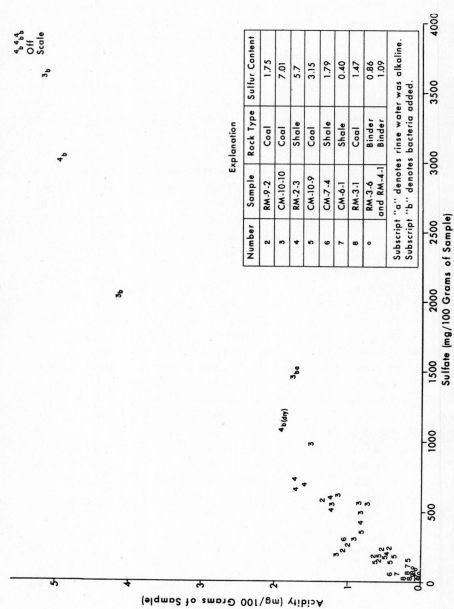

FIGURE 6 Plot of acidity vs. sulfate concentrations of leachates of second leaching experiment.

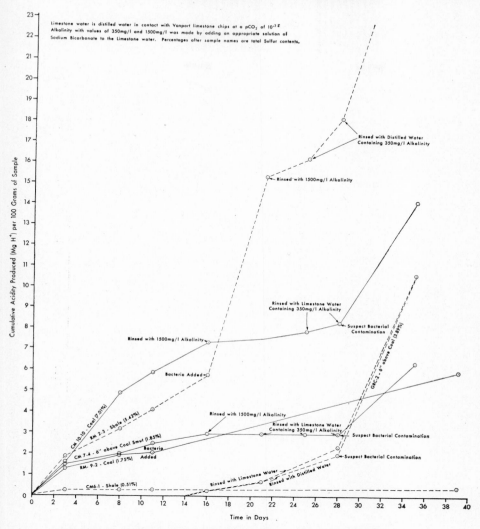

FIGURE 7   Acid-production trends of leaching experiment using limestone water.

The conclusions drawn from all three leaching tests are:

1. acid generation is partly a function of the S content of the sample
and is greatly influenced by the crystallinity of the pyrite, the presence
of bacteria associated with acid mine drainage, and the presence of calcium
carbonate;

14   Hutnik/D (1440)

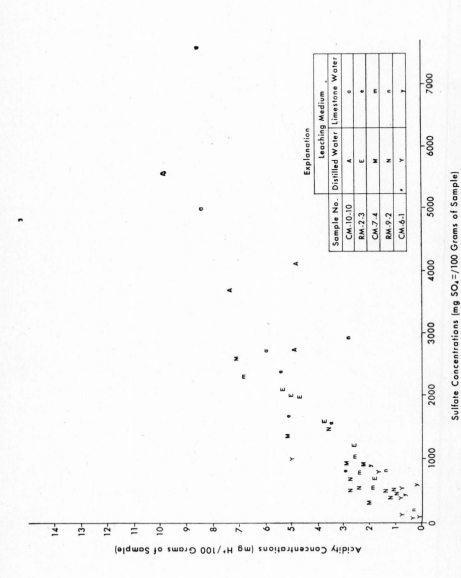

FIGURE 8   Plot of acidity vs. sulfate concentrations of leachates of the second and third leaching experiments.

2. samples inoculated with bacteria remain contaminated despite the use of highly alkaline waters; and

3. waters in contact with limestone at a partial pressure of carbon dioxide equal to $10^{-3.5}$ atmospheres do not generate sufficient alkalinity to effectively offset acid generation.

Aqueous geochemistry

Water samples were collected and analyzed from streams, domestic wells, seepages from mine shafts, and mine pools in the Clearfield and Glen Richey areas. Although not evident at first, water qualities differed for the two areas. Comparison of the water qualities initially was difficult because of an uncertainty of what concentrations and types of ionic species should be ascribed to a particular aquifer of given composition. After the extremes of water quality were established, the subtle variations of the water characteristics of the Clearfield and Glen Richey areas became apparent. Thereafter, water compositions could be grouped according to generalized characteristics associated with certain geologic terrains.

Water qualities of the Clearfield area The samples of groundwater obtained from shallow wells located in the virgin areas of the Clearfield area had a pH range of 4.85 to 5.60 and an average specific resistance of 26,000 ohms which reflected a low concentration of dissolved solids. The water samples had an alkalinity averaging 5 mg/liter (as HCO_3^-) and contained no acidity, sulfate, or Ca ions. Of interest is the low pH, in spite of the fact that the samples contained no potential free acidity.

The samples of groundwater taken from deep and shallow wells in and about the strip-mined areas of the Clearfield area had alkalinities that varied from 3 to 100 mg/liter and Ca ion concentrations that ranged from 0 to 38 mg/liter (as Ca^{++}). Although sulfate concentrations varied from 0 to 85 mg/liter, the samples did not contain potential free acidity. Where calcareous materials were present, the groundwaters had noticeable amounts of alkalinity and the pHs were about 8.0.

The variability in the chemical composition of the groundwaters was explained by the fact that the hydrology of the area was composed of horizontally stratified aquifers of varying chemical composition. The quality of the groundwater was then a function of the horizon from which the water was withdrawn, which in turn was determined by the well's elevation.

The alkalinity found in the groundwaters should cause the strip mines in the Clearfield area to discharge a moderately acid mine drainage. Analyses

14*

of the mine drainages from strip mines in this area showed this to be the case (Table 1).

Generally the acidities were lower than some of those reported in the literature for acid mine drainage. Acidity values common to acid mine drainage are about 20 mg/liter with some values being as high as 50 mg/liter (as H^+). Of interest was the high Ca content of many of the samples. The analyses of the groundwaters had shown that alkalinity was generated at depth in the area, and although alkalinity was not present in the shallow waters, calcium carbonate deposits were noted in the highwall of the mine that could potentially create alkaline waters and in part neutralize the acidity. If significant neutralization were taking place, the samples from the Clearfield area should be high in sulfate and low in acidity. As Fig. 9 shows, however, there is a quasi-linear trend between sulfate and acid concentrations similar to the one obtained from the leaching studies.

TABLE 1

Selected analyses of acid mine drainages from mines CM-6 and CM-10 in the Clearfield study area

Sample	Source	Temp. C	pH	Specific Resistance ohms	Ion concentrations in mg/liter			
					HCO_3^-	H^+	$SO_4^=$	Ca^{++}
CM-6	Pool by wall	22.0	3.80	1,800	0	0.45	330	46
CM-6	Pool # 3	19.0	3.50	1,100	0	1.40	665	76
CM-6	Pool B	16.5	3.50	1,040	0	2.10	720	76
CM-6	Pool C	15.0	3.65	580	0	2.70	1,270	153
CM-10	Pool	15.5	4.10	8,400	0	0.15	40	5

Water qualities of the Glen Richey area   To further evaluate the anomalously low acidities of the Clearfield area, a comparison was made of mine drainages and groundwaters from the Glen Richey area, an area with comparable ranges in S concentrations. Selected analyses are presented in Table 2.

A comparison of mine drainages from the Glen Richey and the Clearfield areas shows obvious differences. Mine drainages from the Clearfield area, although not highly acid, contain measurable acidities; those from the Glen Richey area have none. Sulfate concentrations show a similar pattern. The lack of sulfate anions in the mine drainages of the strip mines and deep mines, old and new, of the Glen Richey area is perplexing. Not only was

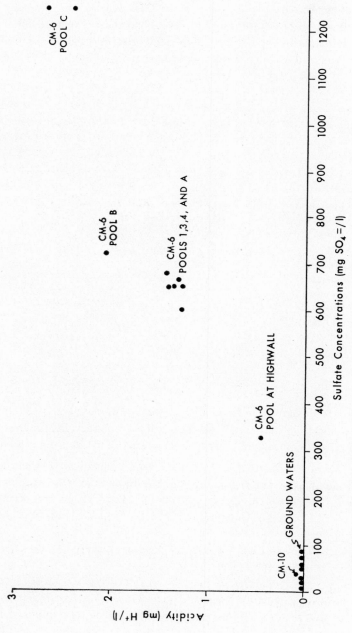

FIGURE 9 Plot of sulfate concentrations vs. acidities of all water samples collected from the Clearfield area.

there an overlap of total S contents of the two areas, but also extensive
pyrite coatings on coals were noted in the Glen Richey strip mines.

To help in the interpretation of samples such as these which are apparently
transitional in nature or comprised of a mixture of various components,
extremely acid and alkaline waters were collected and analyzed.

TABLE 2

Selected analyses of mine drainages and groundwaters of the Glen Richey area

Sample	Source	Temp. C	pH	Specific Resistance ohms	Ion Concentrations in mg/liter			
					HCO_3^-	H^+	$SO_4^=$	Ca^{++}
Groundwaters								
RM-7	Groundwater	13.5	8.30	2,800	75	0	0	50
RM-5B	Groundwater	8.5	6.55	8,600	9	0	0	14
RM-5D	Spring	10.0	7.00	11,000	27	0	—[a]	12
Mine Drainages								
RM-5	Air Shaft drainage (old mine)	8.0	7.25	7,000	25	0	28	19
RM-7	Shaft/Strip drainage (old mine)	11.5	7.4	1,950	123	0	0	66
RM-17	Pool in new mine	—	7.80	4,700	36	0	0	30

[a] Less than 10.

Acid mine drainages from strip mines   The Krebs mine is located approximately 2 miles due east of the northern portion of the Glen Richey area.
The major coal seam mined is the Lower Clarion and has a total S content

TABLE 3

Selected analyses of acid mine drainage collected from the Krebs mine

Sample	Source	Temp. C	pH	Specific Resistance ohms	Ion Concentrations in mg/liter			
					HCO_3^-	H^+	$SO_4^=$	Ca^{++}
KM-1	SE Highwall	12	3.15	480	0	4.05	2860	108
KM-3	West Wall	13	4.15	300	0	7.10	4800	360
KM-4	East Wall	17	3.95	360	0	8.65	5660	198
KM-5	Stream from mine	—	2.80	325	0	8.50	5000	265

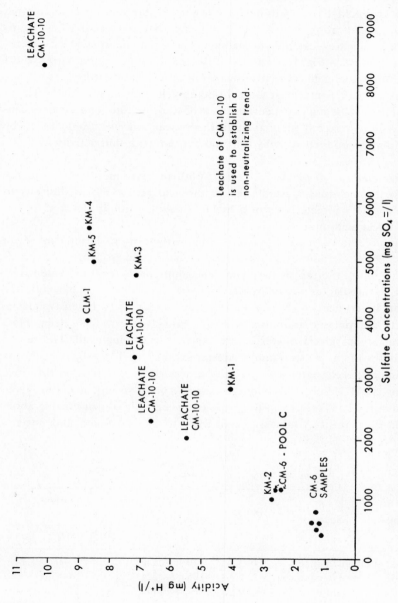

FIGURE 10 Plot of sulfate concentrations vs. acidities of acid mine drainages.

ranging from 0.56 to 12.4% (Reidenouer et al., 1967). Water samples from this mine had compositions presented in Table 3.

Note that KM-1, although having a lower pH, has a lower potential free acidity concentration than KM-3, showing that pH readings alone to determine acidities can be misleading. The sulfate and acidity concentrations plotted in Fig. 10 now extend the graph into a region more typical of acid mine drainage concentrations reported in the literature.

Activity coefficients must be considerably less than unity in order to accommodate the high concentrations of Ca and sulfate ions. The concentrations shown exceed the maximum theoretical concentrations limited by the solubility products of anhydrite and gypsum with unit activities.

Water qualities of the Mercer area   With the extreme of water quality (relative to this study) established in the acid range, it was desirous to determine the characteristics of a highly alkaline groundwater and how it would affect acid mine drainage.

Strip mines in the area of Mercer, Pa. mine the Lower Clarion coal which in this region is about 30 in. thick and contains numerous nodular bands of pyrite along the top of the seam. The joints in the coal are extensively coated by tabular grains of pyrite. The strata above the coal include the Vanport limestone, which may attain a thickness of 20 ft. Extensive glacial deposits are present and often glacial channels about 25 ft deep, filled with calcareous glacial material, are exposed in the highwall. The results of analyses of the water samples are represented in Table 4.

Of interest is the extensive alkalinity generated by the strata in this area. Samples SLM-3 and SLM-4 were collected from a spring emanating from a talus pile. The alkalinity of these samples is capable of neutralizing about 6 mg/liter of acidity; this assumes a mole to mole reaction and neglects

TABLE 4

Selected water analyses of the Mercer area

Sample	Source	Temp. C	pH	Ion Concentrations in mg/liter			
				HCO_3^-	H^+	$SO_4^=$	Ca^{++}
HRM-2	Pool in mine	10.5	7.10	240	0	60	81
SLM-1	Pool in mine	12.0	7.05	224	0	140	98
SLM-2	Pool in mine	11.0	6.45	152	0	740	117
SLM-3	Pool in talus	10.8	6.35	382	0	150	290
SLM-4	Pool in talus	10.8	6.60	388	0	140	300

the dilution factor. Thus, there exists in this area a significant neutralizing mechanism.

Although small pools of water in the mine floor were acid, major pools by the highwall contained no acidity. The high sulfate and low alkalinity content of sample SLM-2 is also evidence that neutralization is taking place. According to Fig. 10, the acidity concentration for a sulfate content of 740 mg/liter should be in excess of 1.5 mg/liter. Sulfate concentration of this magnitude can only be associated with acid mine drainage.

With the exception of SLM-2, the activities of the Ca and bicarbonate concentrations and pH of the water samples in Table 4 show general agreement to the equilibrium relations of a calcium carbonate-bicarbonate system.

Characterization of mine drainage by pyrite grain size and groundwater quality

Pyrite grain size and its relationship to the rock's paleo-environment From the leaching tests, it was concluded that the mineralogy of the iron disulfide (i.e., marcasite versus pyrite) was not in itself the oxidation-rate determining factor. However, variations in the granularity of the pyrite can be readily related to the amount of acidity the sample produced. Samples containing fine-grained pyrite are more "reactive" than samples containing coarse-grained pyrite. To further demonstrate the relationship between the "reactivity" of a sample and the grain size of the pyrite, a point count distribution was made of the pyrite grains of laboratory samples that were obviously decomposing versus those which remained inert.

One sample of the Freeport coal, collected from the Glen Richey area, was noted to remain inert in the laboratory. The sample contained noticeable amounts of pyrite yet the pyrite to this day is still brassy-yellow and shiny.

The other sample was a pyrite layer found at the top of the Clarion coal seam and was collected from a strip mine near Grove City, Pa. This sample oxidized so rapidly that it was necessary to contain the sample in a glass beaker; paper bags containing the sample readily disintegrated due to the acidity on the surface of the sample.

From photomicrographs of the two samples, the variation in grain-size distribution is immediately apparent (Fig. 11). The reactive sample has a preponderance of pyrite measuring less than $2\,\mu$. The grains are microspherules occurring either as spherical agglomerates or layers parallel to bedding and appear to have formed contemporaneously with the coal.

By comparison, the pyrite grains of the Freeport coal tend to be coarser grained and occur both as euhedral (well-defined) crystals parallel to the bedding or as secondary deposits filling joints not parallel to the bedding.

From paleo-geochemical considerations, the strata of the Glen Richey area should be lower in pyritic S than the strata of the Clearfield area because the former's paleo-environment was extensively continental in nature and the common oxidation reactions tended to inhibit the formation of pyrite. On the other hand, the strata of the latter would be deposited in a prevalently reducing environment which was conducive toward pyrite deposition. However, the analyses of samples showed no relation between the S content of the sample and the paleo-environment.

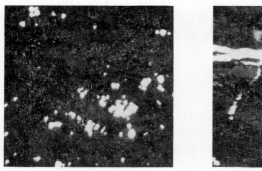

FREEPORT COAL

⊢50 μ⊣

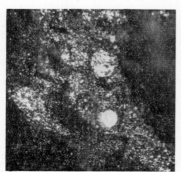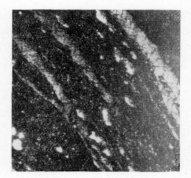

CLARION COAL

FIGURE 11   Photomicrographs of pyrite in the Freeport and Clarion coals.

A possible explanation is that, at the time the Freeport strata were being deposited, conditions were such that limited quantities of pyrite were deposited. By comparison, the paleo-environment of the strata of the Clarion seam appeared to be radically different in that it supported a microbial population which had the faculty to effect pyrite deposition during a stage of its life cycle. The micro-spherules of pyrite had a morphology suggestive of bacterial encasements (Arthur Cohen, personal communication).

Further, if the assumption is made that the pyrite in the Clarion is primary in origin and the preponderance of pyrite in the Freeport is secondary in origin (i.e., the pyrite was deposited after the strata were lithified), then at the close of the depositional stage during the Carboniferous, the pyrite content on the Clarion could indeed have been higher than that of the Freeport.

Coincidentally, the primary pyrite deposits are finer grained, readily decompose, and consequently yield large amounts of acid mine drainage. The Freeport, although containing the same amount of total pyrite sulfur as the Clarion seams, has a preponderance of secondary pyrite which is coarser grained, remains relatively stable, and consequently does not produce significant amounts of acid mine drainage.

The influence of groundwater quality on acid mine drainage production   The role of the iron bacteria in catalyzing pyrite oxidation reactions, thereby increasing acidity, is summarized by Hanna et al. (1963). In the present study, the leaching tests showed that the iron bacteria significantly increased acid production. Data summarized from "Bergey's Manual of Determinative Bacteriology" show that the iron bacteria prefer an environment that has a pH below 6.0 and that their optimum growth occurs in a pH range of 2.5 to 5.8. It is conceivable that, although the bacteria are found under a wide pH range, prolonged exposure to an alkaline environment will eventually lead to their elimination. As a consequence, lower acidity is produced that may be effectively neutralized by the available alkalinity.

While the pyrite grain size is postulated to be controlled by its genesis, which in turn is related to the sedimentary paleo-environment, the alkalinity of the groundwater is a function of the calcium carbonate content of the mine strata and may not be correlative with the paleo-environment. An example of this is the strip-mined area in the northwestern part of Pennsylvania which is covered by a calcareous glacial till and represents a relatively recent event far removed from the strata's paleo-environment.

Characterization of mine drainage   From the preceding discussions it becomes apparent that the variables affecting the quality of mine drainages are primarily the pyrite grain size, which controls the "reactivity" of the sample, and the alkalinity of the groundwaters which controls the presence of the catalyzing bacteria while simultaneously providing a neutralizing medium. Their relationships to the various types of mine drainages found in the areas of study are summarized in Fig. 12 and are the basis for a model (Fig. 13) which facilitates the prediction of the quality of drainage emanating from strip mines in an area. Its use is illustrated in the following discussions.

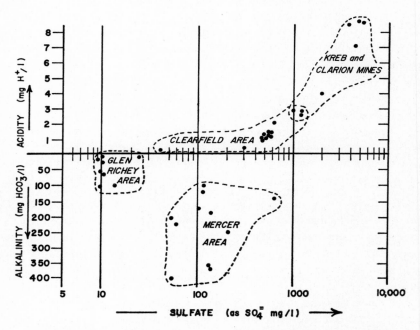

FIGURE 12   Characteristics of mine drainages sampled in this study.

The coal seam mined in the Krebs and Clarion mines is the Clarion coal of a marine-brackish water paleo-environment and should therefore contain primary pyrite of a microbial origin. The grains appear as microspherules and measure 2 to 15 μ in diameter. These grains will readily oxidize and decompose forming the hydrous iron sulfates. In situ calcareous materials are commonly lacking in this horizon; and as a result, the pH and natural alkalinity of the water are low and would support the iron bacteria if present. The bacteria will catalyze the oxidation reaction, and the resulting acidity will be high due to the absence of a neutralizing medium. These interactions will yield a high acid-high sulfate mine drainage.

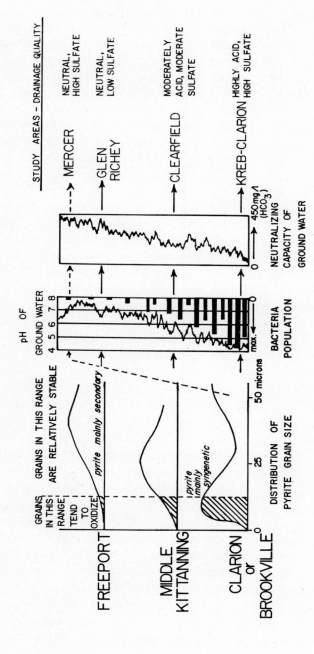

FIGURE 13 Model explaining the occurrence of various mine drainage qualities.

At the other extreme, the Glen Richey area is underlain by strata of a continental paleo-environment. During the depositional phase, conditions did not favor the formation of pyrite. The pyrite present is mainly secondary in origin and appears as tabular coarse grains (50 to 250 μ in diameter) and is relatively inert. The strata also contain significant amounts of calcareous materials which render the groundwaters alkaline. The pyrite will not readily oxidize and the alkaline groundwater will suppress the iron bacteria. The result is a low acid-low sulfate mine drainage.

Where conditions are transitional between the Kreb-Clarion and Glen Richey areas, (e.g. the Clearfield area) moderate amounts of reactive pyrite are present in the strata and moderate amounts of alkalinity are present in the groundwater. These conditions lead to a moderately acid-moderate sulfate mine drainage.

Neutral-high sulfate drainages seem to be prevalent in the Grove City-Mercer region of western Pennsylvania where the Brookville coal strata were deposited in a marine paleo-environment. Much of the pyrite in the strata is syngenetic and composed of micro-spherules 2 to 15 μ in diameter. During the field work, it was noted that a layer of large pyrite nodules capped the coal seam and seemingly contradicted this contention. Further, large nodules (about 5 cm in diameter) readily decomposed and appeared to challenge the relationship between sample stability and pyrite grain size. However, when the nodules were polished and viewed with an oil immersion lens, it was discovered that they were composed of aggregates of micro-spherular pyrite.

In this area, however, the strata of a marine paleo-environment are blanketed by highly calcareous glacial deposits. These glacial deposits give the waters in the area a high neutralizing capacity (effectively able to neutralize on the order of 6–8 mg/liter as H^+). Consequently, although the pyrite in the strata readily decompose and produce copious amounts of acidity, the acid generated is effectively neutralized by the highly alkaline groundwaters. The result is a neutral drainage with high concentrations of sulfate anion.

Iron bacteria may or may not be present in these alkaline areas, and precautions should be taken to avoid inoculation of sterile mines with the bacteria. The leaching tests indicate that once the bacteria are introduced, alkaline waters may not suppress their existence. There is always the possibility that additional acid production by the introduced bacteria may exceed the neutralizing capacity of the alkaline waters. If this happens, the acid environment thus created would tend to support and spread the bacteria which may start a chain reaction and produce even more acid drainage.

CONCLUSIONS

The model presented satisfactorily explains the mine drainage variations seen in the areas of this study. I feel certain that it can be applied to other areas when the pyrite content, its grain-size distribution, and the alkalinity of the groundwater are taken into consideration.

Emerich and Thompson (1968) have shown, on a county basis, a relationship between the character of mine drainages and the age of the coal seam, for the state of Pennsylvania. Younger coals had more alkaline drainages than the older coals. They concluded, "this trend relates closely to the depositional environment." This is in agreement with the hypothesis presented above.

I am currently developing a technique of point counting pyrite grains whereby total S contents of a rock can be converted to percentage of "reactive" S. In this way, the model can be refined so as to permit the prediction of the degree of acid mine drainage pollution that can be expected from a mining operation.

LITERATURE CITED

Carruccio, F. T. 1968. An evaluation of factors affecting acid mine drainage production and the ground water interactions in selected areas of western Pennsylvania. Proceedings, *Second Symposium on Coal Mine Drainage Research*. Mellon Inst., Pittsburgh, Pa. May 14, 1968. p. 107–151.

Caruccio, F. T., and R. R. Parizek. 1967. An evaluation of factors influencing acid mine drainage production from various strata of the Allegheny group and the ground water interactions in selected areas of western Pennsylvania. Special Research Report 65, Coal Res. Sec., Pennsylvania State Univ. 212 p.

Clark, C. S. 1965. The oxidation of coal mine pyrite. *Ph. D. thesis*, Johns Hopkins Univ.

Dutcher, R. R., J. C. Ferm, N. K. Flint, and E. G. Williams. 1959. The Pennsylvanian of western Pennsylvania, *Guidebook for Field Trips*, Pittsburgh Meeting 1959. Geol. Soc. Amer. p. 61–114.

Emrich, G. H., and D. R. Thompson. 1968. Some characteristics of drainage from deep bituminous mines in Pennsylvania. Proceedings, *Second Symposium on Coal Mine Drainage Research*. Mellon Inst., Pittsburgh, Pa. May 14, 1968. p. 190–222.

Ferm, J. C., and E. G. Williams. 1960. Stratigraphic variations in some Allegheny rocks of western Pennsylvania. *Bull. Amer. Assoc. Petroleum Geol.* **44**, 495–497.

Hanna, G. P., and R. A. Brant. 1962. Stratigraphic relations to acid mine drainage production. *Proc. 17th Ind. Waste Conf.* Eng. Est. Ser. No. 112, Purdue Univ.

Hanna, G. P., J. R. Lucas, C. I. Randles, E. E. Smith, and R. A. Brant. 1963. Acid mine drainage research potentialities. *J. Water Pollution Control Fed.* **35**, 275–296.

Mansfield, S. P., and W. Spackman. 1965. Petrographic composition and sulfur content of selected Pennsylvania bituminous coal seams. Special Research Report 50, Coal Res. Sec., Pennsylvania State Univ.

Rainwater, F. H., and L. L. Thatcher. 1960. Methods of collection and analysis of water samples. U. S. Dep. Interior, Geol. Surv. Water Supply Paper 1454.

Reidenouer, D. R., E. G. Williams, and R. R. Dutcher. 1967. The relationship between paleotopography and sulfur distribution in some coals of western Pennsylvania. *Econ. Geol.* **62**, 632–647.

Stumm, W., and G. F. Lee. 1961. Oxygenation of ferrous iron. *Ind. Eng. Chem.* **53**, 143–146.

Williams, E. G. 1960. Marine and fresh water fossiliferous beds in the Pottsville and Allegheny groups of western Pennsylvania. *J. Paleontol.* **34**, 908–922.

Williams, E. G., and M. L. Keith. 1963. Relationship between sulfur in coals and the occurrence of marine roof beds. *Econ. Geol.* **58**, 720–729.

DISCUSSION

HEALD: I am somewhat bothered by all these formulations in which oxygen is the necessary ingredient because in all deeper strata the diffusion of oxygen is very slow. My questions are: (1) How is the needed oxygen obtained at any depth? and, (2) Is the bacterial step an anaerobic reaction?

CARUCCIO: Most of the oxidation occurs at or near the surface. In spoil piles with high permeability oxygen may penetrate to depths of 5 ft, so there is an active oxidation zone below the surface. About 3 years ago, there was support for an anaerobic mechanism of pyrite oxidation, but there are adequate data now to disprove this hypothesis. The chemical nature of the drainages suggests that oxidation is actively taking place, and consequently oxygen must be getting to the pyrites one way or another.

HILL: We have placed pressure-measuring equipment inside and outside underground mines which were sealed with concrete barriers in the known openings, but have never detected a difference between inside and outside pressure. This indicates that equalization of underground air pressure with external barometric pressure is almost instantaneous.

HEALD: You say that bacteria has some role. Do you feel it has a role in the equation you are presenting?

CARUCCIO: My observations in the laboratory show that leachate from sterile material commonly is clear because the Fe is in the ferrous state; in this state the solubility constant is high, and the Fe remains in solution. However, if the bacteria are added, the leachate is invariably deep red and suggests that the Fe is in the ferric state, which is less soluble and consequently is in colloidal form. These observations suggest that the bacteria affect the oxidation of ferrous to ferric iron more so than the oxidation of pyrite to a hydrous iron sulfate complex.

Due to the excellent correlation between the sulfate and acidity concentrations, I believe that equation (1) is the main reaction for the generation of acidity. If you plot sulfate concentrations against acidity, you will find a linear relationship for any group of mine drainages emanating from a particular coal horizon.

CRESSWELL: I was quite interested in the relationship you had with acid production and time in the leachate experiments, and particularly the point of the temperature increase. Do you think this increase in mass production and slight increase in temperature was correlated with bacterial population or increase in the chemical reaction itself?

CARUCCIO: The presence of bacteria would be inferred if the leachate was deep red. However, because the leachate was clear (even during the period of temperature increase) the inference is that the increase in temperature increased chemical reaction rates rather than being related to increases in bacterial populations.

CHADWICK: If I understood your weathering experiment correctly, there was a time lapse before you removed the products of weathering. Now I would imagine that rates of removal of products of weathering would significantly affect the rate of acid production. Could you alter the rates of removal of the products of weathering to determine whether this is so?

CARUCCIO: Yes, in an earlier experiment we studied the mechanics of oxidation. We flushed one sample at daily and another at weekly intervals. Both samples yielded about the same amounts of acid, which suggests that the rate of oxidation is constant regardless of the accumulation of the products of weathering. However, Morth and Smith (Vol. 10, No. 1, 1966, Div. of Fuel Chemistry, Amer. Chem. Soc.) suggested that a limitation of pyrite oxidation occurs as the reactants build up on the reaction site. Possibly, in my experiment, the time interval was too short for a sufficient accumulation of reaction products.

AHARRAH: Did you find an increase in pH with increase in temperature? Might not such factors as temperature at time of sample collection and leaching by rain affect pH readings more so than the actual composition of the spoil?

CARUCCIO: To begin, let me suggest that a more positive relationship could be found between acidity and other parameters than pH. We are dealing with a buffered system, and you can actually increase the total acidity by a factor of ten and only affect the pH by a tenth of a unit. I would rather see a plot of total titratable acidity versus temperature of the spoil banks before making an attempt to answer your question. However, the degree of acidity produced by any spoil bank depends not only on the composition of the bank but on a host of interrelated variables. Temperature is but one. In view of what Borden presented concerning temperatures of the spoils surface, I believe that the high temperature would serve to dry the reactive site and prevent oxidation rather than to provide for an increase in acid production. Conceivably, a short distance below the surface, where water and O_2 are present, the temperature gradient will be such that an increase in acidity is generated.

ACID COAL MINE DRAINAGE EFFECTS ON AQUATIC LIFE

Richard W. Warner

Aquatic Biologist, National Field Investigations Center,
Environmental Protection Agency,
Denver, Colorado

Acidic coal-mine drainage has severely damaged the biota of waters in many areas of the world. Although streams may be affected drastically by drainage from surface mines, the damaging effects from deep-mine discharges are more widespread, of longer duration, and usually more severe. Reaches of Roaring Creek, West Virginia that were severely polluted by acid drainage (pH 2.8–3.8) were inhabited by low diversities of 3 to 12 taxa of benthic invertebrates and 10 to 19 species of attached algae. Stream reaches with median pH values of 4.5 and higher supported communities of 25 or more taxa of invertebrates and 33 or more species of attached algae. Pennsylvania streams damaged by acid mine drainage were inhabited by similar assemblages of organisms, with low diversities in severely polluted reaches.

High concentrations of acidity, total Fe, ferrous Fe, sulfate, hardness, Ca, and Al produced a complex and varying aquatic environment; pH, which was less variable, provides an index of the effects of mine drainage on aquatic life.

INTRODUCTION

Highly mineralized and acidic water draining from coal mines has severely polluted streams in many areas of the world. Pollution by acid mine drainage has been reported in Australia, England, Japan, Korea, South Africa, and the U.S.S.R. (Porges et al., 1966). The problem is especially serious in the Appalachian region of the United States, where 75 to 90% of mine drainage pollution originates from deep mines (Boccardy and Spaulding, 1968). Deep mines, unlike many shallow and surface mines, may continue to discharge pollutants for virtually unlimited periods after mining operations have ceased.

Waters polluted by acid mine drainage may be toxic to many aquatic animals and plants. Such waters constitute highly restrictive environments, capable of supporting only tolerant organisms (Warner, 1971). Because of differences of sensitivity to toxic substances that characterize these polluted streams, aquatic animals and plants are effective monitors of their environments. Some organisms are quite sensitive to mine drainage and do not inhabit streams polluted by it. Other more tolerant forms may flourish in these waters. The composition of biota in streams polluted by mine drainage reflects the chemical character of the water throughout the period of residence of the biota, which may be one year or more.

The biological communities inhabiting Roaring Creek, a mine-drainage polluted stream near Elkins, W. Va., were studied intensively from June 1964 to July 1967. For comparative purposes, shorter term surveys were conducted on Grassy Run, West Virginia and Glenwhite Creek, Clearfield Creek, and Slippery Rock Creek in Pennsylvania (Fig. 1).

FIGURE 1   Locations of acid mine drainage polluted streams surveyed.

METHODS

Qualitative samples of bottom dwelling invertebrate animals were collected by manually removing organisms from rocks and logs and by agitating sediments and debris in a U.S. Standard No. 30 sieve and preserved in

10% formalin solution. Qualitative samples of attached algae were collected by scraping rocks, twigs, and other substrates, examined live at low magnification, and then preserved in 5% formalin for more detailed examination at higher magnification. Diatoms were incinerated in nitric acid and potassium dichromate, and examined at very high magnification (1175X).

Fifteen main stem and tributary reaches of Roaring Creek were sampled during all seasons from June 1964 to July 1967. Chemical sampling was conducted weekly or biweekly (dependent on station location), and analyses performed according to standard methods (American Public Health Association et al., 1965). The chemical data are presented by Warner (1971).

Grassy Run, Glenwhite Creek, Clearfield Creek, and Slippery Rock Creek were sampled from June 1964 to February 1967, July 1966 to April 1967, and in May 1967 respectively. Since chemical analyses from these surveys were incomplete at the time of this writing, only pH values are used in relating water chemistry to biotic diversity in these streams.

RESULTS

Much of Roaring Creek is severely polluted by mine drainage. Such severely polluted stream reaches (median pH 2.8 to 3.8) were inhabited by highly restricted biotic communities, consisting of only 3 to 12 kinds of bottom-dwelling invertebrates and 10 to 19 kinds of attached algae (Table 1). Predominant among these tolerant animals were the larvae of alderflies (*Sialis* sp.), bloodworm midges (*Chironomus plumosus*), Dytiscidae beetles (adults and immatures), and, during the summer months, the caddisfly *Ptilostomis* sp. (Table 2). The distribution of each of these forms was dependent more upon physical habitat preference than upon the chemical nature of the water; e.g., *Chironomus plumosus* prefers a soft stream bed containing leaf litter or other detritus, and *Ptilostomis* sp. generally inhabits slack water reaches. Predominant among the attached algae inhabiting severely polluted reaches of Roaring Creek were the green alga *Ulothrix tenerrima*, the diatoms *Eunotia exigua* and *Pinnularia termitina*, and *Euglena mutabilis*. Also widespread in these reaches were the green algae *Microthamnion strictissimum*, *Microspora pachyderma*, *Closterium acerosum*, and *Chlamydomonas* sp. and the diatoms *Frustulia rhomboides* and *Surirella ovata*. Physical features also affected the diversity of attached algae; stream beds with heavy coatings of iron precipitates were inhabited by fewer species than other reaches of comparable pH, but with clean stream beds.

Headwater and tributary reaches of Roaring Creek not severely polluted by acid mine drainage (pH >4.5) were inhabited by 25 or more species of bottom-dwelling invertebrates and 27 or more species of attached algae.

TABLE 1

Distributions of benthic invertebrates and periphyton at stream stations of various pH; Roaring Creek and selected tributaries

Station	River Mile	pH Range	pH Median	Total No. of taxa	
				Benthic Invertebrates	Periphyton
Mainstream					
R-9	11.9	3.1–6.6	5.7	30	33
R-8	9.6	3.2–5.1	4.5	26	27
R-7	8.8	2.7–4.1	3.5	7	13
R-6	8.1	2.8–4.1	3.6	3	19
R-5	7.5	2.7–4.5	3.6	8	18
R-4	5.1	2.8–4.3	3.5	6	14
R-3	4.0	3.0–4.2	3.8	12	16
R-2A	3.7	2.4–4.0	3.3	5	10
R-2	3.1	2.6–4.3	3.3	5	14
R-1	0.2	2.7–4.1	3.3	7	19
Tributaries					
RT10-1	10.0–1.0	3.1–6.2	5.1	28	35
RT10-2	10.0–0.1	3.1–5.8	4.9	25	34
RT9-23	8.7–0.1	3.0–4.4	3.4	5	17
RT6-1	3.9–0.2	2.2–3.3	2.8	6	10
RT5-1	3.2–0.1	2.0–4.1	2.9	3	10

Although tolerant forms inhabited non-polluted reaches, they were never predominant. Rather, these reaches of higher pH supported communities dominated by stoneflies, mayflies, many species of caddisflies, black flies, crayfish, and complex assemblages of algae never dominated by tolerant forms (Table 2).

Similar to Roaring Creek, severely polluted reaches of the other streams examined (Grassy Run in West Virginia, and Slippery Rock Creek, Glenwhite Creek, and Clearfield Creek in Pennsylvania) each supported biotic communities of limited diversity (Table 3). Also, many of the predominant organisms in these streams were the same forms that dominated polluted Roaring Creek reaches. These included *Sialis* sp., *Ptilostomis* sp., Dytiscidae

TABLE 2

Presence of important taxa of benthic invertebrates and periphyton according to pH class of stream station; Roaring Creek and selected tributaries

Taxon[a]	% of stations at which the taxon is present	
	pH $\geq$ 4.5 (total of 4 stations)	pH $<$ 4.5 (total of 11 stations)

Benthic Invertebrates

Phylum Arthropoda		
Class Insecta		
Order Ephemeroptera		
Ameletus sp.	75	0[b]
Ephemerella sp.	100	0
Hexagenia sp.	75	0
Paraleptophlebia sp.	75	0
Stenonema sp.	75	0
Order Plecoptera		
Allocapnia sp.	75	0
Alloperla sp.	75	0
Brachyptera sp.	100	9[b]
Leuctra sp.	100	0
Nemoura sp.	75	9
Order Trichoptera		
Ptilostomis sp.	0	73
Pycnopsyche sp.	75	9[b]
Rhyacophyla sp.	50	0
Order Diptera		
Family Simuliidae		
Simulium sp.	100	0
Family Chironomidae		
Chironomus sp.	25	100
Order Megaloptera		
Sialis sp.	50	100
Chauloides sp.	75	36
Order Coleoptera		
Dytiscidae	75	55
Order Hemiptera		
Gerridae	100	0
Class Crustacea		
Order Decapoda		
Cambarus sp.	100	0
Phylum Annelida		
Tubificidae	75	9[b]

TABLE 2. (*cont.*)

Taxon[a]	% of stations at which the taxon is present	
	pH $\geq$ 4.5 (total of 4 stations)	pH $<$ 4.5 (total of 11 stations)

Periphyton

Division Chlorophyta
Class Chlorophyceae

Ulothrix tenerrima	100	100
Microthamnion strictissimum	75	91
Microspora pachyderma	100	73
Closterium acerosum	50	73
Chlamydomonas sp.	100	36
Cosmarium sp.	100	27
Ochromonas sp.	100	18
Scenedesmus abundans	75	18
Zygogonium ericetorum	75	18
Cladophora sp.	75	0

Division Chrysophyta
Class Bacillariophyceae

Eunotia exigua	100	100
Pinnularia termitina	100	100
Frustulia rhomboides var. *saxonica*	75	100
Surirella ovata	75	64
Gomphonema sp.	100	64
Achnanthes marginulata	100	36
Navicula sp.	100	18
Fragilaria sp.	100	27
Cyclotella glomerata	75	27
Tabellaria floculosa	75	9
Diatoma hiemale	75	0

Division Euglenophyta
Class Englenophyceae

Euglena mutabilis	100	100
Trachylomonas sp.	100	45

Division Cyanophyta
Class Myxophyceae

Oscillatoria sp.	100	27

[a] Only those taxa in which the presence exceeded 50% in either habitat are included.

[b] Collected at station R-7 only prior to June 1965, when a new acid drainage started at R-7. Not included in values listed in either Tables 1 or 2.

beetles, and *Chironomus* sp. among the invertebrates, and *Ulothrix* sp., *Eunotia* sp., *Pinnularia* sp., and *Euglena* sp. among the algae. Other forms that were tolerant to mine drainage but not predominant in Roaring Creek were sometimes predominant in the other streams. In some reaches of Grassy Run, the larvae of craneflies (*Tipula* sp.) dragonflies, and damselflies were abundant; the attached algae of this stream were the same forms that predominated in Roaring Creek. The invertebrate communities of severely polluted reaches of Glenwhite Creek were composed of the commonly encountered tolerant forms plus large numbers of craneflies. The

TABLE 3

Predominant organisms inhabiting mine drainage polluted streams in West Virginia and Pennsylvania

Stream	Stream reaches with median pH < 4.5			Stream reaches with median pH ≥ 4.5		
	No. of Stations	No. of kinds of organisms per station		No. of Stations	No. of kinds of organisms per station	
		Inverte-brates	Attached algae		Inverte-brates	Attached algae
Roaring Creek, W. Va.	11	3–12	10–19	4	25+	27+
Grassy Run, W. Va.	4	1–4	7–10	3	12–20	18–21
Glenwhite Creek, Pa.	9	2–6	3–16	2	9–25	9–17
Clearfield Creek, Pa	5	3–5	3–10	3	5–7	12–25
Slippery Rock Creek, Pa.	9	2–6	—	3	7–10	—

green algae *Microspora pachyderma* and *Microthamnion strictissimum* and the diatom *Frustulia rhomboides* often dominated the attached algal communities of these reaches; though often collected, they were never abundant in Roaring Creek. The biota of severely polluted reaches of Clearfield Creek was similar to that of neighboring Glenwhite Creek. Slippery Rock Creek also was inhabited by the tolerant invertebrates predominant in Roaring Creek, plus mosquito larvae (*Aedes* sp.) in reaches with pH values less than 4.5. Observations on attached algae were not made in Slippery Rock Creek.

Nonpolluted and moderately polluted (pH >4.5) reaches of each of the streams examined were inhabited by a complex and variable biota, never dominated by tolerant organisms.

DISCUSSION

The toxicity to aquatic organisms of acid mine drainage is undoubtedly a function of a variety of factors. These waters are typically highly mineralized and characterized by low pH. Complex mixtures of free sulfuric acid and the acid salts of Fe, Mn, Al, Zn, Pb, and Cu may be in sufficient concentrations to be toxic to aquatic animals. Smothering blankets of Fe-precipitates may be deleterious to both animals and plants.

The mode of toxicity of acid mine drainage to aquatic animals and plants may be as complex as is the chemical nature of the water. High concentrations of H and sulfate ions may be directly toxic. Mineral salts in high concentrations may be indirectly toxic by upsetting the osmoregulatory mechanisms of animals and plants. The sulfate and hydroxyl salts of Fe

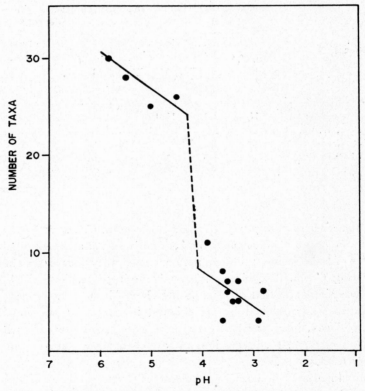

FIGURE 2 Regression of diversity of Roaring Creek bottom-dwelling invertebrates against median pH.

and Al, and possibly Zn, Pb, and Cu, may be of sufficient concentration to be directly toxic. Metallic cations may be directly toxic, and their toxicity may be synergistic. Dissolved O_2 concentrations may be reduced when metals are oxidized. Low pH may cause high carbon dioxide tensions in animals. In laboratory experiments, Lloyd and Jordan (1964) found that 50% of rainbow trout exposed to waters of pH 4.18 (total hardness 320), 4.22 (total hardness 40), and 4.25 (total hardness 12) died within 96 hours. High carbon dioxide levels in the blood of these fish indicated that death was due to acidemia.

In Roaring Creek, high concentrations of acidity, total Fe, ferrous Fe, sulfate, hardness, Ca, and Al produced a complex and varying chemical environment. For this reason, it was not possible to precisely assess the mode of toxicity of mine drainage to aquatic biota. All of the factors

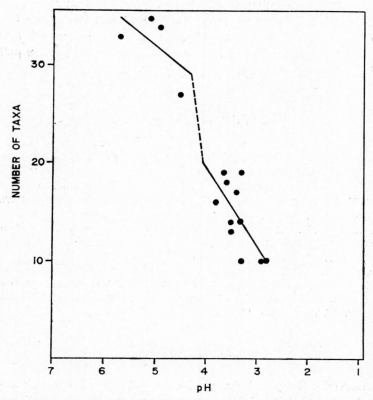

FIGURE 3   Regression of diversity of Roaring Creek attached algae against median pH.

mentioned may be involved. However, pH was less variable, and provides an index of the effects of mine drainage on aquatic life.

Reaches of Roaring Creek with median pH values of 4.5 or higher supported 25 or more taxa of bottom-dwelling invertebrates and 27 or more taxa of attached algae. Stream reaches with median pH values below 3.8 were inhabited by 12 or fewer invertebrate taxa and 19 or fewer algal taxa. Simple regression analyses of these data, plotting diversity of bottom dwelling animals (Fig. 2) and attached algae (Fig. 3) against median pH indicate that, although there are gradual decreases of diversity with decreasing pH within each pH grouping, the diversity decrease from one grouping to the other is not gradual. Rather, an abrupt diversity decrease occurs between pH 4.0 and 4.4. This critical reduction of diversity very likely occurs at pH 4.2, at which point all alkalinity is converted to free carbon dioxide. Thus, high CO_2 concentrations may subject many animals to acidemia and may stimulate the production of tolerant algae (Warner, 1971). Sampling in the other streams examined was inadequate for this type of analysis, but the pH and diversity data at hand suggest that pH may provide a reliable index to damages to the biota of streams polluted by acidic coal mine drainage.

LITERATURE CITED

American Public Health Association, et al. 1965. *Standard methods for the examination of water and wastewater.* Amer. Public Health Assoc., 12th ed. New York. 769 p.

Boccardy, J. A., and W. M. Spaulding, Jr. 1968. Effects of surface mining on fish and wildlife in Appalachia. U.S. Dep. Interior, Bur. Sport Fisheries and Wildlife, Resource Publ. 65. 20 p.

Lloyd, R., and D. H. M. Jordan. 1964. Some factors affecting the resistance of rainbow trout (*Salmo gairdnerii* Richardson) to acid waters. *Int. J. Air. and Water Poll.* **8**, 393–403.

Porges, R., L. A. Van Den Berg, and D. H. Ballinger. 1966. Re-assessing an old problem—acid mine drainage. *Proc. Amer. Soc. Civil Engr.* (San. Engr. Div.) **92** (SA-1), 69–83.

Warner, R. W. (1971). Distribution of biota in a stream polluted by acid mine drainage. *Ohio J. Sci.* **71** (4), 202–215.

DISCUSSION

HOLLAND: Did you find any evidence that terrestrial animals are also affected by the toxicity of the water? Do you have any information about water used for drinking purposes by either wild or domestic animals?

WARNER: I know of no studies on this subject. There have been reports of gastric ulcers in cattle drinking acidic mine water. On the other hand, I have seen people taking it home for drinking purposes because they thought it had therapeutic value.

HOLLAND: Have you investigated how far downstream the effects from acid mine water might be anticipated?

WARNER: Not specifically. The only reasons I can imagine for the water recovering would be dilution or reaction of the acid with alkaline substances. There is not much natural alkalinity in this area. Roaring Creek and Grassy Run pollute the Tygart River for at least 50 miles downstream to Tygart Lake, and I don't know how far beyond that. Some of the acid components are detectable in the Ohio River at least as far as the Cincinnati area. I did calculate that the acidity in Roaring Creek, which averaged around 600 mg/liter, would have to be reduced to around 10 or 11 mg/liter to bring pH up to 4.2 or more.

AHARRAH: In studies on Toms Run in Cooks Forest, Pennsylvania and on Toby Creek near Clarion, Pennsylvania, we found almost identically the same species and the same kind of distribution that you found in the creeks that you were studying.

GOOD: Did you measure dissolved oxygen?

WARNER: Not on a regular basis. Roaring Creek is a small tumbling stream. We assumed it would be adequate in oxygen because preliminary measurements indicated supersaturation.

CARUCCIO: If the water is supersaturated with dissolved oxygen, how does carbon dioxide affect the aquatic life?

WARNER: Carbon dioxide forms carbonic acid in the water, and carbonic acid in the blood can be toxic.

AHARRAH: It may be the lack of bicarbonate; there are no bicarbonates or carbonates where all are in the carbon dioxide range.

PERCOLATE FROM SPOILS TREATED WITH SEWAGE EFFLUENT AND SLUDGE

Larry H. McCormick and F. Yates Borden

Instructor of Forestry and Assistant Professor of Forestry
School of Forest Resources, The Pennsylvania State University,
University Park, Pennsylvania

Small, cylindrical lysimeters were used to measure and observe the chemical changes of the percolate associated with the application of sewage effluent and sludge to strip-mine spoil material. The seven treatments evaluated during this investigation differed in the quantity and method of application of sludge and effluent.

The release of large quantities of ammonia during the decomposition of the sludge accounted for some rather unexpected results. The pH of the percolate resulting from the sludge treatments experienced an increase which was related to both the amount and method of application of sludge. The treatment consisting of 8 in. of sludge mixed in the surface 12 in. of spoils produced the greatest increase in pH, from 4.2 to 7.2. An initial increase in the Ca and K concentrations of the percolate associated with the sludge treatments followed by a gradual decline suggested a partial saturation of the exchange sites of the colloidal portion of the spoils by ammonia. Although initially high, the S concentrations of the percolates resulting from the sludge treatments eventually fell below those of the control treatment which received only demineralized water. In general, the spoils provided satisfactory renovation of most of the major chemical constituents of sludge and effluent.

INTRODUCTION

Application of sewage-plant effluent and sludge in combination or separately to mine spoils could provide a solution to the sewage-disposal problem as well as the problem of revegetation of spoils. The application of large volumes of effluent and sludge, however, might pollute the groundwater since spoils are unconsolidated, often very porous, and chemically quite variable.

A study was, therefore, conducted to determine the chemical composition of the percolate associated with the application of sewage and sludge to spoil material. The basic approach was to use small, circular lysimeters filled with spoil material to which various treatments of sewage sludge and effluent were made. After weekly applications of effluent, percolate samples were collected for chemical analysis. The chemical composition of the percolate was monitored over an extended period of time.

Although spoils tend to be quite variable chemically, high acidity, low fertility, and toxic concentrations of certain elements are the major chemical problems associated with spoils. Acid conditions arise primarily from the oxidation of S-bearing material, such as pyrite. Although spoil bank pH values have been reported as low as 2.0 (Wilson, 1965), a large percentage of the spoil material is above pH 4.0—the value usually given as the critical value for plant survival and growth (Limstrom, 1960). Chemical analyses of spoils associated with six major coal-producing seams in eastern Kentucky (Cummins, Plass, and Gentry, 1965) indicated the nutrient-deficient nature of spoil material. Horn and Ward (1969) found a similar status for the overburden of two major coal seams stripped in Pennsylvania. In addition, they obtained lime requirements which ranged from 5.5 to 8.0 tons/acre, which are very high compared to agricultural soils. Although nutrient deficiency is often believed to cause the failure of plant growth on industrial waste land and deficiency symptoms are often observed, we agree with Knabe (1965) that nutrient deficiency may often be the cause of poor growth but rarely accounts for the complete absence of vegetation.

Perhaps the most important physical property of spoils is the low percentage of soil-size particles (diameter less than 2 mm). Spoils associated with four major coal seams in Pennsylvania contained from 54 to 66% soil-sized particles (Beyer and Hutnik, 1969).

Studies by several municipalities and industries in the United States have recently established that land disposal of sewage sludge and effluent is economically feasible. The alarm over the possibility of groundwater contamination as a result of treatment by sewage effluent has led to several investigations on this subject. Sessing (1961), in a 10-year effluent irrigation study during which an average of 205 acre-inches of an effluent were applied to a muck soil and to a Miami silt loam, found a low bacterial content in the percolate, but concentrations of sulfate, chlorides, and nitrates were higher than in the original effluent. Phosphorus and K decreases were slight.

Pennypacker (1964) in a similar study concluded that: "constituent concentration in the percolate at 6-in. depths was well below levels acceptable under the U.S. Public Health Service standards for drinking water."

Several successful land applications of sewage sludge have also been reported. In addition to providing an economical means of sludge disposal, land application of sludge generally increases the organic-matter content of the soil, improves the soil structure, and increases the water-holding capacity of certain soils (Rudolfs, 1955). The city of New York has reclaimed several areas formerly used for landfills by covering them with materials made by mixing sand and sewage sludge, and preliminary reports indicate that a good turf was easily established on the treated area (Powell, 1956). Knabe (1965) reported on the somewhat successful reclamation of strip-mine spoils in East Germany using activated sludge in combination with lignite ash.

The Rand Development Corporation, Ohio (U.S. Department of Health, Education, and Welfare, 1965) conducted several field demonstrations to show the value of disposing of digested sludge slurries to acidic areas as aids to their restoration without introducing health or nuisance hazards. There was a vigorous grass growth 2 to 4 ft in height on the sludged areas compared to no growth on the unsludged areas.

METHODS

The spoil material used in the present study was taken from an 8-year-old bank containing spoils associated with the Brookville coal seam located approximately 2 miles north of Kylertown, Pa. The spoil material had a pH of approximately 4.0 and a percent soil fraction of roughly 30% of which sand, silt, and clay percentages were 41, 33, and 26 respectively. All fragments not passing through a 1-in. square hole screen were removed by dry-sieving the material at the time of collection. The sieving operation removed roughly 5 to 10% by volume of the original material.

The lysimeters, constructed from galvanized sheet metal, were cylinders 1 ft in diamater, 3 ft high, and closed at the bottom, with a drainage hole 1-1/2 in. in diameter in the side near the bottom for percolate collection. The lysimeters were filled with the spoil material to a depth of 30 in.

A synthetic effluent was prepared in the laboratory using inorganic salts and a biodegradable synthetic detergent component, linear alkylate sulfonate (LAS), obtained from the Soap and Detergent Association. The average chemical composition of treated effluent from the Pennsylvania State University sewage plant as presented by Pennypacker (1964) served as a guide for synthesizing the effluent. The chemical composition of the effluent used in this study is given in Table 1. Milorganite was used as a source of sludge.

Seven treatments were established with three replications of each treatment. A weekly 2-in. application of deionized water served as the control. In the other six treatments, 2 in. of synthetic sewage effluent was applied each week at the rate of 0.75 in./hr. Of these six treatments nothing was added to the first; a 2-in. cap of sludge to the second; a 4-in. cap of sludge to the third; 4 in. of sludge was incorporated into the upper 6 in. of spoil in the fourth; 8 in. of sludge was incorporated into the upper 12 in. of spoil in the fifth; and the equivalent of 8 tons/acre of dolomitic limestone (30% CaO and 20% MgO, guaranteed to pass through a 100-mesh screen) was incorporated into the upper 6 in. of spoil in the sixth.

TABLE 1

Chemical composition of the artificial effluent compared to real effluent

Constituent	Concentration of Real Effluent[a] ppm	Concentration of Artificial Effluent[b] ppm
LAS	3.1	3.0
Nitrate-N	4.3	6.5
P	8.6	8.6
K	13.6	10.8
Ca	31.9	32.3
Mg	17.9	17.0
Na	48.3	48.0
Chloride	44.0	87.8

[a] Concentrations as reported by Pennypacker (1964).
[b] pH of the artificial effluent was 7.4.

At the initiation of the study, a 2-year-old hybrid poplar, *Populus* sp. clone N.W. 388 cutting, was planted in each lysimeter. The rooted cuttings were approximately 5/8 in. in diameter and 12 in. long. A grass mixture, consisting primarily of annual ryegrass (*Lolium* sp.), was also sown in each lysimeter during the tenth week of the study. The primary purpose of these plantings was to study the root-growth patterns as affected by the various treatments.

From the original randomly selected large spoil sample, small samples were analyzed for pH, N, lime requirement, total cation exchange capacity, and exchangeable Ca, Mg and K. The pH of the spoil material was measured using a Corning glass-electrode pH meter with a 1 : 1 solid : water ratio. The percentage of N was determined by the Kjeldahl method. The concentrations of exchangeable Ca, Mg, and K were determined using a Beckman atomic absorption spectrophotometer. The absorption spectrophotometer was also used to determine the cation concentrations in the sludge and percolate. The LAS concentration of the percolate was measured by the methylene blue process (American Public Health Association et al., 1960). An indirect method for measuring sulfate concentrations with the atomic absorption spectrophotometer was developed and used for this study. Basically, this method involved reacting a concentrated solution of barium chloride with the percolate samples and a series of sulfate standards. The resulting barium sulfate precipitate was centrifuged out, and the remaining barium concentration was measured on the absorption spectrophotometer.

RESULTS

The results of the chemical analysis of the spoil material presented in Table 2 are in general agreement with the results of other recent analysis of spoils associated with the Brookville coal seam (Horn and Ward, 1969;

TABLE 2

Chemical properties of the spoil material

Property Measured	Units	Measured Value
pH	pH units	4.14
Cation exchange capacity	meq/100 g[a]	17.31
Exchangeable Ca	meq/100 g[a]	0.29
Exchangeable Mg	meq/100 g[a]	0.54
Exchangeable K	meq/100 g[a]	0.48
Exchangeable H	meq/100 g[a]	16.00
Lime requirement	tons/acre	8.00
Base saturation	%	7.6

[a] Refers to 100 g of soil-size particles—those less than 2 mm in diameter.

Beyer and Hutnik, 1969). The low percentage of base saturation reflects the small amounts of exchangeable Ca and Mg. Although the milliequivalents of exchangeable K also appears to be low, the amount of K reported

16*

is actually comparable to agronomic soils. The high content of exchangeable H is to be expected considering the acidic nature of the spoils.

The chemical analysis of the Milorganite indicated that the percentage of N, P, and K were quite close to the guaranteed fertilizer analysis. The Milorganite did contain a large percentage of Fe (2.4%). The concentration of cations was low and there was no sulfate present.

There was a definite increase in the pH of the percolate associated with the 4-in. sludge cap and the 4- and 8-in. sludge mixed treatments. During the first 26 weeks, the pH of the percolate for the 4- and 8-in. mixed treatments increased steadily from approximately 4.1 to 6.5. Measurements made between the 30th and 45th week indicated that the pH of the percolate for the 8-in. mixed treatment was leveling off near 7.2. The pH of the 4-in. cap percolates and for the mixed treatments decreased gradually to between 4.5 and 5.0.

Linear regressions for the treatments during the first 30 weeks when the pH's of some of the treatments were increasing showed that the 4- and 8-in. mixed treatments were increasing significantly more than the control while the regressions of the others and the control were not significantly different from zero.

Unlike the sludge treatments just mentioned, the control maintained its initial pH of approximately 4.2 throughout the study. Despite the slightly alkaline nature of the effluent, pH 7.4, and the application of lime, the pH of the percolate for the effluent and lime treatment remained essentially the same as the control. The same was true for the 2-in. sludge cap and the effluent treatments.

In general, the average percolate concentrations of Ca for all treatments were below the effluent concentration of 32.3 ppm. The Ca concentrations for the control, effluent, and the lime and effluent, with but few isolated exceptions, remained below 10 ppm. Analyses of the percolate for the effluent treatment indicated that the effluent concentration of 32.3 ppm was reduced to an average concentration of 4.2 ppm which represented an 87% renovation.

Although the Ca concentrations for the 2- and 4-in. sludge cap and the 4 and 8 in. of sludge mixed treatments were quite variable, a definite trend in the Ca concentrations was discernible. Between the 5th and 12th week of the study, the Ca concentrations for the four sludge treatments varied generally between 10 and 25 ppm. Following the 12th week, the Ca concentrations declined until the 25th week when the concentrations were between 4 and 10 ppm. The Ca concentrations remained within these limits thereafter.

The control, effluent, and the effluent and lime treatments had average percolate concentrations of K below the effluent concentration of 10.8 ppm. The control had the lowest average concentration—3.7 ppm. The K concentrations of the percolate associated with the effluent and the effluent and lime treatments remained relatively stable throughout the study and were very similar. For these treatments the reduction represented a 40% K renovation of the effluent.

The K concentrations of the percolate from the four sludge treatments were higher from the beginning than the applied effluent concentration. Although they generally decreased from the 7th week onward, none approached the effluent concentration until about the 40th week. Unlike the Ca concentrations, the K concentrations of the percolate appeared to be associated with the type of sludge application. The 2-in. sludge cap treatment had the lowest average concentration of the four sludge treatments. From low to high average concentrations of K the order of the treatments was the 2-in. sludge cap, the 4-in. sludge cap, the 4-in. sludge mixed and the 8-in. sludge mixed treatments. The concentrations rose sharply from the 4th to the 7th week with maximum values obtained during the 7th week as follows: 2-in. sludge cap—33 ppm, 4-in. sludge cap—50 ppm, 4-in. sludge mixed—72 ppm, and 8-in. sludge mixed—144 ppm. The 8-in. sludge mixed treatment maintained a relatively high concentration until the 18th week. The results during the 30th through the 35th weeks indicated a range in the concentrations for the four sludge treatments from 23 ppm for the 2-in. sludge cap treatment to 80 ppm for the 8-in. sludge mixed treatment.

During the first 30 weeks of the study, Fe was found in the percolate of only three treatments—the 4-in. sludge cap and the 4- and 8-in. mixed treatments. The Fe concentration for the 4-in. sludge cap treatment increased rapidly to a maximum of 46 ppm in the 13th week and then decreased to 0 ppm at the 20th week. The Fe concentrations for the 4- and 8-in. mixed treatments were high during the first 25 weeks with maximums about 30 ppm.

Due to technical difficulties with the atomic absorption instrument, S determinations were only conducted between the 15th and 21st and the 34th and 48th weeks. A comparison of the values obtained during the two periods indicated that the early S concentrations of the percolates were relatively high and quite variable compared to values obtained between the 34th and 48th weeks. Despite the missing data, the values indicated a definite change in the S concentrations during the study. The most notable example is the reduction of the S concentration for the 8-in. mixed treatment from the 250 to 330 ppm range during the first measurement period to an average of 13 ppm for weeks 41 through 44. Except for the 4-in. sludge mixed treatment which continued to have S concentrations ranging from 45 to 75 ppm, subsequent measurements indicated that the S concentrations for the other treatments fluctuated between 35 and 55 ppm.

Analyses during the second, third, and fourth weeks indicated that the concentration of linear alkylate sulfonate (LAS) was reduced from the 3 ppm in the effluent to 0.1 ppm or less, a 97% renovation. The 0.1 ppm concentration of LAS is well below the maximum acceptable concentration of 0.5 ppm under the U.S. Public Health Service drinking-water standards.

The results of the P analyses during the first four weeks and then during the 37th week indicated that the concentration of P in the percolate was 0.10 ppm or less for all treatments. The reduction in the P concentration from 8.6 ppm in the effluent to 0.1 ppm in the percolate represented a 99% renovation.

The percolate resulting from the control, effluent, the lime and effluent, and the 2-in. sludge cap treatments remained colorless and odorless throughout the study. The percolate from the 4- and 8-in. sludge mixed and 4-in. sludge cap treatments, however, became discolored about the 11th week. A pale yellow discoloration of the percolate associated with the 4-in. sludge cap treatment was present until the 20th week. The percolate from the 4- and 8-in. sludge mixed treatments was also pale yellow during the early weeks of the study. The discoloration and an offensive odor of the percolate from the two mixed treatments, however, gradually increased. Ammonia in particular was present. After the 25th week, the percolate from the 8-in. sludge mixed treatment turned from dark yellow to black upon exposure to the air for several days.

The attempts to grow hybird poplar and grass failed. Most of the plants died soon after planting or germination on the sludge treatments. An ammonia odor was detectable above these containers. Although not preplanned, a determination of the ammonium concentrations of the percolates was felt necessary to help explain the sudden death of the hybrid poplar cuttings and other results.

The control, effluent, and lime and effluent treatments contained no ammonia, but ammonia was present in the percolate associated with the four sludge treatments, and the concentration of ammonia appeared to be related to both the amount of sludge applied and the method of application. The percolate from the 2- and 4-in. sludge cap treatments contained respectively 1 and 11 meq/liter of ammonia compared to the 4- and 8-in. sludge treatments which contained respectively 24 and 61 meq/liter.

DISCUSSION

Interpretations of some of the results were quite straightforward, while others were more complicated. The essentially complete removal of P, for example, was not surprising considering the fact that P is readily fixed by the colloidal portion of the spoils and precipitated at low pH's by Fe and Al. Similarly, the breakdown of linear alkylate sulfonate (LAS) was anticipated since LAS is readily decomposed by microorganisms in addition to being adsorbed by the spoil colloids. On the other hand, the reasons for the increase in the pH of the percolates associated with the sludge treatments, the rise and subsequent decrease in the Ca, K, and S concentrations, and the continued presence of Fe in the percolates from the two sludge mixed treatments are not immediately obvious.

The presence of large concentrations of ammonia was associated with many of these rather unexpected results. The ammonia and the ammonium ion concentration, which were probably the result of anaerobic decomposition of the sludge, caused the increase in pH of the percolates associated with the 4-in. sludge cap, 4-in. sludge mixed, and 8-in. sludge mixed treatments through a partial neutralization of the otherwise acid percolate. The percolate from the 2-in. sludge cap treatment did not exhibit an increase in pH simply because not enough ammonia was produced. The continued presence of large concentrations of ammonia was a good indication that the microorganisms responsible for the conversion of ammonia to nitrates were probably destroyed by the initially high concentrations of ammonia. As the microbes gradually became reestablished and began converting the ammonia to nitrates, the pH of the percolates decreased.

The general rise and subsequent decrease in the Ca and K concentrations can also be attributed to the large concentrations of ammonia. Ammonium ions caused a replacement of the other cations through mass action In essence, the rise and subsequent decrease in the non-ammonium cation concentrations simply indicated a partial saturation of the colloidal exchange sites with the ammonium ions. The higher concentrations of K compared to Ca were to be expected since K, a monovalent cation, would be replaced more by the monovalent ammonium ion than Ca, a divalent cation.

The continued presence of Fe in the percolates originating from the two sludge mixed treatments has been taken as an indication of the anaerobic decomposition of the sludge. Anaerobic decomposition created the reduced conditions necessary to keep the Fe in its soluble state. A substantial part of the Fe present in the percolates probably came from the sludge since the sludge contained a large percentage of Fe.

CONCLUSIONS

The results of this project can be summarized in four general statements. First, spoil material appears to be a completely satisfactory renovation medium for sewage effluent. Second, applications of large amounts of sewage sludge and effluent simultaneously may temporarily cause polluting conditions and not furnish a suitable growth medium for plants. This problem can be avoided by applying sludge frequently in small quantities or by allowing an aging period before applying the effluent. Third, pollution of groundwater by Fe and S originating in the spoils does not appear to be a problem as the result of the application of sewage products. Finally, a form of pollution which may be a problem is the offensive odor of the percolate from the sludge material. This problem could be of short duration occurring possibly only during the rapid decomposition of the sludge.

LITERATURE CITED

American Public Health Association et al. 1960. *Standard methods for the examination of water and waste water, including bottom sediments and sludges.* 11th ed., p. 246–248.

Beyer, L. E., and R. J. Hutnik. 1969. Acid and aluminum toxicity as related to strip-mine spoil banks in western Pennsylvania. Pennsylvania State Univ. Spec. Res. Rep. SR-72. 79 p.

Cummins, D. G., W. T. Plass, and C. E. Gentry. 1965. Chemical and physical properties of spoil banks in the eastern Kentucky coal fields. U. S. Dep. Agr., Forest Service, Cent. States Forest Exp. Sta. Res. Paper CS-17. 12 p.

Horn, M. L., and W. W. Ward. 1969. The revegetation of highly acid spoil banks in the bituminous coal region of Pennsylvania. Pennsylvania State Univ. Spec. Res. Rep. SR-71. 65 p.

Knabe, W. 1965. Observations on world-wide efforts to reclaim industrial waste land. In: G. T. Goodman, R. W. Edwards, and J. M. Lambert (Ed.). *Ecology and the industrial society.* Blackwell Sc. Publ., Oxford, p. 263–296.

Limstrom, G. A. 1960. Forestation of strip mined land in the central states. *U. S. Dep. of Agr. Handbook* 166, 74 p.

Lowry, G. L., and J. H. Finney. 1962. A lysimeter for studying the physical and chemical changes in weathering coal spoil. *Ohio Agr. Exp. Sta. Res. Cir.* 113. 17 p.

Powell, T. 1956. World's largest city makes top soil. *Organic Gardening and Farming* 3, 50–53.

Pennypacker, S. P. 1964. Renovation of sewage effluent through irrigation of forest land. *M. S. Thesis.* Pennsylvania State Univ. 94 p.

Rudolfs, W. 1955. Principles of sewage treatment. *Nat. Lime Ass. Bull.* 212. 85 p.

Sessing, J. R. 1961. The physical and chemical properties of soils and growth of plants as affected by irrigation with sewage effluent. *Ph. D. Thesis.* Univ. of Wisconsin. 119 p.

U. S. Department of Health, Education, and Welfare. 1965. *Economic transport and disposal of sludge slurries.* Prepared by Rand Development Corporation. Contract No. PH 86-65-21. 70 p.

Wilson, H. A. 1965. The microbiology of strip-mine spoils. *West Virginia Agr. Exp. Sta. Bull.* 506T, 44 p.

DISCUSSION

ALDON: Because of the presence of toxic concentrations of ammonia, how long do you think you should wait before planting?

McCORMICK: I would say at least three months. Possibly the sludge could be applied in the fall prior to spring planting.

CARRUCIO: When you collected the spoil material from the spoil bank did you crush it in any way?

McCORMICK: No, but it was sieved through a screen having one inch square openings.

CARUCCIO: How did you eliminate wall effects on the lysimeter?

McCORMICK: The inside of each lysimeter was coated with an inert asbestos asphalt coating which formed a spongy layer. We felt that this coating would form a better spoil-container interface.

CARUCCIO: You said you determined S by atomic absorption spectrophotometry?

BORDEN: We used an indirect method, developed for this project, in which the sulfate is precipitated as barium sulfate by addition of barium chloride, the excess Ba is measured on the instrument. This was more satisfactory for routine monitoring analyses than the other well-known sulfate analyses. A publication describing this method is currently being prepared.

RICHTER: Do you feel that raw sludge rather than the Milorganite would have given different results since Milorganite is heat-treated in the drying process?

McCORMICK: No.

RICHTER: You are saying in essence that the release of ammonia was responsible for the increase in pH. Do you feel that after all the ammonia has been released the pH will drop?

McCORMICK: Yes, I feel that the pH of the percolate will eventually drop because of the presence of active acid-producing material.

RICHTER: So actually, in the long haul, we haven't really done a whole lot to effect an increase in pH then?

McCORMICK: Although the pH of the percolate doesn't reflect it, I think the sludge and effluent treatments have had a drastic effect upon the pH of the spoils in the rooting zone. At the end of the study, the pH's of samples from the upper three inches of spoil material under the various treatments were: control – 4.5, effluent – 6.0, 2-in. sludge cap – 4.5, 4-in. sludge cap – 4,8, 4 in. of sludge mixed in the upper 6 in. of spoil – 5.2, 8 in. of sludge mixed in the upper 12 in. of spoil – 5.3, limed – 7.3.

CORNWELL: Many sewages, say in Sheffield, have a very high quantity of heavy metals from pickling plants. Do you have any trials which might show the effect of such levels on your microorganisms? Presumably such levels could kill them.

McCORMICK: No, we have not studied this possibility.

McNAY: On a widespread application of sewage sludge on spoil material, might one anticipate accelerated eutrophication of nearby streams.

McCORMICK: Possibly. However, some of the more detrimental elements involved in eutrophication, such as P, would be effectively removed by the spoil material before reaching the stream unless there was excessive surface runoff.

PART III

BIOLOGICAL CHANGES

INVASION OF TERRESTRIAL PLANTS ON THE NEW VOLCANIC ISLAND SURTSEY

Eythór Einarsson

Director, Museum of Natural History, Reykjavík, Iceland

Surtsey was built up of volcanic material in an eruption lasting from November 14, 1963 to June 5, 1967. Seeds and other parts of about 30 species of vascular plants have been found where they drifted ashore in Surtsey and have been identified. *Cakile maritima* ssp. *islandica* was found growing on the north coast in 1965 and the same species again in 1966, together with *Elymus arenarius*, but in neither year did the plants survive for more than a few weeks. In 1967, the same two species, together with *Honkenya peploides*, *Mertensia maritima* and *Festuca rubra*, were observed growing on the north and northeast coasts. Some of the *Cakile* which started growing in June flowered and were still alive 3 months later and had ripe fruits. *Honkenya* was also found on the southeast coast. Forty-eight percent of the specimens of vascular plants found on the island in 1967 belonged to *Cakile* and 43% to *Honkenya*. Two species of mosses, *Funaria hygrometrica* and *Bryum argenteum*, were also found growing on the island that summer, both on the north coast and in the interior where they succeeded in surviving the next winter; the vascular plants were washed away by the sea. In 1968, four species of vascular plants were found on the coasts of Surtsey, *Atriplex patula*, *Elymus arenarius*, *Honkenya peploides*, and *Mertensia maritima* on the north and northeast coasts; *Honkenya* was also found on the southeast coast. More than 90% of the specimens found belonged to *Honkenya*. Several species of mosses were found on Surtsey in 1968, mainly in the central part, but also on the southeast and west coasts. Of the specimens collected, the most by far belonged to *Funaria hygrometrica*, but *Bryum argenteum*, *B. caespiticium*, *B. capillare*, *Ceratodon purpureus*, *Dichodontium pellucidum* and *Pohlia bulbifera* were also collected. In the early summer of 1969, about 15% of the specimens of *Honkenya peploides* from the previous year were found to have survived as did a single specimen of *Elymus arenarius*. *C. maritima* ssp. *islandica* was observed on Surtsey again in the summer of 1969; one flowering specimen has already been found. Some of the mosses, mainly *Funaria hygrometrica*, also survived the winter on the west coast and in the interior where *B. caespiticium* and *B. capillare* also survived. Two additional species of mosses have so far been found on the island this summer (1969), *Leptobryum pyriforme* and *Polytrichum urnigerum*.

The possible ways by which these plants have been dispersed to Surtsey are discussed. Up to the present, all the vascular plant species found growing on Surtsey are coastal plants.

INTRODUCTION

The volcanic island Surtsey is situated in the sea about 20 km southwest of Heimaey, the main island of the Vestmannaeyjar off the south coast of Iceland, i.e. at approximately 63° 18′ N and 20° 37′ W (Fig. 1). The island was formed in a volcanic eruption which started on November 14, 1963

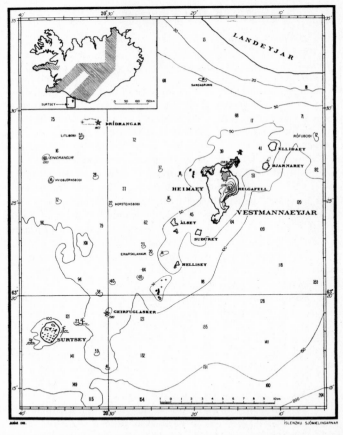

FIGURE 1   Surtsey, Vestmannaeyjar, and the nearest part of the Icelandic mainland in January 1966. Íslenzku Sjómaelingarnar (Icelandic Hydrographic Service).

and lasted until June 5, 1967. The course of events of the eruption and the morphological changes of Surtsey have been thoroughly described by Thórarinsson et al. (1964), Thórarinsson (1965, 1967a, 1967b, and 1968 and 1969) and Th. Einarsson (1967). The island Surtsey itself is partly built up by tephra or volcanic ash formed in the first phase of the eruption, when the activity was explosive; this phase lasted until the beginning of April 1964. Most of the island is, however, covered by lava poured out in an effusive activity from April 1964 to early May 1965 and from the middle of August 1966 to the beginning of June 1967. For more than 15 months there was no activity in Surtsey itself, but two more islands were built up by tephra in an explosive activity in the sea nearby. The first one, called Syrtlingur, was just east of Surtsey, and the other, named Jólnir, was southwest of Surtsey. Neither of these islands lasted long because of heavy marine abrasion. The first one was washed away in 5 months and the second had completely disappeared from the surface of the sea 10 months after it first became visible.

TABLE 1

Composition in percent of recent Icelandic lavas
(from Thórarinsson et al., 1964)

Compound	Katla[a] 1918	Hekla[b] 1948	Askja[c] 1961	Surtsey[d] 1963
SiO_2	47.68	54.25	50.33	46.50
TiO_2	5.01	1.54	2.94	2.28
Al_2O_3	12.54	16.34	12.23	16.80
Fe_2O_3	3.44	2.24	2.37	1.65
FeO	12.34	10.05	13.89	10.80
CaO	9.58	7.09	8.95	9.45
MgO	5.25	3.39	4.99	7.62
MnO	—	0.26	0.27	0.20
P_2O_5	0.23	0.35	0.28	0.33
Na_2O	2.43	3.41	2.81	3.32
K_2O	0.88	0.95	0.68	0.57
H_2O^+	0.44	0.42	0.27	0.03
H_2O^-	0.15	0.08	0.05	0.02
TOTAL	99.97	100.37	100.06	99.57

[a] Tephra from the 1918 Katla eruption (Lacroix, 1923).
[b] Last lava to appear in the Hekla eruption 1947–1948 (Einarsson, 1950).
[c] Askja lava of Nov. 16, 1961 (Thórarinsson and Sigvaldason, 1962).
[d] Tephra from Surtsey, erupted on Dec. 1, 1963 (New analysis by Elísson).

The shape and morphology of Surtsey itself have also changed considerably (Fig. 2). When the eruption ended the area was about 2.8 km² (280 ha), but due to the heavy marine abrasion, it has now been somewhat reduced. The maximum height of the island above sea level had already been reached in April 1964 when it was 173 m, but it has now been reduced to about 160 m. The whole southern part of Surtsey, which comprises about two-thirds of its area, is now covered by lava (Fig. 2). In this lava field, however, many hollows and crevices have been filled with tephra from the Jólnir phase of the eruption; these are especially evident in the southwest part of the island. On the southeast coast, a sandy beach has been formed. The northern part, however (about one-third of the island's area) consists partly of the 150- to 160-m high north rims of the two tephra cones and a small lava field in the valley between the cones, and partly of a broad beach, about 300 m at its widest, with sand and shingle, mostly eroded by the sea from other places on the island; the erosion has been mainly from the northwest coast with deposition on the north coast.

Surtsey is composed of an alkaline olivine basalt, the lava being among the most basic of the lavas erupted in Iceland in recent years (Table 1), according to Steinthórsson (1965 and 1966) and Thórarinsson et al. (1964).

TABLE 2

Meteorological data[a] in Stórhöfdi on Heimaey (Vedráttan 1962. Ársyfirlit)

Month	Mean Temp. C	Mean Precip. mm	\multicolumn{10}{c}{Frequency of Wind Direction in %}
			N	NE	E	SE	S	SW	W	NW	Calm
Jan	1.4	138	16	5	19	12	14	13	11	6	4
Feb	1.6	104	18	5	18	12	12	11	13	7	4
Mar	2.7	109	14	4	23	17	12	10	10	6	4
Apr	3.7	97	15	3	20	17	11	10	12	9	3
May	6.2	81	8	3	22	23	12	8	12	8	4
June	8.5	81	7	2	17	24	13	8	15	9	5
July	10.3	84	7	2	14	21	11	8	16	13	8
Aug	10.2	108	9	2	15	18	13	10	15	11	7
Sep	8.4	132	12	3	18	17	13	10	12	10	5
Oct	5.6	166	16	4	18	16	12	11	11	8	4
Nov	3.8	141	16	4	19	15	13	11	12	6	4
Dec	2.5	156	17	4	21	14	14	11	10	5	4
Year	5.4	1397	—	—	—	—	—	—	—	—	—

[a] Based on the period from 1931 to 1960.

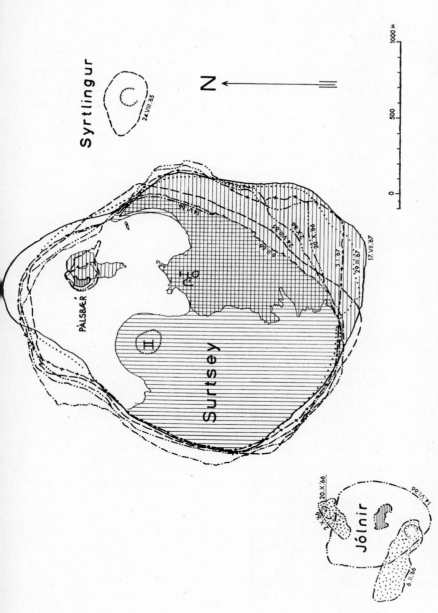

FIGURE 2   The outlines of Surtsey, Syrtlingur, and Jólnir at different times. Legend: I and II—the two main lava craters of Surtsey; vertical and cross striation—areas covered by the 1964-65 lava; horizontal and cross striation—areas covered by the 1966-67 lava; dense striation—lagoon which was filled with sand and disappeared during the winter of 1968-69; dotted areas (Jólnir)—shoals more-or-less visible at low tide (after Thórarinsson, 1968).

Some meteorological observations have been made on Surtsey during the summers since 1967. However, on Heimaey, the main island of Vestmannaeyjar (Fig. 1), such observations have been made for 90 years, the last 46 years at Stórhöfdi, in the southernmost part of Heimaey. The meteorological record for the summer of 1967 from Surtsey has been published by Sigtryggsson (1968). He stated that a preliminary survey of the data showed that the general climate of Surtsey is very similar to Stórhöfdi. Due to the difference in elevation of the two stations, the temperature is generally warmer in Surtsey (0.9 C in April and 0.5 C to 0.6 C in June and July). Precipitation in Surtsey in 1967 was from 60 to 80% of the corresponding values at Stórhöfdi. The mean temperatures together with the precipitation of the months and the whole year and the frequency of wind directions at Stórhöfdi from 1931 to 1960 are given in Table 2. As can clearly be seen, the climate in Vestmannaeyjar is very oceanic, probably the most oceanic in the whole of Iceland. The winters are the warmest in Iceland, precipitation is rather high, and winds are very common.

INVASION OF TERRESTRIAL PLANTS ON SURTSEY

As early as 1964, terrestrial plant material was observed in Surtsey; seeds, leaves, and other parts of vascular plants were found where they had drifted ashore (Fridriksson, 1964 and 1965; Einarsson, 1965). Since then plant parts that had drifted ashore have been found now and then, mainly on the northeast and the east coasts and especially when the wind has been blowing from these directions (Einarsson, 1966; and Fridriksson, 1966 and 1967). All the parts of vascular plants which were investigated and identified are given in Table 3. They belong to about 30 species which are found in one or more of the islands of the Vestmannaeyjar (Johnsen, 1939 and 1948; Fridriksson and Johnsen, 1967). Surtsey is only about 5 km from the nearest island, about 20 km from Heimaey, and not more than 32 km from the Icelandic mainland. Most of this material has without doubt been brought to Surtsey from the other islands of Vestmannaeyjar.

Most of the identified material belonged to the first six species listed in Table 3, which are commonly found growing on the coasts or in the cliffs quite near the coasts of the islands. Material of the next five species, also coastal plants, has frequently been found. Considerable material of the next two species has been observed; these species, especially the first one, are common on many of the islands of Vestmannaeyjar. Material belonging to the remaining sixteen species has been found occasionally.

The germination ability of seeds found drifted ashore in Surtsey has been tested by Th. Einarsson (1966) and Fridriksson (1966). Only the seeds of *Cakile maritima* Scop ssp. *islandica* Hyl. were able to germinate to the extent of about two thirds of the seeds tested. At that time no seeds of *Honkenya peploides* (L.) Ehrh. had been found on the island.

The first species of vascular plants found growing in Surtsey was *C. maritima* ssp. *islandica*; this was on the north coast in early June 1965 (Fig. 3) or more than $1\frac{1}{2}$ years after the beginning of the eruption. About 30 small specimens were found on a mixture of tephra, shingle, and decaying fragments of seaweeds that had drifted ashore at the high-water line. These

TABLE 3

Various parts of the following species of vascular plants found drifted ashore in Surtsey

Species	Plant Part
Angelica archangelica	Shoots with leaves, seeds
Cakile maritima ssp. *isl.* (*Cakile edentula*)	Shoots, seeds, fruits
Cochlearia officinalis coll.	Shoots with inflorescences, leaves
Elymus arenarius	Culms, seeds
Rhodiola rosea	Rhizomes with fresh leaves
Tripleurospermum maritimum	Shoots with leaves
Atriplex patula	Shoots with fruits, seeds
Honkenya peploides	Seeds
Ligusticum scoticum	Leaves
Mertensia maritima	Shoots with leaves
Puccinellia maritima	Inflorescence
Festuca rubra	Culms
Poa pratensis	Culms with rhizomes
Agrostis tenuis	Culms
Alopecurus pratensis	Panicles
Anthoxanthum odoratum	Panicles
Armeria maritima	Leaves, inflorescences
Betula sp.	Twigs
Carex maritima	Shoot with leaves, spikes, and rhizomes
Carex nigra (?)	Perigyniums
Empetrum sp.	Seeds
Euphrasia sp.	Inflorescence with empty fruits
Galium boreale	Shoots with leaves
Juncus arcticus ssp. *intermedius*	A shoot with inforescence
Rumex acetosa	Shoots with leaves
Tricophorum caespitosum ssp. *caesp.*	A shoot with inflorescence
Silene maritima	Shoots with leaves, fruits
Taraxacum sp.	Inflorescences
Trifolium repens	Inflorescences

specimens were completely covered by tephra from the Syrtlingur phase of the eruption 2 weeks later (Fridriksson, 1965).

About a year later some plants were again found growing on the north coast of Surtsey; this time there were a few specimens of *Elymus arenarius* L.

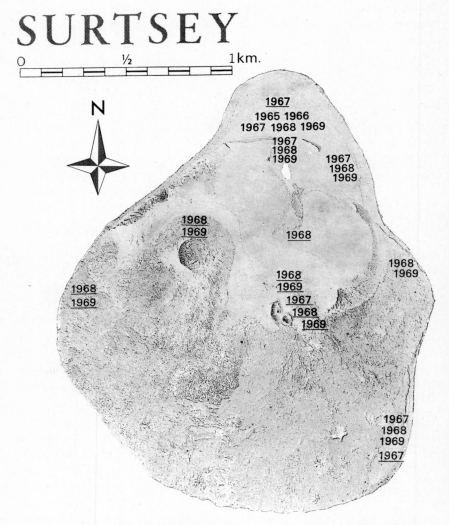

FIGURE 3 A sketch map of Surtsey made after an air photograph taken by the Icelandic Survey Department on July 6, 1968. On the map the years of the discovery of vascular plants and mosses in different parts of the island are shown, the years of the findings of mosses being underlined.

and a single specimen of *C. maritima* ssp. *islandica* (Fridriksson, 1967). All these specimens were washed away within a few weeks by the heavy surf which often pounds the coasts of Surtsey.

About the middle of May 1967, approximately 15 small specimens of *C. maritima* ssp. *islandica* and a single specimen of *E. arenarius* were again found at the high-water line on the north coast of the island (Einarsson, 1967 and 1968). A month later, all of these specimens had disappeared, but at the same time another 6 specimens of *C. maritima* ssp. *islandica* were found on the northeast coast. On June 26, the first flowers were observed in Surtsey on *C. maritima* ssp. *islandica* by the geologist Thórarinsson, more than 3½ years after the eruption started (Einarsson, 1967 and 1968). During the summer of 1967, several more specimens of *C. maritima* ssp. *islandica* and a few of *E. arenarius* (Fig. 4) were found on the northeast coast and a little farther south along the east coast. In the same area, *Honkenya peploides* was found for the first time growing in Surtsey (Fig. 5). Twenty-five specimens were found in all, and furthermore single specimens of respectively *Mertensia maritima* (L) S. F. Gray and *Festuca rubra* L. were observed for the first time. These plants were also found at the high-water line in the northeast part of the island (Einarsson, 1967 and 1968; Fridriksson and Johnsen, 1968). In early September, a single specimen of *H. peploides* was observed on the southeast coast, the first plant to be found in that part of the island. During the summer of 1967, 46 specimens (belonging to 5 species of vascular plants) succeeded in surviving until the autumn, and all the surviving 14 specimens of *C. maritima* ssp. *islandica* had flowered and borne fruits in early September (Fig. 6), but no other specimens flowered (Einarsson, 1967 and 1968). In 1967, the first mosses were found, at first on the north coast, but later I observed mosses in the central part of the island where no plants had been observed before (Einarsson, 1967 and 1968; Jóhannsson, 1968). Two big clusters of mosses were found in the sand on the shore (Fig. 7), and four small ones in the interior on a thin sand or tephra layer covering the still lukewarm edge of the lava field. The mosses, identified by Johannsson, were *Funaria hygrometrica* Hedw. and *Bryum argenteum* Hedw.

As most of the specimens of vascular plants found on Surtsey in 1967 were growing in loose coarse sand at the high-water mark on the relatively flat coast, they were washed away by the sea the following winter as were the mosses on the coast. But *F. hygrometrica* in the interior succeeded as the first terrestrial macroscopic plant species to survive the winter on this island.

In 1968, vascular plants once more started to grow on Surtsey, on the north, northeast, east and southeast coasts of the island. Many of the

FIGURE 4   *Elymus arenarius* on the northeast coast of Surtsey. September 11, 1967.

FIGURE 5   *Honkenya peploides* on the northeast coast of Surtsey, September 11, 1967.

FIGURE 6 The most vigorous specimens of *Cakile maritima* ssp *islandica* found on Surtsey. The specimen is about 70 cm in diameter. September 9, 1967.

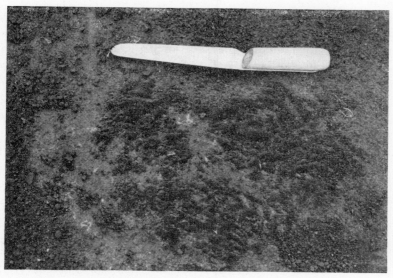

FIGURE 7 *Funaria hygrometrica* growing on the north coast of Surtsey. The small spade is about 30 cm long. September 9, 1967.

specimens observed were growing along the high-water line on the coast, but on the central-east coast several (mostly *Honkenya peploides*) grew in the tephra and sand-covered lava at a distance of 20 to 30 m from the high-water line. Nearly 120 specimens of vascular plants were found on Surtsey in 1968; about 91% of these were *H. peploides*; the remaining specimens were mostly *Mertensia maritima* and *Elymus arenarius*, but one specimen of *Atriplex patula* L. was observed on the northeast coast by Á. Bjarnason, a postgraduate student, and was identified by both him and me. About 83% of these specimens survived until autumn; the remaining ones were blown away by the wind or simply covered by drifting sand and tephra. No plants flowered on Surtsey in 1968. Bjarnason and I discovered more moss localities on the lava in the central part of Surtsey where the island in certain places seemed to be turning green. In all these localities, the mosses grew in a thin tephra layer on still-warm lava. In September, however, I observed three small moss clusters on the top of completely cold lava cliffs close to the sea on the northwest coast, the first terrestrial plants to be found there, and in the sand on the southeast coast where no mosses had been observed previously. All the mosses were identified by Jóhannsson; those from the coasts and most of those from the interior were *Funaria hygrometrica*, but in the interior of the island I collected six additional species: *Bryum argenteum*, *B. caespiticium* Hedw., *B. capillare* Hedw., *Ceratodon purpureus* (Hedw.) Brid., *Dichodontium pellucidum* (Hedw.) Schimp. and *Pohlia bulbifera* (Warnst.) Warnst.

In early July 1969, I visited Surtsey and observed that many of the vascular plants found on the island the previous summer had succeeded in surviving the winter; these included about 15% of the specimens of *Honkenya peploides* found on the island in 1967 and a single specimen of *Elymus arenarius*. Nearly all of these survivals from the previous year are on the east and southeast coasts. This is the first time specimens of vascular plants survived the winter in Surtsey. Some new specimens of *H. peploides* and one of *E. arenarius* were observed at the same time. Furthermore a single specimen of *C. maritima* ssp. *islandica* was observed on the north coast; this specimen was already flowering. The mosses in some of the localities in the interior and on the northwest coast had also survived the winter, but on the southeast coast, no traces of the mosses from the previous year could be found.

As before, *Funaria hygrometrica* was found to be far the most common moss species on Surtsey, but *Bryum caespiticium* and *B. capillare* were observed again. Two species of mosses new to Surtsey were also found, *Leptobryum pyriforme* (Hedw.) Wils. on the northwest coast, where only

Funaria hygrometrica had been found earlier, and *Polytrichum urnigerum* Hedw. in the central part of the island.

All the species of vascular plants and mosses found on Surtsey up to the present time are listed in Table 4.

TABLE 4

Species of vascular plants and mosses found growing in Surtsey

Species	Year[a]				
	1965	1966	1967	1968	July 1969
Atriplex patula				×	
Cakile maritima ssp. *isl*.	×	×	×		×
Elymus arenarius		×	×	×	×
Festuca rubra			×		
Honkenya peploides			×	×	×
Mertensia maritima			×	×	
Bryum argenteum			×	×	
B. caespiticium				×	×
B. capillare				×	×
Ceratodon purpureus				×	
Dichodontium pellucidum				×	
Funaria hygrometrica			×	×	×
Leptobryum pyriforme					×
Pohlia bulbifera				×	
Polytrichum urnigerum					×

[a] In 1966, 80% of the specimens of vascular plants observed belonged to *Elymus* and only 20% to *Cakile*. In 1967, about 48% of the specimens belonged to *Cakile*, 43% to *Honkenya*, 5% to *Elymus* and 2% each to *Mertensia* and *Festuca*. In 1968, about 91% of the specimens belonged to *Honkenya*, about 4% each to *Mertensia* and *Elymus* and scarcely 1% to *Atriplex*. In early July 1969, about 87% of the specimens found belonged to *Honkenya*, 9% to *Elymus* and 4% to *Cakile*. Ever since 1967, *Funaria hygrometrica* has been by far the most common moss species on Surtsey.

DISPERSAL, ESTABLISHMENT, AND REPRODUCTION

As mentioned earlier (Tables 3 and 4) various parts of about 30 species of vascular plants have been observed drifted ashore in Surtsey, but so far only 6 species have been found growing in the island. Five of these are typical halophilous coastal species, and all are found growing on the coasts of Heimaey and some of them in other islands in the Vestmannaeyjar group. Their seeds are relatively large and are known to be able to float and to withstand immersion in salt water (Löve, 1963); thus they are well adapted to dispersal by sea. In Surtsey they have been found growing at the high-water line on the coasts, or not farther from the high-water line than seeds could easily be thrown by the heavy surf which often rages along the coasts. There seems, therefore, no doubt at all about the dispersal of these species to Surtsey—this has been accomplished by the sea. The sixth species, *Festuca rubra*, might also have been dispersed to Surtsey by sea considering the short distance from the nearest islands; e.g. Súlnasker is only about 10 km east-northeast of Surtsey (Fridriksson and Johnsen, 1967). This suggestion is supported by the fact that this species is commonly found on the coasts of Iceland. But it is also possible that *F. rubra* has been dispersed this short distance by birds, as many birds have been observed in Surtsey, especially on the coasts (Gudmundsson, 1966 and 1967).

As might have been expected, the seeds of these coastal plant species do not seem to have any difficulties in germinating on the coasts of Surtsey, but due to the heavy surf, the loose sand and tephra, and the sand drift on the coasts, the plants have some difficulty in establishing themselves and especially in surviving the strong winds and high water during the winter. Only when the seeds succeed in getting some distance from the surf do the plants seem to be able to establish themselves. More species of coastal plants may just as easily be dispersed to Surtsey within a short period and be able to establish themselves on the uniform substrata of the coast. But it is rather unlikely that seeds of non-coastal species would germinate on the coasts and even more unlikely that they would be able to establish themselves there.

Dispersal of light seeds by birds or by wind should also be possible over the short distances between the other islands in Vestmannaeyjar and Surtsey and even across the distance of 32 km from the Icelandic mainland (Van der Pijl, 1969). Some such species might be able to establish themselves in the interior of Surtsey.

In 1967, Fridriksson and his assistants (Fridriksson and Sigurdsson, 1968 and 1969) caught about a hundred migratory birds in Surtsey; about a third of these were snow buntings, *Plectrophenax nivalis*, not belonging to the Icelandic race of the species and therefore probably on migration from the British Isles to Greenland. Almost a third of the snow buntings were found to have seeds as well as grit in the gizzard. Most of the grit was tephra from Surtsey, probably picked up by the birds on the coasts, but some of it was of metamorphic rock types and sediments not found in Iceland and probably of British origin. By far most of the seeds belonged to *Empetrum* sp. but a few belonged to four other Icelandic species of vascular plants and *one single seed* was identified as *Andromeda polifolia* L. which has not been found in Iceland. Single seeds of *Carex nigra* (L.) Reichard and *Polygonum persicaria* L. were found, and they were the only ones from these snow buntings which were able to germinate. From this Fridriksson concluded, because a part of the grit is of foreign origin and because of the single seed of *Andromeda*, that the snow buntings have probably carried the seeds from the British Isles. To me this conclusion seems somewhat doubtful, since if most of the grit had been picked up on the coasts of Surtsey (as seems certain) the seeds may have been picked up there also. The one seed identified as *Andromeda* might have drifted to Surtsey together with litter from passing ships, as the waters around Vestmannaeyjar are common routes for ships sailing to Iceland from abroad.

Many of the specimens of *C. maritima* ssp. *islandica*, an annual, flowered and a number of fruits were formed in the summer of 1967. Nevertheless, not a single specimen of *Cakile* was found in Surtsey the following year. Perhaps the seeds did not become fully ripe or perhaps they were all covered by too much sand to be able to germinate the next year. I have no explanation for the absence of *Cakile* from Surtsey in 1968. No other species have yet flowered on the island, but *Elymus* is known to reproduce vegetatively by stolons and should therefore be expected to reproduce rather soon.

It is of course too early to see any developmental patterns of plant communities in Surtsey as far as vascular plants are concerned because the few specimens which have so far succeeded in establishing themselves on the island are scattered completely at random.

Most of the nine species of mosses which have been found are common in Iceland, mainly in the lowlands; e.g. species like *Bryum argenteum*, *B. capillare*, *Dichodontium pellucidum*, *Funaria hygrometrica*, *Leptobryum pyriforme*, and *Polytrichum urnigerum* (Hesselbo, 1918). *B. argenteum* and *F. hygrometrica* are very common in inhabited areas (Jóhannsson, personal communication). Spores or vegetative parts of these mosses could therefore easily have been dispersed to Surtsey over the short distances mentioned above either by wind, birds, or man. No fertile specimens of mosses have so far been observed on Surtsey.

A certain pattern is apparent in the distribution of mosses in the interior of Surtsey. Most of the moss clusters are growing in thin tephra layers on lava which is still warm and at just the right distance from steam-producing holes in the lava; at these places the tephra is slightly wet from the steam but is not too hot. Where the tephra is too dry, the mosses or other vegetation are not as resistant to the effects of drifting sand.

Airborne microorganisms have been collected in Surtsey and reported by Kolbeinsson (1967 and 1968) and Kolbeinsson and Fridriksson (1965). Only saprophytic bacteria and molds were found.

ACKNOWLEDGEMENTS

Acknowledgements are made to Bergthór Jóhannsson, Museum of Natural History in Reykjavík, for identifying most of the mosses and to the Surtsey Research Society which sponsored this work with a grant from the U. S. Atomic Energy Commission, Biology Branch, under contract No. AT(30-1)3549.

LITERATURE CITED

Einarsson, E. 1965. Report of dispersal of plants to Surtsey. *Proc. Surtsey Bio. Conf.* Appendix II, 19–21.

Einarsson, E. 1966. On dispersal of plants to Surtsey. *Surtsey Res. Progr. Rep.* II, 19–21.

Einarsson, E. 1967. The colonization of Surtsey, the new volcanic island, by vascular plants. *Aquilo. Ser. Bot.* 6, 172–182.

Einarsson, E. 1968. Comparative ecology of colonizing species of vascular plants. *Surtsey Res. Progr. Rep.* IV, 9–22.

Einarsson, Th. 1967. Der Surtsey Ausbruch. *Naturwissenschaftliche Rundschau* 20, 239–247.

Fridriksson, S. 1964. Um adflutning lífvera til Surtseyjar. *Náttúrufrædingurinn.* 34, 83–89.

Fridriksson, S. 1965. Fjörukál (Cakile edentula) í Surtsey og fræflutningur á sjó. *Náttúrufrædingurinn.* 35, 97–102.

Fridriksson, S. 1966. The possible oceanic dispersal of seed and other plant parts to Surtsey. *Surtsey Res. Progr. Rep.* II, 59–62.

Fridriksson, S. 1967. A second species of vascular plants discovered in Surtsey. *Surtsey Res. Progr. Rep.* III, 17–19.

Fridriksson, S. 1969. Snjótittlingar hugsanlegir frædreifendur. *Náttúrufrædingurinn.* 39, 32–40.

Fridriksson, S., and Björn Johnsen. 1967. On the vegetation of the Outer Westman Isles. 1966. *Surtsey Res. Progr. Rep.* III, 20–36.

Fridriksson, S., and Björn Johnsen. 1968. The colonization of vascular plants on Surtsey in 1967. *Surtsey Res. Progr. Rep.* IV, 31–38.

Fridriksson, S., and H. Sigurdson. 1968. Dispersal of seeds by snow buntings to Surtsey in 1967. *Surtsey Res. Progr. Rep.* IV, 43–50.

Gudmundsson, F. 1966. Birds observed on Surtsey. *Surtsey Res. Progr. Rep.* II, 23–28.

Gudmundsson, F. 1967. Bird observations on Surtsey in 1966. *Surtsey Res. Progr. Rep.* III, 37–41.

Hesselbo, Aug. 1918. The Bryophyta of Iceland. In: *The botany of Iceland*, Vol. 1, 4. Copenhagen.

Jóhannsson, B. 1968. Bryological observations on Surtsey. *Surtsey Res. Progr. Rep.* IV, 61–62.

Johnsen, Baldur. 1939. Observations on the vegetation of the Westman Islands. *Soc. Sci. Isl.* XXII, 1–41.

Johnsen, Baldur. 1948. Gródurríki Vestmannaeyja. *Árbók Ferdafelags Íslands.* 1948, 184–190.

Kolbeinsson, A. 1967. A preliminary report on studies of microorganisms on Surtsey. *Surtsey Res. Progr. Rep.* III, 57–58.

Kolbeinsson, A. 1968. Report on studies of microorganisms on Surtsey, 1967. *Surtsey Res. Progr. Rep.* IV, 75–76.

Kolbeinsson, A., and S. Fridriksson. 1965. A Report on the first isolation of microorganisms on Surtsey. *Proc. Surtsey Biol. Conf.* Appendix I, 15–18.

Löve, D. 1963. Dispersal and survival of plants. In: *North Atlantic biota and their history.* p. 198–205. Oxford.

Sigtryggsson, H. 1968. Preliminary report on meteorological observations in Surtsey, 1967. *Surtsey Res. Progr. Rep.* IV, 167–170.

Steinthórsson, S. 1965. Surtsey: petrology and chemistry. *Surtsey Res. Progr. Rep.* I, 41–49.

Steinthórsson, S. 1966. Petrography and chemistry. *Surtsey Res. Progr. Rep.* II, 77–86.

Thórarinsson, S. 1965. Sitt af hverju um Surtseyjargosid. *Náttúrufrædingurinn.* **35**, 153–181.

Thórarinsson, S. 1967a. The Surtsey eruption and related scientific work. *The Polar Record* **13**, 571–578.

Thórarinsson, S. 1967b. The Surtsey eruption, course of events in the year 1966. *Surtsey Res. Progr. Rep.* III, 84–91.

Thórarinsson, S. 1968. The Surtsey eruption, course of events during the year 1967. *Surtsey Res. Progr. Rep.* IV, 143–148.

Thórarinsson, S. 1969. Sídustu thættir Eyjaelda. *Náttúrufrædingurinn.* **39**, 113–135.

Thórarinsson, S., Th. Einarsson, G. Sigvaldason, and G. Elísson. 1964. The submarine eruption off the Vestmann Islands 1963–1964. A Preliminary Report. *Extrait du Bulletin Volcanologique*, XXVII, 1–11 + XVIII, P1.

van der Pijl, L. 1969. *Principles of dispersal in higher plants.* Berlin. Heidelberg. New York.

Vedráttan. 1962. *Ársyfirlit samid á Vedurstofunni.* Reykjavík. 1963.

DISCUSSION

PETERSON: Up to this point, have you made any attempt to prohibit human visitors from bringing in seeds? Will it be possible to separate human-transported seeds from those transported by other means?

EINARSSON: The island has been declared a natural reserve, and visitors are not allowed. Only the working scitiensts are allowed to visit there, but of course, they may carry seeds with them. Some of the mosses might have been dispersed by man, for instance the *Funaria hygrometrica* and *Bryum argenteum* which are common almost everywhere in the islands, even in towns and villages. All the vascular plants growing on the coast of the island have, no doubt, been dispersed by sea, except *Festuca rubra* which might have been dispersed by birds, since it is very common on the nearest islands where birds are nesting. But even this species might have been dispersed by the sea.

CORNWELL: What could be the source of N for these invading plants? Were there ammonium or ammonium salts in the eruptions, and could these be leached out?

EINARSSON: We have tried to collect samples of airborne micro-organisms, but only saprophytic bacteria have been found. The seaweeds carried ashore by the surf and buried in sand and decaying there may be a source of N.

CORNWELL: Is there evidence of ammonium availability from the fresh rock materials?

EINARSSON: No, I don't think so.

BAUER: You have found the same moss species on this volcanic island that I have found on brown-coal dust in the Cologne lignite district.

EINARSSON: Of the nine moss species found on the island, at least seven are common in all of Iceland, especially in the lowlands. Some of them have a cosmopolitan distribution, like *Funaria hygrometrica* which is the most common moss on Surtsey.

HODGSON: The first colonizer of pulverized fuel ashes is *Funaria hygrometrica*; under moist conditions pure cultures completely cover the surface.

TEN YEARS' STUDIES OF BIOCENOLOGICAL SUCCESSION IN THE EXCAVATED MINES OF THE COLOGNE LIGNITE DISTRICT

Hermann Josef Bauer

District Commissioner for Nature Conservation and Landscape Management, Aachen District, and Lecturer in Faunistics, Institute of Zoology, Technical College of Aachen, West Germany.

The rapidly changing landscape of the excavated mines in the Cologne Lignite District presents a rare opportunity for the study of biocenological successions. Many of the biocenoses that came into existence were unknown in the pre-industrial landscape.

The main ecotope groups on the excavated mines are gravel slopes, gravel plains and reclaimed fields, coal-dust areas, and depressions and lakes. On the first three sites, and particularly on the coal-dust areas, edaphic, hydrologic, and microclimatic conditions are often extreme. Nevertheless there is a spontaneous rapid colonization by various plants and animals. Then tree and shrub seedlings become established. The landscape changes appearance from desert-like to grass-steppe and then more gradually to savanna-like. Even later, the tree canopies close, environmental conditions change, and the initial invaders largely disappear. Only then does competition begin to play a dominant role in the determination of the final composition of the plant and animal association.

The new lakes, on the other hand, from the very beginning rapidly develop typical plant associations corresponding to the edaphic-hydrologic zones where conditions are ecologically homogeneous and balanced.

Such studies have disclosed certain laws of plant associations and succession which are of great value in the reclamation of excavated mines.

LANDSCAPE ECOLOGY AND SUCCESSION

The Cologne Lignite District presents a rare opportunity to study the ecology of a rapidly changing landscape. Ten years' continuous detailed analysis of the various ecotopes has provided insight into the sequence of biocenological succession. Not just plant succession but biocenological succession and, after some years, landscape succession take place in these disturbed areas.

The primary disturbance of the excavated areas shows, on a miniature scale, the complete range of fluvial erosion on the bare slopes of the artificial hills with their earthen pyramids, ravines, and landslides. The abiotic factors—extreme edaphic, hydrologic, and microclimatic conditions—render the development of revegetation rather difficult. Nevertheless there is a spontaneous, rapid colonization by various plants. The disturbed areas become—by natural revegetation or by reclamation—ecologically balanced landscapes, even suitable for many types of recreation. Such disturbed areas may be called experimental fields of landscape succession. Our investigations of the dynamics of the ecological factors and conditions, and thereby of the ecosystem, enable us to formulate biocenological rules.

METHOD FOR CONTINUOUS STUDIES

After analysis of the ecological factors, both abiotic and biotic, a synthetic view of the interplay within the ecotopes is made. This permits us to survey the ecosystem, and thereby characterize the ecology of the different ecotopes.

A relevant spatial and temporal change in one of these factors indicates that the border of the adjacent ecotope is reached. A certain amount of tolerance exists and can be recognized in the so-called "differential species" of the plant associations. Within the ecotopes we observe this tolerance as an ecological gradient. Similar ecotopes (for instance lakes and their environment) can be connected as ecotope-groups or ecotope-complexes. The problem of delineation of the ecotopes will be dealt with in my paper on aerial photo interpretation (Bauer, 1973).

THE ECOTOPE-GROUPS OF THE LIGNITE DISTRICT

The excavated mines, which are reclaimed either naturally or by man, include the following main ecotope-groups, each with a different kind of biocenological succession: gravel slopes, gravel plains and reclaimed fields, coal-dust areas, and depressions and lakes.

Gravel slopes

Abiotic factors The important abiotic factors are gravel, sand, and clay contents, low organic-matter contents, all types of erosion, acid soils (pH 5 to 6.2), little water, and extreme microclimatic conditions (high insolation, frequent frosts, strong winds, and daily temperature amplitudes of 40 C).

Pioneer vegetation Pioneer species include: *Calamagrostis epigeios*, *Oenothera biennis*, *Poa annua*, *Bromus sterilis*, and others. A spotty and island-like vegetation indicates the poor conditions for germination. Because the pioneers are mostly annual plants, when their tops die they supply material for humus formation. The added humus improves the soil by increasing its cation exchange capacity and thereby its ability to accumulate nutrients. The dense root growth of the plants inhibits soil erosion, and the leaf cover reduces the soil-drying insolation and promotes an even micro-climate.

Natural reforestation Seeds of woody vegetation (*Salix, Betula, Populus tremula, Robinia*) are carried in by wind or drifted to the site by water and the quickly growing trees prevent further erosion. The pioneer plants soon die out because of increasing shade. After about 8 years, the slopes are covered with a young forest including a group of plants typical of forest-edge communities, for instance the *Melilotus alba – Echium vulgare* association. A strange type of forest, characterized by wide spaces between the trees, develops where there is a source of *Robinia pseudoacacia* seeds. A large portion of the solar radiation reaches the ground, and a dense herb and shrub cover, with climbing plants such as *Clematis vitalba*, *Hedera helix*, *Rubus*, and *Ribes*, is the result. A nitrophilous shrub which appears only in the *Robinia* forests is *Sambucus niger*. *Robinia* shows an allelopathy toward some other plants which is due to poisons (Robin and Robinin) in the roots, bark, seeds, and leaves (Hegi, n.d.; Knapp, 1954; Kohler, 1963). This is evidenced by the low number of species in the herb and shrub layers.

Reforestation by man In most cases the slopes are planted at once. Twenty years ago, *Populus* was most commonly used; now a variety of species are planted. The trees grow very well, and after a few years, we have a young, mixed forest.

Biocenological succession Many insects, birds, and other animals of the open landscape soon appear. With the growing number of plant species, increasing food supply, and better possibilities for breeding in older mixed forests, a larger number of animal species and a greater population density are found.

Gravel plains and reclaimed fields

Abiotic factors Wind erosion, frost, and biochemical conditions are similar to those on gravel slopes. Loess-covered fields are the best agricultural soils (good water permeability and good conditions for the establishment of pioneer vegetation).

Pioneer vegetation and animals Depending upon the type of soil, either xerophilic or hygrophilic plants or weeds (in fields) appear. The unreclaimed areas are totally overgrown after five years or less. The first vegetation is *Calamagrostis epigeios* accompanied by some other pioneer plants.

With the advent of the first plants, the first animals also appear, e.g. the lapwing, which has an unusual breeding place between the gravel stones (Fig. 1). *Charadrius dubius* and many other animals, especially insects and birds, appear.

FIGURE 1   Eggs of lapwing between the gravel.

Natural reforestation The same trees as appear on the slopes become established rather soon on the gravel plains. When *Calamagrostis* is suppressed due to lack of light, species of the forest-edge communities appear.

Gradual development of a soil profile, and later the presence of true forest herbs, can be observed; still later a trend toward an oak-hornbeam, oak-birch or oak-beech forest is noted. An increasing number of forest birds and other forest animals become established in these natural forests.

Reforestation and reclamation of fields Within the variously structured new plant communities, many animal species of field and forest biotopes find ample opportunity for food, breeding, and cover. The fields (loess-covered) are surrounded by wind-sheltering shrubs.

Biocenological succession The biocenological succession develops from single individuals in the first pioneer stages to a closed forest population. Many insects (beetles, bees, and butterflies) occur on the flowering plants of the forest edges and on the wind-sheltering shrubs. Fruit-bearing shrubs, such as *Sorbus*, *Betula*, *Alnus*, and *Prunus*, are important sources of nourishment for birds such as larks, pipits, pheasants, and thrushes.

Coal-dust areas

Until opencast pits are filled with gravel, sand, or loess, their surfaces are covered with coal dust of low economic value.

Abiotic factors The important abiotic factors are acidity (pH 4.2 to 5.7); high content of organic substance and humic acids (22%); wind erosion; below-freezing temperatures, even in summer, caused by settling of cold air in the deep pits; and intense insolation causing temperatures above 40 C with daily amplitudes of 40 C.

Pioneer vegetation Spotty islands of mosses (*Funaria hygrometrica*) are the first to appear. *Ceratodon purpureus* and others come in on moist ground. Even in the areas of higher moisture, only a few species of higher plants can become established (Fig. 2). These are the ones—like *Calamagrostis*, *Tussilago farfara*, *Oenothera biennis*—which are adapted to dry sites by their dense or deeply-penetrating root systems.

Natural reforestation Even on these extreme soils, we find some species of trees: *Betula verrucosa*, *Salix caprea*, *Populus tremula*, and *Robinia pseudoacacia*. The next step in succession might be a heath with *Betula*, except that there is no heather nearby from which seeds could be brought in by animals.

18*

Reforestation by man Planting of trees on these coal-dust areas is useless; such areas must first be covered with gravel, sand, or loess.

FIGURE 2   Pioneer vegetation on coal dust (*Calomagrostis* and *Oenothera*).

Depressions and lakes

In depressions of surface-mined areas, precipitation and groundwater accumulate to form small, or sometimes even large, lakes. This introduces new elements into the landscape; it influences the ecoclimate and the distribution of soil water, and provides a new habitat for many plant and animal species.

Abiotic factors Special types of lakes are formed. They are 0.5 to 15 m deep, with very steep shores and complete circulation (water temperatures are the same at all depths). The pH is between 4.4 and 6.5; they are very low in N, high in Ca (as calcium sulfate), and extremely hard (up to 60° on the German scale although hardness due to carbonate is low).

Pioneer vegetation   Many species of mosses appear at once; these are followed by water plants and swamp vegetation. Wind and birds bring in some rare plants previously unknown in this region. Even in the first year, a zonation according to the edaphic-hydrological requirements of the plants can be observed.

Development of vegetational belts   Within 7 years, a complete series of vegetation belts develops; these range from natural forests through meadows to reeds and water lilies and finally to submerged plants.

Biocenological succession   We soon observe the development of a labile dynamic equilibrium. Dense vegetation belts permit the development of biocenoses with many water birds (such as *Acrocephalus arundinacea*, *Larus canus*, and *Podiceps cristatus*), fishes, toads, and frogs (eggs of which are brought in by waterfowl), and numerous beetles, butterflies, water beetles, and dragonflies. Some of these lakes develop into bogs.

BIOCENOLOGICAL RULES OF LANDSCAPE SUCCESSION

The ten-year study of biocenological succession in the initially disturbed but later regenerated landscape led to the discovery of the dynamics of the ecotopes and their biocenoses. The succession is not limited to the vegetation but involves the whole ecosystem. The following rules give general information concerning the abiotic and biotic conditions and permit comparative research on succession in different landscapes and climatic regions. These rules of landscape succession in disturbed areas outline the possibilities for both natural and man-made regeneration and thereby enable increases in agricultural and forested areas.

Factors of pioneer settlement and plant succession

1)   If we assume that all seeds and animals have an equal chance to reach the site, the community which develops identifies the defined ecotope. The ability to germinate rapidly and low demands on the environment are the factors which select the successful invaders from the multitude of plant species which chance upon the area or are dragged in by animals.

Microclimatic conditions also influence the pioneer vegetation. Animals settle immediately in those ecotopes which are favorable for breeding, living, and feeding.

2) Pfeiffer (1963) called attention to the fact that the new settlement can be compared with the diffusion of single particles according to statistical chance. This supports my observations that the new settlement is a chance combination of species without regard to natural plant associations.

3) The relatively low number of species, frequently present only in vegetational islands, scarcely increases during the following years. The species arriving later do not supplant the first settlers but only fill free niches. Therefore we find a mosaic of different plant species, but not of plant associations.

4) As long as there is no closed vegetation cover the typical pioneer forms (tufts of grasses, stolons, and rosettes) remain.

5) Every association development takes time. After 10 years, firmly established plant associations do not yet exist. Pioneer plants retain their areas and prevent the germination of newly-arrived plants. However in humid ecotopes, as under ecologically homogeneous conditions, all typical species of the various plant associations are present within a few years.

6) After some years, however, bushes or trees begin to grow, and the ecological conditions slowly change. Species which reproduce vegetatively, and hence compete more successfully, persist; the chance settlers disappear because of increasing shade, and forest species are added. Environmental conditions, such as shade and soil properties, are more important than competition as such since there is enough space. A period of quick growth follows the pioneer stage. It is only after more than 10 years that competition begins to play a role in the determination of the final association; this occurs after the vegetational cover is closed or after the microclimate has changed due to shading by trees. Then the only plants that persist are those favored in competition by their physiological constitution or those which can adapt themselves to the changed ecological conditions.

7) Only at the lakes, where ecologically homogeneous and balanced conditions are present from the beginning, do the plant associations typical for the specific edaphic-hydrological zones appear.

8) Because of the greater variety of ecotopes, the disturbed areas support more plant species and final associations than were present in the pre-industrial landscape. This underlines the statement of Tüxen (1960) that the number of primary associations (*Anfangsgesellschaften*) is always greater than the number of climax associations (*Schlußgesellschaften*). In short, there is a trend toward greater uniformity of ecological conditions.

Landscape succession

The desert-like ecotopes of the excavated mines, though initially without plants and animals and with extreme edaphic, hydrologic, and climatic conditions, are nevertheless quickly occupied by various plants (xerophilic

FIGURE 3   An excavated mine (gravel–reed–lake). In the background is the lignite layer and an industrial development.

FIGURE 4   The same mine as in Fig. 3, 5 years later.

species, plants requiring high light intensity for germination, and species which are largely indifferent to ecologic conditions). *Calamagrostis epigeios* is dominant at first, and the landscape resembles a grass-steppe with corresponding animal life (hare, partridge, pheasant, and ground-breeders

FIGURE 5   A *Calamagrostis* "steppe" evolving into a *Robinia* "savanna".

FIGURE 6   A new lake with pioneer vegetation in an excavated mine.

such as plovers and lapwings). The landscape gradually changes into a "savanna" with some of the trees named above (Fig. 3–5). Later the initially disturbed areas are covered by natural forests inhabited by many species of plants and animals, especially insects and birds.

Hygric sites (lakes and bogs) are model cases for studies of landscape ecology and landscape succession. The biocenoses develop in a rapid and regular sequence. Because of the physiological and ecological reactions typical of water and bog plants, they will germinate only in those zones which are favorable for them. The vegational zones at lakes do not result from a gradual selection due to competition between species, but are evident even in the pioneer stage. Only a few species are added later to the different vegetational belts. After 10 to 15 years the biocenoses are complete, with all kinds of waterbirds, fishes, and insects (Figs. 6 and 7).

FIGURE 7   Complete vegetation belts along a 15-year-old lake.

GUIDING PRINCIPLES FOR RECLAMATION

The investigation of natural revegetation and succession of ecotopes over prolonged time periods permits the formulation of guiding principles for reclamation of areas disturbed by mining. A few of these principles, established by Darmer and Bauer (1969), are:

1)   Gravel dumps should not stand isolated and should not be higher than 80 meters. The general inclination should not be steeper than 1 : 3.

2)   For agricultural reclamation, a loess cover at least 1.5 m deep is necessary.

3)   Extreme microclimatic conditions must be modified and a balanced bioclimate developed through formation of a suitable relief and establishment of shelterbelts.

4)   Water controls productivity; regulated irrigation and drainage, shelterbelts, and lakes balance the humidity of air and soil.

5)   Because of the extreme ecological conditions, trees must be planted at once and fields must be seeded promptly while the soil is still loose and well-aerated. One should not wait for weathering of the soil material or formation of humus because fine-textured material may be blown or washed away. At any rate, the soil becomes more dense during any period that reclamation is delayed.

6)   The more varied the plant cover and the better ecologically adapted it is, the better are the opportunities for animal establishment.

7)   In addition, the formerly disturbed areas may become useful for recreation; the varied ecotopes of the forest-field-lake landscape offer ideal conditions for this use.

LITERATURE CITED

Darmer, G., and H. J. Bauer. 1969. Landschaft und Tagebau. Grundlagen und Leitsätze für die landschaftspflegerische Neugestaltung einer ökologisch ausgewogenen rekultivierten Kulturlandschaft im Rheinischen Braunkohlenrevier. In: *Neue Landschaft*, 11/12.

Hegi, G. n. d. *Illustrierte Flora von Mitteleuropa*, Band IV, 3, München.

Knapp, R. 1954. Experimentelle Soziologie der höheren Pflanzen. Ulmer Verlag, Stuttgart.

Kohler, A. 1963. Zum pflanzensoziologischen Verhalten der Robinie in Deutschland. Beiträge naturk. Forsch. SW-Deutschland, Band XXII.

Pfeiffer, H. 1963. Vom gesetzlichen Verhalten der Pioniere bei Neuland-Besiedlung. Mitteilungen d. floristisch-soziologischen Arbeitsgemeinschaft N. F. 10, S. 87–91, Stolzenau.

Tüxen, R. 1965. Wesenszüge der Biozönose. Gesetze des Zusammenlebens von Pflanzen und Tieren. Biosoziologie: *Bericht über das Internationale Symposium in Stolzenau 1960*. Verlag Junk, Den Haag.

Troll, C. 1963. Über Landschafts-Sukzession. Vorwort zu Bauer, H. J.: *Landschaftsökologische Untersuchungen im ausgekohlten rheinischen Braunkohlenrevier auf der Ville*. Verlag Dümmler, Bonn.

DISCUSSION

ROTHWELL: Did you notice any antagonism of the toxins in *Robinia* to the nodulating organisms?

BAUER: *Robinia* nodulate of course.

KNABE: There could be some microorganism in America, which we haven't in Europe, which rapidly decomposes these toxins of the *Robinia*.

SCHLATZER: Have you seen *Populus tremula* growing as seedlings? It has difficulty establishing by seeds.

BAUER: Yes, the seeds come in by wind. It is quite common on all ecotopes, on sand or gravel or even on coal-dust areas.

SCHLATZER: Couldn't it be roots brought up with some part of the topsoil? The young seedling is extremely tender. A heavy rain drop may topple it anytime during the first 3 days. For the first fortnight it cannot stand intensive sunshine, a heavy shower or strong wind, and therefore we consider it particularly ill-adapted for reproduction from seed.

BAUER: Well, I even saw "islands" of 10 to 20 seedlings, especially within canopies of mosses.

SCHLATZER: That is interesting but these could be spots where topsoil containing roots has come in. Young suckers may resemble seedlings very much.

PRETO: Did you study the surrounding natural vegetation and correlate it to the pioneer stages of vegetation on the spoil bank?

BAUER: Yes, I investigated the wooded areas in the vicinity of the disturbed areas. Most of the new species come from these woody areas, but there are many species previously unknown in this area, or even in the whole region of the Rhineland. Waterfowl especially brought many seeds and even eggs of toads, frogs, and fishes from great distances. There are now many lakes in this region where previously there were only woods and fields.

NATURAL REVEGETATION AND CAST OVERBURDEN PROPERTIES OF SURFACE-MINED COAL LANDS IN SOUTHERN INDIANA*

W. R. Byrnes and J. H. Miller

Professor and former Graduate Assistant, Department of Forestry and Conservation, Purdue University, Lafayette, Indiana.

Natural vegetation development was studied on surface-mined coal lands in the unglaciated section of southern Indiana. Cast overburden resulting from surface mining was characterized by an undulating "ridge-trough" topography, a surface mosaic of mixed rock fragments, and variable soil properties. Plant invasion begins during the first year after disturbance on the most favorable spots, with a preponderance of vegetation occurring in the "troughs", while intervening toxic patches of overburden remain devoid of plant cover for up to 45 years. Soil pH below 3.5 and specific conductance above 2 mmhos/cm were apparently toxic and limited plant establishment. Characteristic species with the highest frequency of occurrence were: TREES—*Betula nigra, Populus deltoides, Diospyros virginiana*, and *Sassafras albidum*; SHRUBS—*Rhus glabra* and *R. Copallinum*; VINES—*Rubus* spp., *Rhus radicans*, and *Lonicera japonica*; HERBS— *Eupatorium serotinum, Phytolacca americana, Lactuca* spp., *Diodia teres, Solidago* spp., and *Aster* spp.; and GRASSES—*Aristida* spp., *Andropogon virginicus*, and *Panicum* spp.

INTRODUCTION

By 1969, there were approximately 95,000 acres of land disturbed by surface mining for coal in southern Indiana. In the mining operation the overburden, composed of rock strata and soil mantle above the coal seam,

---

* Based on research conducted by J. H. Miller in partial fulfillment of requirements for the Master of Science degree, Purdue University, Lafayette, Ind. In cooperation with the Midwest Coal Producers Institute, Inc. and Central States Forest Experiment Station Forest Service, U. S. Department of Agriculture.

is removed and deposited in an unconsolidated mass termed cast overburden. The resultant cast overburden is heterogeneous and characterized
by an undulating "ridge-trough" topography with surface features appear-
ing as a mosaic of sandstone, shale, limestone, coal, and residual soil.
Consequently the nature of the cast overburden is dependent upon the type
and quantity of rock and soil material present and the method of mining,
which may result in differential mixing. These variables interacting with
local climate dictate the physical and chemical properties of the cast overburden as a plant growth medium.

Numerous investigations have been conducted to determine the most
suitable plant species and cultural methods to be utilized for artificial
revegetation of cast overburden, but relatively little is known about natural
plant succession that ensues after mining. It is apparent that most surface-
mined coal lands, whether or not they are artificially revegetated, support
some form of local flora. This invasion of natural vegetation, although
possibly competitive with planted species in some areas, may be very
beneficial in amelioration of physical, chemical, and biological soil properties and also contribute much needed plant cover for erosion control
and wildlife utilization.

To provide further insight on ecological relationships of surface-mined
coal lands, an investigation was conducted in 1968 in the unglaciated
portion of Pike County, Ind. Objective of the study was to describe the
natural plant communities in relation to certain site factors on cast overburden of varying ages.

NATURAL REVEGETATION

Early investigations on natural revegetation of surface-mined coal lands
in the Midwest were conducted by McDougall (1918) and Croxton (1928)
in Illinois. McDougall studied plant succession on a glaciated bottomland
site ranging in age from 2 to 18 years following disturbance and concluded
that the site was reverting to a bottomland hardwood forest. Croxton
described a "Polygonum Stage" dominated by smartweed (*Polygonum
pennsylvanicum* L.) with numerous herbaceous associates which invaded
quickly and persisted for 2 to 5 years on cast overburden. The Polygonum
Stage was replaced by white sweet clover* on basic soils and by ragweed,
red sorrel, and partridge-pea on the very acid areas. Croxton found that
tree species such as cottonwood, sycamore, sugar maple (*Acer saccharum*

---

* For species mentioned in the text but whose scientific names are not given, see Table 6.

Marsh.), American elm (*Ulmus americana* L.) and persimmon invaded at various stages of succession.

In Ohio, several studies, mostly of an observational nature, were made of natural revegetation on cast overburden. Graham (1947), working on unglaciated areas of southeastern Ohio, indicated that annual weeds invaded at 1 year, perennial weeds at 3 years, and grasses at 5 years; this was followed by development of a shrub layer at 10 years and a tree layer at 20 years. Merz and Plass (1952) recorded tree species including sycamore, sugar maple, elm, yellow-poplar, and white oak (*Quercus alba* L.) on a bottomland site 2 years after mining. Limstrom (1952) reported on naturally occurring species on surface-mined coal lands in Ohio and also in Illinois and Kansas.

The only previous investigation in Indiana (Deitschman and Lane, 1952) was limited to a study of tree species invading 30-year-old cast overburden in the glaciated region of the state. Deitschman recorded an average of 4631 trees/acre ranging from seedlings under 5 ft in height to sawtimber up to 18 in. in diameter. Eighty percent of the tree species present were reportedly low-value hardwoods and 20% commercially valuable species, but these were mostly open-grown trees with poor form.

PROCEDURE

Study area

The investigation of natural vegetation was conducted in Pike County, Ind., which contains in excess of 21,500 acres of land disturbed by surface mining for coal. The southern portion of the county, located in southeastern Indiana, is unglaciated, while the northern half was subjected to some glaciation during the Illinoian and Wisconsin glacial periods. The stratigraphy above the coal seam exhibits a preponderance of shale and shaly sand, massive sandstone, and some limestone and limestone nodules interspersed within the shale. Calcareous and carbonaceous shale deposits occur immediately above the coal seam, which averages 5 to 6 ft in thickness.

The climate of Pike County is characterized by a mean annual precipitation of 41 in., with good distribution throughout the year but with drought during July and August; mean annual temperature is 55 F, with mean and maximum summer temperatures of 76 and 111 F, respectively. An average frost-free growing season of 184 days extends from April 16 to October 17.

Seventeen study areas were selected for investigation in the unglaciated portion of Pike County on unreclaimed cast overburden of the "Coal V" seam. Selected study areas ranged in age since termination of mining from less than 1 to 45 years. Dependent upon the predominant geologic material of the cast overburden, these areas were designated sandy sites, shaly sites, or mixed sites.

Relief of cast overburden resulting from surface mining is a typical ridge-trough topography with distinct relief positions such as ridge, trough, and slope, differing in aspect and exposure. Topography of the 17 study areas is characterized by mean ridge elevations ranging from 11 to 21 ft, slope angles of 26° to 33°, slope lengths of 22 to 38 ft, and ridge-top widths of 5 to 15 ft. Trough width varied with age of cast overburden due to erosion and subsequent alluviation from less than 1 ft on newly disturbed areas to 17 ft after 34 years.

Properties of cast overburden

On each study area, cast overburden was analyzed by relief position to evaluate surface features and properties of the upper 6 inches of soil that may influence vegetation invasion and development. Surface features were limited to an estimation of the percent of rock fragments (sandstone, shale, and limestone), coal, and soil material free of stones in milacre quadrats. Cast overburden samples of the surface 6-in. layer were sieved to separate fractions of rocks greater than 1 in., rocks between 1 in. and 2 mm, and soil-sized particles less than 2 mm.

Soil-sized particles (less than 2 mm) were analyzed by the revised Bouyoucos (1951) hydrometer method to determine percent sand, silt, and clay; by the pressure plate apparatus at one-third atm for field capacity moisture content; and by the pressure membrane method at 15 atm for moisture content at wilting percentage. Available moisture-holding capacity was calculated as the difference between field capacity and wilting percentage moisture contents.

Analyses of chemical properties included soil reaction of a 1 : 1 soil-water suspension; specific conductance of a 1 : 2 soil-water extract; and extractable P, K, Ca, and Mg.

Natural vegetation

Observations on natural vegetation were made during late June and July, when early summer annual and biennial plants were mature and late season perennials were in initial or rosette stages. Cover and sociability estimates by a modified system of Braun-Blanquet (1932) were made on

0.01-acre plots by relief position and vegetation layer within each of the 17 study areas. Vegetation layers designated were *Ground Layer*, under 4 ft in height, *Shrub Layer*, from 4 to 10 ft, and *Tree Layer*, greater than 10 ft in height. Plants occurring within vegetation layers were classified as herb, grass, shrub and woody vine, and tree species.

Cover, based on a 1 to 7 scale, and sociability, on a 1 to 5 scale, were expressed as the mode of all observations within a study area. Cover classes were: 1 = covering less than 0.1% of the sampled area; 2 = covering 0.1 to 1%; 3 = 1 to 5%; 4 = 5 to 25%; 5 = 25 to 50%; 6 = 50 to 75%; and 7 = 75 to 100%. Sociability classes were: 1 = growing one in a place (singly); 2 = grouped or tufted; 3 = in troops, small patches, or cushions; 4 = small colonies, extensive patches, or carpets; and 5 = great crowds (pure population). Frequency of a species was expressed as the number of plots on which a species occurred divided by the total number of sample plots per study area.

RESULTS AND DISCUSSION

Cast overburden properties

The soil surface free of stones ranges from 12 to 61% among the 17 study areas (Table 1). Rocks lying on the surface of the "Sandy Site" were predominantly sandstone (covering 29 to 35% of the surface area); the "Shaly Site", mostly shale fragments (67 to 74%); and the "Mixed Site," a more balanced mixture of sandstone and shale. Limestone content was very low or absent on all but the two oldest study areas. Small amounts of coal were present on all sites, but it was most abundant on areas designated as mixed site.

These features provide information useful in classifying cast overburden based on surface distribution of geologic material and may be indicators of potential plant invasion. Furthermore, the relative amounts of various rock material will ultimately affect the texture of the residual soil after many years of weathering.

Mean soil content (fraction <2 mm) of the upper 6 in. of cast overburden ranged from 35 to 77% among study areas (Table 2). Although maximum and minimum values among samples within study areas are not included, only three sub-area samples exhibited content of soil-sized material below 20%. Soil content less than 20% has been considered a probable limiting factor to plant invasion on surface-mined coal land (Bramble and Ashley,

TABLE 1

Surface features of cast overburden by study area-age classes

Age class yr	Soil[a] %	Sandstone %	Shale %	Limestone %	Coal %
			Sandy Site		
<1	52	35	11	1	1
1	54	34	11	0	1
2	61	29	8	1	1
3	56	32	9	2	1
			Shaly Site		
<1	12	11	74	1	2
1	12	10	74	1	3
2	22	10	67	0	1
			Mixed Site		
2	18	68	11	1	2
3	50	41	4	1	4
5	18	50	23	1	8
7	18	59	20	1	2
11	23	43	32	1	1
15	28	43	18	1	10
21	27	40	26	1	6
24	31	49	4	1	5
34	55	8	15	15	7
45	26	15	34	24	1

[a] Soil surface free of stones.

1952; Clark, 1954). Particle-size distribution of the soil (< 2 mm) material on the Sandy Site was predominately sand (72 to 79%) resulting in a sandy loam texture with low moisture content at both field capacity and wilting point and correspondingly low available-water-holding capacity (Table 2). The silt plus clay content of soil material on the Shaly and Mixed Sites were generally one and one-half to two times greater than the Sandy Site, resulting in a heavier texture and relatively higher water-holding capacity (Table 2).

To provide some insight on variability of cast overburden within study areas, maximum and minimum as well as mean values are presented for pH and specific conductance (Table 3) and available P and exchangeable K (Table 4). Plantability scales devised for rating areas to be reclaimed in accord with pH (Limstrom, 1960) and specific conductance (Cummins, Plass, and Gentry, 1965) are included for comparative purposes (Table 3).

TABLE 2

Physical properties[a] of upper 6 inches of cast overburden by study area-age classes

Age class yr	Rock Content (%) >1 in.	Rock Content (%) 1 in.-2 mm	Soil (%) <2 mm	Particle Size Distribution (%) Sand	Particle Size Distribution (%) Silt	Particle Size Distribution (%) Clay	Textural Class[b]	Moisture Content[c] (%) Field Capacity	Moisture Content[c] (%) Wilting Point	Moisture Content[c] (%) Available Moisture[d]
Sandy Site										
<1	19	19	62	72	17	11	SL	13.6	3.7	9.9
1	11	12	77	79	12	9	SL	10.3	2.8	7.5
2	13	12	75	77	13	10	SL	11.8	3.3	8.5
3	12	24	64	72	16	12	SL	13.7	4.3	9.4
Shaly Site										
<1	27	40	35	39	39	22	L	21.2	8.0	13.2
1	24	30	46	48	33	19	L	20.7	8.6	12.1
2	23	35	42	47	35	18	L	18.9	6.3	12.6
Mixed Site										
2	18	35	47	50	30	20	L	19.2	7.1	12.1
3	14	21	65	65	22	13	SL	15.1	4.6	10.5
5	14	31	55	49	30	21	L	23.4	10.1	13.3
7	13	30	57	56	38	16	SL	21.9	8.0	13.9
11	11	21	68	44	36	20	L	21.2	8.2	13.0
15	10	30	60	45	32	23	L	23.4	9.9	13.5
21	11	30	59	45	32	23	L	26.1	11.7	14.4
24	10	24	66	45	31	24	L	25.3	10.1	15.2
34	4	23	73	53	25	22	SCL	21.2	8.5	12.7
45	12	22	66	60	24	16	SL	21.3	8.1	13.2

[a] Mean values of all data.

[b] SL = sandy loam, L = loam, SCL = sandy clay loam.

[c] Moisture content expressed in percent oven-dry weight.

[d] Difference between moisture content at field capacity and wilting point.

Limstrom's pH-system is based on the generalization that pH 4 or below is usually toxic to most plants. Cummins' et al. system utilizes Jackson's (1958) findings that specific conductance of 1 mmhos/cm may be critical for seed germination, 2 mmhos/cm critical for the growth of some salt-sensitive plants, and 3 mmhos/cm may result in severe plant injury.

TABLE 3

pH and specific conductance of cast overburden by study area-age classes

Age class yr	pH				Specific Conductance (mmhos/cm)			
	Mean	Max	Min	Plant-ability[a]	Mean	Max	Min	Plant-ability[b]
				Sandy Site				
<1	6.1	7.5	4.3	P	0.9	2.3	0.1	P
1	3.4	4.5	2.7	T	0.6	2.1	0.1	P
2	4.7	6.6	2.5	P	0.3	2.4	0.1	P
3	4.8	7.9	2.7	P	0.4	2.8	0.1	P
				Shaly Site				
<1	6.4	7.8	3.9	P	0.9	1.6	0.1	M
1	5.9	7.6	2.7	P	1.1	3.2	0.1	P
2	5.8	7.9	3.0	P	0.1	1.5	0.1	P
				Mixed Site				
2	7.2	8.2	5.9	P	0.3	2.3	0.1	P
3	5.0	6.7	3.0	P	0.1	0.4	0.1	P
5	4.0	7.2	2.5	T	1.1	2.4	0.3	M
7	4.7	7.6	3.3	P	0.6	2.0	0.1	P
11	4.2	5.8	3.1	P	0.3	1.4	0.1	P
15	4.2	7.4	2.6	P	0.6	2.8	0.1	P
21	3.6	5.3	2.7	T	0.8	3.2	0.1	P
24	4.2	7.2	2.5	M	0.5	3.1	0.1	P
34	4.9	7.6	3.5	P	0.3	2.1	0.1	P
45	5.2	7.0	4.1	P	0.1	0.3	0.1	P

[a] pH Plantability Standards presented by Limstrom (1960):
Toxic (T) – 70% or more of samples with pH less than 4.0.
Marginal (M) – 50 to 70% of the samples with pH less than 4.0.
Plantable (P) – more than 50% of the samples with pH 4.0 or over.
[b] Specific Conductance Plantability Standards presented by Cummins et al. (1965):
Toxic (T) – 70% or more of samples with specific conductance of 1 mmhos/cm or more.
Marginal (M) – 50 to 70% of samples with specific conductance of 1 mmhos/cm or more.
Plantable (P) – more than 50% of the samples with specific conductance of 1 mmhos/cm or less.

Three of the 17 study areas rated "toxic" and one "marginal" in regard to pH. However, it should be noted that those areas that have adverse ratings (toxic or marginal), as well as "plantable" areas, exhibit maximum pH values of 4.5 to 8.2. Conversely, all but three areas show minimum values below pH 4. It is apparent, therefore, that favorable spots for vegetation establishment and also very adverse spots occur within any one area. Further it is apparent that pH, based on values of pH 4 or below, may still be a limiting factor in plant establishment at least 34 years and possibly 45 years after disturbance.

Two study areas rated marginal to planting in regard to specific conductance (Table 3). As with pH, most areas exhibited maximum values possibly detrimental to plant establishment as well as minimum values under the 1 mmhos/cm level.

TABLE 4

Available phosphorus and exchangeable potassium in lb/acre in the cast overburden by study area-age classes

Age Class yr	Phosphorus				Potassium			
	Mean	Max	Min	Rating[a]	Mean	Max	Min	Rating[a]
			Sandy Site					
<1	13	54	2	Low	41	120	15	V. Low
1	14	61	1	Low	24	45	15	V. Low
2	11	67	2	Low	24	30	15	V. Low
3	10	36	2	V. Low	51	120	15	V. Low
			Shaly Site					
<1	3	4	2	V. Low	120	180	60	Low
1	4	10	1	V. Low	85	120	45	Low
2	14	45	4	Low	75	120	15	V. Low
			Mixed Site					
2	15	73	2	Low	78	120	60	V. Low
3	7	14	2	V. Low	50	105	30	V. Low
5	21	162	1	Medium	60	105	30	V. Low
7	5	15	1	V. Low	55	105	30	V. Low
11	7	21	1	V. Low	51	120	15	V. Low
15	5	10	1	V. Low	84	135	30	Low
21	12	23	1	Low	67	105	30	V. Low
24	11	75	1	Low	82	165	60	Low
34	6	21	1	V. Low	114	195	75	Low
45	7	21	2	V. Low	118	210	30	Low

[a] Rating system provided by the Purdue Soil Testing Laboratory for agricultural crops.

Correlation of presence or absence of natural vegetation on areas sampled with corresponding pH values revealed that 31% of the samples with pH values less than 4.0 were vegetated, while only 6% of the samples with pH 3.5 or less supported vegetation. For specific conductance, 28% of samples between 1 and 2 mmhos/cm were vegetated, 9% between 2 and 3 mmhos/cm supported vegetation, and none of the samples above 3 mmhos/cm had plant cover. For invasion and growth of natural vegetation, it appears that plant-growth ratings should be modified to utilize values of pH 3.5 and specific conductance of 2 mmhos/cm as the marginal values.

Variation in P and K content of cast overburden within and among study areas is shown in Table 4. Comparison with the classification system

TABLE 5

Cast overburden properties by relief position[1]

Cast overburden Property	Ridge	Slope	Trough
Physical Properties:			
Percent soil (<2 mm)	56aA	52aA	78bB
Percent rock 2 mm to 1 in.	29aA	30aA	17bB
Percent rock >1 in.	15aA	18aA	5bB
Percent sand (2.00 to 0.02 mm)	54aA	55aA	59bB
Percent silt (0.02 to 0.002 mm)	28aA	27aA	24bB
Percent clay (<0.002 mm)	18aA	18aA	17aA
Percent soil surface[2]	32	21	55
Field capacity (1/3 atm)[3]	20.2	19.7	19.1
Wilting point (15 atm)	7.7aA	7.5aA	7.3bA
Available moisture[3]	12.5	12.2	11.8
Chemical Properties:			
Phosphorus (lb/A)	6aA	12aA	11aA
Potassium (lb/A)	60aA	73aA	71aA
Calcium (lb/A)[4]	2656	1111	2298
Magnesium (lb/A)[4]	475	440	446
pH	4.7aA	4.9aA	4.7aA
Specific Cond. (mmhos/cm)	0.7aA	0.5aA	0.4bA

[1] Values in the same row followed by the same lower case or capital letter are not significantly different. Lower case letters designate differences at the 0.05 level and capital letters designate differences at the 0.01 level.

[2] Means derived from surface characterization data with no analysis of variance performed.

[3] Multiple linear contrasts were not performed on this property because of the presence of interaction at the 0.01 level.

[4] Means derived from limited number of samples from the younger aged areas only with no analysis of variance performed.

of the Purdue Soil Testing Laboratory (1958) for agricultural crops reveals that both P and K are low to very low on practically every area sampled. Analysis of exchangeable Ca and Mg was limited to study areas on the sandy and shaly sites. Mean calcium content ranged from 896 to 2774 lbs/acre and 1587 to 2386 lbs/acre on the sandy and shaly sites respectively. Mean magnesium content was 143 to 184 lbs/acre and 769 to 870 lbs/acre on the sandy and shaly sites respectively.

Comparison of cast overburden properties by relief position for all areas combined is presented in Table 5. Multiple linear contrasts reveal that soil content (<2 mm) is higher and rock content lower in the troughs than on the ridge and slope positions. There also is significantly higher sand and silt present in the trough, while little or no differences were observed among relief positions in other cast overburden properties analyzed.

Natural vegetation

The vegetation profile of the Ground Layer, under 4 ft in height, includes 108 species of herbs; 12 species of grasses, sedges, and rushes; 26 tree species; and 20 species of woody shrubs and vines on all areas. Although 82% of all species in the Ground Layer invaded during the first three years after disturbance, a few new species occurred on most areas in subsequent years.

Characteristic species with highest *frequency* (occurrence on sample plots within study areas) and *constancy* (occurrence among study areas) were as follows (for scientific names, see Table 6):

Tree species
River birch, cottonwood, persimmon, sassafras, black cherry

Shrub species
Smooth sumac, shining sumac

Woody-vine species
Dewberry, poison ivy, Japanese honeysuckle

Herbaceous species
Thoroughwort, pokeberry, wild lettuce, buttonweed, goldenrod, aster, ragweed, evening primrose, Indian hemp, red sorrel, ironweed, Japanese clover, pepper-grass

Grass species
Three-awn grass, broomsedge, panic grass.

The majority of these species, as well as others recorded on the areas under investigation (Table 6), also were associated with plant communities ob-

TABLE 6

Scientific and common names of plant species identified on surface-mined coal lands in Pike County, Ind.

Species		Constancy[a] %
Herbaceous species:		
Acalypha gracilens Gray	three-seeded mercury	47
A. rhomboidea Raf.	three-seeded mercury	23
Acerate hirtelle Pennell	green milkweed	12
Ajuga genevensis L.	bugle	23
Achillea Millefolium L.	yarrow	41
Allium vineale L.	field-garlic	29
Ambrosia artemisifolia L.	ragweed	94
A. trifida L.	giant ragweed	12
Antennaria plantaginifolia (L.) Richards	pussy-toes	59
Apios americana Medic.	wild bean	12
Apocynum cannabinum L.	Indian hemp	88
Asclepias incarnata L.	swamp-milkweed	6
A. purpurascens L.	milkweed	6
A. syriaca L.	milkweed	12
A. tuberosa L.	butterfly-weed	23
Asplenium platyneuron (L.) Oakes	ebony spleenwort	12
Aster spp.	aster	88
Aureolaria flava var. *macrantha* Pennell	false foxglove	6
Bidens aristosa (Michx.) Britt.	beggar-ticks	35
B. frondosa L.	beggar-ticks	41
Campanula repunculoides L.	bellflower	18
Cassia fasciculata Michx.	partridge-pea	41
Centrosema virginianum (L.) Benth.	spurred butterfly-pea	12
Cerastium nutans Raf.	mouse-ear chickweed	6
Chenopodium album L.	lamb's quarters	59
C. ambrosioides L.	Mexican tea	23
Chrysanthemum leucanthemum L.	ox-eye daisy	35
Cicuta maculata L.	water-hemlock	6
Cirsium altissimum (L.) Spreng.	thistle	23
C. vulgare (Savi) Tenore	bull thistle	29
Convolvulus sepium L.	hedge-blind weed	6
Conyza canadensis (L.) Crong.	horseweed	53
Datura Stramonium L.	jimson-weed	18
Daucus Carota L.	Queen Anne's lace	47
Desmodium illinoense Gray	tick-trefoil	18
D. laevigatum (Nutt.) DC.	tick-trefoil	6
D. paniculatum (L.) DC.	tick-trefoil	35
Dianthus ameria L.	deptford-pink	18

TABLE 6 (*cont.*)

Species		Constancy[a] %
Diodia teres Walt.	buttonweed	88
Erigeron annuus (L.) Pers.	white-top	41
Eupatorium altissimum L.	thoroughwort	12
E. coelestinum L.	mist-flower	6
E. perfoliatum L.	boneset	6
E. rugosum Houtt.	white snakeroot	29
E. serotinum Michx.	thoroughwort	100
Euphorbia corollata L.	flowering spurge	23
E. Preslii Guss.	spurge	18
Fragaria vesca L.	strawberry	6
Geranium carolinianum L.	crane's-bill	6
Geum canadense Jacq.	avens	12
Gnaphalium obtusifolium L.	cudweed	6
Helianthus spp.	sunflower	6
H. hirsutus Raf.	sunflower	18
Hepatica americana (DC.) Ker.	hepatica	6
Hieracium Gronovii L.	hawkweed	12
H. longipilum Torr.	hawkweed	12
Ipomoea hederacea (L.) Jacq.	morning-glory	6
I. lacunosa L.	morning-glory	6
I. pandurata (L.) G. W. F. Meyer	wild sweet potato	6
I. purpurea (L.) Roth.	common morning-glory	6
Lactuca spp.	wild lettuce	100
Lepidium densiflorum Schrader	pepper-grass	6
L. virginicum L.	pepper-grass	76
Lespedeza cuneata (Dumont) G. Don.	bush-clover	18
L. hirta (L.) Hornem.	bush-clover	6
L. procumbena Michx.	bush-clover	12
L. striata (Thunb.) H. & A.	Japanese clover	76
L. violacea (L.) Pers.	bush-clover	6
Liatris squarrosa (L.) Michx.	blazing star	18
Linum virginianum L.	flax	18
Melilotus spp.	sweet clover	6
M. alba Desr.	white sweet clover	29
M. officinalis (L.) Desr.	yellow sweet clover	18
Mollugo verticillata L.	carpet-weed	6
Oenothera biennis L.	evening-primrose	88
Oxalis stricta L.	sheep-sorrel	65
Physalis spp.	ground-cherry	6
Phytolacca americana L.	pokeberry	82
Picris hieracioides L.	bitterweed	18
Plantago aristata Michx.	buckhorn	65

TABLE 6 (*cont.*)

Species		Con-stancy[a] %
P. lanceolata L.	ribgrass	35
P. major L.	plantain	6
Polygala sanguinea L.	milkwort	12
Polygonum Convolvulus L.	black blindweed	47
P. cuspidatum Sieb. & Zucc.	Mexican bamboo	6
P. lapathifolium L.	smartweed	29
P. orientale L.	prince's feather	6
P. Persicaria L.	smartweed	65
P. punctatum Ell.	smartweed	65
Potentilla canadensis L.	cinquefoil	53
Pycnanthemum flexuosum (Walt.) BSP.	mountain-mint	18
Ranunculus abortivus L.	small-flowered crowfoot	12
Rumex Acetosella L.	red sorrel	82
R. crispus L.	sour dock	41
R. obtusifolius L.	bitter dock	6
Solanum carolinense L.	horse-nettle	23
S. nigrum L.	black nightshade	29
Solidago spp.	goldenrod	94
Strophostyles helveola (L.) Ell.	wild bean	6
S. umbellata (Muhl.) Britt.	wild bean	18
Symphytum officinale L.	comfrey	6
Taraxacum officinale Weber.	dandelion	35
Trifolium pratense L.	red clover	18
T. repens L.	white clover	41
Verbascum Thapsus L.	mullein	41
Verbena hastata L.	vervain	6
Vernonia missurica Raf.	ironweed	82
Viola spp.	violet	12
Grasses, Sedges and Rushes:		
Agrostis hyemalis (Walt.) BSP.	redtop	76
Alopecurus carolinianus Walt.	foxtail	12
Andropogon virginicus L.	broom sedge	100
Aristida spp.	three-awn	100
Bromus spp.	brome grass	88
Carex spp.	sedge	82
Cyperus strigosus L.	galingale	23
Echinochloa muricata (Beauv.) Fern.	barnyard grass	29
Juncus Dudleyi Wieg.	rush	6
J. effusus L.	rush	6
Panicum spp.	panic grass	100
Phleum pratense L.	timothy	6

TABLE 6 (*cont.*)

Species		Con-stancy[a] %
Tree species:		
Acer negundo L.	boxelder	6
A. rubrum L.	red maple	35
Betula nigra L.	river birch	41
Catalpa speciosa Warder	northern catalpa	18
Cercis canadensis L.	eastern redbud	—
Cornus florida L.	flowering dogwood	29
C. stricta Lam.	stiffcornel dogwood	—
Diospyros virginiana L.	persimmon	70
Fraxinus americana L.	white ash	23
Fraxinus pennsylvanica Marsh.	green ash	6
Juniperus virginiana L.	eastern redcedar	—
Liriodendron tulipifera L.	yellow-poplar	6
Pinus strobus L.	eastern white pine	18
P. virginiana Mill.	Virginia pine	18
Platanus occidentalis L.	American sycamore	35
Populus alba L.	white poplar	12
P. deltoides Bartr.	eastern cottonwood	82
P. grandidentata Michx.	bigtooth aspen	—
Prunus spp.	plum	—
P. angustifolia Marsh.	Chickasaw plum	6
P. Persica Patsch	peach	—
P. serotina Ehrh.	black cherry	59
Quercus imbricaria Michx.	shingle oak	41
Q. palustris Muenchh.	pin oak	23
Q. rubra L.	northern red oak	18
Q. stellata Wangenh.	post oak	12
Q. velutina Lam.	black oak	6
Robinia pseudoacacia L.	black locust	18
Salix interion Rowlee	sandbar willow	18
S. nigra Marsh.	black willow	18
Sassafras albidum (Nutt.) Nees	sassafras	76
Ulmus rubra Muhl.	slippery elm	35
Shrubs and Woody Vines:		
Campsis radicans (L.) Seem.	trumpet creeper	53
Celastrus scandens L.	bittersweet	12
Hypericum prolificum L.	St. John's-wort	18
H. punctatum Lam.	St. John's-wort	6
Lonicera japonica Thunb.	Japanese honeysuckle	82
Parthenocissus quinquefolia (L.) Planch.	Virginia creeper	29

TABLE 6 (*cont.*)

Species		Constancy[a] %
Rhus Copallinum L.	shining sumac	23
R. glabra L.	smooth sumac	47
R. radicans L.	poison ivy	100
Rosa carolina L.	pasture rose	23
R. multiflora Thunb.	multiflora rose	35
R. palustris Marsh.	swamp rose	6
Rubus flagellaris Willd.	dewberry	100
R. allegheniensis Porter	blackberry	53
R. occidentalis L.	raspberry	6
Sambucus canadensis L.	common elder	6
Smilax Bona-nox L.	greenbrier	6
S. glauca Walt.	greenbrier	70
Vitis aestivalis Michx.	summer grape	29
V. palmata Vahl.	catbird grape	59

[a] Constancy is the number of areas on which a species occurs divided by total number of study areas.

served on surface-mined coal lands in Illinois, Ohio, Kansas, and Pennsylvania. Furthermore, as one would expect, the plant community on cast overburden had many species in common with the community that invades old fields and roadsides in southern Indiana.

The process of invasion by migration and ecesis was not in waves or stages as noted by Croxton (1928) and Graham (1947) but in the manner described by Bramble and Ashley (1955). Vegetation first invaded the more favorable spots and in subsequent years the pioneer plants, through propagation and aggregation, continually encroached on the intervening bare patches. With highly vegetated spots (some exhibiting well defined tree, shrub, and ground layers) coexisting with bare patches on areas 11 years old and older, several stages of succession occur simultaneously in close proximity to one another.

A distinct Shrub Layer, 4 to 10 ft in height, had developed within a period of 7 years, with a few individual tree species attaining this height after 3 years. The most common species in the Shrub Layer were trees such as cottonwood, river birch, persimmon, sycamore, sassafras, slippery elm, black cherry, flowering dogwood, and shingle oak; woody shrubs and vines such as trumpet creeper, Japanese honeysuckle, poison ivy, and sumac; and the tall-growing herbaceous perennial, pokeberry, which was evident in the Shrub Layer after one to two years.

A prominent Tree Layer, over 10 ft in height, was evident on most study areas after 11 years. Light-seeded species such as cottonwood, river birch, sycamore, and catalpa were the first to attain a height of 10 ft. Conversely, the heavier-seeded species, which are also characterized by a slower growth rate, such as oaks, black cherry, persimmon, and dogwood were not present in the Tree Layer until 15 to 21 years after disturbance. Two of the most common species in the Tree Layer on younger aged areas were cottonwood and river birch, with the latter having the highest frequency of occurrence. On older areas, pin oak and persimmon along with river birch are most common, while cottonwood decreases in frequency.

From cover estimations made for individual species, the percent cover on cast overburden provided by annual, biennial, and perennial plants in the Ground Layer was ascertained by study area-age classes (Fig. 1). Fluctuation among the proportions of annuals at the younger ages is due primarily to the small amount of cover present at these ages and consequently the heavy weight given to the occurrence of one or two perennial species. The increase in cover with age afforded by biennials and perennials is not caused by an increase in invasion of new species, but rather an expan-

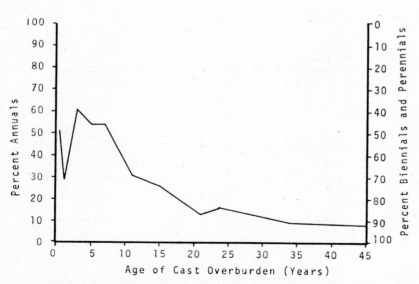

FIGURE 1 Percentage of vegetation ground cover composed of annual plants and biennial and perennial plants by age of cast overburden.

sion in cover and increase in frequency of previously established tree and shrub species with a corresponding decline in herbaceous annuals.

The cover provided by each vegetation layer, based on mean values weighted by the total number of sample plots per study area, is presented in Fig. 2. The Tree Layer exhibits a marked increase between 15 and 34 years, mainly due to the influx of the heavier-seeded hardwood species. Cover provided by the Shrub Layer remains static for many years but on the 45-year-old area is very prominent due to the occurrence of sumac species and increase in frequency of several tree species such as persim-

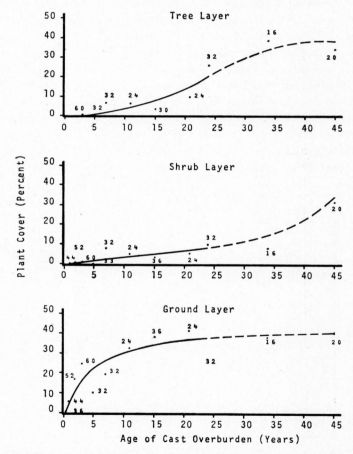

FIGURE 2 Trends in plant cover by vegetation layer and age of cast overburden. Curves adjusted by weighted means in respect to number of plots per study area and extended by dash lines for ages represented by few observations.

mon, slippery elm, flowering dogwood, and red maple. Percent cover of the Ground Layer reflects a rapid invasion in the initial years after disturbance followed by a gradual leveling-off. Some species of the Ground Layer that do increase in frequency and cover over time are the herbaceous perennials such as goldenrod, aster, and Indian hemp; grasses such as three-awn grass and broom-sedge; and woody vines such as raspberry and poison ivy. Tree species which exhibit a trend in frequency of occurrence with age of cast overburden are sassafras, persimmon, red maple, black cherry, flowering dogwood, and shingle oak.

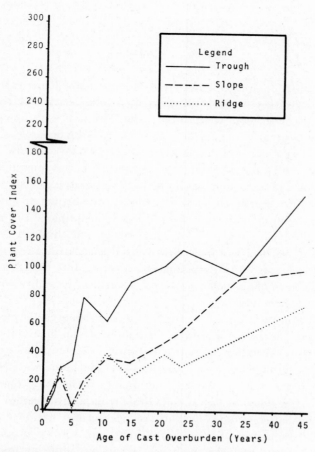

FIGURE 3   Plant cover index (0 to 300) derived by adding percent cover of the three vegetation layers (Tree, Shrub, Ground) by relief position in relation to age of cast overburden.

Based on a "plant cover index" for the Tree, Shrub, and Ground Layers combined, there was little differentiation in cover on cast overburden up to 3 years among the three relief positions (Fig. 3). However, after the third year, plant cover in the trough surpasses the ridge and slope which have similar values up to 15 years. Differences in plant cover among relief positions reflect differences observed in properties of the respective cast overburden. More vegetation occurs in the trough with lesser amounts on the slopes and ridges. A further comparison of tree species by relief position and slope aspect reveals that most trees occurred in the troughs, the second largest number on the north slopes, and the fewest on south slopes and ridges with little difference between these latter categories.

CONCLUSIONS

One of the most obvious conclusions revealed in the soil analysis data and the vegetation survey is that with both cast overburden properties as well as vegetation cover and composition, the variation existing within an area may be as great as that existing between two or more areas of different ages. The presence of this large variance necessitates the use of many samples for evaluation of soils and vegetation if meaningful and conclusive results and deductions are to be obtained on specific species or cast overburden types. Furthermore, a more practical method to obtain such information would be the establishment of permanent plots. In conjunction with studying a particular cast overburden type, the difficult task would be the derivation of a workable cast overburden classification system for surface-mined areas. Many reclamation investigators and practitioners have tried to formulate such systems to correlate plantability and site but have not been very successful.

The importance or value of the vegetation cover being established through natural plant succession on surface-mined lands in Pike County is unanswered. Any vegetation present will furnish some erosion control and also aid in screening the barren and desolate appearance of these areas. However, on the areas examined, this quality of masking the disturbed land to a degree where it was unnoticeable from a distance did not occur until 34 years after mining. Due to the open-grown nature of the trees present on these disturbed lands, a resultant poor form is produced. This poor form, coupled with the small size and uneven stocking found on the two oldest areas (34 and 45 years old), makes any profitable economic return in timber production of naturally occurring species doubtful.

Several abundant and lesser occurring, seed-producing species such as ragweed, Japanese clover, tick-trefoil, beggar-ticks, wood sorrel, and partridge-pea along with species from the *Compositae* family, are actual or possible food sources for quail and songbirds. Quail, as well as deer, also may utilize certain fruit-bearing tree, shrub, and woody-vine species such as sassafras, persimmon, oaks, black cherry, dewberry, and black-berry (*Rubus* spp.). Approximately 45% of all species recorded on the study areas rated usable for fruit, forage, or cover by wildlife. The majority of the plants that were not usable were the less common and abundant species of herbaceous plants and almost all of the grasses. Consequently, the value of these lands for wildlife purposes shows promise and should be investigated more closely.

LITERATURE CITED

Bouyoucos, G. J. 1951. A recalibration of the hydrometer method of making mechanical analysis of soils. *Agron. J.* **43**, 434–437.

Bramble, W. C., and R. H. Ashley. 1955. Natural revegetation of spoil banks in central Pennsylvania. *Ecology.* **36**, 417–423.

Braun-Blanquet, J. 1932. *Plant sociology.* (Transl. by G. D. Fuller and H. S. Conard). McGraw-Hill Book Co., New York. 439 p.

Clark, F. B. 1954. Forest planting possibilities on strip-mined land in Kansas, Missouri, and Oklahoma. U. S. Dep. Agr., Forest Serv., Cent. States Forest Expt. Sta. Tech. Paper 141, 33 p.

Croxton, W. C. 1928. Revegetation of Illinois coal-stripped land. *Ecology.* **9**, 155–175.

Cummins, D. G., W. T. Plass, and C. E. Gentry. 1965. Chemical and physical properties of spoil banks in the eastern Kentucky coal fields, U. S. Dep. Agr., Forest Serv., Cent. States Forest Expt. Sta. Research Paper CS-17, 11 p.

Deitschman, G. H., and R. D. Lane. 1952. Forest planting possibilities on Indiana coal-stripped lands. U. S. Dep. Agr., Forest Serv., Cent. States Forest Expt. Sta. Tech. Paper 131, 57 p.

Graham, E. H. 1947. *The land and wildfire.* Macmillan Publ. Co., New York, 232 p.

Jackson, M. L. 1958. *Soil chemical analysis.* Prentice Hall, New Jersey, 498 p.

Limstrom, G. A. 1952. Effects of grading strip-mined lands on the early survival and growth of planted trees. U. S. Dep. Agr., Forest Serv., Cent. States Forest Expt. Sta. Tech. Paper 130, 36 p.

Limstrom, G. A. 1960. Forestation of strip-mined land in the Central States. *U. S. Dep. Agr. Handbook* 166, 74 p.

McDougall, W. B. 1918. Plant succession on an artificial bare area in Illinois. *Trans Ill. State Acad. of Sci.* **11**, 129–131.

Merz, Robert W., and W. T. Plass. 1952. Natural forestation on a strip-mined area in Ohio. U. S. Dep. Agr., Forest Serv., Cent. States Forest Expt. Sta. Note 68, 2 p.

Purdue University. 1968. Soil test report explanation sheet. Agron. Dept. Soil Testing Laboratory, 4 p..

DISCUSSION

REPP: Did you find any indicator value of the natural vegetation?

BYRNES: We were not specifically looking for indicator species in this study. We could, however, look at our data with this in mind; for example, red sorrel seems to be a species that will invade and establish on more acid conditions. Further, it appears that little or no vegetation occurred on areas with pH below 3.0. From that viewpoint, absence of vegetation may be an indicator.

AHARRAH: In a similar study in western Pennsylvania, I came up with the idea that possibly the lack of vegetation on slopes and ridges was more the matter of the seed skidding over these shale areas than moisture collecting in the trough. What do you think about this situation?

BYRNES: I think this is definitely part of the picture, although you do have little crevices and cracks in which seed can and do fall and germinate. I have also observed the condition that you are referring to. I think it is a combination of factors that results in more vegetation in the more favorable spots, which may include troughs and other physiographic positions.

DICKINSON: Did you consider aspect?

BYRNES: We did attempt to collect the data with this stratification in mind, but we did not analyze and present it in that manner.

CORNWELL: Did you find any *Bryophyta* there?

BYRNES: There were mosses present, but we did not attempt to include them in this investigation.

CORNWELL: In the anthracite region, we recognized that mosses and lichens were probably the last things to establish. For example, *Cladonia* species occurred with other vegetation—like poverty grass. Classical succession was not observed, and I was interested to compare this with the succession described for the island of Surtsey.

INVESTIGATIONS OF SOILS AND TREE GROWTH ON FIVE DEEP-MINE REFUSE PILES IN THE HARD-COAL REGION OF THE RUHR*

Wilhelm Knabe

Regierungsdirektor, Northrhine-Westphalian Institute for Air Pollution Control and Land Use Protection, Essen, West Germany

Soil development and revegetation were investigated on five refuse piles from underground coal mines in the Ruhr. Burned and unburned material, and young and old stands were included in the 87 sample plots and 107 soil profiles studied.

Soil conditions varied greatly due to differences in the origin of tipped material, the degree of burning, and the soil-forming processes. Soil types can be described as *Halden-Rohboden* (raw refuse-soil, with no A horizon) and *Halden-Ranker* (immature refuse-soil, with an A horizon above a C horizon). Large pores (even at considerable depth), thermal activity, and weathering of pyrites are considered essential for this special kind of soil development, which is also affected by the dustfall and acid precipitation which are prevalent in the Ruhr. Acidity varies less in the surface layers of revegetated old dumps than in the subsoil. Available nutrients are higher in this surface layer (from 0 to 5 or 0 to 12 cm) than at a depth of 30 to 35 cm. Detailed information on tree growth was obtained from sample plots and increment borings. Broad and narrow annual rings of old and young black locust trees show good correlation and confirm the reliability of annual ring chronology, even on spoil heaps. On favorable sites open forests of birch and willow may result from natural seeding, but planting of pioneers such as *Alnus glutinosa*, *A. incana*, *Robinia pseudoacacia* and *Betula pendula* appears more promising. Additional species are also suggested.

INTRODUCTION

Refuse piles are a common feature of most regions where coal is deep mined, because only a small part of the colliery waste is used underground to

---

* The experimental work was carried out at the Federal Research Organization for Forestry and Forest Products, Reinbek, West Germany.

refill mined seams. These piles, because of their height, are visible from all directions and, in spite of the relatively small area they occupy, they either loom as ugly eyesores or improve the landscape as picturesque wooded hills.

The Planning Authority of the Ruhr (*Siedlungsverband Ruhrkohlenbezirk*) has, since 1951, sponsored many planting projects on refuse piles (Berthold, 1953; Mellinghoff, 1959 and 1965); these followed earlier attempts by individual mining companies. The Federal Research Organization for Forestry and Forestry Products at Reinbek supported investigations to gain a better understanding of soil development and revegetation on these sites. The objectives of these investigations were to facilitate further planting and to encourage international exchange of experience in this field. Earlier reports on the afforestation of refuse piles in the Ruhr included valuable results but omitted detailed analyses of soil and of stands already established (Berthold, 1953, 1954, and 1957; Roosen, 1959), whereas results of the scientific work of other deep-mining districts had already been published e.g. by Wünsche (1963) for Saxony and Whyte and Sisam (1949) for Great Britain.

Results of the recent investigations in the Ruhr have heretofore been published in German only (Knabe et al., 1968). Reviewers suggested publication in French and English (Petsch, 1969) to facilitate international comparisons.

DESCRIPTION OF INVESTIGATIONS

Choice of sites

Bare and afforested refuse piles of the Ruhr were first visited. They showed great differences in many respects. Various materials had been tipped: coal refuse, topsoil, overburden, fuel ash, domestic refuse, and industrial waste. Texture ranged from stones above 80 mm to silt and clay. Steep cones, dams, irregular mounds, table mountains, or nearly level spoil banks of different age were found; these were bare or covered by grass or trees of different heights. Some heaps were still expanding due to continued waste dumping; others were being hauled away; some had been burned or were still burning; others remained unburned. Because there were great differences within individual refuse piles, it seemed best to choose sites representative of the most common or most interesting types, such as wooded refuse piles consisting of both burned and unburned soft shales and sandstone of the Carboniferous age, more or less in the form of table mountains. The age and composition of the stands on these heaps varied.

Description of sites

The following sites were chosen:

Halde Zollverein (*site Z*)   A stand of black locust (*Robinia pseudoacacia* L.) was planted about 70 years ago on weathered but unburned carboniferous shales (Middle Westphalian). The plateau of this table mountain was covered by a 2-in. layer of airborne dust deposits, humus, and litter.

Halde Möller (*site M*)   Pure and mixed stands of birch (*Betula pendula* Roth), poplar (*Populus nigra* hybrids), and speckled alder (*Alnus incana* Moench) were planted about 22 and 10 years ago on mostly unburned carboniferous shales (Lower and Middle Westphalian). Airborne dust deposits were present in small quantities only; the younger stands contained almost none.

Halde Bismarck (*site B*)   A 20-year-old natural birch stand was growing on burned red shales and sandstone (Middle and Upper Westphalian) in the area designated B1. Birch stands were planted less than 10 years ago on the unburned gray shales of seams Q and T (Middle Westphalian) in the area designated B2. Dust deposits formed a layer over the burned material similar to that on site Z. General characteristics and the progress of revegetation on site B can be seen in aerial photos taken in the summers of 1952 (Fig. 1) and 1962 (Fig. 2).

Halde Prosper (*site P*)   Mixed hardwoods were planted on predominantly unburned Carboniferous shales (Lower and Middle Westphalian) 9 years ago. A shallow layer of dust covered parts of the plateau.

Halde Oberhausen (*site O*)   Mixed stands of hardwoods were planted on predominantly burned Carboniferous shales covered with deposits of dust. Unfortunately this spoil heap was hauled away before investigations could be completed.

FIGURE 1   Aerial photograph of site B in 1952. Lower left: Site B1, refuse pile tipped before 1903, burned until 1922, and naturally seeded with birch, willow, and grasses since then. Center: basin filled with dark coal refuse. Upper part: Site B2, bare gray shales from coal washeries, tipped 1942 to 1945; severe erosion. Left side North.

FIGURE 2 Aerial photograph of site B, 10 years later (1962). Note progress of revegetation as a result of natural seeding at B1 and in the basin, and of partially successful plantations at B2; erosion is still active. The adjacent community, south of heap, benefits from the afforestation.

Investigations

After preliminary reconnaissance of sites and stands, including study of aerial photographs and analysis of several soil profiles, 85 circular sample plots were located according to a 40- by 40-m grid. A different plot radius was used for each diameter class; the larger the tree diameter, the larger the plot radius.

Samples of the topsoil and subsoil (30 to 35 cm) were taken from the center of each plot. The pH in H_2O and KCl solution, the lime requirement according to Schachtschabel (Thun et al., 1955), loss on ignition, and available P and K in lactic acid solution were determined for all samples. Additional soil investigations were carried out on selected profiles at six rather than two depths. As part of the same study, Schmidt-Lorenz investigated soil micromorphology and Meyer studied the development of vegetation and mycorrhizae (Knabe et al., 1968, chapters BIIb, BIIIa, and BIIIc).

RESULTS OF SOIL INVESTIGATIONS

The composition of refuse piles

Burned and unburned carboniferous shales were the main constituents of all piles, but sandstone, coal, ash, residues from sunken shafts or construction work, topsoil, and domestic refuse were also present. Sites Z, B1 and B2 were relatively uniform within themselves; sites M, P, and O showed great variation in both composition and soil characteristics.

Changes in the soil profiles

The accumulation of dust and litter under the first tree cover has effectively changed the original spoil material and formed an A horizon which contains more organic material and available nutrients than the subsoil. The enrichment with available K (soluble in lactic acid) of the topsoil of a wooded refuse pile of medium age is shown in Fig. 3. There the subsoil consists of poor gray shale except for some plots marked "r" (red burned shale) or "a" (ash). In the topsoil of an old wooded refuse pile there is an even greater enrichment of P than of K (Fig. 4). The ratio of the mean contents between topsoil and subsoil amount to 5.5 : 1 for P and 1.6 : 1 for K.

Great variation in the pH of different soil layers was observed at the refuse pile of medium age (Fig. 5). When the subsoil is strongly acid it shows a lower pH than the topsoil; when the subsoil is about neutral or alkaline, it shows a higher pH than the topsoil. Hence there is less variation of pH in the topsoil than in the subsoil.

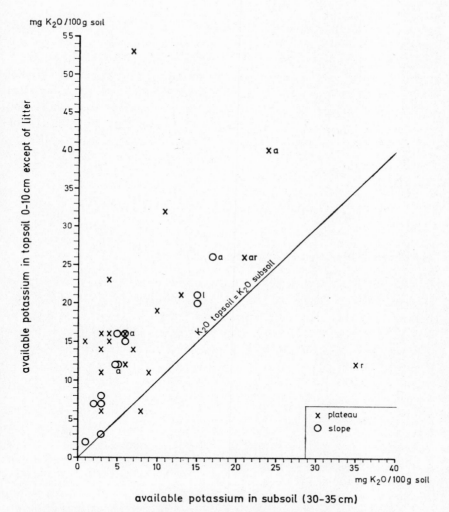

available potassium in subsoil (30-35 cm)

FIGURE 3 The enrichment of available K (soluble in lactic acid) in the topsoil of an old wooded refuse pile above the poor gray shales of the subsoil; a = ash; r = red burned shales; unlettered = gray unburned shales; Site M, Gladbeck.

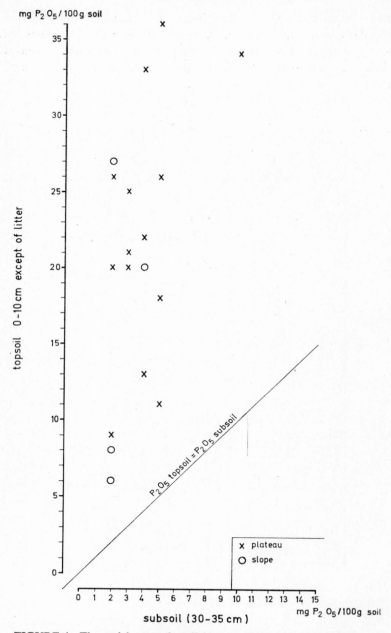

FIGURE 4   The enrichment of available P (soluble in lactic acid) in the topsoil having a high content of dust and humus above a poor subsoil that consists of gray shales; Site Z, Essen.

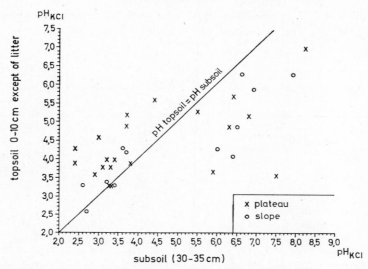

FIGURE 5 Changes of pH values in weathered spoil material after 10 to 25 years of exposure; Site M, Gladbeck.

Characteristics of various soil constituents

The main constituents of individual refuse piles differ in their characteristics and suitability for tree growth (Table 1).

Airborne dust After a few decades, substantial amounts of airborne dust accumulate on refuse piles under the protection of established tree cover or occasional felts of mosses; on bare sites, it is blown away. It contains more organic matter and soluble nutrients than the subsoil. The cation exchange capacity reaches 35 to 40 meq/100 g soil. The quality of the dust is influenced by the kind of industry nearby. The variations, e.g. in pH, can be seen in Table 1. The dust layer usually contains a dense network of roots and seems to promote both soil development and tree growth. The decay of litter is rapid and earthworms are found only on refuse piles with a developed layer of dust and litter.

Recent humus Recent humus formed from the litter of growing tree stands is incorporated into the topsoil. Surprisingly, recent humus—determined by the method of Gerretsen and Campen (1958)—accounted for only 1/3 to 1/6 of the total loss on ignition of oven-dry samples of the layer under the litter; the rest was coal and bound water. The wide C/N ratio of 30 to 37 at site M indicates the predominance of fossil organic matter, because the N content of bituminous coal and coal ash is very low.

TABLE 1

Acidity and available nutrients of major soil-forming constituents of five refuse piles in the Ruhr

Site	Material[a]	No. of Samples	pH in H_2O	pH in KCl	Lime require.[b] tons/ha	Avail. P_2O_5 mg/100 g	Avail. K_2O mg/100 g
		Topsoil without litter to depth of about 10 cm					
Z	Gray Shale	2	4.1	3.7	5.2	7.0	23
M	Gray Shale	10	4.1	3.9	6.1	0.9	12
B	Gray Shale	8	3.8	3.1	7.4	1.3	11
P	Gray Shale	1	4.0	3.5	4.2	4.0	9
O	Burned Shale	1	5.2	5.0	1.5	21.0	44
Z	Humus-dust	16	3.7	3.7	16.8	23.0	23
M	Humus-dust	3	5.1	5.0	2.1	5.0	24
B	Humus-dust	9	4.5	4.2	8.2	7.0	27
P	Humus-dust	9	5.2	5.0	2.2	17.0	25
O	Humus-dust	4	7.1	6.7	0.0	35.0	>50
M	Fly ash	2	6.2	6.0	0.0	11.0	23
		Subsoil at depth of 30 to 35 cm					
Z	Gray Shale	18	4.2	3.6	5.1	4.0	16
M	Gray Shale	19	4.1	3.9	6.5	0.7	5
B	Gray Shale	8	3.2	2.9	7.4	1.3	3
P	Gray Shale	13	4.6	4.0	5.2	3.0	9
M	Burned Shale	1	7.3	7.5	0.0	18.0	35
B	Burned Shale	14	5.0	4.5	2.8	2.0	22
O	Burned Shale	4	6.4	5.9	1.9	17.0	19
M	Fly ash	4	7.0	6.4	0.0	17.0	19
M	Loam	2	4.1	3.7	7.1	3.0	17

[a] Some non-shale samples included a small proportion of shale.
[b] Lime requirement by method of Schachtschabel.

Gray shales Gray shale, the main constituent of the refuse piles studied, is usually acid or very acid. The fine waste of coal washeries (with pH below 3.0) proved to be toxic to poplars, black locust, and red oak (*Quercus rubra* L.), whereas European white birch was successfully planted after liming. These toxic shales contain free acids and salts. Under these conditions, as already reported for toxic spoil of lignite opencast mines (Knabe, 1959 and 1965), the sum of the H-value and the S-value is higher than the cation exchange capacity which is only 3 to 15 meq/100 g soil in more-or-less weathered gray shales. Although soluble P is very low, old weathered shales may contain sufficient soluble K. In levelled areas, weathered gray shales may show a zone of compaction formed by the precipitation of Fe at a depth of about 2 ft.

Red burned shales　Burned shales have lost part of the S originally present and are hence less acid than unburned ones. Their content of soluble nutrients is also higher, which confirms the results of Wünsche (1963). Their loss on ignition and exchange capacity are, however, lower. Poplars, black locusts, birches and willows (*Salix caprea* L.) are growing in this material. No toxic spots were observed.

Ashes　Ash has been dumped on some sites. It is also the main component of airborne dust. The reaction of the dumped ash varies around neutral. Available P and K are sufficient, but only 0.9 % N was found in one sample which resulted in a C/N ratio of 47. The growth of poplars, speckled alder, and birches on ash has been good. Therefore dumping of ash on toxic gray shales can be recommended as a means of soil improvement.

Loam　Loam was occasionally found on a few sample plots. Wünsche (1963) has already mentioned its good ameliorative effect on gray shales in Saxony. The observations in the Ruhr tend to confirm his findings, but there were too few samples to justify any general conclusions.

RESULTS OF STAND INVESTIGATIONS

Natural revegetation

The natural vegetation of the refuse piles studied is described in detail by Meyer (Knabe et al., 1968, chapter B IIIa). Burned shales are usually easily colonized by grasses (mainly *Agrostis tenuis* Sibth.) or European white birch and willow. These trees sometimes form closed stands, especially on northern slopes or plateaus, but slopes from southeast to southwest show hardly any naturally seeded trees. Unburned gray shales, especially toxic gray shales from coal washeries, also remain bare for a longer period. Naturally seeded birches and willows are, however, found in gaps between artificial plantings of poplars on gray shales. No young birches are present in old stands of black locust, but there is often a shrub layer of *Sambucus racemosa* L. and *Holcus mollis* L. *Poa annua* L., *Urtica dioica* L., and *Athyrium filix femina* (L.) Roth are predominant in the ground layer. *Agrostis tenuis* and *Epilobium angustifolium* L. are growing on all the investigated sites; they are well-known pioneers in Great Britain also (Brierley, 1956; Hall, 1957).

There are many reasons for the lack of vegetation on industrial waste (Knabe, 1965). In the Ruhr, completely barren areas on older piles were found on fine material that was either toxic, or exposed to the sun on steep slopes, or both. Brierley (1956) suggested that the ability of plants to become established on pit heaps depends upon mechanical rather than chemical factors, but he provided no soil analyses to exclude soil toxicity as a primary factor.

Artificial plantations

The oldest tree stand on any refuse pile in the Ruhr was planted at site Z about 1890. A pure stand of black locust, it has provided a green cover for this heap ever since then. Other successful plantations include hybrid poplars, birch, speckled and European black alder, black locust, and intermixed other hardwoods. Plantations failed on toxic waste and heaps that were still burning. At site M, they were once destroyed by fumes from a nearby factory.

Data from stand measurements

The number of stems per ha varied considerably. The lowest values (200) were found on sites with scattered natural growth or where artificial plantations had failed. Dense stands of naturally seeded birches on open sites or under scattered poplars reached values of 11,000, 25,000, and 32,800. Fifty-four percent of all sample plots were between 1200 and 4800. Because of the spotty occurrence of naturally seeded birches, the variation in numbers of stems was greatest within individual spoil heaps rather than between them or between age classes. The basal area of the stands, however, differed more between piles or age classes than within them. The youngest stands had basal areas of 6 m^2/ha; stands aged 10 to 30 years, about 12 m^2; and the 50- to 70-year-old stand of black locust at site Z, 28 m^2. The older the stand the more the growth differed from that in general yield tables. Basal areas corresponded to those of good yield classes, and heights to those of medium or low yield classes.

Site conditions and tree growth

Some relationships between site conditions and tree growth were revealed. Birch accounted for a greater proportion of mixed stands on acid soils (below pH 4.0) than on less acid or neutral soils, but grew faster on less acid sites. Competition with other species on the better sites may be the reason for this oddity, because the others do not grow well on very acid shales. For birch, the ecological optimum pH is not the same as the physiological one. Also, birch generally grew on sites lower in nutrients than those covered with poplar and alder. Height and diameter growth of speckled alder increased with rising pH (between 4.1 and 6.2) and decreased with rising lime requirement. On site Z, basal area and mean and maximum heights of black locust rose with the content of available P in the topsoil. Stands of the same age generally had a higher basal area on red burned shales than on gray shales. Individual refuse piles showed differences in growing potential; however, these were not always significant because of the great variation. Maxima and minima of annual rings corresponded well between old and young stands of black locust, thus showing the suitability of annual ring chronology even on refuse piles. These measurements showed that many of the 60- to 70-year-old black locusts were still vigorous in spite of the acid soil and considerable air pollution.

DISCUSSION OF SOME PECULIARITIES OF REFUSE PILES

Some refuse piles are relatively uniform in composition, but in most cases a great heterogeneity of material is typical. Hence taking one sample per pile, as has sometimes been done, is generally unsatisfactory. Hall (1957) concluded that there was a relation between age of spoil and pH without mentioning whether there was any variation within the investigated pit heaps.

Effects of precipitation

Soil development on Ruhr refuse piles was strongly influenced by dustfall, N, and acids contained in precipitation. The deposited dust provided the trees with nutrients, especially P which is rare in gray shales (but essential for earthworms). Plant species regarded as indicators of a good N supply often occur on these sites. Based on measurements made over a period of

1 year, a relationship between the pH of the precipitation and the soil reaction is evident. At site O, the only one with a neutral humus-dust layer, the precipitation had a mean pH of 6.0; at the other sites (with acid topsoil) it had pH values between 3.5 and 4.7.

Occurrence of free mineral acids and water-soluble salts

Polluted precipitation affects all sites in industrial areas, but is by no means the only important factor on refuse piles. They can be influenced as much or even more by burning. Sulfur, in the gases released by burning within the heap, may be precipitated near the surface and then react with O_2 and water as in the case of pyrites in unburned shales. Both reactions lead to the production of sulfuric acid, which may reach a normality of 0.01 to 0.1. Iron sulfates are also formed by the weathering of pyrite $(2FeS_2 + 7O_2 + 2H_2O = 2H_2SO_4 + 2FeSO_4)$. Sulfuric acid rapidly dissolves cations from the crystal-lattice of silicates and changes sparingly soluble calcite into soluble gypsum. It can also dissolve films of precipitated iron and aluminum hydroxides. Schmidt-Lorenz (Knabe et al., 1968, chapter B IIb) showed the results of these processes in microphotos of soil thin sections. He stressed the importance of the special Fe dynamics of these raw soils, which can be easily seen in the microphotos. He shows recently formed crystals of gypsum and films of hydrated iron oxides and jarosite. Sulfuric acid, though not visible in the photos, is active in the translocation of Fe. Free mineral acids and excessive quantities of salts are rarely found in natural soils in humid climates.

Deep drainage systems

All refuse piles consisting of coarse material have large air-filled pores even at great depths. These pores prevent waterlogging, at least during the first few decades after dumping. Percolation of precipitation is good, and chemical weathering, increased by sulfuric acid, extends to depths far beyond physical weathering (mainly a result of freezing and thawing). Biological influences do not reach as deep. In spite of high percolation rates, established plantations on refuse piles do not suffer from droughts.

Origin of organic matter

There are more sources of organic material on refuse piles than on undisturbed soils: (a) litter, (b) fossil organic matter from shales or coal, and (c) partly coked fossil organic matter from dumped ash or dustfall.

Variation in soil profiles

There are more reasons for the variation in the profiles of refuse-soils than in those of natural soils: (1) tipping of various materials one upon the other, e.g. loam over fly ash, or ash over shales, (2) erosion and deposition of material, (3) dustfall, and (4) soil-forming processes. Most of the differences between topsoil and subsoil listed in Table 1 are caused by (3) and (4), because (1) and (2) were almost excluded by stratification of the samples.

Thermal activity

Refuse piles containing S and coal show a thermal activity unknown to most natural sites. If the surface temperature is not too high, plant growth may be stimulated. On actively burning heaps, vegetation may be killed by lethal temperatures and noxious fumes. The chemical soil conditions become better for plant growth after burning because of decreased acidity and better availability of nutrients; the water-holding capacity and cation exchange capacity are, however, not as good as before.

Soil types

The soils studied were either *Halden-Rohboden* (raw refuse-soils) with no marked A horizon developed, or *Halden-Ranker** (immature refuse-soils) with both A and C horizons, but no intervening B or (B) horizons. The special Fe and S dynamics justify special names for these soils in the early stages of development.

CONCLUSIONS AND RECOMMENDATIONS

The investigations showed that refuse piles of the Ruhr, whether burned or unburned, can be successfully afforested. The existing stands of hardwoods have proved capable of reproducing themselves. These stands promote soil development as already stated by Hall (1957) and Wünsche (1963) for other regions. Earthworms were found in refuse piles only under tree cover and especially where a thick dust layer had accumulated. Planting

---

* "Ranker" according the nomenclature of Kubiena (1953).

pioneer species such as black and speckled alder, black locust, and European white birch seems to be the best method of revegetation.

Black locust did especially well on burned shales, and speckled alder on fly ash. Hybrid poplars of the Section Aigairos are recommended for burned shales and ashes only. Balsam poplars and aspen should be used instead on gray shales. Red oak, sycamore maple (*Acer pseudoplatanus* L.), ash (*Fraxinus excelsior* L.), cherry (*Prunus avium* L.), and linden (*Tilia platyphyllos* L.) trees should be planted along with the pioneer trees for permanent cover. Species of *Sorbus*, *Prunus*, *Pyrus*, and *Crataegus* are helpful for planting edges and borders. Tree willows can be tried at the bases of the heaps. So far, few shrubs have been planted on refuse piles in the Ruhr; they could be used to control erosion. *Elaeagnus umbellata* and *E. angustifolia*, *Rhus typhina* L. and *Lycium halimifolium* Mill. appear to be the most promising shrubs for such plantations.

Conifers, extensively used in plantations on industrial waste land in the U.S.A. and the U.K., are hardly worthy of trial in the Ruhr because of the heavy air pollution. *Taxus baccata* L. and *Pinus nigra* L., which can tolerate a certain degree of air pollution, are the only exceptions.

Leaving the sites as they are does not seem the proper way of dealing with the problem. The Ruhr area has the densest population in Germany. Nature alone is too slow in revegetating these ugly refuse piles, but they can become really attractive if they are wooded. Economic returns cannot be expected from artificial plantations. Aesthetics, welfare functions, and recreation are the only reasons for planting refuse piles in the Ruhr, but they are important enough to justify finishing the project that has been started, even if many of the heaps may be hauled away for road building purposes or industrial development.

LITERATURE CITED

Berthold, H. J. 1953. Haldenaufforstung in Nordrhein-Westfalen. *Die Holzzucht* **14**, 2–3.

Berthold, H. J. 1954. Erfahrungen bei der Aufforstung von Halden auf dem Gelände des westdeutschen Steinkohlenbergbaus. *Forschung und Beratung.* **1**, 146–150.

Berthold, H. J. 1957. Die Begrünung der Halden des westdeutschen Steinkohlenbergbaus. *Kulturarbeit.* **9**, 29–31.

Brierly, J. K. 1956. Some preliminary observations on the ecology of pit heaps. *J. Ecol.* **44**, 383–390.

Gerretsen, F. C., and W. A. C. Campen. 1958. Die Bestimmung der Haushaltkohle im Müllkompost. Int. Arb. Gem. Müllkompost. Zürich Inf. Bl. Nr. 5, 1012.

Hall, I. G. 1957. The ecology of disused pit heaps in England. *J. Ecol.* **45**, 689–720.

Knabe, W. 1959. Zur Wiederurbarmachung im Braunkohlenbergbau. Deutscher Verlag der Wissenschaften. Berlin. 154 p.

Knabe, W. 1965. Observations on world-wide efforts to reclaim industrial waste land. In: *Ecology and the Industrial Society*. G. T. Goodman, R. W. Edwards and J. M. Lambert (Ed.) Blackwell Sci. Publ., Oxford. p. 263–296.

Knabe, W., K. Mellinghoff, F. Meyer, and R. Schmidt-Lorenz. 1968. Haldenbegrünung im Ruhrgebiet. Schriftenrh. Siedlungsverb. Ruhrkohlenbez. **22**, 146 p.

Kubiena, W. L. 1953. Bestimmungsbuch und Systematik der Böden Europas. Enke-Verlag. Stuttgart. 392 p.

Mellinghoff, K. 1959. Grünes Werk auf grauem Grund: Die Begrünungsaktion Ruhrkohlenbezirk. *Unser Wald.* **3**, 65–66.

Mellinghoff, K. 1965. Aus grauen Halden werden grüne Hügel. Über Aufgabe, Problematik und Ergebnisse der Haldenbegrünung im Ruhrgebiet. *Unser Wald.* **7**, 171–172.

Petsch, G. 1969. Haldenbegrünung im Ruhrgebiet (book review). *Schweiz. Z. Forstwesen* **120**, 208–209.

Roosen, H. 1959. Probleme und Möglichkeiten bei der Aufforstung von Halden und anderen Aufschüttungen im Ruhrgebiet. *Forst- und Holzwirt.* **14**. 4–10.

Struthers, P. H. 1964. Chemical weathering of strip-mine spoils. *Ohio J. Sc.*, **64**, 125–131.

Thun, R., R. Herrmann, and E. Knickmann (Ed.) 1955. Die Untersuchung von Böden. Neumann, Radebeul and Berlin, 271 p.

Whyte, R. O., and J. W. B. Sisam. 1949. The establishment of vegetation on industrial waste land. *Comm. Agr. Bur. Joint Publ.* No. 14. Aberystwyth, Wales and Oxford. 78 p.

Wünsche, M. 1963. Die Standortsverhältnisse und Rekultivierungsmöglichkeiten der Halden des Zwickau-Lugau-Ölsnitzer Steinkohlenreviers. Freiberger Forschungshefte, C 153, p. 1–88.

DISCUSSION

SCHIMP: Could you be more explicit on the time required for soil development after revegetation?

KNABE: It depends on the species you use. We found very nicely developed soil under locust stands, 60 to 70 years old.

ONOSODE: Did you find any changes in the soil due to the presence of earthworms?

KNABE: Earthworms were observed only on those spoil heaps which were either covered with a layer of fly ash or loam, or which were old enough to be influenced by dust precipitation. In these soils earthworms mixed the thin top layer of ash and dust with the substratum which consisted of weathering shales. The 'Losung' of the *oribatidae* was then worked through by *enchytraeae*. The relatively quick development of the Halden-Ranker on heavy clay soils are hence partly due to earthworms.

ONOSODE: Did you find any chemical changes in the soil due to the weathering of pyrites?

KNABE: I think the experiments which have been done at Wooster where they leached out the spoil material in lysimeters (Struthers, 1964) could help you more because we have only investigated the refuse piles once. Differences may result from different tippings or from weathering. We think some differences are due to weathering, but you will have to prove it.

DAVIS: In studying about 75 deep-mine refuse piles in Pennsylvania we noticed differences between samples taken from near the surface and from 2 ft beneath the surface. On new spoils which have had a chance to weather a little, we might have a pH of 2.5 near the surface and 7.8 at 2 ft underneath.

BENGTSON: Did you say that the films around the spoil particles are clay? If so, do you think this is formed in place or is it suspended clay that has percolated down through the profile?

KNABE: The real films were Fe or other minerals. The clay was only shale weathered in situ which had adsorbed water and become plastic, and could then be compressed. It adhered very loosely. There were no very hard films, but a loose connection between the fragments of coal.

THE MICROFLORA OF DUMPED SOILS IN TWO OPENCAST BROWN-COAL MINING REGIONS OF POLAND*

Krystyna Müller

Scientific Research Enterprise, Upper Silesian Industrial Area,
Polish Academy of Sciences, Zabrze, Poland

The part played by microflora in the transformation of dumped material was studied in 1966 and 1967 in two opencast brown-coal mining regions of Poland. The areas selected for research included uncultivated dump soils and soils that had been influenced for many years by plant life, introduced either as part of a reclamation program or by natural succession. In the two regions, different factors govern both the rate and manner of transformation of dump material by the microflora. In the Konin region (where the dump lands are formed of predominantly basic soils), differentiation in microbiological activity in the soils is dependent principally on the species of plants introduced under the reclamation plan but also on the age of the dump and weather conditions. In the Turoszów region (where the soils are mostly acid with pH less than 6.0 in H_2O), both the geological origin and chemical composition of the rock material limit the activity of the soil microflora. With gradual neutralization of the soil, there is an increase in the influence of external factors—vegetation and climate—on the microbiological processes in the dumped soil.

INTRODUCTION

During the opencast mining of brown coal, the rock formations in the overburden become intermixed and toxic formations frequently occur on the surface of the dumped soils. Reclamation of these barren areas is hindered by these toxic elements (Illner and Katzur, 1964; Knabe, 1962; Skawina and Zubikowska-Skawinowa, 1964), whose occurrence is determined by the geological structure of the coal deposit and the lithological

---

* An invited paper; not presented at the symposium because the author was unable to attend.

and mineralogical composition and chemical properties of the overburden. These factors govern both the quantitative and qualitative occurrence of the microflora which assist in the biochemical transformation of these dump materials (Drzał and Smyk, 1968; Smyk, 1967; Zajcew, Sawicz, 1967).

The purpose of this research was to characterize the processes by means of which the microflora and plants transform the raw soil formed by the mining waste. Research sites were chosen to represent both young, unimproved dump soils and areas that had been influenced for several years by vegetation—introduced either as part of a reclamation program or by natural succession.

The research was centered in two of the Polish brown-coal mining areas; Konin, in Poznań province, and Turoszów, in Wrocław province. In these two regions, both the natural conditions and the lithological and chemical composition of the dominant overburden formations differ considerably.

PROCEDURE

Microbiological characteristics were studied in the summers of 1966 and 1967. Meteorological conditions in 1967 were generally more favorable for the development of microflora than in 1966.

Samples for microbiological tests were taken at 6-week intervals (i.e. five times from April to November), and the following determinations were made:

1) total number of microorganisms (bacteria, in active and spore form, actinomycetes, and fungi);
2) total number of microorganisms associated with N metabolism (nitrifiers, ammonifiers, and atmospheric-N assimilators);
3) total number of microorganisms associated with S metabolism;
4) activity of microorganisms in the decomposition of cellulose;
5) P bacteria activity; and
6) systematic and frequency relationships in the occurrence of the most common genera of microorganisms.

Three parallel tests were carried out for each determination. The quantitative results were analyzed statistically, and the significance of the differences was assessed by the Dunnett (1955) test.

The most frequently occurring genera of microorganisms were identified on the basis of microscopic observations and biochemical analysis, using the standard systematic tables for microorganisms (Breed et al., 1957; Gilman, 1956; Skerman, 1959).

RESULTS

The Konin region

Test sites in this region were on dumped soils of Tertiary and Quaternary formations. The dumped material showed a neutral or mildly alkaline reaction (pH 7.2 to 8.0 in H_2O) and exhibited no significant differences in chemical composition.

Predominant microorganisms in the sampled dumps of the Konin region were (numbers in parentheses indicate dump locations as shown in Fig. 1):

Bacillus megaterium (1, 2, 3, 4, 5)
B. cereus (1, 2, 3, 4, 5)
B. lentus (1)
B. pumilus (1)
B. mycoides (2, 3, 4, 5)
B. subtilis (4, 5)
Mucor griseo-cyanus (1, 4, 5)
Penicillium chrysogenum (1, 2, 3, 5)
P. lilacinum (4)
Fusarium orthoceras (1, 2, 4)
Oospora variabilis (1, 2, 3)
Alternaria tenuis (1, 2, 3, 4, 5)
Azotobacter chroococcum (2, 3, 4, 5)
Streptomyces globisporus (2, 4)
S. fumosus (2, 3)
S. ruber (2, 3, 5)
S. oidiosporus (4, 5)
S. cylindrosporus (4, 5)
Stysanus medius (2, 3)
Flavobacterium rigense (3, 4)
Arthrobacter tumescens (3)
A. globiformis (4)
Botrytis cinerea (3)
Rhizopus nigricans (5)
Thamnidium elegans (5)
Torula alli (5)
Verticillium cellulosae (5)

The results do not indicate any considerable differences among the Konin region dumps in the genus composition of the microfloral communities

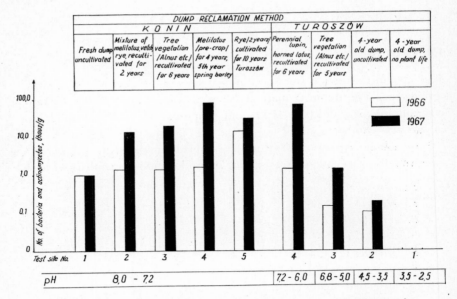

FIGURE 1   Variations in numbers of bacteria and actinomycetes in dump soils in the regions of Konin and Turoszów in 1966 and 1967.

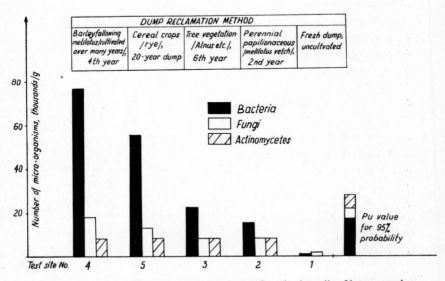

FIGURE 2   Variations in numbers of microflora in the soils of brown-coal dumps in the Konin region in 1967.

characterizing the particular environments. In all the areas sampled, transformation of the dump material is assisted by microorganisms associated with N, P, and C metabolism; however, no active S-metabolizing microorganisms were found. Differences among the dumped soils of the Konin region in both the quantity of microorganisms present and their biochemical activity were observed (Fig. 1). These are probably due to the influence of agrotechnical factors, since the majority of the tested dump sites in the Konin region are now cultivated lands. The growth in intensity of the microbiological processes in the dump material is proportional to the length of cultivation time and depends on the species of plants introduced (Fig. 2). In this region, the microbiological activity should theoretically be at its highest after about 10 years of agricultural cultivation of the dump soil. Therefore, Test Site 5 can be used as a standard with which the other test sites can be compared.

Analysis of the results shown in Fig. 2 justifies the following observations:

1) At Test Site 3, there are markedly fewer microorganisms (bacteria and fungi) than at Test Site 5. The influence of tree growth on the quantity of microflora found in the dump material is clearly weaker than that of leguminous plants.

2) On the dump cultivated with a perennial leguminous mixture (Test Site 2), the number of microorganisms is lower than at Site 5; Site 5 has been cultivated for a long time, with cereals, whereas Site 2 has been farmed for only 2 years.

3) Test Site 4, covered with perennial legumes (preliminary crop: *Melilotus alba* for a 4-year period), has a markedly higher total number of microorganisms than Site 5.

4) Only insignificant differences were noted in the numbers of actinomycetes on the various test areas.

The Turoszów region

In the Turoszów dump areas, both Tertiary formations (pH 2.5 to 4.5) and Quaternary formations (pH 4.5 to 6.0) may be found (Fig. 1). Non-homogeneity in the mineralogy and lithology of the dump material, and hence in its chemical properties, has a decisive influence on both the numbers and genus composition of the microflora. With a rise in the pH of the dump material, activity of the microorganisms in the N and C metabolism cycle increases, while that of the chemosynthetic microorganisms associated with S metabolism decreases.

Microorganisms characterizing the samples dumps of the Turoszów region were (numbers in parentheses indicate dump locations as shown in Fig. 1):

Thiobacillus thiooxidans (1, 2)
T. ferroxidans (1, 2)
T. thioparus (2, 3)
Mucor griseo-cyanus (3)
Penicillium chrysogenum (3, 4)
Bacillus megaterium (3, 4)
B. pumilus (3)
B. cereus (4)
B. mycoides (4)
Flavobacterium sp. (3)
Streptomyces globisporus (3, 4)
Alternaria tenuis (3, 4)
Aerobacter aerogenes (4)
Arthrobacter tumescens (4)
Cladosporium epiphyllum (4)

The pH also influences the numbers of microorganisms in the dump material (Fig. 3). Fungi are less sensitive to the acidity of the environment than bacteria, particularly in the pH range from 2.0 to 4.9. When pH increases to 7.0, the numerical superiority of the bacteria over the fungi is increased, and at the same time, there is an overall rise in the number of microorganisms in the dump soils. Assuming that pH is one of the factors affecting the microflora of the Turoszów dump grounds, we can distinguish the following groups:

Group I Dumps with very acid soils (pH less than 4.0) and usually without vegetative cover. The total number of microorganisms* varies with pH from 0 to 1000 cells/g. The number of S bacteria is sometimes as high as 10,000 cells/g. In this pH range, ammonification does not take place. The dumps at Test Sites 1 and 2 are in this group.

Group II Dumps with an acid or weakly acid soil reaction (pH of 4.5 to 6.0) and with little vegetative cover. The total number of microorganisms* does not exceed 10,000 cells/g. Traces of ammonification are found in such dumps (Site 3).

---

* Excluding chemo-synthetic bacteria and atmospheric-N assimilators.

Group III Dumps with a mildly acid or neutral soil reaction (pH over 6.0) and usually bearing a varied plant cover from either natural succession or reclamation efforts. The number of microorganisms usually exceeds 10,000 cells/g; the number of ammonifiers usually goes up to 100,000 cells/g. Dumps covered with perennial legumes are in this group (Site 4). The genus composition of the microbiocenose is broader than that of the microfloral

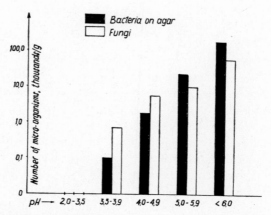

FIGURE 3   The influence of pH on the number of soil microorganisms in the dumps of the Turoszów region.

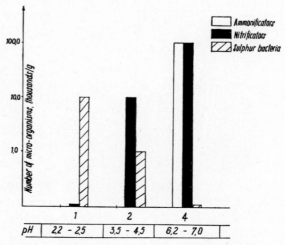

FIGURE 4   The influence of fertilization and neutralization on the activity of the soil microorganisms.

communities characteristic of most of the test sites in the Turoszów region. Neutralization of the soil results in increased activity of the microorganisms associated with N metabolism (ammonifiers, nitrifiers, and symbiotic assimilators of atmospheric N), while the microorganisms associated with S metabolism play a smaller role (Fig. 4).

DISCUSSION

Comparison of the results from the two regions demonstrates that in the different environments, different factors are responsible for deciding both the initiation and the progress of the microbiotic transformation of the virgin dump material.

In the Konin region, where the dominant rock formations show a basic reaction, the major factor influencing both the number and the biochemical activity of the microorganisms is the reclamation method. Perennial leguminous plants as a pre-cultivation crop have a beneficial influence on the activity of microorganisms associated with the metabolism of N, P, and C. The results obtained confirm those of many authors (Balicka and Sobieszczański, 1964; Hazuk, 1967; Müller, 1967; Smyk, 1967; University of Illinois, 1953).

The overall test results from dump sites in the Konin region show that transformation of the dump material by the microflora is principally dependent on external factors (plant life and climate). The structure of the rock substrata, which differs little in the tested environments, is of minor importance.

Among the groups of microorganisms tested, bacteria and actinomycetes reacted most noticeably to the presence of vegetation. For fungi, the quantitative differences observed between young, uncultivated dumps and re-cultivated dumps were not so distinct. The development of microflora under gramineous-leguminous plants is generally more active than under tree vegetation.

In the Turoszów region, the chemical properties of the dump material limit, to a certain extent, the activity of the microorganisms in the transformation process. This is particularly applicable to very acid Tertiary formations (pH 2.5 to 4.5) and to a lesser degree to Quaternary (pH 4.5 to 6.0). This conclusion is confirmed in numerous scientific papers on the bio-toxicity of acid soils (pH less than 4.0) (Limstrom and Deitschman, 1951; Knabe, 1962; Skawina and Zubikowska-Skawinowa, 1964).

For dump areas with a pH above 6.0, due to the improvement measures applied in these districts in 1960 (spreading slag, fertilizing with NPK, planting perennial legumes, etc.), a markedly beneficial effect was observed on the formation of certain microfloral communities and on their biochemical action.

The tests and results presented suggest the hypothesis that, on dump areas consisting of acid formations (the majority of the Turoszów dumps), the lithological and chemical composition of the dump material governs the development of the particular groups of microorganisms and the nature of their biochemical activity. With gradual neutralization of the soil (rise in pH) there is an increase in the importance of the external factors (including plant cover) in the shaping of the microbiological processes in the dump material.

LITERATURE CITED

Balicka, N., and J. Sobieszczański. 1964. Rola mikroflory w rekultywacji terenów poeksploatacyjnych kopalni węgla brunatnego w Turoszowie. *Roczniki Nauk Rolniczych* 88-A-3, 711–722.

Breed, R. S., E. G. D. Murray, and N. R. Smith. 1957. *Bergey's manual of determinative bacteriology*. Bailliere, Tindal Cox, Ltd. 7th ed. London.

Drzał, M., and B. Smyk. 1968. Rola czynnika mikrobiologicznego w kształtowaniu struktur i form podłoża skalnego. *Przegląd Geograficzny* 13, 425–430.

Dunnett, C. W. 1955. A multiple comparison procedure for comparing several treatments with a control. *J. Amer. Statist. Ass.* 50, 1096–1121.

Gilman, J. D. 1956. *A manual of soil fungi*. Constable and Co., Ltd. London.

Hazuk, A. 1967. Gestaltung der enzymatischen Aktivität von Versatzsand-Restlöchern. *III. Int. Symposium über Rekultivierungen der durch den Bergbau beschädigten Böden.* Ref. Sammlung 88–94.

Illner, K., and J. Katzur. 1964. Zur Wiedernutzbarmachung kulturfeindlicher Kippen und Halden im Braunkohlentagebau. *Bergbautechnik* 14, 403–412.

Knabe, W. 1962. The reclamation of lands stripped for brown coal. Ohio Agr. Exp. Sta., Forest. Dep. Ser. 49, 11 p.

Limstrom, G. A., and G. H. Deitschman. 1951. Reclaiming Illinois strip coal lands by forestry planting. *Univ. of Illinois Agr. Exp. Sta. Bull.* 547, 201–251.

Müller, K. 1967. Mikrobiologische Untersuchungen von Braunkohlenkippen im Industriegebiet von Konin. *III. Int. Symposium über Rekultivierungen der durch den Bergbau beschädigten Böden.* Ref. Sammlung 302–307.

Simon, W., and E. Brüning. 1964. Über Anbaumöglichkeiten von Gräser- und Kleearten als Pionierpflanzen bei der Kippenrekultivierung im Bereich des Braunkohlenwerkes Finkenherd bei Frankfurt/Oder. *Zeitschr. f. Landeskultur* 5, 133–150.

Skawina, T., and L. Zubikowska-Skawinowa. 1964. Zagadnienia teksyczności i rekultywacji na rekultywowanych zwałowiskach kopalni węgla brunatnego "Turów." *Węgiel Brunatny* 2, 135–142.

Skerman, V. B. D. 1959. *A guide to the identification of the genera of bacteria, with methods and digests of generic characteristics*. The Williams and Wilkins Company, Baltimore, Md. 217 p.

Smyk, B. 1967. Gestaltung der mikrobiologischen Aktivität auf einigen Bergbauneulandskippen und Versatzsand-Restlöchern entstehender Böden. *III. Int. Symposium über Rekultivierungen der durch den Bergbau beschädigten Böden*. Ref. Sammlung 353–359.

University of Illinois. 1953. The potentialities of revegetating and utilizing agronomic species on strip mine areas in Illinois. A progress report covering the sixth year of work on a cooperative investigation conducted by Univ. of Illinois, Urbana.

Zajcew, Sawicz. 1967. Chimiko-biołogiczeskij process okisslenija sulfidow żeleza w gruntach otwałow i terrikonow ugolnych rozrabotok Podmoskownowo basejna. *III. Int. Symposium über Rekultivierungen der durch den Bergbau beschädigten Böden*. Ref. Sammlung 163–168.

SUCCESSION OF SOIL FAUNA
IN AFFORESTED SPOIL BANKS
OF THE BROWN-COAL MINING
DISTRICT OF COLOGNE

Ulrich Neumann

*Cologne, West Germany**

In the reclaimed areas of the Cologne Brown-Coal Mining District, a succession can be observed from raw spoil banks to approximately 30-year-old afforestations. Carabid beetles, millipedes, and woodlice were chosen for investigation. The progress of succession of the three groups is different. On spoil banks a pioneer association of Carabids develops with a very great number of species and individuals. With the growth of trees and other vegetation the pioneer association gradually decreases and finally disappears. The fauna which follows is one of the transition stages (10- to 20-year-old afforestations); this in the end is replaced by a forest association.

The fauna of millipedes and woodlice does not develop a pioneer association. On the contrary, new species gradually appear with the growth and development of the new forest stands. The great number of species and specimens decrease in undisturbed forest stands. The most important factors influencing immigration are the microclimatic conditions and the moisture of the soil. The microclimate of spoil banks and young afforestations is a very extreme one; that of 11-year-old afforestations can be similar to that of ordinary woodland. Other factors important for immigration are food supply and distance from the afforestations to undisturbed forest sites.

INTRODUCTION

Just as important as the problem of which species of trees should be grown on spoil banks is the problem of the future growth and productive capacity of the new forest sites. Good growth is guaranteed when a fertile soil has developed. Soil fauna and soil microorganisms in a stand are exclusively responsible for the formation of a fertile soil.

---

* The research reported was conducted at the Zoological Institute of the University of Cologne.

Nutrients, originating from minerals or from fertilizers, are assimilated by plants and carried back to the soil as leaf litter. They are then accumulated in the litter, and must again be made available to the plants by breakdown of the litter. This breakdown is caused by soil fauna together with microorganisms. Without soil fauna, thick layers of *Rohhumus* (raw humus) develop. In this way nutrients become unavailable and aeration and moistening of the soil are also impeded (Thiele, 1964b). Normally as a first step litter is eaten and reduced to small pieces by primary decomposing animals (especially Diplopoda, Isopoda, and other species of the macrofauna). Then smaller animals (mesofauna) and microorganisms are capable of further decomposition to humus.

Many authors have proved that the presence of primary decomposing animals is a necessary condition for quick breakdown of litter (Thiele, 1964b). The rate of breakdown of litter depends on a soil fauna which is rich in species and individuals. A poor soil fauna causes incomplete and slow decomposition and undesirable humid acids develop, causing an acid soil. Acid soil is a poor environment for soil animals and results in more *Rohhumus*. Under these conditions, circulation of nutrients is insufficient. Thus N may become deficient in reclaimed areas, whereas the other nutrients can be supplied if the original soil material is of good quality (Jacoby, 1963). The lack of N retards tree growth. Soil fauna both start and maintain N circulation, provided N has been initially supplied by fertilizer application or by N-fixing bacteria.

I want to demonstrate the development of the soil fauna in reclaimed areas. (Dunger (1968) also investigated and recently published upon the soil fauna on reclaimed sites in mideastern Germany.) This development can show whether the new forest sites will be of poorer quality, the same quality, or even better quality than the original ones. Carabid beetles, millipedes, and woodlice were chosen for investigation. Carabids are important because they can regulate the abundance of harmful insects; moreover, being highly sensitive, they show the changes in the elementary conditions of the site; and finally, the succession of carabids particularly shows the factors determining the formation of a new soil fauna in the reclaimed site. Millipedes and woodlice were included in the study because they are primary decomposing animals.

METHODS

Succession was traced through the use of pitfall traps exposed throughout the year in stands of various ages. (It would of course be possible to trace succession in a single stand, but this would require many years, and it would not be possible to recognize the generally effective factors.) Two sites that had not been afforested were also included. Information about the sites is given in Table 1.

TABLE 1

The study sites

Site	Condition of site or type of afforestation	Age yr
K 0	raw spoil bank	1
K 3	spoil bank	3
P 2	hybrid poplar and beech (increasing vegetation)	2
P 3	hybrid poplar and beech (surface-covering vegetation)	3
P 5	alder (*Alnus glutinosa*)	5
P 7	hybrid poplar and alder	7
P 11	hybrid poplar and alder (canopy closed)	11
R 28	red oak (*Quercus rubra*)	28
P 28_2	hybrid poplar and alder	28
P 25	hybrid poplar and alder	25
P 28_1	hybrid poplar and alder	28
Bk	beech (*Fagus silvatica*)	undisturbed woodland
Ek	oak (*Quercus robur*)	undisturbed woodland

FACTORS DETERMINING SUCCESSION

Distance between afforestation and undisturbed woodland

If an old afforestation is distant from original forest sites, development of a soil fauna takes a long time because of the relatively slow migration of the animals. Additional spoil banks or young afforestations between an old afforestation and undisturbed woodland act as barriers which small forest animals cannot cross. The distances between some of the afforestations studied and undisturbed forest are as follows (Fig. 1):

Site	Distance
K 0	1 km
K 3 through P 11	from 2.5 km (P 5) to 6.5 km (P 2)
R 28 and P 28_2	1 km
P 25	300 m (surrounded by pine stands)
P 28_1	adjoining undisturbed woodland

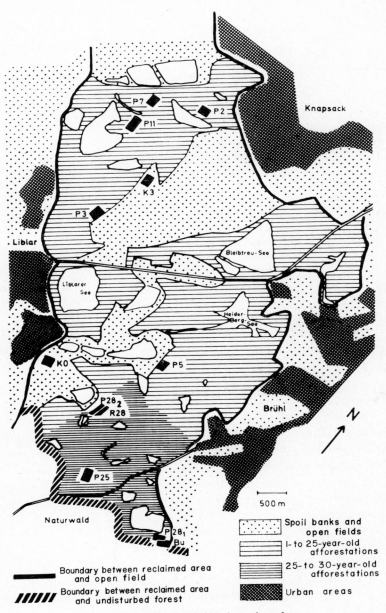

FIGURE 1   The sites in the investigated area.

Development of afforestation

The canopy of the stand must soon close because animals of the forest soil do not like sunlight. A forest soil fauna develops more slowly in open woodland.

Food supply

In an afforestation composed of trees supplying leaf litter that is particularly digestible, the reproduction rate of animals which decompose organic matter will be higher than in sites which produce less-digestible foliage. Trees having preferred foliage are poplar, alder, linden, hornbeam, elm, ash, and others (Dunger, 1958). Carnivorous animals must find other animals, which have previously immigrated, for their prey.

Microclimate

Many authors (Thiele, 1959, 1964a; Lauterbach, 1964; and others) have shown that microclimate is one of the most decisive factors for the "*Biotopbindung*" (restriction to the site) of Carabidae, Diplopoda, and Isopoda. Microclimate depends mainly on type and density of vegetation, but also on soil characteristics and moisture content. Naturally, woodland animals prefer a humid and cool microclimate.

Temperature The daily temperature curve (Fig. 2) becomes more balanced as the stands develop. The great difference between P 7 and P 11 is remarkable; it results from the much higher density of site P 11, where the canopy is almost closed.

Relative humidity of the air Also note that the humidity of the air (Fig. 3) of P 7 is similar to that in the spoil bank K 0, whereas P 11 shows forest conditions similar to old afforestations.

Evaporation Naturally, K 0 has the highest evaporation (Fig. 4). Again we see a great difference between P 11 and P 7. But there is also a difference between P 7 and K 0, because vegetation on P 7 has reduced the wind influence.

General Spoil banks have an extreme microclimate on summer days. Young afforestations (P 2 through P 7) very much resemble spoil bank sites in their microclimate. But evaporation is reduced by vegetation even

22*

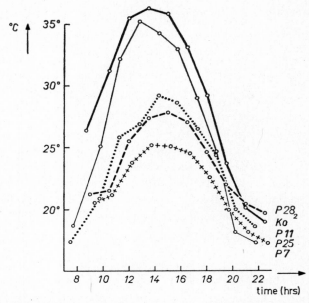

FIGURE 2   Daily march of the temperature in summer, 5 cm above
soil surface.

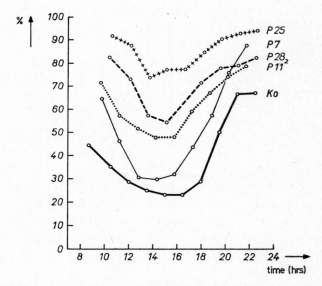

FIGURE 3   Daily march of the relative humidity of the air in summer,
5 cm above soil surface.

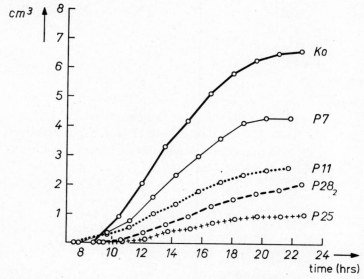

FIGURE 4 Cumulative evaporation in summer, 5 cm above soil surface.

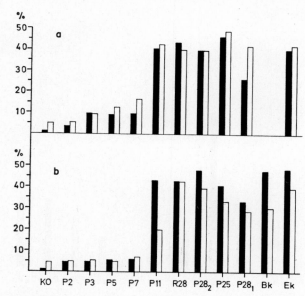

FIGURE 5 Soil moisture on two different days (a and b) in summer
(black bar is for soil surface; white bar, for 5-cm depth).

on young afforestations. The microclimate of wooded sites is more balanced; an 11-year-old site, thickly grown, can already have a woodland micro-climate.

Soil moisture

Soil moisture is very important to the groups of animals which were studied because they live mostly in the soil or in the litter. Besides soil type, moisture depends on the density of vegetation. In P 11 (Fig. 5) the results of stand density are again evident as the soil moisture is equal to that in the oldest afforestations and undisturbed forest.

DESCRIPTION OF SUCCESSION

Carabidae

The number of species and individuals living on spoil banks is relatively small but changes after afforestation (Fig. 6). When increasing vegetation covers the surface of the soil, many new species immigrate; some of these reproduce rapidly (e.g. in P 3). On such sites, the highest number of species

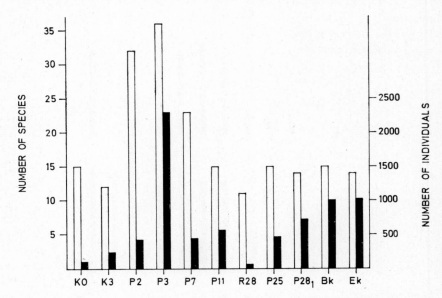

FIGURE 6   Carabidae (black bars represents number of individuals; white bar, number of species).

and individuals can be found. This is a pioneer fauna. In the course of site development, the number of species and individuals of the pioneer fauna decrease; the species of the young afforestations no longer find suitable living conditions and therefore disappear. But from P 11 on, woodland species could find suitable living conditions. Nevertheless we do not find them there because woodland species, in contrast to those living in newly afforested sites, are mostly unable to fly, and P 11 is too far from undisturbed forest sites. The species living in P 11 belong to a transitional community. R 28 is also too far from the original forest sites; at this stage and site, all species of young afforestations have disappeared and therefore the number of species and individuals is at its lowest. The number of individuals of woodland species may be low as compared to the original forest sites, because some animals on which carabids prey have not yet immigrated.

Diplopoda

Depending on age and the distance of a stand from the original woodland the number of species and individuals increase successively from the raw spoil bank to the oldest afforestations (Fig. 7). This is shown by the fact that the diplopod fauna consists of woodland species. A pioneer fauna does not develop. In P 11, one woodland species reproduces prolifically; in P 28_1, the highest number of species and individuals can be found. Comparatively low numbers of species and individuals are found in the original

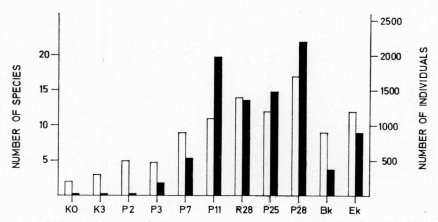

FIGURE 7   Diplopoda (black bar represents number of individuals; white bar, number of species).

forest sites because, on one hand, the kind of leaf litter is not very good food for these animals and, on the other hand, these sites lack the synanthropic character which the oldest afforestations still have.

Isopoda

Isopods do not develop a pioneer fauna either. Mainly two species (*Trachelipus rathkei* and *Armadillidium vulgare*) invade spoil banks and young afforestations. These two species, and only these, can also be found in woody afforestations (e.g. P 11) because the usual woodland species are not able to migrate over long distances. R 28 shows a richer isopod fauna (Fig. 8). *T. rathkei* reaches its highest reproduction rate in P 7; the highest for *A. vulgare* is in R 28. The number of species and individuals is highest in P 28_1 and, as a result of the better food (litter) in the afforestations, is far higher than those in the original forest sites. Site P 25, with the same favorable conditions, provides lower numbers, probably because the surrounding pine stands are a barrier for some species.

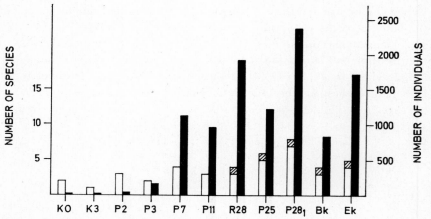

FIGURE 8   Isopoda (black bar represents number of individuals; white bar, number of species; and diagonally hatched bar, the subfamily Trichoniscinae, which is considered here as one species).

COMPARISON

The immense significance of leaf litter is clearly shown in the numbers of diplopods and isopods of site Ü (Table 2). These data are from a set of pitfall traps exposed along a line extending from site Bu (undisturbed forest) into P 28_1 (Fig. 1); the values are based on two pitfall traps each.

The differences between the numbers of individuals in Bu and P 28$_1$ are extraordinarily great and reveal the importance of the food factor.

Comparing the woodland species of the three examined groups in regard to their ability to spread, diplopods rank first; they can be found in sites far from natural woodlands. Even though they are not able to fly, a few carabids compare favorably to the diplopods in this respect. The woodlice rank lowest in mobility; no woodlouse has spread farther than R 28 (1 km).

TABLE 2

Numbers of individuals in species of Diplopoda and Isopoda trapped on a transect extending from a natural forest into an afforestation

Species	Site Ü (P 28$_1$)	Site Ü (Bu)
Diplopods		
Brachydesmus superus Latzel	19[a]	0
Chordeuma silvestre Latzel	5	21
Craspedosoma rawlinsii Leach	8	14
Cylindroiulus nitidus Verhoeff	3	13
C. londinensis C. L. Koch	12	3
C. punctatus Leach	10	2
Glomeris marginata Villers	45	50
Julus scandinavius Latzel	141	8
Leptoiulus belgicus Latzel	93	6
Microchordeuma gallicum Latzel	12	0
Polydesmus angustus Latzel	16	0
P. denticulatus C. L. Koch	52	11
P. inconstans Porat	1	1
P. testaceus C. L. Koch	23	5
Schizophyllum sabulosum L.	2	0
Tachypodoiulus niger Leach	91	30
Total	533	164
Isopods		
Armadillidium opacum C. L. Koch	31	1
A. vulgare Latr.	1	1
Ligidium hypnorum (Cuv.)	195	31
Oniscus asellus L.	289	107
Philoscia muscorum (Scop.)	20	0
Porcellio scaber Latr.	2	0
Trachelipus rathkei Brdt.	1	0
Trichoniscinae Verh.	189	18
Total	839	158

[a] Italicized values are considerably greater than those of the other site.

Compared to the carabids, diplopods and isopods play an unimportant part in young afforestations. After the soil has been vegetated for some time, the proportions are reversed. While the abundance of carabids decreases to a very low level and the numbers for even the old afforestations adjoining original woodland are less than those of the original forest, the numbers of diplopods and isopods increase rapidly and exceed that in the undisturbed forest sites. This can be attributed to the fact that diplopods and isopods prefer the food supply of the oldest afforestations to that of the original forests. These afforestations favor the decomposer animals.

CONCLUSIONS

What conclusions can we reach concerning the new sites like P 28_1, and to what degree have natural conditions been reached? In the first place the afforestations are, with respect to tree species, nurse crops. Considering the fauna (diplopods and isopods), the new sites are better than the old ones. There is the possibility that, from the point of economics, the new forest areas will develop in the future into better sites than they were before disturbance. To grow better forests for utilization we must encourage a rich soil fauna which effects a faster transformation of leaf litter and thus a sufficient supply of plant nutrients. Fertilizer must be used to start the forest culture because, at the beginning, there is no soil fauna and there is a severe lack of N. Afterwards, lupine, alder and other plants with nodules containing N-fixing bacteria must bridge the gap until the time when a substantial soil fauna has developed. To develop a rich soil fauna in a short time, the trees of an afforestation should be planted close together to keep sunlight from the surface. In recent forest cultures, this effect has been achieved by growing lupine; grass is useless for this purpose. An afforestation should be established in three strata (herbaceous, shrub, and tree). This kind of afforestation creates the necessary microclimate for the fauna of a woodland.

The trees planted first should be those whose litter is preferred by soil animals, e.g. poplar, alder, elm, linden, hornbeam, or ash. These species at least should be mixed in with the major species at the site.

A proper microclimate enables soil fauna to migrate into a site; a good food supply guarantees their survival. In spite of all this, soil fauna will hardly migrate into a site if it is too far away from one originally inhabited. Here man must introduce the animals into the new suitable site. The best way to do this is to transport soil from a site with rich soil fauna to the new site. This soil will help start a new population which might later spread throughout the new site.

LITERATURE CITED

Dunger, W. 1958. Über die Zersetzung der Laubstreu durch die Boden-Makrofauna im Auenwald. Zool. Jb. (Syst.) 86, 129–180.

Dunger, W. 1968. Die Entwicklung der Bodenfauna auf rekultivierten Kippen und Halden des Braunkohlentagebaues. Abh. Ber. Naturkundemus. Görlitz, 43, Nr. 2. 1–256.

Jacoby, H. 1963. Zur forstlichen Rekultivierung im Rheinischen Braunkohlenrevier. Dipl.-Arbeit Hann. Münden.

Lauterbach, A. W. 1964. Verbreitungs- und aktivitätsbestimmende Faktoren bei Carabiden in Sauerländischen Wäldern. Abh. Landesmus. Naturkde. Münster i. W. 26, 1–103.

Thiele, H. U. 1959. Experimentelle Untersuchungen über die Abhängigkeit bodenbewohnender Tierarten vom Kalkgehalt des Standorts. Z. ang. Entom. 44, 1–21.

Thiele, H. U. 1964a. Experimentelle Untersuchungen über die Ursachen der Biotopbindung bei Carabiden. Z. Morph. Ökol. Tiere 53, 387–452.

Thiele, H. U. 1964b. Bodentiere und Bodenfruchtbarkeit. Naturwiss. Rundschau 17, 224–230.

DISCUSSION

MORGAN: Are millipedes and woodlice which you have studied of much importance to the mineralization or mobilization of nutrients for use of plants?

NEUMANN: Millipedes and woodlice are primary decomposing animals. Lacking these animals, only microorganisms (fungi, bacteria, etc.) remain to perform the decomposition. The breakdown by these organisms is too slow. The result is a thick layer of litter in which the nutrients are accumulated.

E. PETERSON: Is it known how to encourage definite generic groups to enhance a particular part of litter breakdown or a particular part of a biogeochemical cycle?

NEUMANN: We know that millipedes are very important animals for the breakdown of litter, especially the family "Glomeridae"; but it is not known how to encourage one special group or how to influence a particular part of litter breakdown.

KNABE: Did you investigate whether a balance between predators and plant-eating soil animals had already been achieved at that time? Could it be that the high frequency of individuals is due to the lack of predators?

NEUMANN: On the contrary, the high frequency of individuals in P 3 is due to one of the carabids, which are carnivorous animals. They reproduce in such great numbers because the site P 3 was fully covered with vegetation providing favorable living conditions for many species of many different groups. In older afforestations the numbers of individuals of the carabids decrease.

AHARRAH: You mentioned the earthworm as you started. When do you find these invading or haven't you found any?

NEUMANN: Earthworms normally spread about 4 to 8 m per year, and I have found earthworms at a distance of 1 km. That means that these species had to spread more than 30 m/year. A possible explanation for this fact could be that these earthworms are species associated with the litter and not with the soil.

NODULATION BY VARIOUS STRAINS OF *RHIZOBIUM* WITH *ROBINIA PSEUDOACACIA* SEEDLINGS PLANTED IN STRIP-MINE SPOIL

Frederick M. Rothwell

*Department of Life Sciences, Indiana State University,
Terre Haute, Indiana*

Sixteen strains of *Rhizobium* were investigated to determine their ability to nodulate with *Robinia pseudoacacia* L. seedlings which were grown in four eastern Kentucky strip-mine spoils. Three of the bacterial strains were effective in all spoil types and two strains nodulated in three of the four spoil types when the seedlings were grown under controlled conditions. Plastic planting bullets were selected as the most efficient means of growing and examining the seedlings for nodulation. The use of planting bullets may contribute significantly to studies of rhizospheric as well as symbiotic and mycorrhizal micro-organisms associated with tree species used in revegetating drastically disturbed areas.

INTRODUCTION

One of the most important aspects to be considered in the reclamation of drastically disturbed sites is the choice of cover species. May (1965) has outlined a few considerations to insure the best possible revegetation of coal strip-mined areas, including the study of site stability, texture, and acidity; choice of species or mixtures to suit conditions and desired land-use; and selection of varieties and seed sources adapted to spoils and climate. An additional consideration which might be added to the above is the continued investigation and understanding of the microbiological ecology associated with the vegetative species as they become established on these "soil" conditions.

Although mineral nutrition is rarely a limiting factor for establishment of cover species, the lack of available nitrogen, humus, and a desirable microflora in these areas has favored the selection of species which have a known bacterial or fungal associate. In his excellent study of plant colonization on mining wastes, Schramm (1966) concluded that the only generally successful original colonists of bare and nitrogen-deficient wastes were either nitrogen-fixing plants or certain ectotrophically mycorrhizal species. As noted by Silver (1969), many of the nodulated non-leguminous species have considerable ecological importance as pioneering plants as a result of biological nitrogen fixation. In the past, *Robinia pseudoacacia* L. has been one of the nodulated nitrogen-fixing species widely used as a nurse crop in the revegetation of strip-mined lands, and even though it is losing favor with reclamation foresters in this role, it may be a satisfactory research species in determining interactions between host and endophyte under these conditions.

Hoffmann (1963) demonstrated that the total nitrogen level of *R. pseudoacacia* can vary depending upon the strain of nodulating bacterium which infects the plant. He concluded from the results of four cross-inoculation series in which strains of *Rhizobium* from several types of leguminous plants were used, that *Robinia* exhibits a broad spectrum of infectivity with these strains, and that the nitrogen-fixing efficiency varied with the strain. Since *Robinia* is still planted for erosion control, and on some of the most acid of strip-mined areas, the following study was made to determine the ability of various strains of *Rhizobium* to nodulate with *Robinia pseudoacacia* seedlings which were grown from seeds planted in four different eastern Kentucky spoils.

MATERIALS AND METHODS

The spoil materials and previous history of spoil characteristics shown below, and the *Robinia pseudoacacia* seeds used in this study were supplied by the U.S. Department of Agriculture's Forest Service, Northeastern Forest Experiment Station, Berea, Ky.

Spoil B1 – Hazel Green; pH 4.8; moderate phosphate level; no apparent manganese toxicity; no previous history of legumes grown in this spoil.
Spoil B2 – Quicksand 5; pH 5.0; low phosphate level; no manganese toxicity; previous legume experimental plantings all nodulated well.

Spoil B3 – Quicksand 2; pH 3.9; low phosphate level; no manganese toxicity; no legume nodulation from previous plantings.

Spoil B4 – Hardburley 6; pH 4.2; phosphate level unknown; no apparent manganese toxicity; previous *Robinia* experimental plantings had some nodulation.

All of the experiments were conducted using native spoil which had been screened through a 0.635-cm mesh and otherwise untreated except for additions noted below. Two sizes of plastic planting bullets, 6.35 × 2.2 and 13.97 × 2.2 cm were obtained from the Forestry Division, The Tennessee Valley Authority, Norris, Tenn. These were filled with spoil material thoroughly moistened with distilled water, placed in test-tube racks and set aside to drain; following equilibration, a single scarified *Robinia* seed was planted to a depth of approximately 0.6 cm in each of the planting bullets. The bullets were subsequently placed in sterilized sand to a depth of 2.54 cm of the rim of the bullet in containers which permitted a 5.08-cm sand layer beneath the bottom of the bullet. Two replicates of five planting bullets for each spoil type and bacterial strain were used routinely throughout the study. The following host plant information was supplied with lyophilized strains of *Rhizobium* obtained from the U.S. Department of Agriculture, Agricultural Research Service, Peoria, Ill.

NRRL L-258 *Rhizobium* sp. (*Glycine hispida*)
NRRL L-259 *Rhizobium* sp. (*Glycine hispida*)
NRRL B-326 *Rhizobium Leguminosarum* (*Pisum* sp.)
NRRL B-509 *Rhizobium Leguminosarum* (None given)
NRRL L-234 *Rhizobium* sp. (*Vicia villosa*)
NRRL L-235 *Rhizobium* sp. (*Vicia villosa*)
NRRL L-26 *Rhizobium* sp. (*Lupinus perennis*)
NRRL L-31 *Rhizobium* sp. (*Lupinus luteus*)
NRRL L-58 *Rhizobium* sp. (*Medicago lupulina*)
NRRL L-65 *Rhizobium* sp. (*Medicago officinalis*)
NRRL L-187 *Rhizobium* sp. (*Robinia pseudoacacia*)
NRRL L-113 *Rhizobium* sp. (*Trifolium* sp.)
NRRL L-116 *Rhizobium* sp. (*Trifolium spadiceum*)

Three of the strains used as inoculants represented recent isolates from nodules of plants during the time the study was being made. Two of these, C4 and C6, were from a farm field of *Trifolium pratense* and the other, RQ2B, was from a 2-year-old *Robinia pseudoacacia* plant growing on a strip-mine site in western Kentucky. A standardized inoculum was obtained for each of the bacterial strains by centrifuging a 20-ml aliquot from 48-hour shake flask cultures. The cells were washed with saline, centrifuged again, and resuspended in 25 ml of 200 ppm monobasic calcium phosphate. A 30% transmittance value was obtained for each of the cultures using a B & L Spectronic 20 with phosphate as a control. On the 10th and 24th days following seed germination, 1 ml of the *Rhizobium* strain and 1 ml of a 200 ppm monobasic calcium phosphate solution were added to the planting bullets; 1 ml of distilled water was substituted for the bacterial strain in the control series. Plant growth was observed over a 60-day period under controlled conditions in a Percival Model PGC-78 growth chamber. Relative humidity was set at 70%, day temperature at 82 F, night temperature at 60 F, and 3300 foot-candle illumination was used for 18 hrs out of each 24-hr period.

RESULTS

It was necessary to ascertain the presence or absence of *Rhizobium* in the spoil before addition and evaluation of known strains could be made. Spoils used in this experimental study were obtained from sites in which locust is generally seeded in mixtures of the lespedezas, crownvetch, or birdsfoot trefoil seeds which are treated with their respective commercial inoculants. As noted in Table 1, bacterial strains capable of forming nodules with *Robinia* were either absent, non-infective, or present in insufficient numbers to bring about an infection.

TABLE 1

Robinia *seed germination and nodulation in spoil material from four eastern Kentucky locations*

Spoil location	Germination %	Nodulation %
B1	68.8	0
B2	45.3	0
B3	59.0	0
B4	61.8	0

After a preliminary screening of the 16 strains added to each of the spoil materials, five were selected as the most effective in producing nodules with *Robinia* under conditions of this study. Qualitative platings of spoil replicates indicated the survival of L-58, C4, and RQ2B strains. Even at this early stage of development, the appearance of coralloid nodules was particularly evident in L-58 replicates (Table 2).

TABLE 2

Robinia *nodulation*[a] *following addition of active* Rhizobium *strains*

Bacterial strain	Spoil locations			
	B1	B2	B3	B4
L-58	+	+	+	+
RQ2B	+	+	+	+
C4	+	+	+	+
L-187	+	+	+	−
L-26	+	−	+	+
Control	−	−	−	−

[a] Nodules observed = (+); nodules absent = (−).

DISCUSSION

According to Nutman (1963) wherever a nodulating species of legume occurs naturally, its nodule bacteria are found, and that conversely, nodule bacteria are not found in soil where their host plants are not naturalized or have only recently been introduced. Since nodulation of *Robinia* has been obtained on some of the strip-mine sites which were seeded with the mixtures noted previously (Davis, personal communication), it apparently can serve as a host plant for one or more strains of the commercial inoculants. The absence of nodules on seedlings grown in native spoils in this study would indicate either a low level of infective cells or an adverse effect on viability by the spoil material.

Nutman (1963) has pointed out that a large rhizoidal population in the rhizosphere would provide for a reserve to survive unfavorable soil conditions, and that nodule bacteria may take part in the process of bringing into solution and subsequent utilization by plants of mineral phosphate. These advantages were taken into consideration in selecting the plastic planting bullets; they were not only useful in evaluating the infective potential of *Rhizobium* strains added to seedlings grown in spoil, but they also offered a convenient means for studying the rhizosphere levels of the inoculum.

From a microbiological viewpoint, the planting bullet offers an excellent means for studying the rhizoplane and rhizosphere interaction of natural and induced associates. Continued investigations under field conditions of the microbial succession associated with a number of different revegetation species would permit one to determine those organisms which are of importance in the establishment of the tree species and those which are involved in a microbial symbiosis. Tree species planted on spoil banks are typically obtained from nursery stock and usually have the rhizoplane associates well established; however, removal of the seedling from a desirable rhizosphere environment may have a significant effect on the early development of the transplant. A summation of these effects may be found in a recent article by Wilde (1968) who points out: "At the present state of knowledge it may not be entirely metaphoric to state that a tree removed from the soil is only a part of the whole plant, a part surgically separated from its rhizospheric absorptive and digestive organ."

LITERATURE CITED

Hoffmann, Günter. 1964. Effektivität und Wirtsspezifität der Knöllchenbakterien von Robinia pseudoacacia L. *Archiv für Forstwesen* **13**, 563–576.

May, Robert F. 1965. Strip mine reclamation research—where are we? *Mining Congress J.* (April) **51**, 52–55.

Nutman, P. S. 1963. Factors influencing the balance of mutual advantage in legume symbiosis. In: *13th Symp. Soc. Gen. Microbiol.* "Symbiotic Associations". Cambridge Press. p. 51–71.

Schramm, J. R. 1966. Plant colonization studies on black wastes from anthracite mining in Pennsylvania. *Trans. Am. Phil. Soc.* **56**(1), 1–189.

Silver, W. S. 1969. Biology and ecology of nitrogen fixation by symbiotic associations of non-leguminous plants. *Proc. Roy. Soc.* (London), B, **172**, 389–400.

Wilde, S. A. 1968. Mycorrhizae and tree nutrition. *Bioscience* **18**(6), 482–484.

DISCUSSION

AHARRAH: We have previously discussed the possibilities of inhibition with *Robinia pseudoacacia* which we have not noticed in America. Do you suppose that this might hinge on the nodulating bacteria or some other microorganisms that infect this legume in the European areas?

ROTHWELL: I would rather believe that the inhibition to which you refer is not associated with *Rhizobium*; however, it is quite possible that other microorganisms may be producing toxic materials which are disseminated throughout the area in which the species are growing. Inhibition may be the result of these metabolic products in the soil rather than from the tree itself.

BAUER: It is not the effect of nodulation. Several German authors found toxic material called robine and robinin in all parts of *Robinia*, including the bark, leaves, and flowers. This toxic material hinders other species (herbs, grasses, etc.) from growing in these *Robinia* forests. This condition is found all over Europe, not just on spoils. I wonder if you find this antagonism in your *Robinia* forests in America as well, either in the natural or planted forests?

ROTHWELL: Do you have a procedure for the isolation and detection of robine?

BAUER: Yes, I did not do it myself, but there is some literature about it. The kind of toxicity and its effect on germination are given in some experimental plant physiology and plant sociology books.

CRESSWELL: With regards to the different types of nodulation on the *Robinia*, fixer and non-fixer, could one distinguish these visually by color due to the presence of hemoglobin or not?

ROTHWELL: Yes, although the external color differences between the effective and non-effective strains are not as apparent as one might hope for. On the other hand, morphological differences are quite distinct. One may observe numerous nodules in the non-effective strains as small spheres scattered throughout the root system, whereas the effective strain may occur less frequently but are large tortuous or coralloid types of nodules.

CRESSWELL: Have you any indication of the relative importance on these recolonization areas between symbiotic and non-symbiotic N fixation?

ROTHWELL: I would think the symbiotic N-fixing would be the more important and probably the major source of fixation based on the success with which plants with such microbial associates can compete in these areas.

EFFECT OF ALDER AND ACACIA ON DEVASTATED LAND

Nobuyoshi Hashimoto, Toshiro Kojima, Makoto Ogawa, and Tadashi Suzuki

Chief and Research Officers, Division of Soils, Government Forest Experiment Station, Tokyo, Japan; Research Officer, Shizuoka Prefectural Forest Experiment Station, Hamakita, Shizuoka, Japan, respectively

In Japan, nitrogen-fixing trees such as alder (*Alnus tinctoria* Sarg. var. *glabra* Call) and acacia (*Acacia dealbata* F. Muell.) are planted for erosion control. It was determined that Hinoki (*Chamaecyparis obtusa* Sieb. and Zucc.), which is an important silvicultural tree in Japan, can grow vigorously on the poor site present on devastated land when it is planted with alder. Alders affect soil conditions and growth of co-planted trees. Soil structure has strongly developed during the 7 years since alders were planted. Consequently, other physical conditions of the soil have improved and have affected microbial activity. Although changes in the chemical properties of the soil have occurred, in such an early stage of the alder stand they have not been great. After alder planting, the cation exchange capacity apparently increased and the N and C content of the surface horizon, but not in the lower horizons, also increased. Planting of acacia has also changed the soil conditions, but not so favorably.

INTRODUCTION

Alder species are planted to control erosion, to attain rapid covering of denuded land, and to promote the growth of conifers which are planted with the alders. Hinoki (*Chamaecyparis obtusa* Sieb. and Zucc.) which is an important silvicultural tree in Japan, can not grow well on devastated land. The effect of an alder plantation on the growth of Hinoki and Momi (*Abies firma* Sieb. and Zucc.) was examined on severely eroded diluvium soil. The improvement of soil conditions by alder and acacia plantations was also studied.

The experimental site was located in Hamakita, Shizuoka, Japan. It was a severely eroded site on the upper part of a gentle slope in hilly land facing west at an elevation of 100 to 120 m. Before planting, the site was occupied by a natural 17- to 63-year-old pine (*Pinus densiflora* Sieb. and Zucc.) forest. The trees averaged 5.5 m in height, 9 cm in diameter; there were 2200 trees per hectare. In this area the mean annual temperature is 15.2 C, the maximum temperature is 37.2 C, the minimum temperature is −6.0 C, and the annual precipitation is 1941 mm.

The acacia plot (0.2 ha), control plot (0.06 ha, no trees), and alder plot (0.1 ha) were set along the edge of a hill from south to north.

EXPERIMENTAL PROCEDURE

At a density of 5000 trees/ha, acacias and alders were planted on separate plots in 1960 and 1961, respectively. Fifty-seven g ammonium sulphite, 75 g superphosphate, 37 g potassium sulfite, and 180 g rice-straw were applied to each tree in each plot. In 1964 after half the alders (alternate rows) were cut, 2500 trees/ha of Hinoki were planted on the upper half and the same number of Momi on the lower half of both the alder and control plots. When Hinoki and Momi were planted, 50 g/tree of fertilizer (N : P : K = 15 : 8 : 8) were applied. Height and diameter of all planted trees have been measured annually.

In 1968, a morphological soil survey was made in each plot, an dsoil samples were taken for physical, chemical and microbial analyses. Field moisture content, moisture equivalent, maximum water-holding capacity, pore-size distribution, and three-phase (solid, water, and air) composition were measured. Chemical properties such as pH, exchange capacity as measured by the Daikuhara method (y_1), cation exchange capacity (CEC), and exchangeable Ca and Mg were analyzed. Microbial analyses of the soil were made by the dilution plate method on glucose-peptose-yeast medium (GPY) and the soil-smear method on GPY + antibiotics medium.

RESULTS AND DISCUSSION

Tree growth

Height growth of alder and acacia are presented in Fig. 1. These two species grow rapidly while young even on such poor sites. However, it is assumed that the growth of both species will decrease in the future.

Height and diameter growth of Hinoki and Momi are also shown in Fig. 1. In comparison with the control, these trees grow extraordinarily well when mixed with alders. The growth of Hinoki under alders is equivalent to the growth in commercial Hinoki forests. Although it is doubtful whether this growth rate will continue in the future, the effect of the alder plantation on the growth of Hinoki is apparent.

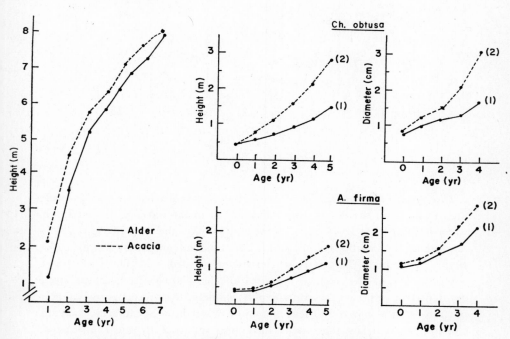

FIGURE 1   Growth of trees on devastated land: (1) = growth on the control plot; (2) = growth on the alder plot.

Soil conditions

Profile descriptions   Although the profile features of each plot had not been surveyed before the alders and acacias were planted, the control plot was placed so that it would have the same characteristics as the others. The present diagnostic features of the surface horizon are apparently different in each plot (Fig. 2). The soil of the control plot is in an eroded condition, has a nutty structure, and is compact even at the surface.

Structure and compactness of the soil under the planted trees changed remarkably, but there were no differences in soil color. The soil of the alder plot has a loose and crumb structure while the soil of the acacia plot is dry and has a fine nutty or loose granular structure.

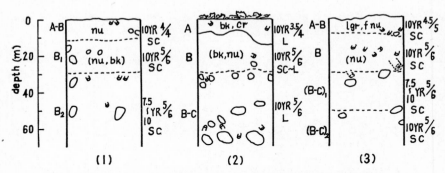

FIGURE 2   Soil profile of each plot: (1) control; (2) alder; and (3) acacia.

Three-phase composition   Undisturbed core samples from each plot were used to measure the three-phase composition of the soil and the maximum water-holding capacity (Fig. 3). In the control plot, the solid phase occupies more than 50% of the volume of all horizons, and the minimum air capacity is very small. This is characteristic of eroded soil. The three-phase compositions of the surface horizons of the plantation plots are quite different from that of the control plot; namely, they have a smaller proportion of solid phase and less maximum water-holding capacity than the control. This means these soils have been affected by the influence of nitrogen-fixation in the tree stands. These results are due to the development of soil structure under these stands. Under the acacia stand, the soil was especially low in moisture content and in water-holding capacity. But after a steaming treatment, an increase in water-holding capacity was recognized. This fact is due to the water-proofing characteristics of the soil, probably caused by the abundant mycelia of basidiomycetes in the F layer or the surface mineral horizon.

Tadaki (1968) summarized the results of past studies and pointed out that the net production of *Acacia mollissima* was 25 to 35 ton/ha/year, significantly higher than the 11 to 23 ton/ha/year net production of other evergreen broadleaf trees in Japan. The great amount of transpiration associated with this high net production combined with the water-proofing phenomenon probably causes the very dry soil under the acacia stand.

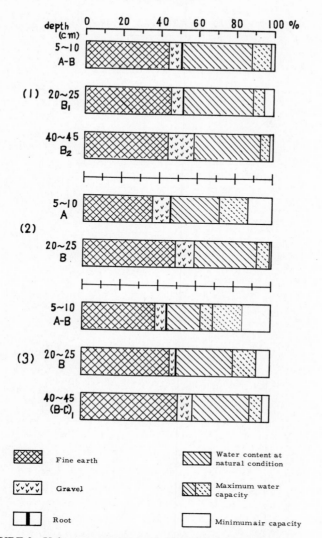

FIGURE 3   Volume composition of soils: (1) control plot; (2) alder plot; and (3) acacia plot.

Aggregates The aggregate-size distribution, analyzed by sieving soil samples of natural condition, prove that the soil of the devastated land does not develop a favorable structure but remains as large clods at the surface horizon (Fig. 4). The decrease of large-size aggregates and the increase of small-size aggregates under alder and acacia trees indicate

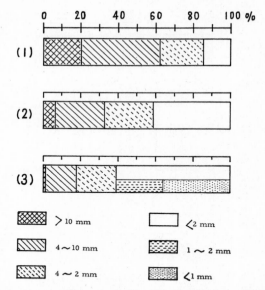

FIGURE 4   Aggregate-size distribution of soils: (1) control plot; (2) alder plot; and (3) acacia plot.

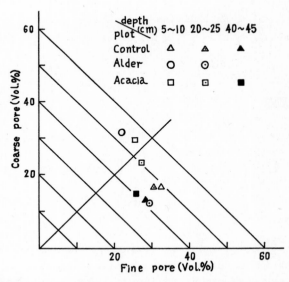

FIGURE 5   Pore-size analysis of soils in the control, alder, and acacia plots; for water in fine pores the pF is 2.7 or higher; in coarse pores the pF is less than 2.7.

development of crumb or loose granular structure during the 7 years after planting. Very fine structures have developed, especially under the acacia stand.

The pF-moisture curve was determined by the suction membrane method up to pF 2.7 under undisturbed conditions, and the moisture content at pF 4 was measured by the centrifugal method. Mashimo (1960) estimated the pore-size distribution of soils by the shapes of pF curves and defined their relationships to the characteristics of soil structure (Fig. 5). The curves of surface horizons shown in Fig. 6 indicate the development of a crumb structure on the alder plot and a nutty and massive structure on the control plot.

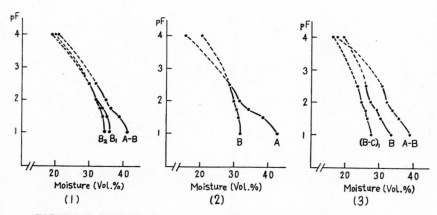

FIGURE 6   pF-moisture curves of soil: (1) control plot; (2) alder plot; and (3) acacia plot.

Chemical characteristics   The data on chemical properties of the experimental plots are shown in Table 1. Although pH and y_1 values are not evidently different between plots, chemical conditions on the alder plot are more favorable and those on the acacia plot are less favorable than those on the control plot.

In spite of the apparent effect of alders on tree growth and physical conditions, improvement of chemical conditions is not so evident. In the case of forest fertilization, Tsutsumi (1962) also recognized the similar fact that the chemical condition of fertilized soil did not change, while physical properties improved in the early stages after fertilizer application.

When additional nutrient substances are put into the nutrient circulating system between trees and soil, the growth of trees apparently increases, and inevitably a larger amount of fallen leaves is turned back to the soil.

TABLE 1

Chemical properties of the soils

Plot	Soil Horizon	pH (in H2O)	pH (in KCl)	y_1	N %	C %	C/N	CEC meq/100 g	ex. Ca. meq/100 g	ex. Mg. meq/100 g
Hinoki (Control)	A–B	4.79	3.75	21.9	0.08	2.02	25	9.50	0.99	0.24
	B_1	4.87	3.81	24,7	0.04	0.56	14	8.46	0.31	0.17
	B_2	4.92	3.81	23.1	0.03	0.35	12	7.84	0.29	0.17
Alder	A	4.49	3.70	19.0	0.13	2.58	20	12.76	0.98	0.31
	B	4.80	3.81	22.4	0.03	0.65	22	11.69	0.43	0.11
	B–C	4.89	3.81	23.2	0.03	0.28	9	11.99	0.26	0.12
Acacia	A–B	4.55	3.70	21.6	0.05	1.47	29	11.70	0.41	0.20
	B	4.70	3.80	22.5	0.04	0.74	19	7.44	0.31	0.17
	$(B–C)_1$	4.85	3.79	23.5	0.02	0.69	35	7.44	0.24	0.20
	$(B–C)_2$	4.86	3.79	28.0	0.02	0.35	18	7.41	0.22	0.21

TABLE 2

Results of microbial analyses

Plot	Depth cm	Dilution-plate method (no. in 100's)			Soil-smear method for fungi (appearance %)							
		Bacteria	Actino-myctes	Fungi	No. of Species	Tricho-derma	Peni-cillium	Asper-gillus	Phyco-mycetes[d]	Others	Total
Control	1	29	122	0.7	4	76.8	21.6	4.8	0	7.2	110.4
	10	21	120	0.2	3	62.4	26.4	0	0	7.2	96.0
	16	3	83	0.2	3	33.6	19.2	0	0	2.4	55.2
	26	1	62	0.3	2	12.0	0	0	0	4.8	16.8
	34	4	38	0	4	14.4	9.6	0	2.4	2.4	28.8
Alnus	4[a]	16	59	1.7	7	88.8	14.4	0	7.2	7.2	117.6
	4	3	29	1.6	7	81.6	24.0	0	12.0	12.0	129.6
	7	3	21	2.5	7	64.8	36.0	4.8	21.6	4.8	127.2
	13	6	20	4.7	6	31.2	24.0	0	12.0	7.2	74.4
	18	7	20	0.6	8	28.8	60.0	0	9.6	4.8	103.2
	26[b]	2	40	1.3	7	88.8	52.8	0	12.0	0	153.6
Acacia	F layer[c]	19	54	2.4	4	100.0	2.4	0	0	4.8	107.2
	2	16	44	1.3	8	76.0	38.4	7.2	14.4	7.2	143.2
	5	3	28	2.2	4	95.2	4.8	0	0	4.8	104.8
	12	2	22	3.9	3	91.2	4.8	0	0	0	96.0
	23	2	26	1.0	5	50.4	19.2	0	33.6	0	103.2
	33	1	25	2.1	1	100.0	0	0	0	0	100.0
	44	0.4	23	0.2	6	16.8	7.2	0	4.8	2.4	31.2

[a] Dark-colored spot.

[b] Root rot and adjacent dark-colored spot.

[c] funus mantle of *Basidiomycetes*.

[d] *Phycomycetes: Mucor, Mortierella, Absidia, Rhizopus*, etc.

However, we believe the additional nutrient substances are decomposed and absorbed by the trees rather than fixed in the soil; consequently, although the amount of circulating nutrients is increased, the greater proportion is in the trees. The increase in the amount of circulating nutrients indirectly promotes the development of soil structure. Great improvement in the chemical characteristics apparently takes many more years.

On the other hand, fallen leaves of *Acacia dealbata* are very small and are washed away by surface water which does not infiltrate due to the properties of the soil; thus the nutrient substances are likely to be lost from the cycle. This is one of the reasons for poorer chemical conditions on the acacia plot compared with the control plot.

Microbial tests   Because a great change in microbial flora with the planting of nodule-bearing trees was expected, microbial analyses were made (Table 2).

As physical and chemical conditions of devastated lands are poor, kinds and numbers of microbes in devastated soils are less than those of matured soils. The results of the control plot confirm this fact. On the other hand, many fungi are found in the acacia plot, and many bacteria, in the alder plot. The soil-smear method is applied for examining the existence of fungal hyphae. In the alder plot, many more kinds of fungi are found throughout the profile than in the other plots. Many *Trichoderma* are found in the acacia plot. Fine roots are abundant in this plot, and *Trichoderma* first colonize the dead fine roots. In general, the alder plot has the most well-developed microbial flora. The soil under alders will soon acquire the characteristics of mature soil. On the other hand, the kinds of microbes in the acacia plot are rather simple owing to the dryness of the soil. It is a question whether or not the soil has improved; it will probably revert to the devastated state if the acacia are cut.

LITERATURE CITED

Tadaki, Y. 1968. Primary productivity and stand density control in *Acacia molissima* stand. *Bull. of the Gov. Forest Exp. Sta.* No. 216, p. 99–125.

Tsutsumi, T. 1962. Studies on nutrition and fertilization of some important Japanese conifers. *Bull. of the Gov. Forest Exp. Sta.* No. 137, 158 p.

Mashimo, Y. 1960. Studies on the physical properties of forest soil and their relation to the growth of Sugi (*Cryptomeria japonica*) and Hinoki (*Chamaecyparis obtusa*). *Forest Soils of Jap.* No. 11, 182 p.

DISCUSSION

BENGTSON: Were these single plots, or were they part of a replicated experiment?

HASHIMOTO: They were single plots.

GOOD: Did you observe a comparable increase in production of shrubs and herbs in the *Alnus* plots, as compared with the *Chamaecyparis*.

HASHIMOTO: No, I could not observe any increase in production of shrubs and herbs, which were rather poor in the *Alnus* plot compared with the control plot. I suppose it was caused by the shading from the dense canopies of *Alnus* and *Chamaecyparis* in the *Alnus* plot. But in my branch station, the effect of scattered planting of *Alnus* trees on herb production was studied.

SMALL MAMMALS ON SURFACE-MINED LAND IN SOUTHWESTERN INDIANA*

R. E. Mumford and W. C. Bramble

Professor and Head, Department of Forestry and Conservation,
Purdue University, Lafayette, Indiana

A study of small mammals on surface-mined land in southwestern Indiana indicated that mice were abundant and important factors in the ecosystem. The white-footed mouse (*Peromyscus leucopus*) was the most abundant of nine species trapped. Its food habits indicated that it consumed seeds of important trees as well as of many other plants on mined land. Five of the nine species trapped showed their highest indices on mined land and together comprise a significant segment of the wildlife food chain found on such areas.

INTRODUCTION

Small mammals are an important part of the ecosystem of most disturbed land areas where animals and vegetation compete for living room. As several studies made on small mammals on surface-mined land in other states have indicated their probable importance on such land (Yeager, 1940 and 1942; Verts, 1957; Bramble and Sharp, 1949), the present study was initiated to describe the situation in Indiana. This paper is concerned with the occurrence of seed-eating mice and their possible effects both on direct seeding as a means of reforestation and on game food and cover establishment.

Other wildlife was studied, but will only be mentioned to indicate that a diverse population does exist of which small rodents are but a segment.

---

* Based on M. S. thesis by Gwilym Strong Jones, Purdue University, 1967; directed by Professors R. E. Mumford and W. C. Bramble. In cooperation with the Midwest Coal Producers and the Central States Forest Experiment Station of the U. S. Forest Service.

Four species of fish, nine species of amphibians, and ten species of reptiles were recorded on the study area. One hundred and thirty-nine species of birds were observed. Thirty species of mammals were recorded, only two of which were not found on spoil banks on mined land. Common game species found on the mined land included deer, cottontail rabbits, and bobwhite quail. Only the quail were in lesser abundance on mined than on unmined land.

METHODS

The study was carried out on a $7\frac{1}{2}$-square-mile area in southwestern Indiana which had been surface mined for coal from 1921 to 1961 (Fig. 1). The original topography, before surface mining, was rolling with low, wet marshy areas interspersed throughout. About half of the total area had been mined.

The cover types may be briefly characterized as follows:

1)   Pines – composed of eight species of planted conifers;
2)   Pine-hardwoods – composed of mixed plantings of pines and hardwoods;
3)   Pine-hardwood saplings – composed of planted pines invaded by native hardwoods, mostly cottonwood, sycamore, and river birch;
4)   Hardwoods – includes natural and planted stands of hardwoods;
5)   Bottomland hardwoods – pin oak, river birch, red maple, and shingle oak;
6)   Black locust – planted black locust overgrown with Japanese honeysuckle;
7)   Brush – early stage of natural invasion made up typically of cottonwood, sycamore, sassafras, red maple, persimmon, shingle oak, and river birch; and
8)   Weeds – access roads and abandoned fields invaded by shrubs, herbs and grasses.

The small mammal (shrews and mice) population of the study area was studied by means of random trapping. A grid was drawn on a map from which 100 grid squares were selected at random. Three transects were placed systematically in each grid square selected. Trap stations containing three snap traps each in a $2\frac{1}{2}$-ft radius were spotted at 25-ft intervals on each transect; a total of 54 traps were then placed in each selected grid square. Stomachs of animals caught were preserved for a food study.

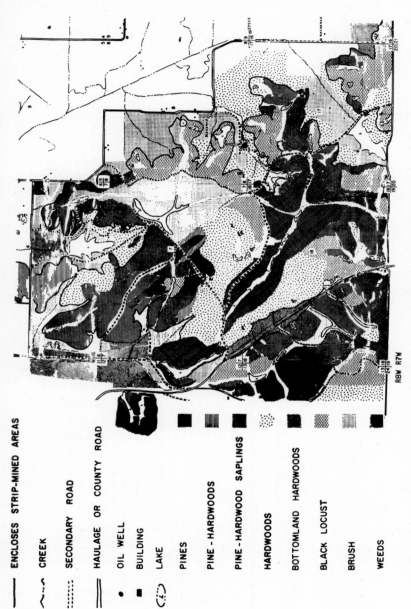

ENCLOSES STRIP-MINED AREAS

CREEK

SECONDARY ROAD

HAULAGE OR COUNTY ROAD

OIL WELL

BUILDING

LAKE

PINES

PINE - HARDWOODS

PINE - HARDWOOD SAPLINGS

HARDWOODS

BOTTOMLAND HARDWOODS

BLACK LOCUST

BRUSH

WEEDS

FIGURE 1 Map of the study area in southwestern Indiana showing the cover types used in this study.

A "trap night," which was the unit used as an index of population, is one trap set for one night. The number of trap nights required to catch one animal gave "trap nights per animal." This value was converted to animals per 100 trap nights.

RESULTS

Of the 100 grid plots chosen for the small mammal study, 94 were used. The other six plots were discarded because owners refused to grant permission to use them, cattle grazing occurred, etc.

The white-footed mouse (*Peromyscus leucopus*) was by far the most frequently captured animal (Fig. 2). Its population index was higher on all cover types on the mined area than on the unmined or on cropland.

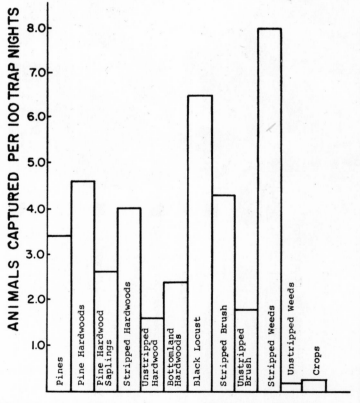

FIGURE 2 Population indices of the white-footed mouse (*Peromyscus leucopus*) in various cover types.

In five cover types, it had an index of 4, or higher, indicating an unusually high population for the species. An excellent low cover, as well as abundant rocky areas, on the mined area indicated that habitat conditions favored by the white-footed mouse were an important factor.

The other eight species of small mammals trapped on the study area showed indices of less than 1.0 (Figs. 3 and 4), except for the house mouse which had an index of 2.0 in cropland near dwellings. Only one species, the meadow jumping mouse, was not found on mined land.

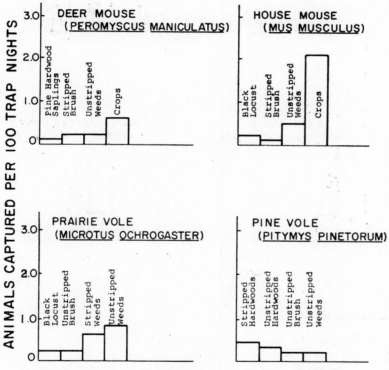

FIGURE 3 Population indices of four species of mice in various cover types.

In general, five of the nine species trapped had their highest indices on mined land. The most abundant species, the white-footed mouse, had indices on mined land which were two to three times higher than those on unmined land. This means that small mammals are, as suspected, present in high abundance on mined land and must be considered an important factor in any competition between plants and animals.

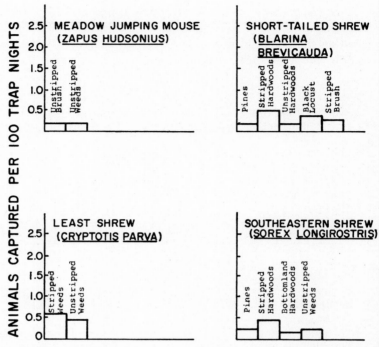

FIGURE 4   Population indices of jumping mice and three species of shrews in various cover types.

Food habit analysis

Examination of the stomach contents from trapped, white-footed mice indicated that this most abundant species did feed on seeds of desirable forest trees (Table 1), as well as on seeds of many other plants. The identified food shows that a remarkable variety was available and helps explain the abundance of this mouse on mined land. When only a few seeds of a valuable tree species are planted for reforestation, however, the feeding by mice will be a destructive factor to be seriously considered. On the other hand, seeds of legumes, such as crown vetch, sericea lespedeza, and partridge pea, planted in medium density on spoil banks developed into dense stands for good game food and cover.

TABLE 1

Average percent volume and percent frequency of foods, 489 white-footed mice (Peromyscus leucopus) *stomachs, September 1965 to August 1966*

Food	Volume	Frequency
Starchy material	30.1	77.3
Insects	14.5	78.6
Lepidoptera or Hymenoptera larvae	9.2	42.2
Unidentified seeds	7.5	41.0
Wild cherry (*Prunus*) seeds	5.3	21.4
Rubus (sp.) seeds	3.7	10.0
Yellow wood sorrel (*Oxalis*) seeds	3.6	9.4
Unidentified plant	3.3	23.3
Hair	2.2	41.2
Chilopoda	1.9	13.7
Green vegetation	1.8	12.7
Indian hemp (*Apocynum*) seeds	1.6	7.9
Cranesbill (*Geranium*)	1.5	5.0
Mollusca	1.2	8.9
Maple (*Acer*) seeds	1.2	8.3
Unknown	0.9	8.3
Arachnida	0.8	9.8
Flesh	0.8	4.8
Pine (*Pinus*) seeds	0.8	4.8
Endogone	0.7	6.0
Ash (*Fraxinus*) seeds	0.7	4.4
Sumac (*Rhus*) seeds	0.6	2.3
Elm (*Ulmus*) seeds	0.5	3.3
Bush clover (*Lespedeza*) seeds	0.5	3.1
Rose (*Rosa*) seeds	0.5	2.9
Rumex (sp.) seeds	0.4	3.7
Bittersweet (*Celastrus*) seeds	0.4	2.9
Cottonwood (*Populus*) seeds	0.4	2.5
Poison ivy (*Rhus*) seeds	0.4	2.5
Sassafras (*Sassafras*) seeds	0.4	1.5
Pebbles	0.3	7.3
Honeysuckle (*Lonicera*)	0.3	1.5
Unidentified grass seeds	0.2	3.3
Panic grass (*Panicum*) seeds	0.2	2.7
Dogwood (*Cornus*) seeds	0.2	2.1
Unidentified animal	0.2	1.5
Everlasting pea (*Lathyrus*) seeds	0.2	0.6
Unidentified fungus	0.1	3.5
Grape (*Vitis*) seeds	0.1	1.5
Greenbriar (*Smilax*) seeds	0.1	1.2
Sedge (*Carex*) seeds	0.1	1.2

TABLE 1 (*cont.*)

Food	Volume	Frequency
Feathers	0.1	1.0
Peppergrass (*Lepidium*) seeds	0.1	1.0
Foxtail (*Setaria*) seeds	0.1	0.6
Black locust (*Robinia*) seeds	0.1	0.6
Sweet clover (*Melilotus*) seeds	0.1	0.6
Apple (*Pyrus*) seeds	0.1	0.2
Compositae seeds	a	0.8
Crowfoot (*Ranunculus*) seeds	a	0.6
Annelida	a	0.6
Touch-me-not (*Impatiens*) seeds	a	0.6
Pupae cases	a	0.4
Pokeberry (*Phytolacca*) seeds	a	0.4
Tick trefoil (*Desmodium*) seeds	a	0.4
Metal	a	0.4
Trumpet creeper (*Campsis*) seeds	a	0.2
Coleoptera larvae	a	0.2
Flower petals	a	0.2
Bones	a	0.2
Redbud (*Cercis*) seeds	a	0.2
Oxeye daisy (*Chrysanthemum*) seeds	a	0.2
Avens (*Geum*) seeds	a	0.2
Sedge (*Scirpus*) seeds	a	0.2
Daisy fleabane (*Erigeron*) seeds	a	0.2
Lettuce (*Lactuca*) seeds	a	0.2
Bluets (*Houstonia*) seeds	a	0.2
St. John's-wort (*Hypericum*) seeds	a	0.2
Plantain (*Plantago*) seeds	a	0.2

[a] Trace.

LITERATURE CITED

Bramble, W. C., and W. M. Sharp. 1949. Rodents as a factor in direct seeding on spoil banks in central Pennsylvania. *J. Forest.* **49**, 477–478.

Verts, B. J. 1957. The population and distribution of two species of *Peromyscus* on some Illinois strip-mined land. *J. Mammal.* **38**, 53–59.

Yeager, L. E. 1940. Wildlife management on coal stripped land. *Trans. 5th N. Amer. Wildlife Conf.*, p. 348–353.

Yeager, L. E. 1942. Coal-stripped land as a mammal habitat, with special reference to fur animals. *Amer. Midl. Nat.* **27**, 613–635.

WILDLIFE BENEFITS FROM STRIP-MINE RECLAMATION

Frank R. Holland

Wildlife Biologist, Division of Forest Development,
Tennessee Valley Authority, Norris, Tennessee

Four widely separated Appalachian coal strip-mined areas reclaimed with various trees, shrubs, and grasses were compared with adjacent untreated spoils the third year after test plantings. Ecological succession on the test areas was estimated to be 10 years advanced over the unreclaimed controls. Vertebrate animals were not sampled although several species were observed. Treated spoils had 43% more insects per unit area. Herbaceous plants were twice as dense in terms of ground area shaded by crowns, four times as dense measured by basal area of stems. Woody plants showed 13% greater plant number, 57% greater basal area, 62% greater canopy area, and 155% more new leaders per unit area on the reclaimed lands. Wildlife cover and food were also evaluated.

INTRODUCTION

Surface mining for coal is common in the Tennessee Valley states of Alabama, Virginia, Kentucky, and Tennessee. The overburden is displaced to expose coal for removal, leaving rows of steep-sided, poor quality, acidic, unvegetated rubble piles subject to erosion. Such wastes often remain for years as barren eyesores which destroy much of the aesthetic quality of the wooded surroundings. Primary productivity of coal spoil banks is extremely low and offers a minimum of cover or food to most forms of wildlife.

Seepage and runoff waters from stripped areas are usually acidic because of the oxidation of exposed sulfur-rich minerals. Catch basins, whose pH may be as low as 2.5 or 3, are generally devoid of both plant and animal life. Runoff water is frequently silt-laden where vegetation is absent. The approximately 50,000 acres of abandoned strip-mine wastelands in the Tennessee Valley have a significant potential for polluting natural drainages with silt and acid.

The Tennessee Valley Authority has the general responsibility for natural resource conservation within the Tennessee River drainage basin. TVA's interest in increasing the productivity of areas left barren by coal mining led to the opportunity to learn how reclamation can improve wildlife habitat.

In 1963, TVA established four demonstrations of strip-mine reclamation, one each in Wise County, Va. and Claiborne, Morgan and Sequatchie Counties, Tenn. The major erosion problems were eliminated, stream pollution was reduced, and the stripped lands were planted to grasses, shrubs, and trees in combination with several fertilizers. It was hoped the areas would experience greater wildlife use and present an aspect more pleasing to the eye.

OBJECTIVE

The major objective of this study was to ascertain if wildlife benefitted from reclamation of the project areas. It was pursued from four directions:

1. identification of plants and evaluation for wildlife;
2. identification and enumeration of all wildlife and evidence of wildlife;
3. identification of the ways reclamation plantings attract wildlife; and
4. evaluation of any ecological advance attributable to reclamation.

SURVEY METHOD

One hundred forty-one permanent 100-ft^2 (5 by 20 ft) sample plots, selected by random placement of a grid over maps of each area and located in the field by compass and tape, were used to measure plant basal and canopy areas, identify plants, collect insects, measure litter, determine pH, and evaluate new growth. Two 1-ft^2 subplots, systematically located along a diagonal line crossing each plot, provided data on soil invertebrates and annual plants. Forty check plots, 10 adjacent to each treated area, were sampled by the same procedure, permitting comparison between un-reclaimed and reclaimed portions of each mine.

Data on woody plants, pH, litter, browse, and wildlife cover were collected during the winter of 1966–67. Soil invertebrate, insect, and non-woody plant data were collected in the summer of 1967.

To help determine wildlife use and presence, each area was cruised after fresh snows. Organisms sighted, tracks, and other signs were recorded during all phases of the study. No attempt was made to census vertebrates.

RESULTS

Vertebrates

Several species of wildlife were found on both treated and untreated areas. No reliable comparison of vertebrate-use frequency between the two kinds of areas is possible because of sampling procedures. A total of 9 species of mammals, 18 species of birds, and 3 species of reptiles and amphibians were observed.

Invertebrates

Insects were collected by sweeping each plot 20 times with a hand net. Thirteen orders were identified. Fossorial invertebrates were collected from the 1-ft² subplot located closest to the southwest corner of each larger sample plot. Five insect orders, two other classes of mandibulate arthro-

TABLE 1

Insects and other invertebrates collected per acre

Organism	Treated areas	Untreated areas
Thysanura	10,481	4,356
Collembola	121,693	91,476
Orthoptera	191	22
Isoptera	4,174	0
Psocoptera	51,276	41,382
Thysanoptera	162	87
Hemiptera	1,300	958
Homoptera	5,710	3,703
Neuroptera	90	65
Coleoptera	2,098	1,590
Lepidoptera	588	414
Diptera	3,322	2,439
Hymenoptera	168,221	113,288
Diplopoda	16,741	15,246
Chilopoda	16,696	2,178
Pseudoscorpionida	5,036	4,356
Acarina	44,590	37,026
Phalangida	601	153
Araneida	226,504	160,584
Gastropoda	6,941	6,534
Annelida	8,394	0
Total	694,813	485,857

pods, four orders of chelicerate arthropods, gastropods, and annelids were represented in invertebrate soil samples (Table 1). Totals ran 695,000/acre for the treated plots and 486,000/acre for the untreated ones, a 43% superiority for the treated areas (Table 2).

TABLE 2

Numbers of invertebrates (in thousands per acre)

County	Treated areas			Untreated areas		
	Litter	Sweeps	Total	Litter	Sweeps	Total
Wise	566	23	589	436	17	453
Claiborne	1,135	23	1,158	410	14	424
Morgan	737	14	751	810	15	825
Sequatchie	270	11	281	240	2	242
Mean	677	18	695	474	12	486

Non-woody plants

Each non-woody plant occurring in the 362 subplots was identified and its basal and canopy diameters were measured. For the treated areas, the number of plants averaged 170,000/acre. Untreated areas had an average of 189,000/acre. Basal area (BA) and canopy areas (CA) are shown in Table 3.

TABLE 3

Non-woody plants per acre

County	Treated areas			Untreated areas		
	No. (thousands)	Basal Area ft²	Crown Area ft²	No. (thousands)	Basal Area ft²	Crown Area ft²
Wise	352	1,227	28,000	318	89	10,700
Claiborne	120	49	28,700	57	21	5,900
Morgan	83	438	12,200	266	275	19,100
Sequatchie	126	13	4,000	118	9	2,300
Mean	170	432	18,000	189	98	9,500

Woody plants

Woody plants in each 100-ft^2 plot were counted, identified, and measured for basal area and canopy area at or below 4½ ft above ground. All new plant leaders below 4½ ft were counted by species. On a per-acre basis, the treated areas showed a 13% greater plant number, 57% greater basal area, 62% greater canopy area, and 155% more new leaders than the untreated areas (Table 4).

TABLE 4

Woody plants per acre

County	Treated Areas				Untreated Areas			
	Number	BA ft^2	CA ft^2	No. of leaders (thousands)	Number	BA ft^2	CA ft^2	No. of leaders (thousands)
Wise	3,400	6.0	6,800	130	800	0.1	1,200	6
Claiborne	5,100	39.7	12,600	117	2,300	4.8	5,100	14
Morgan	9,500	26.1	19,900	194	14,100	44.2	19,900	195
Sequatchie	3,000	6.1	6,700	114	1,600	0.4	2,200	3
Mean	5,300	19.5	11,500	139	4,700	12.4	7,100	54

Litter

Two litter measurements were taken on each plot—the percentage of cover and, where litter was present, the average depth. The treated areas showed 52% greater cover than the untreated areas (Table 5). Average litter depth was 0.07 ft for both treated and untreated areas.

TABLE 5

Litter

County	Treated Areas		Untreated Areas	
	Cover %	Depth ft	Cover %	Depth ft
Wise	45.7	0.07	23.7	0.07
Claiborne	46.6	0.09	7.1	0.04
Morgan	43.9	0.10	62.0	0.13
Sequatchie	9.4	0.03	2.8	0.03
Mean	36.4	0.07	23.9	0.07

Acidity

At least one, but generally two, random soil pH readings were taken on each plot. All readings showed acid soil conditions with pH ranging from 3.9 to 5. The treated plots averaged 4.5; the untreated ones, 4.2.

Wildlife cover

Plant density measurements cannot be directly converted to cover values because plant distribution is such a major factor. Each plot was therefore evaluated visually for ground cover (surface to 1 ft) and above-ground cover (1 ft to $4\frac{1}{2}$ ft). Arbitrary ratings of good (3), fair (2), poor (1), and none (0) were then assigned each plot. Average cover ratings for the various areas are shown in Table 6.

TABLE 6

Winter wildlife cover

Area (county)	Treated Areas			Untreated Areas		
	No. of plots	Above-ground cover[a] rating[c]	Ground cover[b] rating[c]	No. of plots	Above-ground cover[a] rating[c]	Ground cover[b] rating[c]
Wise	41	0.37	1.51	10	0.00	0.60
Claiborne	31	0.28	1.40	10	0.00	0.20
Morgan	30	0.87	1.63	10	0.08	1.60
Sequatchie	39	0.23	0.41	10	0.00	0.30
Mean	35	0.44	1.24	10	0.02	0.68

[a] In the layer between 1 to $4\frac{1}{2}$ ft above the surface.

[b] In the layer between the surface and 1 ft above.

[c] Figures are qualitative; derived by visual evaluation of plant density and distribution. Good = 3, Fair = 2, Poor = 1, None = 0.

Wildlife food values

Wildlife food evaluation was limited to winter deer browse and to summer forage and seed-producing plants used by birds and small mammals. The importance of browse plants was determined by combining available data from five sources: (1) U.S. Forest Service (1959), (2) Pugh and Whitehead (personal communication), (3) Moore and Strode (1966), (4) Burbank (1967), and (5) Halls and Ripley (1961).

Deer herds show local differences in browse preference. Since the area in question has not been studied, the combined lists from the above sources were presumed to include the majority of browse plants favored by white-tailed deer in the eastern Tennessee Valley.

TABLE 7

Deer browse ratings

Preferred	Secondary	Tertiary (may be locally important)
Honeysuckle	Red maple	Coral berry
Strawberry bush	Chestnut	Lespedeza
Greenbrier	Sourwood	Swamp ironwood
Buffalo-nut	Grape	Sweet shrub
Blackberry, etc.	Hydrangea	Sumac
Huckleberry	Viburnums	Persimmon
Dogwood	White ash	Birch
Yellow-poplar	Black locust	Hawthorn
Black gum	Rhododendron	Butternut
	Sassafras	Basswood
		Grasses
		Mountain laurel
		Hickory
		Carolina silverbell
		American beautyberry
		Trumpet creeper
		Buttonbush
		Ilex
		Willow
		Serviceberry
		Witch-hazel
		Oaks

Browse species were graded *preferred* if they were so designated by at least two of the five sources, *secondary* if they appeared on two lists as desirable or on one as preferred and on one as desirable, and *tertiary* if they were not listed as preferred or desirable on any of the lists. Table 7 shows the ratings of the browse species found on the sample plots.

Numbers assigned to the rated browse species—3 for preferred, 2 for secondary, and 1 for tertiary or undesirable—were multiplied by leader number for each species on each plot. The resulting products thus contained elements of both quality and quantity and were used as an index of winter food conditions (Table 8).

TABLE 8

Winter deer browse index

County	Treated Areas rating/100 ft²	Untreated Areas rating/100 ft²
Wise	339	16
Claiborne	356	81
Morgan	576	761
Sequatchie	296	24
Mean	392	220

One hundred leaders, from less than 4.5 feet above ground, from the previous year's growth of each woody species were clipped, oven dried, and weighed. Weights were converted to pounds per acre. Treated areas averaged 404 lb/acre as compared with 185 lb/acre for untreated areas (Table 9).

TABLE 9

Dry matter in lb/acre of browse produced by woody plants

Area	Treated area	Untreated area
Wise	304	2
Claiborne	235	34
Morgan	758	692
Sequatchie	320	13
Mean	404	185

For grasses and forbs, the food values developed by Martin et al. (1951) were used to evaluate non-woody plants for wildlife. The sum of stem numbers, animal users, and amount of use yielded a food value index for each plant. On a unit area, the treated area plant value totaled 1,104, while the untreated area plants totaled 1,551 (Table 10). By this measure, food value was greater on the untreated areas.

TABLE 10
Food importance of grasses and forbs

Plant	Number	Users	Use	Index
Treated Areas				
Grasses				
Wheat grass	69	1	2	72
Paspalum	40	12	11	63
Panic-grass	38	62	36	136
Bluegrass	31	5	6	42
Fescue	23	6	6	35
Ticklegrass	6	1	1	8
Three-awned grass	9	3	3	15
Muhly	3	4	4	11
Woolgrass	1	2	5	8
Forbs				
Common lespedeza	82	11	6	99
Sericea lespedeza	59	1	1	61
Dogmint	35	1	1	37
Goldenrod	24	10	10	44
Whitlow grass	22	1	1	24
Lily	19	1	1	21
Poke	10	28	27	65
Snakeroot	8	1	1	10
Hawkweed	6	4	4	14
Aster	5	7	7	19
Violet	4	8	8	20
Milkweed	4	1	1	6
Ragweed	3	67	37	107
Batchelor's buttons	3	1	1	5
Buttercup	3	11	12	26
Crownbeard	3	1	1	5
Sunflower	3	29	23	55
Yarrow	2	3	3	8
Mayweed	2	3	3	8
Horseweed	2	1	1	4
Bedstraw	1	1	1	3
Joe-pye-weed	1	2	2	5
Jewel-weed	1	5	4	10
Plantain	1	1	1	3
Heal all	1	1	1	3
Goose foot	1	23	19	43
Knawel	1	1	1	3
Southern harebell	1	1	1	3
Virgins' bower	1	1	1	3
Total	528	322	254	1,104

TABLE 10 (*cont.*)

Plant	Number	Users	Use	Index
Untreated Areas				
Grasses				
Paspalum	187	12	11	210
Panic-grass	52	62	36	150
Three-awned grass	30	3	3	36
Fescue	15	6	6	27
Broomsedge	120	6	7	133
Forbs				
Wild strawberry	277	15	19	311
Common lespedeza	112	11	6	129
Goldenrod	210	10	10	230
Whitlow grass	75	1	1	77
Aster	15	7	7	29
Violet	67	8	8	83
Bidens	22	5	5	32
Beggars tick	7	4	4	15
Dock	7	1	1	9
Thyme	7	1	1	9
Venus looking-glass	7	1	1	9
Virgins' bower	60	1	1	62
Total	1,270	154	127	1,551

DISCUSSION

Most contour strip-mine operations remain practically devoid of vegetation for several years following mining. Toxic minerals, unstable substrata, lack of surface organic material, absence of soil organisms, excessive stoniness, overly steep slopes, and extremes of temperature, moisture, light, and wind combine to present a rigorous habitat. It may be 10 years or more before substantial revegetation can occur naturally. Reclamation reduces the time required for revegetation and almost immediately increases the attractiveness of the land for wildlife.

Development of biologic communities on contour strip-mined lands should be viewed as a definite wildlife asset. The edges of stripped areas become ecotones between biotic communities, and hence support a mixture of animals and plants characteristic of the two communities (the well-known "edge effect"). One habitat may compensate for deficiencies in the other; thus, the combination is able to support more kinds and larger numbers of animals. Less-mature plant communities can support a greater animal biomass because they produce more available energy (Margalef, 1963). Therefore, we would expect to find more animals of more different kinds using revegetated strip-mine lands in a forest than using a homogeneous mature oak-hickory association.

This study has shown that reclamation: (1) improved soil conditions by increasing ground litter and pH; (2) increased the basal and canopy areas of annual and biennial plants; (3) increased the numbers, basal areas, canopy areas, winter deer browse, and total leader production of woody plants. Only in food value did the untreated area seem to be superior to the treated area. This may be explained by the preponderance of pine species used in revegetation. Less pine would be desirable if maximum wildlife benefits are to be achieved. Even so, wildlife should respond to greatly improved habitat conditions by substantial increases in both numbers and varieties.

LITERATURE CITED

Burbank, J. H. 1967. Deer browse studies at Land Between the Lakes; pilot study: Barnes Hollow. Unpublished. Tennessee Valley Authority, Div. of Forestry Development.

Halls, L. K., and T. H. Ripley. 1961. *Deer browse plants of southern forests*. U. S. Dep. Agr., Forest Service, S. & SE Forest Exp. Sta., and SE Sect. Wildlife Soc.

Margalef, R. 1963. On certain unifying principles in ecology. *Amer. Natur.*, **97**, 357–374.

Martin, A. C., et al. 1951. *American wildlife and plants—a guide to wildlife food habits*. McGraw-Hill Book Co., New York. 500 p.

Moore, W. H., and D. D. Strode. 1966. Deer browse resources of the Uwharrie National Forest. U. S. Dep. Agr., Forest Service, *SE Forest Exp. Sta. Res. Bull.* SE-4.

U. S. Forest Service. 1959. Guide to timber management and wildlife coordination, Region 8. U. S. Dep. Agr., Forest Service.

DISCUSSION

DOWNING: How long would you expect this beneficial effect of strip mines on wildlife to be felt? I would imagine it would be a very short time.

HOLLAND: I would expect the succession rates of newly planted strip mines would be so slow that the beneficial effects of the ecotone establishment may last 100 years.

DOOLITTLE: You mentioned that these stripped areas were very good for wildlife. How about squirrels?

HOLLAND: Stripped areas are not good for squirrels. The eastern gray squirrel occasionally uses blackberry, dewberry, or raspberry which may occur on older stripped areas, but these foods are a minor part of their diet.

DARMER: Did you compare wildlife in mixed forests with forests of only one species?

HOLLAND: No, I did not do that. The major comparison used in making the present study was between reclaimed and nonreclaimed sections of strip mines. Most of the forest in east Tennessee has a closed canopy. Therefore, a very limited amount of browse and fruiting vegetation is available at the ground level. Since revegetated strip-mine land is fully open to the sunlight, browse material as well as seed-producing plants thrive. All of these are available to animals in the region.

BAUER: Was there a succession of invertebrates, insects, and mammals; or did they invade at the same time? Which landscape areas or ecotopes were most favored for wildlife, the drier slopes or plateaus or where there was water? We found the highest wildlife count in wet areas.

HOLLAND: I did not look at the elements of succession specifically. However, I found that on the check areas, where no reclamation had been done, very little wildlife was present except fossorial invertebrates. Peculiarly, two of the most common invertebrates were spiders and ants. Spiders are predators, but I don't know what they were preying on. I also noticed a greater abundance of wildlife using wet areas than dry areas, although no specific study was made on this aspect.

PART IV

EFFECTS ON PLANTS

GROWTH AND NUTRITION OF BEECH TREES ON SITES OF DIFFERENT SOIL TEXTURE IN THE LIGNITE AREA OF THE RHINELAND

Hermann Jacoby

*Forester, Ministry of Agriculture, Viticulture and Forests in Mainz,
Rheinland-Pfalz, Division of Forest Inventory, 5238 Hachenburg,
Westerwald, West Germany*

Because of widespread surface-mining for lignite in the Rhineland, large areas are being reclaimed for both agriculture and forestry. The growth and nutrition of beech on mined lands were investigated utilizing six experimental areas including three spoil bank sites with different spoil types, an undisturbed forest soil, and two sites on a toxic portion of a spoil bank.

Nutrient analysis of the various soil materials showed that pH is a reliable indicator of nutrient status, and is strongly related to both the equivalent fraction of Al in the spoil and the ratio of actual to maximum cation exchange capacity. The most deficient nutrient was N, while P was low on the toxic spoils.

Root system development was strongly influenced by spoil texture, with long, mostly vertical roots in the loose, coarse-textured spoils, and shorter, more numerous roots in the fine-textured spoils. However, total length of first-order roots did not differ significantly.

Though statistically significant, differences among plants in height growth were small. Differences in plant weight were greater, but significant correlation with soil nutrients was found only for P..

Nutrient analysis of the plant tissues disclosed little difference among plant parts in concentration of Ca, Mg, or Na. However, N, P, and K were higher in leaves, and Al and Fe higher in roots. Tissue concentrations were not correlated with concentrations in the soil. Equivalent fractions in the plant ash, however, were related to equivalent fractions in the soil solution, all ions showing selective uptake by the plant parts.

Beech appears to be well-suited for planting on alkaline spoil sites, requiring only fertilization with N.

INTRODUCTION

In the Rhine lignite area, there are great deposits of Tertiary (Miocene) brown coal. In the primeval North Sea, sands of various granulation were layered over the lignite toward the end of the Tertiary (Pliocene) period. In the vicinity of the lignite layers they often contain fossils. During the Quaternary (Pleistocene) Period, the ancient Rhine deposited gravel over the sand; the gravel came from all areas and strata of the Rhineland mountains and hills. We find quartzite, slate, graywacke, and variegated sandstone.

A long mountain ridge, called "Ville", was formed by the raising of the ancient Rhine riverbed by tectonic forces during the Pleistocene period. During the first Intermediate Ice Age (Elster-Saale-Interglacial) the loamy topsoil decayed very intensively and dense gleyed zones were formed which are today known as fossil pseudogleys; loess layers (between 0.5 m thick in the south and 20 m in the north) were then deposited during the following ice ages. In the southern part of the Ville, these loess layers, depending on their depth, developed into more-or-less well-defined, impermeable, wet soils originally stocked mostly with oak (*Quercus*) and hornbeam (*Carpinus*) forests. In the north, they developed into very fruitful agricultural soils.

Since early in this century, lignite has been surface mined over large areas. In the southern part of the Ville, where exploitation is almost complete, reclamation for forestry prevails. In the north, the open mining pits are now pushing into the fertile farmlands. There, on the widespread and high spoil dumps, the plateaus are reclaimed for agriculture and only the slopes for forests. As of January 1, 1969, the total area of spoil banks reclaimed amounted to 7374 ha and was distributed as follows:

Agriculture	2750
Forestry	3586
Housing and Industry	422
Roads	180
Lakes	436

The reforested area is made up of stands approximately as follows:

Hybrid poplar (*Populus*) and alder (*Alnus*)	55%
Beech (*Fagus*), ash (*Fraxinus*) and maple (*Acer*)	35%
Pine (*Pinus*), Douglas-fir (*Pseudotsuga*), and spruce (*Picea*)	10%

Six experimental areas on spoil banks and one on a nearby old gley forest soil of the Ville were studied. Each area contained three plots, each with 10 beech trees which were 8 years old in 1965, when the study was begun.

From the experimental areas, I selected three typical spoil sites, the old forest soil, and two plots on a toxic portion of a spoil bank which had been studied by Ulrich (1965). All plots are named by the dominant characteristic of the soil.

SOIL RESEARCH

Experimental plot sites

The first of the selected spoil sites consists of sandy, loamy *Rhine Gravel*. In 1945, the spoil was reforested with larch, beech, hornbeam, red oak, and red alder mixed by rows. The mixture by rows did not do well, and except for a thin cover of larch and red oak, the stand was cut in 1960. The area was replanted with 3-yr-old beech in the spring of 1961.

The other two plots lie on a bank upon which spoil was being dumped until the fall of 1960. One part of this spoil consists of *Sand*. The other part is so-called *Forest Gravel* (*Forstkies*); this is a mixture of loess and Rhine. Gravel and is a sandy, loamy silt in texture. Both plots were planted to 3-yr-old beech and filled in with hybrid poplar in the spring of 1961.

A plot on an old forest soil of the Ville served for comparison with the spoil banks. It consisted of *Pseudogley*, a gleyey loess-loam over ancient Rhine gravel. After the old stand of 120-yr-old oak and hornbeam was harvested, the area was replanted (as were the other plots) with beech.

All of the beech were planted at a spacing of 1.0 by 0.8 m and fertilized with 200 kg/ha N. Lupine was seeded on the spoil between the beech rows.

The spoil bank of toxic *Tertiary Sand* was first planted with maple and beech; these promptly died and the area was immediately replanted with locust and red alder. These also died. This spoil proved to be completely hostile to vegetation and was later covered with a loamy soil. Usually, toxic *Tertiary Sand* is dumped and then covered with layers of gravel or loess.

Nutrition analysis

The total exchange capacity (Ak$_t$, dimension: mval/kg of soil)* was found with Ba at pH 8.1. Ak$_t$ is a measure of the maximum nutrient capacity of a soil.

---

* mval/kg is the same as meq/kg.

The exchangeable cations (H, Na, K, Ca, Mg, Al, Fe, and Mn) were determined at almost identical pH through percolation of the soil with 1 N NH_4Cl. Their sum is the real (actual) exchange capacity (Ak_r, dimension: mval/kg of soil).

Ak_r/Ak_t is, according to Ulrich (1966), along with pH a measure of the acidity of a soil. Ak_r is less than Ak_t when exchange spaces are blocked by non-exchangeable polymeric aluminum hydroxide, $Al_6(OH_{15})^{3+}$.

A sample of the equilibrium soil solution (ESS) was extracted from the liquid phase of an aqueous soil paste, and the cations were determined in the same manner. The results of the analysis are shown graphically (Figs. 1–5) as equivalent fractions of the individual cations in percent of Ak_r.

The equivalent fraction X of a cation is calculated as follows:

$$X_i = \frac{Z_i \cdot C_i}{\sum Z_i \cdot C_i} \cdot 100$$

where Z_i is the valence of cation i; C_i is the concentration of cation i; and $\sum Z_i \cdot C_i$ is the sum of all exchangeable cations. In the calculation, Fe and Mn are considered to have a valence of 2, and Al, a valence of 3. Further, X_i^s is the equivalent fraction of cation i in the soil as a percentage of Ak_r, and X_i^L is the equivalent fraction of cation i in the soil solution (ESS) as a percentage of the total exchangeable cations. With the conversion to intensity parameters, all values are comparable.

Phosphorus was fractionated according to Watanabe and Olsen (1965). For the total content (P_t, dimension: mg/kg of soil), the percentages of P_{Al}, P_{Fe}, P_{Ca}, P_{okk} and P_{org} are shown graphically in Figs 1–5 ($P_{okk} = P_{occluded}$, and $P_{org} = P_{organic}$).

Nutrient condition of the experimental plots

Windblown ash containing CaO from nearby briquette factories is contained in the humus cover of the 20-yr-old spoil bank of Rhine Gravel (Fig. 1). Because of this, unusually high quantities of nutrients are stored therein, $Ak_r = 977$ mval/kg of soil. A pH of 8, an X_{Ca}^s of 92%, and 6% $CaCO_3$ also indicate this. The result is confirmed by a P_t of 490 mg/kg of soil, of which P_{org} is 47% and P_{Ca} is 25%.

The nutrient content in the mineral portion of this spoil bank is substantially lower; Ca and Mg dominate in the soil and in the soil solution (ESS). The high X_{Na}^L in the ESS is explained by the spoil material. P_t is high and has a favorable fractionation. Acidity begins in the subsoil; Ak_r is less than Ak_t.

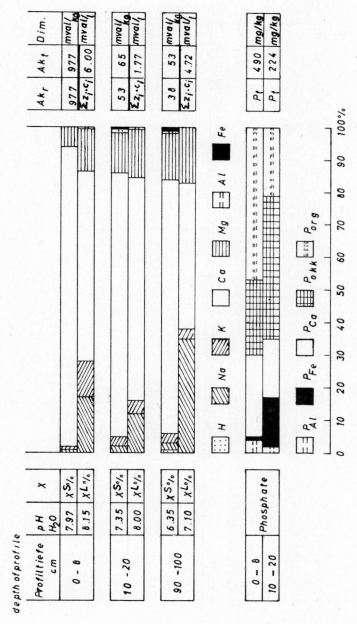

FIGURE 1   Profile of Rhine Gravel at Gruhlsee.

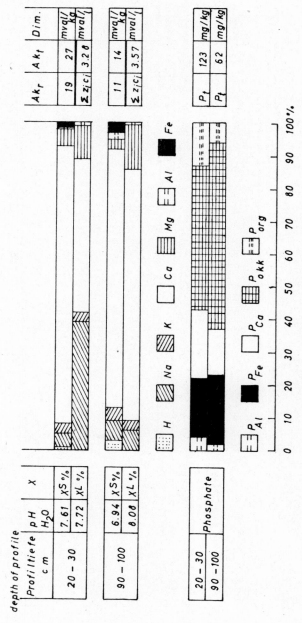

FIGURE 2   Profile of Sand at Fortuna.

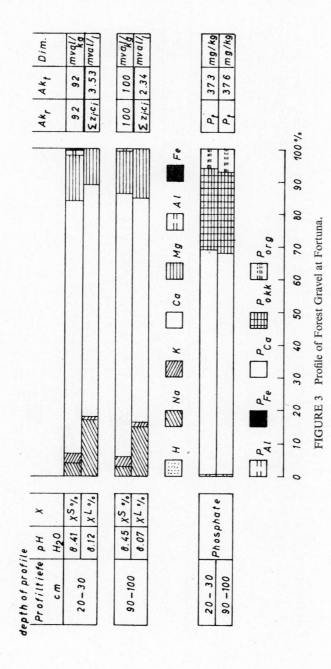

FIGURE 3   Profile of Forest Gravel at Fortuna.

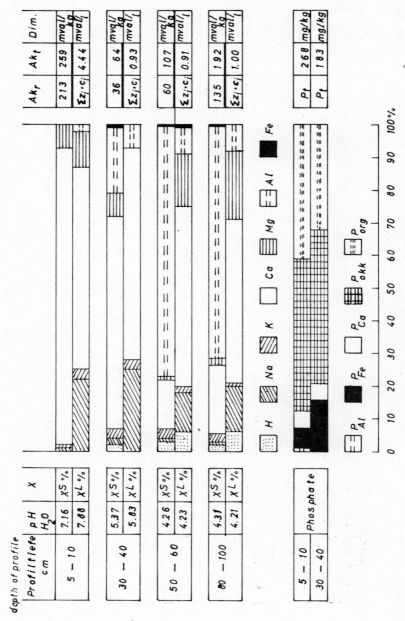

FIGURE 4   Profile of Pseudogley at Weilerswist.

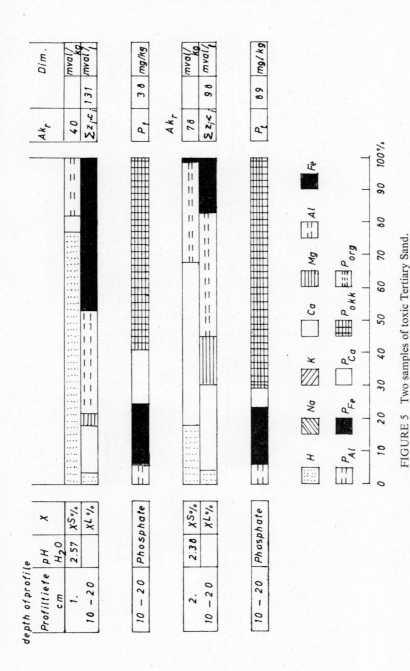

FIGURE 5   Two samples of toxic Tertiary Sand.

On the young spoil bank of Sand (Fig. 2), the Ak_r values of 11 and 19 mval/kg of soil, are very low, and the humus layer is missing. The nutrient distribution, however, is comparatively very good (mostly Ca). Blocking of cation exchange positions by Al and Fe has begun. Nutrient concentration in the soil solution (ESS) is very high, but this is precarious, because the total nutrient supply of sand with only 2% clay content is small and will be quickly exhausted. P_t is also small, but $P_{Al} + P_{Fe}$ make up more than 20%.

The Forest Gravel (Fig. 3) with its loess content has a very favorable nutrient content and distribution, although no humus has been built up yet. The content of 8% $CaCO_3$ and a P_t of 375 mg/kg of soil with a P_{Ca} of 68%, also indicate its favorable status. $P_{Al} + P_{Fe}$ of less than 1% is not favorable for the nutrient supply, but is typical for loess. Here, as for the sand, P_{org} is insignificant because of the lack of humus on these young spoils.

On the slightly alkaline spoils, the equivalent fraction of K ranges from 2 to 5% in the soil, but somewhat lower in the soil solution, indicating a selectivity in adsorption of the K ion. The Na ion, because of its particular nature, is consistently higher in the soil solution than in the soil. Relative concentrations of Al and Fe are low (0 to 2%), and that of Mn even lower (0 to 0.05%).

The profile of the Pseudogley (Fig. 4) is surprising for an old forest soil. A pH of 7 and an X_{Ca}^s of 91% show that this site is also profoundly altered down through the topsoil by the CaO from the nearby briquette factories. Only below 50 cm is the distribution of the cations such as would be expected of an old forest soil. The pH falls to 4, X_{Al}^s climbs to 70% and Ak_r is 50% of Ak_t. In the soil solution, Ca is less than in the spoils. In spite of large Ca additions, P is mostly unchanged. As with the Rhine Gravel, 40% of the phosphates are present in organically bound form.

The N reserve of all the spoil banks is very low, only 0.02% in the mineral portion. The C/N ratio is about 10 to 20 and is comparable to the Pseudogley at a depth of 50 to 90 cm. On the spoil banks, N is the most deficient of all nutrients. Nitrogen fertilizer and seeding with lupine are being used to combat their deficiency.

The spoil bank of toxic Tertiary Sand with pH 2.5 (Fig. 5) differs considerably from the other spoils in its nutrient condition. Ak_r is still comparable to other sandy spoils, but X_{H+Al}^s reaches 95%. In the soil solution, H, Al, and Fe become dominant in the extreme. Together they comprise 83% of the total cation concentration of 131 mval/liter in the ESS. Calcium and Mg are less significant and Na and K sink below 1%.

Phosphorus is very low and is 60 to 70% P_{okk}. The Tertiary Sand, enriched with organic material, lies close to the lignite layer. After it is dumped, oxidation of H_2S to H_2SO_4 causes a drop in the pH. At a pH of 2.5, toxic concentrations of H, Al, and Fe appear and the low percentage of clay is further reduced. On such strongly acid spoil banks, growth of forest trees is impossible without prior amelioration.

The nutrient condition of spoil banks can be judged quickly and positively on the basis of pH measurement. According to Ulrich (1966), pH is related to X^s_{Al} and Ak_r/Ak_t in the manner shown in Fig. 6.

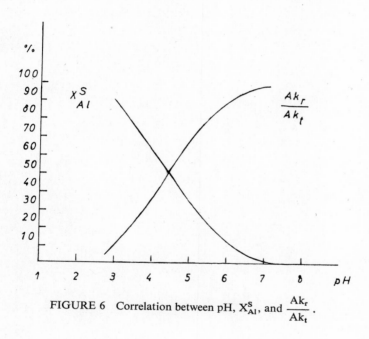

FIGURE 6   Correlation between pH, X^s_{Al}, and $\dfrac{Ak_r}{Ak_t}$.

RESEARCH ON THE BEECH TREES

Mapping the root system

Root maps were prepared for the three plots in each experimental area; each map shows the surface root systems (to a depth of 30 cm) of the ten 8-yr-old beech trees. The point of root penetration into the subsoil is indicated by a small arrow. The drawings also show the stumps of harvested trees, and the stems and crown projections (dashed lines) of existing trees.

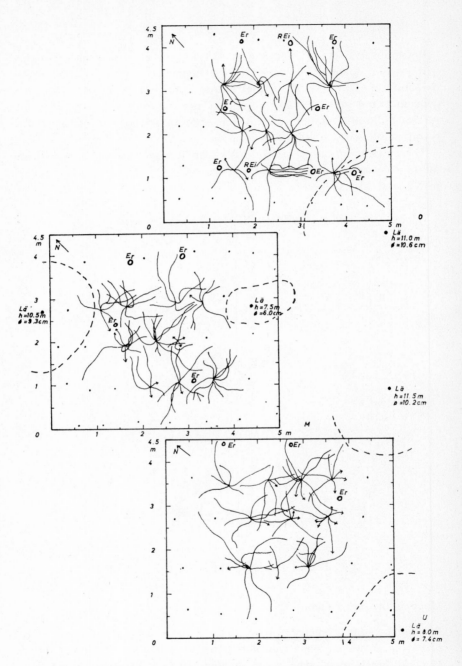

FIGURE 7 Surface-root system on the plot of Rhine Gravel (at Gruhl-see). (Lä = larch; REi = red oak; Er = alder; h = height; Ø = diameter; and O = upper, M = middle, and U = lower plots respectively.)

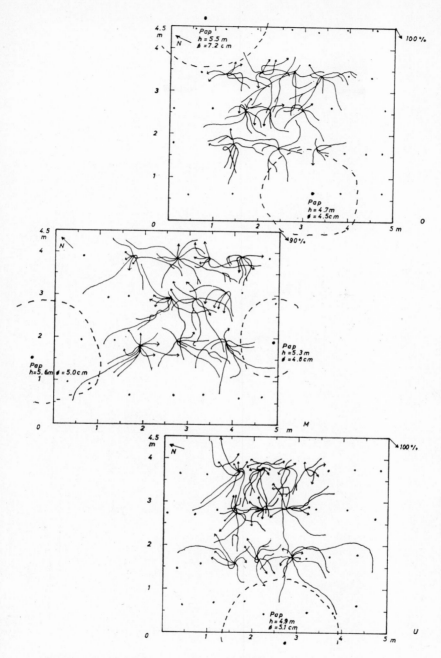

FIGURE 8 Surface-root system on the Sand plot. (Pap = poplar; h = height; Ø = diameter; and O = upper, M = middle, and U = lower plots respectively.)

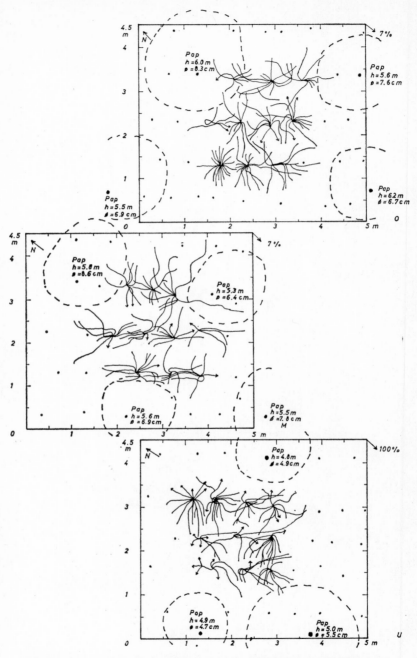

FIGURE 9   Surface-root system on the plot of Forest Gravel (at Fortuna).
(Pap = poplar; h = height; Ø= diameter; and O = upper, M = middle,
and U = lower plots respectively.)

404

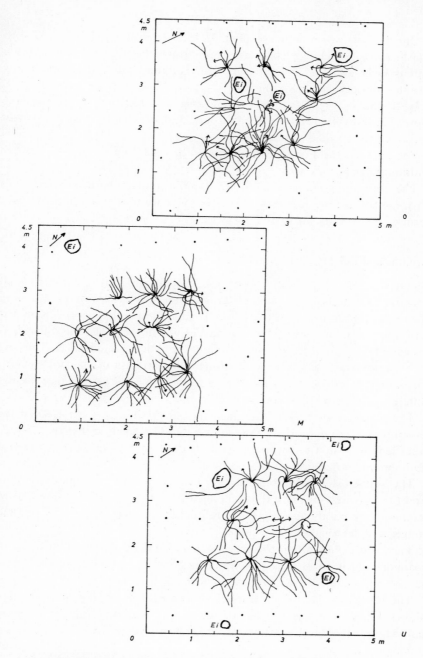

FIGURE 10 Surface-root system on the Pseudogley plot. (Ei = oak;
and O = upper, M = middle, and U = lower plots respectively.)

On the plot of Rhine Gravel (Fig. 7), the root system is quite long with considerable branching. Roots are concentrated between the nutrient-rich humus layer and the mineral soil. Many of the roots are conspicuously oriented toward the alder stumps.

In the Sand (Fig. 8) the roots were able to spread widely through the loose soil. Individual roots pushed through 3 plant rows in 5 years. The root network was oriented downslope.

The roots in the Forest Gravel (Fig. 9) are more numerous, but shorter and more densely grown.

The roots in pseudogley (Fig. 10) exhibit similar characteristics. Here also, the soil texture exercises a decisive influence on the development and form of the root network.

Lengths and weights of the beech trees

Figure 11 gives the mean top lengths and mean root lengths from all experimental plots. After 5 yr of growth, there is little difference among the plots in mean height of trees, even though these differences are statistically significant. Because of large variances within the plots, the differences in height growth for 1965 are without statistical significance. The site factors, however, cause relatively strong differentiation in the root systems. Depth and length of roots are influenced more by soil texture than by the difference between spoil-bank and old-forest soil.

The greater root lengths found on the sandy sites are compensated for by more numerous roots on the loamy sites. The result is that the average total length of first-order roots in the surface root system lies between 4 and 6 m and differences are not significant.

The statistical relationship between average length and depth of roots and the looseness of the soil, exemplified here by the sand fraction (2.0 to 0.02 mm), is parabolic (Fig. 12). The higher the percentage of sand, the longer and deeper the root system.

The ratio of horizontal to vertical roots also depends on soil texture. In loam and silt most of the roots are in the topsoil; in sandy soils they tend to be deeper and the majority are vertical.

The results of the weight measurements from all experimental plots are shown in Fig. 13. The weights of the beech roots and tops differ more among plots than do the lengths. Average leaf weight showed no significant differences among plots.

The site, up to now characterized by the soil texture, does not exercise a decisive influence on weight development. A correlation between plant weight

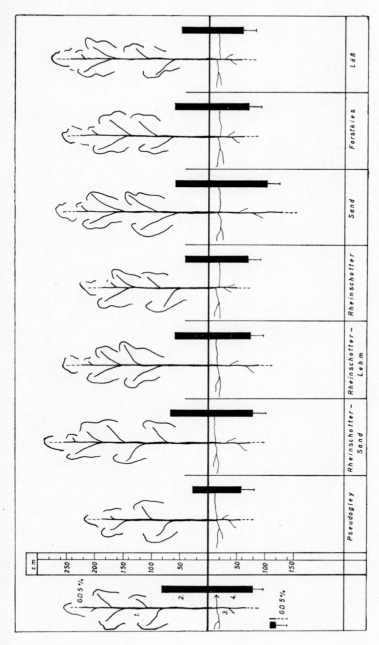

FIGURE 11 Average tree height and root length. 1. total height in the fall of 1965; 2. height increment in 1965; 3. maximum depth of roots; and 4. average reach of the surface roots of the first order. (English equivalents of plot names from the left to right are: Pseudogley; Rhine Gravel-Sand; Rhine Gravel-Silt; Rhine Gravel; Sand; Forest Gravel; and Loess. G D 5% = statistical error at the 5% probability level.)

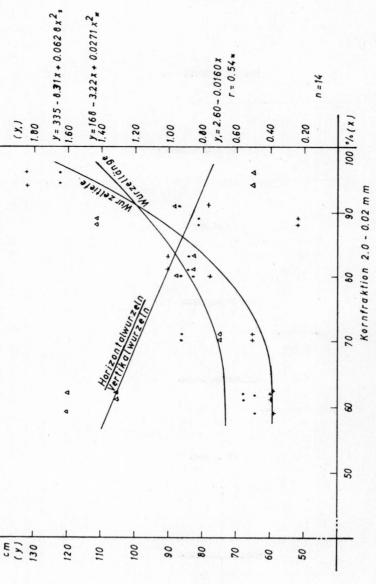

FIGURE 12 Relationship between the root depth (*Wurzeltiefe*, +), the root length (*Wurzellänge*, •), the ratio of horizontal to vertical roots (*Horizontal/Vertikalwurzeln*, △) and the sand fraction (*Kornfraktion* 2.0–0.02 mm).

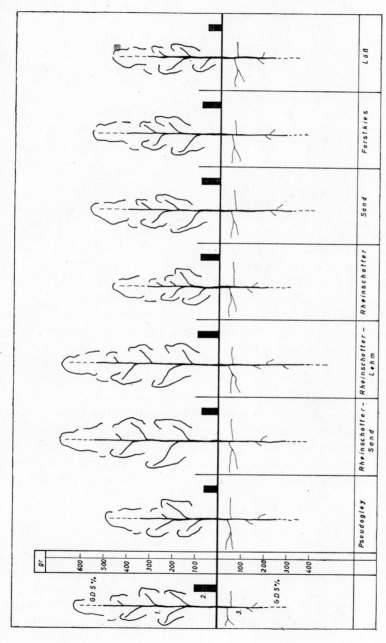

FIGURE 13   Average weight measurements of the beech. 1. total weight of the tops; 2. total weight of the leaves; and 3. total weight of the roots. (English equivalents of plot names from the left to right are: Pseudogley; Rhine Gravel-Sand; Rhine Gravel-Silt; Rhine Gravel; Sand; Forest Gravel; and Loess. G D 5% = statistical error at the 5% probability level.)

and soil nutrients could be found only for P. The total weight increases
with the ratio of $P_{Al} + P_{Fe}$ to total available P according to the function:

$$Y = 671 + 4.10\,X$$

where Y is total weight and X is $\dfrac{P_{Al} + P_{Fe}}{P_t - P_{okk}}$. The correlation coefficient
is 0.58 and the explained variation is 33%.

Of all soils examined, the Forest Gravel is, on the basis of nutrient supply
and distribution as well as texture, the best-suited for planting deciduous
trees.

NUTRIENT CONTENT OF THE BEECH

On soils generally rich in metal cations, the concentrations of Na, Ca,
and Mg do not vary much among samples within the plant parts of leaves,
branches, bark, and roots. Concentrations of N, P, and K are higher in
the leaves; those of Al and Fe are higher in the roots; and Mn concentrations vary widely, both among plant parts and among plots. There is
no correlation between ion concentrations or equivalent fractions in the
soil or soil solution (ESS) on the one hand, and nutrient concentrations
in the beech tissues on the other.

After analogous conversion of the nutrient contents in the plant parts
into equivalent fractions X_i^A, we can show a statistical relationship between
the ratio of plant ash X_i^A to ESS X_i^L and the ratio of soil X_i^S to ESS X_i^L.
Potassium and Ca are adsorbed selectively by the soil, while Na is discrimi-
nated against. However, all have a selective ion uptake to the plant parts,
and K is dependent on pH. Because of the low concentrations of Al, Fe,
and Mn in the soil and in the soil solution, no correlation could be found,
which, according to Ulrich (1966), is also the case for acid forest soils.

SUMMARY

On alkaline spoil sites, beech is suitable for establishing a healthy forest.
Favorable results can also be obtained with ash and maple on nutrient-
rich spoil banks. With the addition of N, the spoils made up of Rhine
gravel, loess, and, above all, forest gravel can be rated better than the old
gley forest soil.

Reforestation of spoils in the Rhine lignite area is more important for outdoor recreation, of people from nearby industrial areas, than for wood production. Management for timber production, however, facilitates administration and care of the forest and in the long run reduces the cost that must be charged to recreation.

LITERATURE CITED

Knabe, W. 1964. Methods and results of strip-mine reclamation in Germany. *Ohio J. of Sci.* **64** (2), 75–105.

Jacoby, H. 1968. Wachstum, Wurzelausbildung und Nährstoffversorgung von Buchenkulturen auf Standorten mit verschiedenen Bodenarten im rheinischen Braunkohlenrevier. Dissertation Univ. Göttingen 162 p.

Ulrich, B. 1965. Bericht über bodenkundliche Untersuchungen im Tagebau Garsdorf und im Forstamt Rheinbraun. Institut für Bodenkunde, Univ. Göttingen 18 p.

Ulrich, B. 1966. Kationenaustausch-Gleichgewichte in Böden. *Zeitschrift für Pflanzenernährung, Düngung und Bodenkunde*, **66**, 141–159.

Ulrich, B. 1966. Selectivity and discrimination in ion uptake under field conditions. Tech. Rep. No. 65 Int. Atomic Energy Agency, Vienna.

Watanabe, F. S., and S. R. Olsen. 1965. Test of ascorbic method for determining phosphorus in water and $NaHCO_3$-extracts from soil. *Soil Sci. Soc. Amer. Proc*, **29**, 677–678.

DISCUSSION

GOOD: Was there no difference in growth between the *Fagus* on the waste soils and that in the old forest soils?

JACOBY: The difference was not very great. The old forest soil has dense layers of roots to 50 cm depth; but on spoils, roots are able to penetrate to a greater depth.

ABNORMALITIES IN THE ROOTS OF TREES GROWING ON TOXIC DUMP MATERIAL*

Zdzisław Harabin and Jan Greszta

Scientific Research Enterprise, Upper Silesian Industrial Area
Polish Academy of Sciences, Zabrze, Poland

The relationship of the morphological and anatomical development of tree roots to certain chemical characteristics of industrial waste material was studied on waste dumps in three regions of Poland.

In toxic soil environments, all tree species formed flat root systems with virtually all root development in the surface and near-surface layers. Under these conditions, the underground parts of most species develop only in a considerably reduced form, and as a consequence, the functioning of the root system is severely restricted.

Anatomical changes in the roots of trees growing on toxic dump material were principally in the secondary bark (i. e. the phloem), the phloem rays, the pith, and the sclerenchyma. Although these changes may have been caused directly by toxicity, they may also have developed because the roots grow very close to the surface on toxic sites.

INTRODUCTION

The dynamic development of industry has made the problem of reclamation of various types of dump grounds one of major importance, particularly in developed areas. In many cases, reclamation by tree planting is the cheapest and quickest method of soil stabilization and hence protection against wind and water erosion. Research was carried out on industrial dumps of a great variety of materials, many of which may be toxic. The toxic

---

* An invited paper; not presented at the symposium because the authors were unable to attend.

formations may appear as homogeneous layers or dispersed in the form of inserts of varying sizes.

Studies were made in three different regions of Poland with varied mineralogical and lithological, and hence physico-chemical, conditions. In the region of Turoszów, old dumping grounds were chosen, where the predominant constituents are toxic Tertiary clays with an admixture of dusty Quaternary loam. In the region of Żary, studies were conducted on levelled external dumps almost 30 years old in which the predominant constituents are loose Tertiary sands with an admixture of fragmented brown coal. Also included were flotation-waste tailings ponds of fragmented dolomites with a fine-sand texture. This waste was transported hydraulically to the tailings ponds, which were banked with mineral earth.

Both on the dumps left after brown coal exploitation and on the flotation-waste tailings ponds, the soil toxicity prevents natural plant succession. This process can be restarted, or even accelerated, by neutralizing the phytotoxic constituents and sowing a suitable mixture of grasses and legumes.

Our purpose was to demonstrate the relationship between the root-development of the introduced tree species and certain chemical properties of the dumped material.

PROCEDURE

Chemical properties

In the area of the rhizosphere, soil samples for chemical analysis were taken from depths of 1 to 10, 20 to 30, and 40 to 50 cm, and in the case of deeply-rooted trees, from depths of more than 2.0 m. The following properties were determined:

1. pH, by a potentiometric method using a glass electrode;

2. exchangeable acidity, by the Daikuhara method;

3. hydrolytic acidity, by the Kappen method;

4. free acidity, by a method by Thun-Herrmann;

5. exchangeable Al, by the Sokołow method; and

6. exchangeable Zn, by the Rinkis and Peire dithiazone extraction-colorimetric method.

Root systems

To demonstrate the effect of toxicity of the soil on the root system formation of selected tree species, both field and laboratory investigations were conducted.

On the described waste dumps, root systems of the following species were investigated: *Alnus glutinosa* (L.) Gaertn., *Betula verrucosa* Ehrh., *Populus robusta* Schn., and *Populus Simonii* Carr. The root systems were excavated, whitewashed, and then photographed. The following elements of the exposed roots were studied: number and length, position and penetration of the root in the dump material, and the boundary zone of root range.

Anatomical changes

The anatomical structure of the roots of *Alnus glutinosa, Populus berolinensis* Dipp., and *P. robusta* trees growing on both toxic sites and in natural habitats were studied. The trees on the two different sites were the same age. Sections were taken from first-order lateral roots at a distance of 0.5 m from the trunk and were preserved in alcohol. Transverse sections were stained as follows:

1. differential staining with alum carmine and iodide green to show up cellulose membranes, and the prepared sections were sealed in Canadian balsam;
2. PAS coloring (periodic acid and Schiff reagent staining cellulose membranes); and
3. Feulgen staining method (1 N HCl plus Schiff reagent at 60 C).

For microphotography, sections prepared by the Feulgen method or after the Sudan III reaction were used. Photographs were made with a "Praktiflex" camera on narrow *"mikrofilm negatywowy"* film, using an Nfpk microscope (panachromatic lens, 6.3X; periplanet eyepiece, 10X). The prints were enlarged to 90X.

RESULTS AND DISCUSSION

Chemical properties

The toxicity of coal tip dumps is governed primarily by the presence in the soil of exchangeable Al and free H_2SO_4.

Although there are many opinions on the effect of exchangeable Al on plant life, there is complete agreement that an increased concentration in

TABLE 1

Certain chemical properties of dump material

Dump	Description of material	Depth cm	pH		Hydrolytic acid.	Exch. acid.	Exch. Al	Free acid.
			in KCl	in H$_2$O	in meq/100 g of dumped material			
Toxic Material								
Turów-Jasienica	Tertiary clays with large content of organic matter (brown coal), and a slight admixture of light dusty Quaternary loams.	1–10	3.6	4.0	7.05	4.55	2.74	1.20
		20–30	3.4	3.9	7.05	4.38	2.31	1.45
		50–60	3.6	4.0	4.86	2.80	1.17	0.95
Turów-Jasienica	Tertiary clays with a large content of organic matter and a slight admixture of light dusty Quaternary loams.	1–10	3.6	3.9	7.02	4.20	2.14	1.05
		20–30	3.6	3.9	6.75	4.03	2.16	1.10
		40–50	3.5	3.7	6.89	4.20	2.15	1.25
Żary-"Czapla" dump	Loose dark-colored Tertiary sands with a slight admixture of organic material mixed with glacial-water Quaternary sands.	1–10	3.1	3.2	10.13	6.12	3.44	3.45
		20–30	2.9	3.1	11.07	5.25	3.77	3.00
		60–80	2.8	3.0	12.23	7.35	4.46	4.10
"Nowy Dwór"	Loose fine-grained dolomite sands with a grain diameter 0.02 to 1.0 mm	1–10	7.7	8.3	0.11	0.09	0.00	0.00
		20–25	7.9	8.4	0.11	0.09	0.00	0.00
		40–50	7.5	7.8	0.15	0.13	0.00	0.00
"Nowy Dwór"	Loose fine-grained dolomite sands with a grain diameter 0.02 to 1.0 mm	1–10	7.5	8.1	0.11	0.09	0.00	0.00
		15–20	8.2	8.4	0.19	0.15	0.00	0.00

Non-Toxic Material

Turów	Tertiary clays with a considerable admixture of rock rubble	1–10	5.0	5.8	0.44	0.41	0.13	0.20
		20–30	5.4	5.8	0.53	0.27	0.25	0.00
		60–80	5.1	5.7	0.54	0.35	0.30	0.50
Turów	Tertiary clays with an admixture of slag, and gravels of diameter from 0.5 to 1.0 cm	1–10	5.6	6.1	0.81	0.35	0.05	0.05
		20–30	4.8	5.3	0.70	0.54	0.06	0.00
		60–80	5.1	5.6	0.41	0.35	0.10	0.00
Turów	Brownish Tertiary clays with an admixture of slag, and gravels.	10–20	4.7	5.2	0.54	0.53	0.17	0.15
		20–30	5.1	5.9	0.41	0.09	0.11	0.60
		40–50	3.8	4.5	2.03	1.59	0.52	0.60
		100–110	5.4	5.7	1.35	0.26	0.08	0.15

the soil causes permanent changes in the root system (Russell, 1958; Ragland and Coleman, 1959; Lisiewska, 1960; Foy and Brown, 1964; and others). The exchangeable-Al content in samples taken from near the trees' roots ranged up to 4 meq/100 g of dump material (Table 1), while spot samples from other locations had values as high as 10 meq/100 g or even more.

In this environment the pH indicates, to a certain extent, the phytotoxic properties of the dumped material. On toxic coal tip dumps this value varies between pH 2.8 and 3.6 in KCl. The high pH found in flotation tailings ponds, and the toxicity in this type of dumped soil, is governed principally by the high content of exchangeable Zn (from 2.20 mg/kg of dump material in the surface layers up to 11.50 mg/kg in lower layers).

Root systems

The analyses showed a clear relationship between the development of the root systems and the chemical properties of the tested soils. The root systems of most tree species growing in natural soils or on non-toxic dumps are well-developed both horizontally and vertically. Where toxic constituents are present, the roots develop only in the surface and near-surface soil. The greatest changes in morphological structure of the root sytem are observed in deep-rooting species such as *Populus* and *Alnus*.

In a toxic soil environment, all the tested tree species exhibited flat root systems, the roots spreading out just below the surface in a soil layer no more than 10 cm deep (Fig. 1). Only certain individual secondary roots penetrated the soil to a depth of 25 to 30 cm. This type of root system in trees may be the result of compactness of the soil or of the presence of toxic compounds in the soil. Under the test conditions, the first eventuality may be discounted since investigations made on soils of similar compactness but with insignificant quantities of free acidity and exchangeable Al showed that these same species developed a tap root system (Fig. 2).

The trees growing in toxic material exhibited changes both in the length of lateral roots and in the number of branch roots of higher orders. In a toxic environment *Alnus glutinosa* always developed notably shortened lateral roots (Fig. 3); the remaining species show a root formation depending on the nature and type of the dump.

Populus berolinensis and *P. Simonii* growing on coal tip dumps form markedly reduced root systems; in a flotation tailings pond environment, the same species develop abnormally thin, elongated, string-like lateral roots

(Fig. 4). Average annual increase of primary lateral roots on ordinary sites is 10.3 m/tree compared to 1.2 m on coal tip dumps.

Differences in planting depths in tailings pond dumps resulted in a particularly interesting behavior of the roots of *Populus berolinensis* and

FIGURE 1   Root systems of trees on toxic dumps: (top) *Populus robusta* (Turoszów-Jasienica); (bottom) *Betula verrucosa* (Żary-"Czapla").

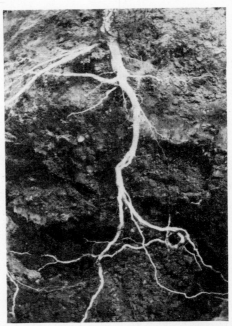

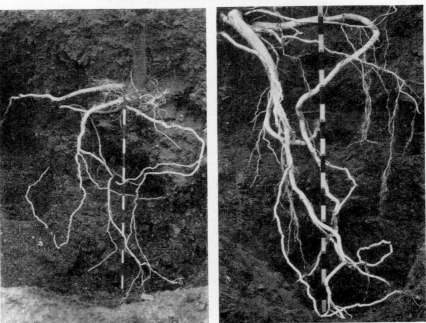

FIGURE 2 Root systems of trees on a non-toxic dump (Turoszów): (top) *Betula verrucosa*; (bottom left) *Populus berolinensis*; (bottom right) *P. robusta*.

P. robusta. Deep planting (holes more than 40 cm deep) caused complete inhibition of root development of *P. berolinensis*, and the trees died immediately. With shallow planting (holes 20 to 25 cm deep), the trees formed lateral roots growing towards the upper layers and spreading horizontally at a depth of only 0 to 5 cm.

FIGURE 3   Root system of an *Alnus glutinosa* tree on a flotation tailings pond.

Standard-type *P. robusta* was generally planted in holes 40 to 50 cm deep. The first direct contact between the roots and the toxic material has a decisive effect. The roots react in various ways to the change in soil environment (nursery to toxic dump material), e.g.:

1) The root system, reduced before planting out, may not develop at all.
2) The main root does not increase in length; only the lateral roots develop.
3) Both main root and lateral roots develop and increase in length, at least in the initial vegetation period.

The first two examples of modified behavior of the root systems in a toxic soil environment occur very frequently; although the third is found only sporadically, it is worthy of discussion.

In the first growth stage, the trees develop irregular, deformed, short main roots, and single lateral roots of the first order. At the end of the first year, the growth of the main root is arrested, loosened tissues are

FIGURE 4   Root systems of *Populus berolinensis* trees in toxic material: (top) coal tip dump (Turoszów-Jasienica); (bottom) flotation tailings pond ("Nowy Dwór").

visible on its surface, and at the end of this stage, a thick layer of bark is formed. Both growth and physiological functions are taken over by the first-order lateral roots and a few small rootlets. Near the end of the second growing season, most of the side roots develop surface deformations, similar to those of the main root described above, and then die off. At the beginning of the third season, there is an increase in the number of rootlets in comparison with the previous year, and several lateral roots also survive (Fig. 5). Dying and subsequent shedding, of the bark on many parts of the roots was also observed.

This type of root deformation, as well as the changes in the surface tissues of the root have been attributed by some authors to the harmful action of exchangeable Al in the soil (Ganża, cited by Lisiewska, 1960). Virtually identical phenomena were observed in *Populus robusta* in an environment that did not contain exchangeable Al, which indicates that such morphological-anatomical changes can be caused by other toxic compounds as well.

FIGURE 5 Severely deformed root system of a *Populus robusta* tree on a flotation dump. ("Nowy Dwór".)

Anatomical changes

Although initial investigations detected certain anatomical changes in the roots, it could not be established whether these changes were caused directly by the toxic soil base or by other factors. Concentration of the

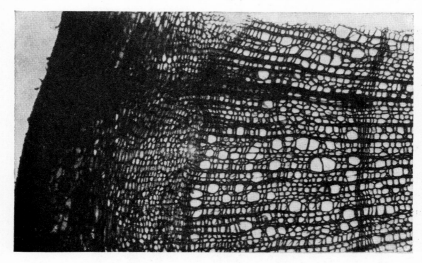

FIGURE 6   Cross sections of roots of *Alnus glutinosa*: (left) toxic environment; (right) non-toxic environment.

roots in a thin surface layer of soil exposes them to the harmful effects of extreme temperatures and hence to considerable disturbances in their water balance. At this stage, therefore, caution is advisable in interpreting the observed phenomena.

Anatomical changes were found principally in the secondary bark (i.e. the phloem), the secondary phloem rays, the pith, and the sclerenchyma.

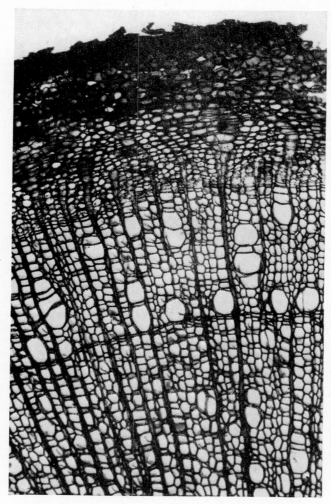

FIGURE 7 Cross section of a root of *Alnus glutinosa* from a toxic environment showing changes in the phloem rays.

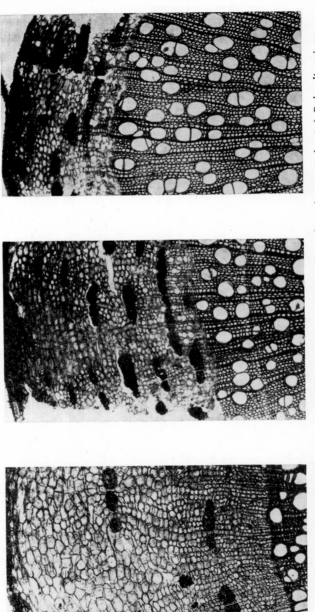

FIGURE 8   Cross sections of roots of *Populus*: (left) *P. robusta* on a severely toxic environment; (center) *P. berolinensis* on a slightly toxic environment; (right) *P. robusta* on a non-toxic environment.

The secondary bark of roots of *Alnus glutinosa* growing on
and on flotation tailings ponds was about twice as thick as th
of the same species growing in a natural habitat (Fig. 6). Mor
trees growing on toxic formations, the phloem rays were distinctly v
towards the outer side (Fig. 7).

In the roots of *Populus robusta* from a severely toxic flotation tailings
pond, there was a considerable increase in the width of the secondary
bark, both in comparison with the roots of the same species growing outside the toxic environment and with the roots of *P. berolinensis* growing
in a weakly toxic soil environment (Fig. 8). Also, there was a distinct decrease
in the number of sclerenchyma layers in the secondary bark zone, and groups
of irregular cells occurred on the outside of the compact layers of the
phloem.

However, comparison of the transverse sections of roots from trees
growing in toxic soils with those from trees growing in natural habitats
did not indicate significant differences in the structure and size of the
cells of the particular tissues. Investigation of the cork layers also showed
a very similar anatomical structure, and the microchemical reaction
(Sudan III) showed no differences whatsoever.

CONCLUSIONS

1) With a pH below 2.5 in KCl, root development by either trees or herbs
is impossible. With a rise of pH to 3.0, some trees survive, but develop
poorly and their root systems are completely deformed.

2) Concentration of the whole root system in a thin layer of soil near the
surface (a depth of barely 10 cm) is most probably the result of the leaching
of toxic substances from the surface layers to the deeper-lying soil.

3) Development of root systems of trees, regardless of species, is affected
more by the chemical than by the physical properties of the dumped
material.

4) The severe cutting back of the root systems before planting, thus
reducing the numbers of rootlets and root hairs to a minimum, probably
contributes to the rapid death of trees on spoil dumps. In a toxic environment trees are unable to replace with sufficient speed these important
organs.

LITERATURE CITED

Foy, C. D., and J. C. Brown. 1964. Toxic factors in acid soils. II. Differential aluminum tolerance of plant species. *Soil. Sci. Soc. Am. Proc.* **28**, 27–32.

Lisiewska, M. 1960. Systemy korzeniowe roślin grądowych a podłoże. Poznańskie Towarzystwo Przyjaciół Nauk. **23** (1), 1–84.

Ragland, J. L., and N. T. Coleman. 1959. The effect of soil solution, aluminum and calcium on root growth. *Soil Sci. Soc. Am. Proc.* **23**, 355–357.

Russell, J. E. 1958. Warunki glebowe a wzrost roślin. Państwowe Wydawnictwo Rolnicze i Leśne, Warszawa.

SURVIVAL AND GROWTH OF RED PINE ON COAL SPOIL AND UNDISTURBED SOIL IN WESTERN PENNSYLVANIA

Ernest C. Aharrah* and Richard T. Hartman†

Pymatuning Laboratory of Ecology, University of Pittsburgh, Pittsburgh, Pennsylvania

Comparisons were made of 20-year-old red pine (*Pinus resinosa* Ait.) plantations growing on spoil of the Kittanning coal measure and on an adjacent old-field site in Clarion County, Pa. Estimated volume increment, total cubic volume, total height, length of five-year intercept immediately above breast height, and diameter at breast high are reported for each stand. The old-field plantation showed greater growth for all of these parameters. Red pine is shown to have grown very well on these spoils however, and compares quite well in many parameters with those reported in the literature. Percentage survival is higher on the spoil than in the old-field situation. The old-field site quality as measured by five-year intercept exceeds that of the Kittanning spoil. Some measurements of red pine growing on Clarion coal seam spoil are also reported.

INTRODUCTION AND DESCRIPTION OF STUDY AREA

Although much has been written about the growth and survival of tree species on strip-mine spoils, authors often find themselves in contradiction with one another; in fact, authors often find conflicting results when data from several spoils are compared. (Chapman, 1944; Bramble, 1950, 1952, 1953; Rogers, 1951; Limstrom and Deitschman, 1951; Finn, 1958.) The difficulty has arisen in part from the great variability in spoils, and from the difficulty of making meaningful comparisons with growth occurring on undisturbed lands.

---

* Associate Professor of Biology, Clarion State College, Clarion, Pa.

† Professor of Biology, University of Pittsburgh, Pittsburgh, Pa.

An unusual opportunity was presented for the study of the survival and growth of red pine (*Pinus resinosa* Ait.) in plantations on a spoil and on an adjacent "undisturbed" old-field area. The trees were planted at the same time and from the same nursery shipment. Casual observation of the two plantations suggested that survival and growth on the spoil was equal to or exceeded that of the undisturbed area. Several parameters were evaluated and compared by a variety of standard procedures.

Some other investigators have made comparative growth studies of trees growing on spoil. Tryon and Markus (1953), reporting on the growth of tree species on century-old ore banks in West Virginia, stated: "The abundance of woody vegetation above 0.6 inches d.b.h. showed no real difference between the spoil and the control on three of the units. On one unit, the control had a higher number of stems than the spoil." DenUyl (1962) found cottonwoods to have reached crop tree size in 11 years, but he was not able to recommend other species for planting on the basis of growth at that age. Potter, Weitzman, and Trimble (1951) examined an old spoil dating back more than 30 years. Their results suggested that at least some spoils have maintained good growth through several decades.

All of these studies dealt with natural revegetation. However, Potter and his co-workers make the following statement concerning West Virginia spoils which have been artificially revegetated: "The average growth for most of the planted species was about the same on the spoils as on undisturbed soil. In a few places, black locust and red pine showed exceptionally fast growth."

Chapman (1944) studied plantations which were eight years old. He cited shortleaf pine (*Pinus echinata* Mill.) and pitch pine (*P. rigida* Mill.) as growing better on spoils than on adjacent old fields in Ohio. Rogers (1951) reported that black walnut (*Juglans nigra* L.) on Kansas spoils had averaged an increase in height of 2 ft/year and a radial increment of 0.25 in. The same species is reported to grow faster than average on the spoils of Missouri.

The study area is located about two miles north of Sligo, Pa. in Piney Township, Clarion County. The two plantations are separated by an unimproved road, Legislative Route 16069 (Fig. 1). Land use in the area prior to the coal stripping operations was general farming with some forest production. In many cases this was only marginally profitable, and much of the farmland had been abandoned before the stripping began. The original soil types for the area belong to the Gilpin series (U.S. Department of Agriculture, 1958). These are shallow to moderately deep well-

FIGURE 1   The photo shows the two plantations (arrows) as they appeared at the time of sampling. The road visible between them is Legislative Route 16069. Photo by Taylor Engineering, Clarion, Pa.

drained upland soils developed on mixed-acid materials weathered from shales and sandstone.

The soil of the undisturbed old-field area is classified as a Gilpin shaly silt loam with 12- to 25-% slopes. This type is described as moderately acid and moderately low in plant nutrients. Because it is shallow, it has a low water-supplying capacity. Forest tree growth is considered slow, and this soil is recommended for Christmas-tree production because the slow growth favors a dense bushy tree.

The original soil in the stripped area was classified as a Gilpin silt loam with slopes of 5 to 12%. This soil type has been characterized as acid, moderately low in plant nutrients. Its water-supplying capacity is moderate to moderately low. It is unlikely that the mining had an appreciable effect on this characteristic, for spoils are usually well-drained and low in their capacity to supply water. None of the structure of the original soil is retained in the spoil, but the new parent material is very similar to that of the original soil.

The native cover of the area was mixed hardwoods, with a few pines and hemlocks. Wooded areas now have second-growth stands in which white and red oaks (*Quercus alba* L. and *Q. rubra* L.) and red maple (*Acer rubrum* L.) predominate. The growth on idle land and neglected pastures is mostly poverty grass (*Danthonia spicata* (L.) Beauv.) and broomsedge (*Andropogon virginicus* L.). Spoils which were not planted or on which survival was minimal are slowly being revegetated with these species in addition to the aspens (*Populus tremuloides* Michx. and *P. grandidentata* Michx.).

Clarion County receives approximately 40 inches of rainfall yearly. The area is exposed to high summer temperatures, i.e. 90 to 100 F on summer days, and the soil often freezes to a considerable depth in winter. Winds often blow much of the snow cover from the exposed spoils and may leave small seedlings exposed to the elements throughout the winter.

The spoil under investigation was created in 1944 with the strip mining of the Kittanning coal measures. The stripped area entirely circles the hill top leaving an undisturbed area in the center where the coal was too deep to be mined with the equipment available at that time.

The banks were not treated, i.e. not graded or prepared in any way, and were not planted upon completion of the operation, as there were no state laws in Pennsylvania to require post-stripping operations on private lands until 1945. The act passed at that time, called the "Bituminous Coal Open Pit Mining Conservation Act," required operators to reclaim land stripped for bituminous coal. It called for rounding off the spoil piles to permit the planting of trees, shrubs, or grass and required that planting be carried out as soon as possible in accordance with a plan approved by the Secretary of Mines and Mineral Industries. This law was not retroactive and no physical correction was carried out on the spoils involved in this study.

The banks presently consist in most parts of a rather broad ridge with very steep slopes, exceeding 60° on either side. The height of the spoil ridge is approximately 35 ft. The surface is quite well weathered, being covered with fine shale particles. The entire spoil has a somewhat homogeneous appearance as demonstrated in a cut made by a bulldozer cutting a road through the bank to the depth of the coal seam. Soil pits dug at various sites on the spoil to depths of 6 ft and greater show the same homogeneous structure. The spoil is a mixture of coarse shale, a few inches in diameter, interspersed with a few larger pieces, with much of the material already weathered to finer soil particles. Certainly the entire spoil contains greater than 20% soil-size particles (<2 mm in diameter) which Bramble (1952) reported as required for revegetation.

Mechanical analysis of soil on another Kittanning spoil a short distance away showed the percentage of soil-size particles in the upper 3 in. of soil varied from 45 to 75%, with a mean of 60% (Aharrah, 1962). Nine soil pits were dug in that spoil to a depth of 2 ft. Mechanical analysis of the upper 8 in. in these pits showed a mean of 31% soil-size particles. Only the 2-ft level had less than 20% soil-size particles. The mean at this depth was 16%.

The trees involved in this study were planted by the Department of Forest and Waters in 1950 as part of a program for revegetating these mounds of disturbed earth. Red pine and jack pine (*P. banksiana* Lamb.) were utilized in the plantation on the spoil with 6- by 6-ft spacing. The red pine were planted on the outside slope and on the top of the spoil. Survival of both species is extremely good. Jack pine has reproduced to some extent on the spoil, and numerous seedlings are to be found. There has been no noticeable regeneration of the red pine, however, and only a few cones have been observed on the red pine trees cut in the conduct of this study.

The old-field plantation lies immediately across the unpaved road and was planted at the same time and from the same stock with the same 6-by 6-ft spacing. This plantation contains only red pine and consists of approximately 8000 trees. At present the C & K Coal Company of Clarion, Pa. is stripping the immediate area and will soon be destroying these plantations. It was for this reason that destructive sampling could be carried out without violating good conservation practices.

The soil surface under both plantations is covered with from 2 to 3 in. of litter. There is very little humus beneath this litter but a small amount has mixed with the soil surface to produce an A horizon a few hundredths of an inch in thickness.

METHODS

Plots, approximately 12- by 36-ft in size, were laid out in both the spoil and old-field study areas. This size was selected so that each plot would include the space occupied by 12 trees in the original 6- by 6-ft spacing of the planting. On the spoil the size and shape of the plots was varied somewhat so that only red pine was included in each plot. Four plots from each area were chosen by lot for destructive sampling.

Trees within each plot were cut as close to the ground as possible with a chain saw. Branches were removed and separated as dead or living and each group was bundled and tied. These bundles were weighed and the weights recorded. The bole was measured and then sectioned and weighed. Weighing was done with a steelyard with a maximum load capacity of 140 lb and an accuracy of 1 lb. Lighter weights, less than 30 lb, were determined on the reverse side of the beam where accuracy reaches 0.5 lb. Samples of both the living branches and the bole were removed and placed in large paper bags which were returned to the laboratory and weighed. These are being oven dried to determine percent dry weight in order to convert the field weights to dry weights which are readily comparable.

A handbook of the International Biological Program (Newbould, 1967) contains an excellent summary of methods for estimating forest production. Many of the methods discussed have been adapted to the present study. Immediately after felling the following measurements were made: (1) height to top of tree, (2) crown depth (measured height of lowest living branch), (3) crown radius (measured length of longest living branch), (4) diameter at breast high (dbh), (5) fresh weight of branches and needles, (6) total weight of the bole, (7) length of each internode above breast height, and (8) diameter at 1-m intervals beginning with basal diameter.

All diameter measurements were made with a steel tape. It is realized that many investigators prefer calipers to tape for such measurements, but Newbould (1967) declared tape to be far superior to calipers. Furthermore, the use of the tape would make the study more comparable to those done under the International Biological Program.

The length of the five-year intercept (the aggregate length of 5 internodes) immediately above breast height was calculated as an index of site quality for the red pine growing on the two sites (Ferree, Shearer, and Stone, 1958; Wakeley and Marrero, 1958).

Ferree and his coworkers in measuring the intercept of red pine began their measurements with the node above breast height. Wakeley and Marrero used the node below breast height as a point of origin. To permit better comparison, the method of the former investigators was adopted for the present study which included only red pine. By using the five-year intercept method of measuring site quality, inequities of growth during the period of establishment which result from factors other than those of the soil itself can be at least partly eliminated. Such factors on the open spoils consist of high surface temperatures, poor planting stock, poor planting practices, desiccation as a result of the high temperatures, and the exposure to winter winds and frosts. Some of these factors certainly differ between the spoils and the adjacent old-field site.

Cubic volume of the bole was estimated by recognizing each one-meter log as a truncated cone and the tip as a true cone. The volume of each of the sections was calculated from the diameter measurements and the results were summed. A program for the Wang calculator series 370 was written to simplify the calculations.

Whittaker (1961) chose estimated volume increment (EVI) as the one expression which combines tree size and growth rate and is strongly correlated with the various aspects of tree production. In the present study, estimated volume increments were calculated for each tree for each of the past five years, according to the formula of Whittaker and Woodwell (1969):

$$EVI = 0.5 \, \pi h (r^2 - c^2)$$

where h is the height, $r = \frac{1}{2}$ dbh, $c = r - i$, and i is the annual wood radial increment at breast height. The value for i was determined in our samples by averaging four measurements made at the points where diameters drawn at right angles to each other intersect the annual rings. The sections on which these measurements were made were removed from the bole at breast height and preserved in a 70% solution of half alcohol and half glycerin. This solution reduces shrinkage which often occurs when the small sections are dried. This method of preservation also improves the visibility of the annual rings.

Height in each of the years of growth was calculated by subtracting the succeeding internode lengths from the total height. Values for r for each

28*

subsequent increment was the c value from the preceeding calculation. Only trees with a single stem were used in calculating volume, estimated volume increment, and five-year intercept. Trees which had two stems below breast height were also eliminated from dbh measurements. Where two stems existed, only the longest was included in the analysis of total height.

Foliar analyses are being conducted for calcium and iron. The material is digested with nitric and perchloric acids in a Kjeldahl apparatus. The resulting mineral solution is being analyzed in an atomic absorption spectrophotometer, Perkin-Elmer 290. Additional analyses of foliage extracts are being conducted colorimetrically with a Beckman Model B spectrophotometer. These analyses include aluminum, with a hematin reagent, and phosphorus, with a molybdate reagent.

RESULTS AND DISCUSSION

Survival of trees from planting to 19 years was greater on the Kittanning spoil than on the adjacent undisturbed land, Table 1. The lowest survival on the spoil in any single plot occurred in Sample No. 1 in Table 2. This group of trees, located on a steep outside slope, exhibited a stunted growth form in addition to a low survival rate.

TABLE 1

Comparison of survival on Kittanning spoil with that on the undisturbed land

Location	Basal Area ft²/acre	Survival	
		no./acre	%
On spoil	100	1091	91
Off spoil	92	924	77

The survival rates of 91 and 77% exceed those reported for red pine on spoil banks in most areas. Hart and Byrnes (1960) reported survival on a single spoil in Clarion County as 21%. Other investigators have found good survival of red pine but usually less than 80%. Brown (1962) found survival of 71.6% on spoils in West Virginia while Limstrom and Deitschman (1951) report survivals of 55 and 81% in two 9-year-old plantings in Perry County, Illinois. The latter also studied 2-year-old plantations where survival rates of 50 and 41% were obtained. The average heights of the dominant trees in the former study were 16 and 18 ft respectively. These trees were probably taller than those of the present study, but use of only dominant trees by these authors makes comparison with the present data difficult.

TABLE 2

Comparison of growth on the Kittanning spoil with that on undisturbed land adjacent to the spoil

Sample No.	No. of Trees	Mean DBH m	Mean Volume m³	Mean Height m	Mean 5-yr Intercept m	Mean EVI (5-yr period) m³
			On Spoil			
1	10	0.071	0.018	3.47	1.41	0.008
2	12	0.124	0.048	6.73	2.69	0.005
3	9	0.117	0.058	7.70	3.05	0.013
4	12	0.104	0.046	7.21	2.68	0.016
			Off Spoil			
5	10	0.119	0.053	7.38	2.93	0.020
6	9	0.102	0.042	7.52	3.10	0.011
7	8	0.104	0.037	6.31	2.71	0.013
8	11	0.109	0.043	7.43	2.85	0.015

The calculations of basal area per acre were made following the procedures of Lundgren (1965). The original planting spacing of 6- by 6-ft provides for 1200 trees per acre. This figure was multiplied by the survival rate to estimate the number of trees per acre surviving. Basal area was then read from the chart presented in Lundgren's paper. These data (Table 1) did not lend themselves to statistical analysis. The difference of 8 ft² is not very large, however it is the only growth parameter measured in which the spoil plantation exceeded the old field.

The experimental design is based on a three-ranked hierarchy. Each plot is designated as a minor group and each site a major group. This design permits the analysis of the unequal groups resulting from the variable survival (Li, 1964). All the parameters shown in Table 2 exhibited greater range on the spoil than in the old field situation. This is probably indicative of similar range in site quality throughout the spoil.

The five-year intercept data, which give the most effective measure of site quality, indicate that the old field is a better site for red pine than the spoil. The mean intercept in the old field is 0.44 m greater than that of the spoil. Analysis of these data demonstrated that this difference is significant at the 1% level. Ferree et al., (1958) reported intercept values for 37 plantations in New York state. These ranged from 2.7 ft to 11.4 ft with a mean value of 8.7 ft (2.65 m). The mean values of 2.46 m on the spoil and 2.90 m in the old field compare favorably with the New York mean.

Height measurements support the conclusion that the old field is the better site. The mean height of the trees in the old field exceeds that of the trees on the spoil by 0.89 m. This difference is also significant at the 1% level. No significance was shown in the differences within the plantation on the spoil or the old field in either of these parameters. When growth of these trees is compared with growth of red pine in Michigan by means of the growth curves of van Eck and Whiteside (1963, Fig. 5), the mean height of the trees in the present study fall above their curves when plotted on the same axes.

Stiell (1965) found the average height from actual measurement in one 16-year-old plantation of red pine in Canada to be 22.8 ft (6.9 m), and in a second plantation of the same age to be 24.9 ft (7.6 m). In the present study the mean height at 18 years of the trees included in the spoil plots was 6.3 m and those of the old field 7.2 m. Thus the trees appear to be slightly more than two years behind those of Stiell in height. Bramble, Cope and Chisman (1949) found red pine 16 years of age and planted with 6- by 6-ft spacing to have achieved a height of 22.0 ft (6.7 m). This compares favorably with the measurements of Stiell and is somewhat taller than the trees of the present study.

Estimated volume increments are expressed in Table 3 in units of cm^3/tree/yr and in cm^3/m^2/yr for each situation. The estimates per square meter were calculated from values in Table 1.

Whittaker and Woodwell (1969) report an estimated volume increment of 2100 cm^3/tree for *Pinus rigida* in the Brookhaven forest. Estimated volume increments of 1900 cm^3 and 3000 cm^3 in the present study compare favorably with this figure. These authors carried out a series of regressions on estimated volume increment which led to the conclusion that EVI was advantageous as an independent variable to estimate production because it includes an expression of growth rate of the individual tree.

Rudolph (1957) reported mean annual increments for the entire rotation age (140 years) for red pine in unmanaged plantations as being 28.5 ft^3/acre or approximately 2.0 m^3/ha. The figure of 0.0019 m^3 per tree on the spoil in this study gives an estimate of 4.2 m^3/ha.

Whittaker (1966) calculated estimated volume increments for a variety of forest types in the Great Smoky Mountains. He says that the values converge in the range of 530 to 590 cm^3/m^2 for a wide range of forest types.

As can be seen in Table 3, the values in this study lie just outside that range on either side; the spoil value being slightly below and the non-spoil above the values given by Whittaker. Whittaker found the increments to decrease along a moisture gradient which may indicate a reason for the difference between spoil and old-field situations. Moisture studies must be included in additional research.

TABLE 3

Comparison of estimated volume increments on Kittanning spoil and undisturbed land with those of Whittaker and Woodwell

Forest type or species	Location	Author	Estimated Volume Increment	
			cm^3/tree/yr	cm^3/m^2
Red pine	Pennsylvania spoil	Present study	1900	512
Red pine	Pennsylvania old field	Present study	3000	685
Pitch pine	Brookhaven forest	Whittaker & Woodwell	2100	
Mixed hardwoods	Cades Cove[a]	Whittaker		532
Mixed hardwoods	Cades Cove[a]	Whittaker		900
Tuliptree forest	Greenbrier Cove[a]	Whittaker		1444
Spruce-fir	North slope, Mt Collins[a]	Whittaker		534
Spruce-fir	South slope, Mt. Mingus[a]	Whittaker		528
Fraser fir	North slope, Mt. Le Conte[a]	Whittaker		239
Fraser fir	South slope, Mt. Le Conte[a]	Whittaker		268
Oak-Hickory	Oak Ridge	Whittaker		455
Redwoods	California	Whittaker		1314

[a] These forests in the Great Smoky Mountains National Park.

Preliminary foliar analysis for P, Ca, and Fe indicate very little difference in the nutrient content of the needles from trees on the spoil and in the old field. A far larger difference appears to exist between needles from different locations on the same tree than exists between the needles of trees in the two locations.

Sample No. 1 on the spoil (Table 2) contained trees which were definitely chlorotic as well as stunted. The needles of the trees were small, sparse and yellowed. Horton and Brown (1960) described trees of a similar appearance on old-field sites in Canada which are high in lime and low in either

K or Mg. There is certainly no abundance of lime or Ca in this spoil but deficiencies may exist in either Mg or K or both.

A nearby Kittanning spoil which was analyzed in 1961 proved to be low in K while Ca content ranged from very poor through fair with a maximum of 750 lb/acre available (Aharrah, 1962). Magnesium was not included in this analysis. The overburden on the Kittanning coal seams is reported to be very consistent throughout most of Perry and Piney Townships. It is assumed that mineral analyses in the present study will prove similar to those of the earlier investigation. These analyses showed a maximum K concentration of 0.03 mg/g of air-dried soil. The mean K content however was approximately 0.0025 mg/g of air-dried soil.

At that time no correlation was recognized between chemical analysis of the soil and site conditions such as exposure of slope or topography. Frequency data for plants showed some correlation with soil nutrients.

In the present study the largest dbh and volume on the spoil occurred in the two plots on the more level surface of the ridge top. Height, however, reached its maximum on one of these plots and one of the plots on the slope. The slope plot was located only a few yards from the plot containing the stunted, chlorotic trees. There is no reason to suspect the chlorotic trees to be the effect of exposure or degree of slope.

TABLE 4

Comparison of growth means from Kittanning and Clarion spoils and the undisturbed old field

Location	Intercept m	Volume m³	Height m
Clarion spoil	2.348	0.0317	6.39
Kittanning spoil	2.457	0.0413	6.27
Old-field	2.898	0.0438	7.16

Measurement of the same parameters of a group of trees cut from a spoil of the Clarion coal seams, Table 4, indicates these coal seams produce spoil less suitable to the survival and growth of red pine. These trees were not included in the statistical analysis as they were cut before the experimental design had been prepared. They were cut, prior to being destroyed by additional stripping, for the purpose of determining regression constants for estimation of volume from measurements of height and dbh. These data do, however, indicate that the spoils of the Clarion coal seams are poorer sites for red pine than those of the Kittanning seams, and are included here for that reason.

In our opinion, the results of the investigation of Tryon and Markus (1953) should not be compared to strip-mine spoils. Many researchers have made such comparisons in the past because the century-old ore banks were the only examples of disturbed and reclaimed land that had existed for a long period. The comparisons were unfortunate, for these iron ore operations in West Virginia were mere pick-and-shovel operations compared to the equipment in use today. The overburden of bituminous coal measures, at least in the vicinity of Clarion, Pennsylvania, differ in both physical and chemical characteristics from that of the West Virginia iron ore. The mounds of earth resulting are much higher and steeper in the coal fields. When these spoils are leveled, the compaction by the heavy machinery adds another variable to the soil characteristics.

There is reason, however, to agree with Bramble (1952) that the coal measure spoils of Pennsylvania will eventually be revegetated with oak-hickory forests, not because of similarity with the site of the Tryon and Markus study, but because of the similarity of the conditions other than soil which govern the climax vegetation of the area. Man, by planting forest species, has not altered the final outcome of succession on unmanaged lands but has only succeeded in changing the course of events leading to that final result.

Although its growth in the old field exceeds that on the spoil, red pine is an effective species for use in revegetating disturbed lands in northwestern Pennsylvania. Survival is adequate on many spoils, and when it survives it produces a usable product in a relatively short time.

It will be interesting to see if this exotic species will reseed itself in the years to come on these sites. Most of the plantations in western Pennsylvania are just now beginning to produce cones. Very few of these cones will escape the red squirrels which have been attracted to the cones of other species in the mixed plantations.

The spoil in this study is well covered with an excellent plantation of red pine which has produced a remarkable litter. This cover of the forest floor inhibits run off and increases the infiltration of water into the soil. At present there is no erosion from this spoil. There is little doubt that this disturbed land has been reclaimed satisfactorily although individual tree growth is exceeded by that in the adjacent old-field plantation.

Similar studies now under way in newly established plantations may shed some additional light on the causes of these differences. It will be interesting to follow the development of plantings on spoils resulting from present coal mining in the area. This mining will create a spoil larger than any in Clarion County. Has 20-years experience led to improved survival and growth? That is a question for future research.

LITERATURE CITED

Aharrah, E. C. 1962. Revegetation and soil chronosequence of strip-mine spoil banks of the Lower Kittanning coal measure in Clarion County, Pennsylvania. *M.S. Thesis*. Univ. Pittsburgh.

Bramble, W. C. 1952. Reforestation of strip-mined bituminous coal land in Pennsylvania. *J. Forest*. **50**, 308–314.

Bramble, W. C., and R. N. Ashley. 1950. Spoil bank planting—fall, 1949. Pa. Agr. Exp. Sta. Progr. Report 24.

Bramble, W. C., H. N. Cope, and H. H. Chisman. 1949. Growth of red pine in plantations. *J. Forest*. **47**, 726–732.

Bramble, W. C., and A. E. Stamers. 1953. Early height growth and survival of trees planted on spoil banks. *Sci. for the Farmer* **1**(1), 15–16.

Brown, J. H. 1962. Success of tree planting on strip-mined areas in West Virginia. *W. Va. Agr. Exp. Sta. Bull*. 473.

Chapman, A. G. 1944. Forest planting on strip-mined coal lands with special reference to Ohio. U. S. Dep. Agr., Forest Serv., Central States Forest Exp. Sta. Tech. Paper 104.

DenUyl, D. 1962. Survival and growth of hardwood plantations on strip-mine spoil banks of Indiana. *J. Forest*. **60**, 603–606.

Ferree, M. J., T. D. Shearer, and E. L. Stone, Jr. 1958. A method of evaluating site quality in young red pine plantations. *J. Forest*. **56**, 328–332.

Finn, R. F. 1958. Ten years of strip-mine forestation research in Ohio. U. S. Dep. Agr., Forest Serv., Central States Forest Exp. Sta. Tech. Paper 153.

Hart, F., and W. R. Byrnes. 1960. Trees for strip-mined lands. U. S. Dep. Agr., Forest Serv., Northeast. Forest Exp. Sta. Paper 136.

Horton, K. W., and W. G. E. Brown. 1960. Ecology of white and red pine in the Great Lakes-St. Lawrence forest region. Can. Dept. North. Affairs and Nat. Resources, Forest. Branch Tech. Note 88.

Li, C. C. 1964. *Introduction to experimental statistics*. McGraw-Hill Book Co., New York.

Limstrom, G. A., and G. H. Deitschman. 1951. Reclaiming Illinois coal lands by forest planting. *Ill. Agr. Exp. Sta. Bull*. 547.

Lundgren, A. L. 1965. Alignment chart for numbers of trees-diameters-basal areas. U. S. Dep. Agr., Forest Serv., Lake States Forest Exp. Sta. RN-LS-67.

Newbould, P. J. 1967. Methods for estimating the primary production of forests. *IBP Handbook* No. 2. Blackwell Sci. Publ., Oxford. 62 p.

Potter, H. S., S. Weitzman, and G. R. Trimble. 1951. Reforestation of strip-mined lands in West Virginia. U. S. Dep. Agr., Forest Serv., Northeast. Forest Exp. Sta. Paper 43.

Rogers, N. F. 1951. Strip-mined lands of the western interior coal province. *Mo. Agr. Exp. Sta. Res. Bull*. No. 475.

Rudolph, P. O. 1957. Silvical characteristics of red pine (*Pinus resinosa*). U. S. Dep. Agr., Forest Serv., Lake States Forest Exp. Sta. Paper 44.

Steill, W. M. 1965. Height sampling in red pine and white spruce plantations. *Forest. Chron.* **41**, 175–181.

Tryon, E. H., and R. Markus. 1953. Development of vegetation on century-old iron ore spoil banks. *W. Va. Agr. Exp. Sta. Bull.* 360.

U. S. Department of Agriculture. 1958. Soil Survey, Clarion County, Pennsylvania. Superintendent of Documents, Washington, D. C.

van Eck, W. A., and E. P. Whiteside. 1963. Site evaluation studies in red pine plantations in Michigan. *Soil Sci. Soc. Am. Proc.* **27**, 709–714.

Wakeley, P. C., and J. Marrero, 1958. Five-year intercept as site index in Southern pine plantations. *J. Forest.* **56**, 332–336.

Whittaker, R. H. 1961. Estimation of net primary production of forest and shrub communities. *Ecology* **43**, 357–377.

Whittaker, R. H. 1966. Forest dimensions and production in the Great Smoky Mountains. *Ecology* **47**, 103–121.

Whittaker, R. H., and G. M. Woodwell. 1969. Dimension and production relations of trees and shrubs in the Brookhaven Forest. *J. Ecol.* **56**, 1–25.

DISCUSSION

DAVIS: I conducted a study of older plantations of several species on spoils similar to your study, and I compared their growth to natural stands reported in the literature. Red pine was the fourth fastest growing species. Japanese larch had the fastest growth over a 25-year period, and it was producing 118 ft^3/yr. Scotch pine was second with 113 ft^3 followed by white pine (77 ft^3) and red pine (67 ft^3). All 11 species measured grew at least 1 ft in height per year, and Scotch pine and Japanese larch grew almost 2 ft.

AHARRAH: I noticed the same thing in some of the other species that we have not had time to measure. We are going to show the same thing, I am sure, with the species that you have mentioned. One of the things that also surprises me is the number of cones that jack pine is producing on some of these. They are just going wild and have reseeded all over the place. The first seeds are being produced on the red pine in the area at the present time, but the red squirrels eat them up as fast as they are produced, so I don't know if or when we will get viable seed or germination. We haven't seen any of it yet.

NEUMANN: The differences between these two sites—could they be because of different soil fauna? Did you investigate anything in this direction, i.e. a difference in the layer of litter?

AHARRAH: I wouldn't say that they couldn't be. I have a feeling that soil fauna may have some effect upon this; however, we do not have the problem of distance for invasion that you had in Germany. In other words, the old fields grow on one side of this tract and trees on the other, we are right in the middle.

NEUMANN: Soil animals invade pine woods more slowly than hardwoods because pine litter is not so readily decomposable. Normally it is eaten only if some litter of herbaceous vegetation or hardwood species is mixed in. Therefore, small distances in pine woods play the same role as large distances in hardwoods in the rate of invasion of soil fauna.

AHARRAH: Then in this case we may not have an invasion because of distance too, since pine forest is some short distance away. It is hardwood that immediately surrounds them.

GOOD: I'm not surprised that your figures are at least as great as Whittaker's from Brookhaven, Long Island. The pitch pine that we saw on the spoils last week were growing much better than they do in Brookhaven or anywhere else on that part of Long Island.

AHARRAH: I have not seen the Brookhaven forest.

CYTOECOLOGICAL INVESTIGATIONS WITH REGARD TO THE MECHANISM OF CHEMICAL RESISTANCE OF PLANTS

Gertraud Repp

University Professor, Plant Physiological Institute,
University of Vienna, Vienna, Austria

Cell-physiological resistance tests of protoplasm may be of considerable value in the revegetation of chemically adverse sites. In addition to the clear relationships of desiccation tolerance and heat tolerance to prevailing climatic conditions, investigations in Vienna have shown similar adaptations to chemical conditions of the sites (e.g. halophytes and heavy-metal plants). This "ecological resistance" of the protoplasm is thus a very important factor in plant growth under adverse conditions.

When such sites are to be revegetated, cell-physiological resistance tests can be used as a rapid method for preliminary selection of suitable plant species. In comparative tests, plasmatic salt-tolerance results agreed well with the results of concurrent field tests. This method has since been used successfully to test the salt tolerance of woody-plant seedlings.

The author has studied the plasmatic resistance of plants in saline soils and in Cu-containing soils. In both cases, "shock resistance" was a decisive factor in the mechanism of plasmatic resistance. Both the difference between internal and external concentrations of the chemical and the rate of permeation are important. Within the genetic limits of a species, plasmatic resistance is variable to some extent, which offers possibilities for "hardening" against damaging site factors.

GENERAL ECOLOGY OF CHEMICALLY ADVERSE SITES

Drastic disturbances of sites can be caused naturally (e.g. by volcanic eruptions, landslides, or floods), or artificially, by man. Where drastic chemical or physical changes are caused by mining or industry, restoration of vegetative cover is a problem of both economic importance and of

445

human ecology. Difficulties in the revegetation of such areas may result from the generally poor soil structure, but the main difficulty is contamination of the soil with toxic substances such as acids or heavy metals (e.g. Cu, Zn, Mn, Cr, or Ni).

Attempts are often made to revegetate such sites with species which grow naturally on undisturbed sites in the same locality. However, from the ecological point of view, one must realize that conditions have often been altered so drastically that they are no longer suited to the original vegetation, but need first to be improved by pioneer plants. On such sites, the use of pioneer plants is of practical importance in two respects: (1) to prevent further soil erosion or water pollution, and (2) to increase the humus content of the soil and, by reducing evaporation from the soil, minimize the accumulation of toxic substances on the surface where they are particularly harmful to seedlings. Once the chemically disturbed soil has been stabilized and improved biologically by resistant pioneer vegetation, it will be easier to establish more useful trees or shrubs.

In the search for such pioneer species, plant introduction is much more promising than breeding; the latter has already been done by nature. In natural habitats with extreme chemical soil conditions—whether ore soils or saline soils—long-term natural selection has resulted in many plants with specific resistance capacities. The plants of such natural sites throughout the world should be studied and compared with native pioneer species on the chemically adverse sites created by man.

The natural flora of the heavy-metal habitats consists almost exclusively of herbs and grasses. Many of them are especially adapted to the site, but there are also some which apparently occur in these habitats only by accident and thus very often show poor vitality. Such accidental plants should not be neglected, however, because they represent a kind of orientating experiment of nature itself.

Most of the true heavy-metal plants are not limited to only one type of metal soil but are reported from rather different metal habitats. Experiments have shown that this is not usually a true combined resistance in the sense that one could transfer mature plants directly, for example, from a Zn soil to a Cu soil. Evidently, it is merely the general adaptive capability of a species to heavy metals which enables it to develop a specific tolerance for the metal which is present.

The search for suitable pioneer plants should be international, and a list of species adapted to heavy-metal soils should be prepared after careful analysis of the natural occurrence of such plants. This list should include herbs and grasses as well as woody plants, and the more primitive

TABLE 1

List of plant species with adaptive capability to heavy metals

Plant species	Site resistance (found growing in soil containing:)
Mosses growing in the Austrian Alps on sulfuric copper ore soils:	
Mielichhofera elongata Hornsch.	Cu (0.43%)[a]
Mielichhofera nitida Hornsch.	Cu (0.01%)[b]
Pohlia sp.	Cu (0.93%)
Nardia scalaris	Cu (0.3%)
Marsupella emarginata	Cu (∼0.01%)
Merceya ligulata	Cu
Grimmia atrata	Cu
Gymnocolea acutiloba[c]	Cu (0.01%)
Cephalociella phyllacantha[c]	Cu
Grasses growing on different mine spoils of North Wales:	
Agrostis tenuis	Zn (4.0%), Pb (3.6%) Cu (2.3%), Ni (1.1%)
A. tenuis × *stolonifera*	Zn, Pb (2.88%)
A. stolonifera	Zn, Cu, Ni, Mg
A. canina	Zn (0.12%)
Festuca rubra	Zn, Pb (8.0%)
F. ovina	Zn, Pb (3.2%), Al, Cu (1.0%)
F. glauca	Zn
Grasses on other heavy-metal sites:	
Poa alpina	Zn, Cu
P. badensis	Zn, Cu
Lolium perenne	Mn, Al, Na
L. multiflorum	Mn, Al
Dactylis glomerata	Mn, Al, Na
Herbs found in various heavy-metal soils in Europe:	
Armeria maritima	Cu (1.0%), Zn, Pb (0.44%), Mg
Thymus Serphyllum	Cu, Zn, Pb, Mg
Silene dioica	Mg, Cu
Minuartia verna subsp. *hercynica*	Cu (0.46%), Zn (5.0%), Pb (0.4%)
Anthoxanthum odoratum	Zn, Pb (4.8%)
Iberis subsp. *cepaefolia*	Zn, Pb
Thlaspi alpestre subsp. *calaminaria*	Zn (5.0%), Pb (0.4%), Mg
Plantago lanceolata	Zn (5.0%), Pb (0.4%)
Viola lutea Hudson	Zn (6.0%)
Vicia calaminaria	Zn
Cardaminopsis Halleri	Zn (6.0%)
Armeria Halleri	Zn
Armeria plantaginea	Zn

TABLE 1 (*cont.*)

Plant species	Site resistance (found growing in soil containing:)
Linum catharticum	Zn (6.0%)
Campanula rotundifolia	Zn (6.0%)
Leontodon autumnalis	Zn
Rumex Acetosa	Mg, Zn, Pb (0.44%), Cu (1.0%)
Trifolium repens	Mn, Al, Na
Medicago sativa	Mn, Al
Gilia capitata	Mg

Herbs found in ore and mine spoils in Katanga (West Africa), U.S.S.R., U.S.A., and United Kingdom:

Acrocephalus robertii	Cu
Becium humblei	Cu
Polycarpa spirostyles	Cu
Astragalus pattersoni	U, Se
A. preussi	U, Se
Crotalaria cobalticola	Co
Silene cobalticola	Co

Herbs in Cu soils in Austria:
Obligate:

Silene vulgaris Moench.	Cu (0.5%), Zn (8.9%)[d]

Accidental:

Rumex Acetosella	Cu (0.5%)[f]
Taraxacum officinale	Cu (0.5%)[e]
Tussilago Farfara	Cu (0.5%)[e]

Trees found growing on serpentine soils in California (Kruckeberg, 1951):

Quercus durata	Mg
Cupressus sargentii	Mg
Ceanothus pepsonii	Mg

[a] In a laboratory experiment, cells still living in 0.1 M $CuSO_4$ after 48 hours (Url, 1956).
[b] Cells still living in 0.05 M $CuSO_4$ after 48 hours (Url, 1956).
[c] Especially on dry sites.
[d] Cells still living in 0.005% $CuSO_4$ and 0.04 M $ZnSO_4$ after 48 hours (Repp, 1963).
[e] Cells still living in 0.0001% $CuSO_4$ after 48 hours (Repp, 1963).
[f] Cells still living in 0.0005% $CuSO_4$ after 48 hours (Repp, 1963).

plants like mosses should not be neglected. Some plant species which have a distinct tendency to develop heavy-metal tolerance are listed in Table 1.

THE ROLE OF "PROTOPLASMIC ECOLOGY" IN RESISTANCE PROBLEMS

Protoplasmic ecology or "cytoecology" is a line of research dealing with the ecophysiology of protoplasm only (Biebl, 1962). Numerous investigations have shown significant relationships between specific physiological qualities of the protoplasm and its adaptation to climatic and edaphic factors. For instance, in higher plants (Höfler, 1942, 1943; Iljin, 1930), algae (Biebl, 1938; Höfler, 1931), and mosses (Höfler, 1950, 1954), the desiccation tolerance of the protoplasm is distinctly related to prevailing moisture conditions of the site. The same is true for resistance to high or low temperatures (Biebl, 1939, 1958, 1964, 1967, 1968; Döring, 1933; Lange, 1957, 1959, 1961).

Similar relationships are found in plants subject to chemical extremes. For instance, the protoplasmic salt-tolerance of marine algae was much higher in those species which are exposed to increasing salt concentrations during ebb tide (Biebl, 1939a, 1958; Höfler, 1931), and the well-known generally high salt tolerance of the halophytes is based mainly on high protoplasmic salt-resistance (Iljin, 1932; Repp, 1939, 1958, 1959). Similarly, specific protoplasmic resistance against heavy-metal cations has been found in mosses (Url, 1956) and in higher plants growing on heavy metal soils (Gries, 1966; Repp, 1963). Thus, the specific resistance of the protoplasm is a very important factor in general tolerance of plant species to adverse site conditions.

Can protoplasmic ecology facilitate, by quick preliminary screening, selection of other plant species for extreme habitats? This has been possible for saline soils. Gradients in protoplasmic salt-tolerance corresponding to the site conditions were found in halophytes and, to a lesser extent, in glycophytes. Once the roles of physiolgic and morphologic adaptations in general salt tolerance of plants have been analyzed, these adaptations could be used as a test in pre-selection of resistant plants for agriculture and forestry. The results of such cell-physiological tests have agreed satisfactorily with concurrent field experiments (Repp, 1958; Monk and Wiebe, 1967).

However, to apply our experience with salt tolerance to the resistance problems arising on the heavy-metal sites, we must first consider some basic differences between them:

1) In saline soils—which are mostly reclaimed for agriculture—the plants introduced are expected to provide a reasonable yield. In heavy-metal soils, any vegetative cover has value, regardless of productivity.

2) Except grasses, all those halophyte species which do not excrete the uptaken salts develop morphological adaptations, such as an increase in succulence combined with cell enlargement. Succulence thus regulates the rise of internal salt concentration (Steiner, 1934; Repp, 1939, 1951, 1958) up to a degree which is genetically fixed (Repp, 1958). Although no such morphological regulation has been found in heavy-metal plants, considerable internal metal storage has been reported (Baumeister, 1967; Ernst, 1966), with maximum storage in the large roots (Ernst, 1966). Recent investigations (Turner, 1969) indicated strongly that the roots may even act to some extent as a kind of "physiological barrier" by storing the metal in a biologically inactive form.

3) If in saline habitats uptake of water is inhibited osmotically, halophytes tend to develop xeromorphic adaptations such as stunted growth. Heavy-metal (Zn and Cu) plants also show a distinct tendency toward small growth. However, unlike the halophytes, this tendency is gentically fixed, since it is retained in normal soil (Schwanitz and Hahn, 1954b).

4) Salinity, provided it is not combined with high alkalinity as in the case of $NaCO_3$ soils, cannot be considered as physiologically toxic. Cations like Mg, K, and sometimes Na are important nutrients. It is merely their excess in the tissues and in the soil, as well as the possible osmotic inhibition of water intake, which matters. Although the heavy metals are also important to plants as bio-catalysts, only traces are found in normal soils; in higher concentrations, they are truly toxic to protoplasm. Therefore the high resistance of heavy-metal plants (Baumeister, 1954, 1967; Gregory and Bradshaw, 1965) is all the more surprising. Both salt tolerance and heavy-metal resistance of the protoplasm are a genetically fixed result of long-term natural selection on such sites.

5) In halophytes, the osmotic pressure of the internally stored salts helps maintain cell turgidity, reducing the amount of photosynthate needed for that purpose. This "saving" of organic material for growth may be the reason that halophytes grow better with moderate quantities of salt (Repp, 1951, 1958). Heavy-metal plants may also grow better if the metal is present in the soil, but this is not an osmotic but a metabolic effect. In Zn-tolerant plants, for example, assimilation is stimulated by Zn, an important bio-catalyst in photosynthesis (Baumeister, 1954). Evidently their higher Zn-resistance permits use of this bio-catalyst in quantities toxic for normal plants.

Most studies of heavy-metal tolerance concern Zn- or Cu-plants, but specific resistance to Pb or Ni (Gregory and Bradshaw, 1965) and to Mn, Cr, and V (Url, 1965) has also been investigated.

Some species show combined resistance to two or more metals. For example, Cu and Cr cause similar cell-physiological reactions (Url, 1956). Such combined resistance has also been found where different metals occur together naturally, e.g. Zn plus Pb or Zn plus Ni (Baumeister, 1967; Bradshaw, 1965; Ernst, 1966). Combined resistance is evidently based on either (1) similar chemical response of the protoplasm, or (2) acquired tolerance by natural exposure of the plant to two or more metals.

In addition to the typical metal species, natural heavy-metal habitats usually contain many species which, though also found in normal habitats, have an inherent adaptability to metal soils. One can therefore assume that there are many more plant species with similar, yet undiscovered, adaptive capability. The suitability of plants for sites contaminated by heavy metals, high acidity, or both is usually determined by growing them on the spot— a procedure which, for woody plants, may take years. Cell-physiological tests should be tried as a means of screening plants for use on such sites. They would not replace field experiments but could certainly simplify them.

CELL-PHYSIOLOGICAL EFFECTS OF ACIDS AND HEAVY METALS

Cell-physiological testing is done by immersing tissue cuttings in graduated aqueous solutions of the contaminating chemical, e.g. NaCl or $CuSO_4$. After a standard period of 48 hours, the survival rate of the cells is tested by plasmolysis in 1.0 M glucose (Repp, McAllister, and Wiebe, 1959) or in tetrazolium (Monk and Wiebe, 1961). Since the chemical acts directly on the protoplasm, there is no delayed action as a result of protective anatomical structures.

Evaluation of the results, however, requires knowledge of the specific response of the protoplasm to acids and to heavy metals.

Acids

In cell-physiological acid-resistance tests (Becker, 1936; Brenner, 1920; Küster, 1929; Schindler, 1938), two toxic effects were found:

(1) Weak acids permeate relatively easily through the protoplasm and rapidly attack its internal and most sensitive portion.

29*

(2) Strong acids first increase the viscosity of the protoplasm, as can be seen from the concave form of the plasmolysis. By solidification of the external surface of the protoplast—which is probably due to coagulation—permeability is temporarily reduced. Afterwards, however, fast permeation takes place, which in cells containing anthocyanin, is visible as a sharp and sudden change in color.

Weak acids, surprisingly, may thus be more harmful than the strong acids, as the following sequence of damage indicates (Schindler, 1938):

Oxalic acid > Acetic acid > Lactic acid > Hydrochloric acid

What is the cell-physiological mechanism involved in this unexpected reaction? Protoplasm has both external and internal membranes, the plasmalemma and the tonoplast. The tonoplast is a barrier to the permeation of substances from the protoplasm into the cell sap; the plasmalemma is a barrier to the entrance of substances into the protoplasm from the external environment. The solidification effect of strong acids evidently strengthens the plasmalemma, delaying entrance of the toxic substance into the protoplasm. Thus, during the standard 48-hour period, strong acids had less acute damaging effect than weak acids.

It is significant that the toxicity of strong acids can be reduced by adding neutral salts (chlorides, sulfates and nitrates of Na, K, Mg and Ca). Brenner (1920) found that protoplasmic resistance to hydrochloric acid increased by 6 times with the addition of $CaCl_2$, 2 times with $Ca(NO_3)_2$, 3.5 times with $MgCl_2$, and 1.5 times with KCl. Such cell-physiological tests on the antagonistic effect of neutral salts can be of practical importance, especially in acid spoils.

Heavy metals

According to cell-physiological experiments with different salts of heavy metals, the sulfate ion is the least damaging anion. The effects of heavy-metal cations can thus be best determined in sulfate solutions.

Aqueous solutions of heavy-metal sulfates cause reactions similar to those of strong acids (Repp, 1963; Schindler, 1943). Plasmolysis is delayed and concave in form, indicating increased viscosity of the protoplasm. With heavy metals however, damage is first seen in the chloroplasts, which become angular. Granulation of the protoplasm follows. The harmful effects of the different heavy metals on the protoplasm are not identical, but depend on their differential capability to coagulate protein. Cell-physiological experiments have confirmed that Cu is more toxic than Zn or Mn (Url, 1956; Repp, 1963).

The increased viscosity and temporary solidification of protoplasm which take place on contact with the heavy metals probably result from coagulation and dehydration of the protoplasm, and form an additional barrier similar to that caused by strong acids. This effect occurs only at higher concentrations, making the course of necrosis in the cell-physiological tests rather irregular (Table 2).

TABLE 2

Vitality tests in aqueous solutions of heavy metal sulfates

Species	Duration of test hrs	Cell damage classification[a] for concentrations of						
		0.0001%	0.001%	0.01%	0.1%	1.0%	3.0%	5.0%
		Vanadium Sulfate (Url, 1956)						
Arthrodemus								
convergens	48	0	2	2	2	0	0	0
Closterium	48	0	2	2	0	0	1	1
		Copper Sulfate (Repp, 1963)						
Aspidium felix-mas	24	1	0	2	2	2		
Tropeaolum majus	24	1	0	2	2	2		
Tropeaolum majus	48	2	1	2	2	2		

[a] 0 = all cells living (except cells on the border of the cuttings).
 1 = about 50% of cells dead.
 2 = all cells dead.

Only at the lowest concentrations, (which can be considered the true resistance limit) is the protoplasm really undamaged. Survival at the higher concentrations (indicated by enclosed values in Table 2) is, however, only temporary. Damage is delayed because of the external "coagulation barrier" formed by the protoplast.

This reaction to strong acids and heavy metals is very common; it was also found with $MnSO_4$ (Biebl and Rossi-Pillhofer, 1954) and with $ZnSO_4$ (Baumeister, 1967). Some authors (Lepeschkin, 1937; Schindler, 1943; Kaho, 1933) considered it to be a "protective layer." Its benefit is questionable, however, since any irreversible obstruction to permeability would also have a retarding effect on normal physiological processes such as transpiration and assimilation. Nevertheless, low concentrations of the metal or acid, because they do not create such a barrier, can sometimes damage plants faster than higher concentrations, even under field conditions.

Cell-physiological experiments (Repp, 1963) have also shown that smaller round cells of the same cutting are more resistant than longer cells. For example, in epidermis cuttings of *Amaranthus* after 24 hours in 0.01% $CuSO_4$, all the short round cells were still living while all the longer cells were dead. The cell-physiological effects of other heavy metals are similar to Cu only less toxic. Therefore, the tendency, in the natural flora of heavy-metal habitats, to develop small cells (Schwanitz and Hahn, 1954) may be of some importance. The smaller and the rounder the cells, the more and better the protoplasmic barriers existing in the body of the plant. Although this tendency to small cells may be related to the aridity of many heavy-metal soils, it may be an adaptation to their chemistry as well.

In general, both cell-physiological reactions and morphological structures of the heavy-metal plants give the impression that they have a rather modest vegetative development in order to ensure regeneration.

SHOCK RESISTANCE AS A FACTOR IN CHEMICAL TOLERANCE

The previously mentioned coagulation layer was found only in species with low basic protoplasmic resistance and never in resistant heavy-metal plants (Repp, 1963; Url, 1956). It evidently forms only when there is a sufficient difference between the specific metal resistance of the protoplasm and strength of solution. Thus this reaction is one typical example of a "difference effect", i.e. it is the result of the intensity of the chemical "shock" to which the protoplasm is exposed.

My investigations have shown that resistance to chemical shock is in general very decisive in determining the total chemical resistance of the protoplasm. In halophyte species without salt excretion, for example, the internal salt concentration of leaves increases steadily with age as salts taken up with the water are left behind by transpiration. Since these salts are dissolved in the cell sap and increase the osmotic pressure of the cells, one can assume that the osmotic value, as measured by "limiting plasmolysis" (i.e. always in the same and comparable state of cell turgidity) also indicates the relative extent of salt storage inside the cells. This was confirmed by cryoscopic analysis of the expressed cell sap (Repp, 1951).

Table 3 shows the effect of 1.0 M NaCl on younger and older leaves of two halophytes, *Salicornia* (an extreme type) and *Plantago* (a moderate type). In both plants, the cells of the older parts lived significantly longer than those of the younger parts. Because they had already become "accustomed" to the salt during a period of slowly increasing salt storage, the difference between the salt concentration inside and that acting from outside the cell was smaller, and thus the "shock" was less intense. Of

TABLE 3

Protoplasmic salt resistance in 1.0 M NaCl (from Repp, 1958)

Plant species and part	Osmotic value by limiting plasmolysis 1.0 M glucose	Cell damage classification[a] for immersion periods of			
		2 hr	19 hr	49 hr	82 hr
Salicornia herbacea					
young parts	1.60	0	0	1	2
old parts	1.95	0	0	0	2
Plantago maritima					
young leaves	0.70	0	2	2	2
old leaves	0.95	0	0	2	2

[a] 0 = all cells living (except cells on the border of the cuttings).
 1 = about 50% of cells dead.
 2 = all cells dead.

TABLE 4

Comparison of osmotic resistance and chemical resistance of the protoplasm (from Repp,1958)

Plant species and part	Osmotic value by limiting plasmolysis 1.0 M glucose	Cell damage classification[a] after immersion in					
		2.0 M glucose for			1.5 M NaCl for		
		10 hr	30 hr	150 hr	10 hr	30 hr	150 hr
		(osmotic resistance)			(chemical resistance)		
Salicornia herbacea							
young parts	1.50	0	0	0	0	1	2
old parts	1.95	0	0	2	0	0	1
Plantago maritima							
young parts	0.85	0	0	0	2	2	2
old parts	1.25	0	1	2	2	2	2

[a] 0 = all cells living (except cells on the border of the cuttings).
 1 = about 50% of cells dead.
 2 = all cells dead.

course, the cells of the older leaves died too, but much later than those of the younger leaves. This indicates that resistance is not only a function of the "physiological shock" for a given concentration but also a function of time, and short-term exposures can be survived easier.

To make sure that the shock phenomenon is a true chemical effect and not due only to the hypertony of the solution used, the effects of the strongly hypertonic solutions 2.0 M glucose and 1.5 M NaCl were compared (Table 4). These concentrations are nearly equal in osmotic effect, but in glucose only water loss and plasmolysis occur, while in NaCl an additional chemical effect takes place. The considerably higher resistance in glucose, in which young cells were still living after 150 hours, proves that it is really the chemical, not the osmotic effect, which injures the protoplasm.

Surprisingly however, in glucose, where salt resistance acquired during life time is unimportant, the older leaves had a lower protoplasmic resistance than the younger parts! The only plausible explanation is that the salt concentrations in the oldest leaves were initially so high that the water loss due to the plasmolysis resulted in internal concentrations which exceeded the threshold values above which damage occurs. Thus, with increasing age, a possible chemical shock upon the protoplasm is more and more "absorbed" by the increasing internal storage of the chemical and the resulting reduction of difference effect, but only until the internal concentration reaches a critical stage. Any additional permeation of the chemical or increase of its internal concentration by water loss (either wilting or plasmolysis) is then fatal for the protoplasm. In old age, the chemical damage is not due to "difference effect" as in the young stage, but to "summation effect" by which the specific tolerable internal concentration of salts or metals is exceeded.

Similar chemical shock phenomena also occur in heavy-metal plants. The shock resistance of Cu plants was 2 to 16 times higher than that of other plant species (Repp, 1963). In the case of Cu—which is very toxic— duration of exposure was, however, particularly important. In cell-physiological experiments with heavy metals, it is advisable to check the cuttings at 2 to 3 intervals before the standard time of 48 hours is reached.

Most heavy-metal plants are also storing types. For instance, Baumeister (1967) found that eight species of the Zn-tolerant plants on Zn soil contained from 686 to 12,000 ppm of Zn compared to 17 to 96 ppm for three plant species on normal soil. Generally, Zn resistance is higher due to "shock reduction" in the older and more Zn-storing parts of Zn plants (Rüthner, 1966; Gries, 1966). In some experiments with Zn plants, the cells of older parts were found to be more resistant, but in other experiments, less resistant (Biebl and Rossi-Pillhofer, 1954). According to Gries (1966), the protoplasmatic Zn-resistance can change; it is low in the young stage, then increases up to ten times, and finally decreases again in the oldest stage. Likewise the Zn resistance of plants from natural Zn habitats is usually higher where the soil Zn content is high. However, some experiments (Rüther, 1966), in which the Zn content of the soil was maintained at various levels, showed lower resistance in soil with more Zn.

For plants with some internal chemical storage, these contradictory relationships can be explained by the following theory, which is illustrated in Fig. 1.

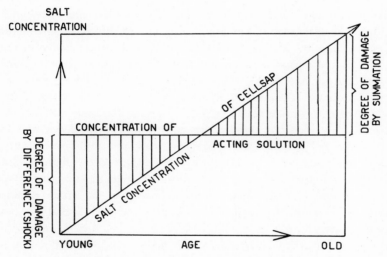

FIGURE 1   A theory of the cell-physiological mechanism of salt resistance.

In soils containing above-normal quantities of water-soluble substances, these substances are taken up and (if not used for growth) gradually accumulate as transpiration takes place. In young tissues, their concentration in the cells is low. Thus in cell-physiological resistance tests, there is a greater difference in concentration of the chemical between the cells and the solution outside. This means a bigger chemical shock and thus greater damage to the protoplasm.

In older tissues, the internal concentration has become higher. For a given concentration of solution, this difference is therefore smaller, and consequently the chemical shock and damage are less intense. However, as more of the internal concentration reaches the critical stage, danger of damage from summation effect increases, be it by any additional uptake or just by water loss!

The same principles apply in the habitat, where chemicals in the soil water act on the roots. In the case of Zn and Cu plants the metal is stored in the roots more than in the leaves, thus reducing the chemical shock.

Time, however, is also a factor, influencing chemical shock in two ways: (1) by sudden contact of the protoplasm with the chemical at a concentration considerably higher than the protoplasm is accustomed to, and (2) by very rapid intake of the damaging agents, even at relatively low concentrations.

An example of the first kind is given by Repp (1958) in an experiment involving two halophytes, *Aster tripoleum* and *Plantago maritima*. One set of cuttings of each species was placed directly into 1.5 M NaCl; the other was placed into 0.2 M NaCl and the concentration gradually increased to 3.5 M over a period of 24 hours. After 21 hours, all cells of cuttings placed directly in the 1.5 M solution were dead, but all were alive in the solution gradually increased to 3.5 M. Similar reactions were found in experiments with Cu plants (Repp, 1963) as mentioned earlier.

An example of the second kind occurs when plants which have a high transpiration rate (and thus fast water passage) grow on a moist soil containing injurious chemicals. For instance, halophytes are often damaged when rainy weather is followed by high evaporation due to sun, strong wind, and heat (Repp, 1958). Such climatic circumstances can likewise become dangerous when water-oriented species grow in soil containing heavy metals or acids.

Although the physiological activity of stored chemicals is still in question, a recent report suggests that heavy metals may be stored to some extent in cell walls in insoluble, and thus physiologically inactive, form (Turner, 1969). This may explain the growth of plants at metal concentrations in the field that are fatal when applied directly to protoplasm in cell-physiological experiments.

ECOLOGICAL HARDENING

As we have seen, the climatic or chemical tolerance of plants is based mainly on the resistance capacities of the protoplasm, the biological adaptability of which is astonishing. We must, however, differentiate between two kinds of resistance (Stocker, 1954):

1) *Genotypical* resistance, the genetically fixed potential resistance of a plant species based on specific chemical or physical qualities of the protoplasm. It involves the general basic level of resistance as well as the additional potential for modification. Genotypical hardening can be attained only by breeding, or selection, or both, similar to the long-term selection of nature itself.

2) The *phenotypical* resistance, which can change but only within the boundaries of the potential resistance. The actual level is not fixed genetically and involves only those adaptations to the environment which can, but need not, occur during the lifetime of the individual plant. In Fig. 1, for instance, the chemical resistance related to "difference effects" and "summation effects" is phenotypic; the basic starting level, however, and the boundaries of the diagram are genotypic. Only within the scope of this phenotypical resistance can short-term "hardening" and "weakening" due to ecological influences occur.

TABLE 5

Phenotypical increase in protoplasmic heavy-metal resistance due to reduction of chemical shock

Species	Heavy-metal content in soil	Resistance limit of protoplasm
	Zn plants (Gries, 1966)	
Silene cucubalus	6000–7000 ppm (Zn)	0.04 M $ZnSO_4$
	1500 ppm (Zn)	0.004 M $ZnSO_4$
	Invaders on Cu soil (Repp, 1963)	
Tussilago Farfara	0.5% (Cu)	0.005% $CuSO_4$
	0.006% (Cu)	0.0001% $CuSO_4$
Taraxacum officinale	0.5% (Cu)	0.0005% $CuSO_4$
	0.006% (Cu)	0.0001% $CuSO_4$

Many examples of hardening against adverse site conditions or temporary stresses are known, but the physiological mechanism involved can not yet be explained. However, Lange (1961) found younger leaves less heat resistant than the older ones, which had been exposed longer to heat, indicating that climatic difference effects may occur. Cytoecological studies of chemical resistance may be the best approach to this problem, since confounding due to morphological adaptations is less likely. Chemical hardening has also been found frequently in heavy-metal habitats (Table 5). Plant individuals grown in either high Zn or high Cu soils showed greater protoplasmic resistance than those of the same species grown under more moderate conditions.

Thus, the physiological mechanism of hardening is mainly based on the avoidance or reduction of the chemical shock to which plants are or could be exposed. This applies to both true "metal plants" and other plants to be introduced into heavy-metal soils. There are, however, some points to consider with respect to such hardening:

1) *Hardening and the time factor* Phenotypical hardening is a dynamic process, occurring slowly with the gradual internal accumulation of the metal. Experiments would be necessary to determine whether this adaptation time could be shortened for non-metal plants.

2) *Hardening to specific metals* Natural hardening to a metal occurs only when it is present in the soil. Metal plants, within the boundary of their general genotypical metal resistance, are able to evolve tolerance to a specific metal in their environment. The physiological effects of Zn and Ni, however, are so closely related that resistance to them is reciprocal.

3) *Hardening and plant species* Plants other than the typical metal plants may also have a large potential for phenotypical hardening, although basically at a lower level. Numerous plant species can probably be induced to tolerate chemically adverse conditions.

Can protoplasmic ecology indicate such possibilities of hardening? Theoretically, chemical shock could be avoided by accelerating the gradual protoplasmic adaptation of the plant. One possibility, applicable to both heavy metals and strong acids, is precultivation of seedlings in a soil with a small content of the chemical in question.

It seems, however, to be more promising to consider, during screening, other adaptations of plants which may act as "shock-absorbers." For vascular plants, these may include:

1) *Physiology* Low transpiration rates avoid too-rapid accumulation of toxic substances and the consequent premature shedding of leaves and loss of assimilating surface. Transpiration rates can be reduced artificially by shelter from wind or sun, but may be increased by irrigation.

2) *Morphology* Small leaves are an advantage, since, if shedding occurs, the loss of assimilation surface is more gradual. On the other hand, a tendency to large vegetative growth and a high water-content: surface-area ratio may also help by extending the capacity for internal chemical storage and thus reduce or delay damage. Schwanitz and Hahn (1954) found, for example, that when cut leaves or cut plants were exposed to Zn solution,

the larger leaves and plants survived longer. Deep rooting is also an advantage (frequently seen in halophytes), allowing the roots to avoid the surface soil horizons where chemical concentrations are usually highest. Also, since the roots seem to act as a kind of barrier by storing the heavy metal, a well-developed root system should prove beneficial.

3) *Anatomy* Small cells would be preferable to large cells in view of the greater number of cell-physiological barriers against the damaging substance.

So far, these considerations are largely theoretical, but they may stimulate further observations which could facilitate the advance screening of plants for revegetation of chemically adverse sites. Just as in resistance problems, nature itself is the great teacher, and by analyzing the excellent examples given by it, man can learn how to improve his own environment.

SUMMARY

From ecological studies of heavy-metal habitats, many resistant plant species are known. When a pioneer species is needed to prevent erosion and to prepare the soil for reforestation, these "heavy-metal" plants should be the first to be tried. It is therefore suggested that an international list of such heavy-metal plants be prepared.

In chemically extreme environments, the resistance capacities and the adaptability of the protoplasm itself are decisive. Studies have shown that plants tolerant to saline or heavy-metal conditions have in common a higher resistance of the protoplasm than normal plants; they also internally store the salt or metal up to a certain limit. While salt tolerance can be augmented to some extent by morphological adaptations, such as an increase in succulence which retards the increase of the internal salt concentration, heavy-metal tolerance is mainly based on the resistance capacities of the protoplasm itself.

Multiple heavy-metal resistance of the protoplasm is possible through either (1) a similar physiological response of the protoplasm to different heavy metals (e.g. Zn and Ni), or (2) protoplasmic adaptation of the plant to metals which are present in the site but only within the range of general heavy metal tolerance of the species.

Possibly, cell-physiological test methods can be used in screening plant species to be introduced on acid or heavy-metal soils as was done in the case of saline soils. However, since both heavy metals and acids are more toxic to the protoplasm than salts, such cell-physiological testing will have to be carried out using finer graduations of concentrations.

The toxicity effect of weak and strong acids is different. Weak acids permeate easily and damage occurs fast, whereas in strong acids damage is temporarily delayed by solidification of the external protoplast (plasmalemma). By addition of water-soluble neutral salts, particularly $CaCl_2$, the damaging effect of acids can be counterbalanced by ion-antagonism.

The cell-physiological effect of heavy metals seems mainly to depend on the capacity of the specific metal to coagulate proteins (sequence e.g. Cu > Zn > Mn). Additional solidification of the external plasmalemma as in strong acids occurs, however, only in case of contact with relatively high metal concentrations; lower concentrations permeate and damage rapidly. This may be of some importance in the habitat, e.g. when the concentration is temporarily lowered by rain. The tests indicated that small, round cells are more resistant than big, long cells.

Chemical resistance must also be considered from the dynamic point of view (difference effect and chemical "shock"). Cells of younger tissues have lower internal content of salts or heavy metals and are less resistant to these substances. On the other hand, in older tissues with the internal concentration already near its threshold value, damage can be caused by additional permeation or water loss (summation effects).

Based on these observations, a theory of the mechanism of chemical resistance was developed taking into account both the static basic level of resistance and the limits of its possible modification.

There are two kinds of protoplasmatic resistance: (1) the genotypical resistance, or potential resistance, which includes the general basic level of resistance and additionally the possible range of its modification (adaptive capability) and (2) the phenotypical resistance, which can develop in the habitat within the boundaries of this adaptive capability during the lifetime of the plant. The stage of resistance which is actually achieved is thus not genetically fixed only but depends also on the ecological conditions. Ecological "hardening" is possible only with this phenotypical resistance. Hardening in this respect is closely connected to shock avoidance and is also time dependent. Plants can be selected with respect to physiological, morphological, and anatomical characteristics which can act as "shock absorbers."

LITERATURE CITED

Abel, W. O. 1956. Die Austrocknungsresistenz der Laubmoose. Sitzgsber. Wien Akad., Math. Natur. Wiss. Kl., Abt. 1. **165**, 619–707.

Alexandrow, W. J., M. J. Ljutowa, and N. L. Feldman. 1959. Jahreszeitliche Änderungen der Resistenz von Pflanzenzellen gegenüber der Wirkung verschiedener Agenzien (in Russian) *Cytologia* (Moskau) **1**, 672–691.

Ashida, J. 1965. Adaptation of fungi to metal toxicants. *Ann. Rev. Phytopathol.* **3**, 153–174.

Baumeister, W. 1954. Über den Einfluß des Zinks bei *Silene inflata* Smith, *Ber. Deut. Botan. Ges.* **67**, 205–213.

Baumeister, W. 1967. Schwermetall-Pflanzengesellschaften und Zinkresistenz einiger Schwermetallpflanzen. *Angew. Botan.* **40**, 185–204.

Becker, Z. 1936. A comparison between the action of carbonic acid and other acids upon the living cells. *Protoplasma* **25**, 161–175.

Biebl, R. 1938. Trockenresistenz und osmotische Empfindlichkeit der Meeresalgen verschieden tiefer Standorte. *Jahrb. Wiss. Botan.* **86**, 350–386.

Biebl, R. 1939. Über Temperaturresistenz von Meeresalgen verschiedener Klimazonen und verschieden tiefer Standorte. *Jahrb. Wiss. Botan.* **88**, 389–420.

Biebl, R. 1958. Temperatur- und osmotische Resistenz von Meeresalgen der bretonischen Küste. *Protoplasma* **50**, 217–242.

Biebl, R. 1962. Protoplasmatische Ökologie der Pflanzen. 1. Wasser und Temperatur. Protoplasmologia XII, Springer Wien. 344 p.

Biebl, R. 1964. Temperaturresistenz tropischer Pflanzen auf Puerto Rico. *Protoplasma* **59**, 133–156.

Biebl, R. 1967. Temperaturresistenz der Urwaldmoose. Flora 157, Abt. B, 25–30.

Biebl, R. 1968. Über Wärmehaushalt und Temperaturresistenz arktischer Pflanzen in West-Grönland. Flora 157, Abt. B, 327–354.

Biebl, R., and W. Rossi-Pillhofer. 1954. Die Änderung der chemischen Resistenz pflanzlicher Plasmen mit dem Entwicklungszustand. *Protoplasma* **44**, 113.

Bradshaw, A. D., T. S. McNeilly, and R. P. Gregory. 1965. Industrialization, evolution and the development of heavy metal tolerance in plants. In: G. T. Goodman, R. W. Edwards, and J. M. Lambert (Ed.). *Ecology and the industrial society.* Blackwell Scientific Publ., Oxford, p. 327–343.

Brenner, W. 1920. Über die Wirkung von Neutralsalzen auf die Säureresistenz, Permeabilität und Lebensdauer der Protoplasten. *Ber. Deut. Botan. Ges.* **38**, 277.

Clark, J. A., and J. Levitt. 1956. The basis of drought resistance in the soybean. *Plant. Physiol. Plantarum* **9**, 598–606.

Döring, H. 1933. Beiträge zur Frage der Hitzeresistenz pflanzlicher Zellen. Planta. **18**, 405–434.

Ernst, W. 1966. Ökologisch-soziologische Untersuchungen an Schwermetall-Pflanzengesellschaften Südfrankreichs und des östlichen Harzvorlandes. Flora 156, Abt. B, 301–318

Gregory, R. P., and A. D. Bradshaw. 1965. Heavy metal tolerance in populations of *Agrostis tenuis* and other grasses. *New Phytol.* **64**, 131–143.

Gams, H. 1966. Erzpflanzen in den Alpen. Jahrb. d. Vereines z. Schutz der Alpenpflanzen, München, 37, IV R, 1–9.

Gries, B. 1966. Zellphysiologische Untersuchungen über die Zinkresistenz bei Galmei-Ökotypen und Normalformen von *Silene cucubalus* Wib. Flora 156, Abt. B, 271–290.

Henckel, P. 1954. Sur la résistance des plantes à la sécheresse et les moyens de la diagnostiquer et de l'augmenter. Soc. Botan. USSR. Acad. Sci. USSR, Moskau, p. 436–453.

Höfler, K. 1931. Hypotonietod und osmotische Resistenz einiger Rotalgen. Österreich. Botan. Zeit. **80**, 51–71.

Höfler, K. 1942. Über die Austrocknungsgrenzen des Protoplasmas. Anz. Akad. Wiss., Wien, Math. Natur. Kl. Jahr 1942 Nr. 12.

Höfler, K. 1943. Über die Austrocknungsfähigkeit des Protoplasmas. *Ber. Deutsch. Botan. Ges.* **60**, 94–106.

Höfler, K. 1950. Über Trockenhärtung des Protoplasmas. *Ber. Deutsch. Botan. Ges.* **63**, 3–10.

Höfler, K. 1951. Zur Kälteresistenz einiger Hochmooralgen. Verhand. Zool. Bot. Ges., Wien **92**, 234–242.

Höfler, K. 1954. La résistance du protoplasme à la sécheresse. VIII. Int. Congr. Botan., Paris, Rapport et Comm., Sect. **11**, 239–241.

Iljin, W. S. 1930. Die Ursache der Resistenz der Pflanzenzellen gegen Austrocknen, *Protoplasma* **10**, 379–414.

Iljin, W. S. 1932. Die Anpassung der Halophyten an konzentrierte Salzlösungen. *Planta* **16**, 352–366.

Kaho, H. 1933. Das Verhalten der Pflanzenzellen gegen Schwermetallsalze. *Planta* **18**, 664–682.

Küster, E. 1929. Die Pathologie der Pflanzenzelle. 1. Pathologie des Protoplasmas. Monographien, 3, Berlin.

Lange, O. 1957. Hitzeresistenz und Blattemperaturen mauretanischer Wüstenpflanzen. Abstract in *Ber. Deutsch. Botan. Ges.* **70**, 31–32.

Lange, O. 1959. Untersuchungen über Wärmehaushalt und Hitzeresistenz mauretanischer Wüsten- und Savannenpflanzen. *Flora* **147**, 595–641.

Lange, O. 1961. Die Hitzeresistenz einheimischer immer- und wintergrüner Pflanzen im Jahresablauf. *Planta* **56**, 666–685.

Lepeschkin, W. W. 1937. Zell-Nekrobiose und Protoplasmatod. Protoplasma-Monograph, 3, Berlin.

Levitt, J. 1958. Frost, drought and heat resistance. Protoplasmologia, Handbuch d. Protoplasmaforschung, 8, 6. part, 87 pp.

Levitt, J., C. Y. Sullivan, and E. Krull. 1960. Some problems in drought resistance. *Bull. Res. Counc. Israel*, Sect. D, Botany, 8 D 173–180.

Kruckeberg, A. 1951. Intraspecific variability in the response of certain native plant species to serpentine soil. *Amer. J. Bot.* **38**, 408–419.

Monk, R. W., and H. Wiebe. 1961. Salt tolerance and protoplasmic salt hardiness of various woody and herbaceous ornamental plants. *Plant Physiol.* **36**, 478–482.

Pribik, E. 1947. Das Resistenzverhalten verschiedener pflanzlicher Plasmen gegenüber einigen Spurenelementen. *Dissertation* Univ. Wien (unpublished).

Repp, G. 1939. Ökologische Untersuchungen im Halophytengebiet am Neusiedlersee *Jahrb. Wiss. Botan.* **88**, 554–632.

Repp, G. 1942. Wasserökologische Untersuchungen an einigen Kulturpflanzen. *Landwirt. Jahrb.* **92**, 155–192.

Repp, G. 1943. Zum Wasserhaushalt der Sojabohne. *Landwirt. Jahrb.* **93**, 732–758.

Repp, G. 1950. Untersuchungen über die Kultivierung von Salzböden, *Die Bodenkultur* **4**, 329–354.

Repp, G. 1951. Kulturpflanzen in der Salzsteppe. Experimentell-ökologische Untersuchungen zur Salzresistenz verschiedener Nutzpflanzen. *Die Bodenkultur* **5**, 249–294.

Repp, G. 1958. Die Salztoleranz der Pflanzen, 1. Salzhaushalt und Salzresistenz von Marschpflanzen an der N-Seeküste Dänemarks in Beziehung zum Standort. *Österreich. Botan. Zeit.* **104**, 454–490.

Repp, G. 1959. The salt tolerance of plants. Basic research and tests. Publ. *UNESCO Salinity Symp.*, Teheran, 1958, 153–161.

Repp, G. 1963. Die Kupferresistenz des Protoplasmas höherer Pflanzen auf Kupfererzböden. *Protoplasma* **57**, 643–659.

Repp, G. 1964. L'Ecophysiologie des Halophytes au niveau cellulaire. *Bull. Société Francaise Physiol. Végétale* **10/4**, 209–228.

Repp, G. 1967. Ecological investigations on some forest trees in W-Pakistan. Report No. 2, UNDP-FAO Research and Training Project, Peshawar, Pakistan.

Repp, G., and Ch. Killian. 1956. Recherches écologiques sur les rélations entre le climat, les sols et les plantes irriguéés des Oasis Sahariennes. *J. d'Agr. Trop. et Botan. Appl.* **3**, 109–319.

Repp, G., D. R. McAllister, and H. Wiebe. 1959. Salt resistance of protoplasm as a test for the salt tolerance of agricultural plants. *Agron. J.* **51**, 311–314.

Repp, G., and A. H. Khan. 1961. Some ecological observations in irrigated plantations and riverian forests of Pakistan. *Pakistan J. Forest.* p. 1–13.

Rüther, F. 1966. Vergleichende physiologische Untersuchungen über die Zinkresistenz von Schwermetallpflanzen. Dissertation Münster, (ref. in Baumeister 1967).

Schindler, H. 1938. Der Säuretod der Pflanzenzellen. *Protoplasma* **30**, 547–569.

Schindler, H. 1943a. Protoplasmatod durch Schwermetallsalze. I. Cu-Salze. *Protoplasma* **38**, 225–244.

Schindler, H. 1943b. Protoplasmatod durch Schwermetallsalze. II. Co und Ni–Salze. Ebenda, 245–273.

Schwanitz, F., and H. Hahn. 1954. Genetisch-entwicklungsphysiologische Untersuchungen an Galmeipflanzen. *Zeit. für Botan.* **42**, 179–190.

Schwenker, H. 1959. Das Resistenzverhalten von Tiefen-Rotalgen bei ökologischen und nicht-ökologischen Temperaturen. *Kieler Meeresforschg.* **15**, 34–50.

Steiner, M. 1934. Zur Ökologie der Salzmarschen im NO der USA. *Jahr. wiss. Botan.* **81**, 94–202

Stocker, O. 1954. Die Trockenresistenz der Pflanzen. VIII. *Int. Cong. Botan.*, Paris, Rapport et Comm. Sect. **11** et **12**, 223–232.

Stocker, O. 1956. Die Dürreresistenz. In: Ruhland, *Handbuch der Pflanzenphysiologie*, Bd. **3**, 696–741.

Turner, R. G. 1969. Heavy metal tolerance in plants. *Brit. Ecol. Soc., Symp.* No. 9. Blackwell Scientific Publ. Oxford and Edinburgh.

Url, W. 1955. Resistenz von Desmidiaceen gegen Schwermetallsalze. Sitzgsber. Wiener Akad. Wiss. Math. Natur. Kl., Abt. 1, Bd. **4**, 207–230.

Url, W. 1956. Über Schwermetallresistenz, zumal Cu-Resistenz einiger Moose. *Protoplasma* **46**, 768–793.

DISCUSSION

BENGTSON: Dr. Repp, do you know of any examples where seedlings grown under extremely acid conditions in the nursery have shown unusual resistance to extreme acidity in outplanting situations?

REPP: The seed tissue may be accustomed to the site where it was produced and thus be less subject to shock in the first stage of the plant. I have not made such experiments, but I have been told that seeds from plants on saline soil grow better in saline conditions than seeds from a non-saline soil.

GOODMAN: Cultivated clones grown in boxes seem to become box-bound and lose tolerance, but we have never been able to induce tolerance in apparently non-tolerant clones. Every bit of tolerance that we have picked up has always been genetic based.

REPP: Yes, but you should not exclude the possibility of acquired tolerance because it has been shown in cytoecological investigations.

GOODMAN: In working with Al toxicity, we often found that plants were tolerant to Al because it never penetrated into the cells. In this case tolerance to Al would result from the plant's ability to keep Al out of the cell. It may have been a mechanical or physiological process.

REPP: Aluminum is a special case because it induces sudden increase in viscosity. It does, however, go through the cell wall, but solidifies the protoplasm on contact. This same effect happens with other heavy metals but only at high concentrations. It may also be possible at low concentration if, by high transpiration, the plant takes up too much metal per unit of time.

GOODMAN: We have always found that recovery from plasmolysis is a better indicator than plasmolysis itself.

REPP: This depends on the substance.

CHADWICK: When you make the ecocytological tests, how do you partition between the effect of the cell wall and the effect of the protoplasm as far as tolerance is concerned? Turner, when he looked at this, concluded that much of the mechanism of heavy metal tolerance could be attributed to cell wall constituents.

REPP: I didn't consider the cell wall conditions, but it would be well to do so.

TRANSPIRATION OF NATIVE AND INTRODUCED GRASSES ON A HIGH-ELEVATION HARSH SITE

Ray W. Brown

Plant Physiologist, USDA Forest Service,
Forestry Sciences Laboratory, Logan, Utah

Transpiration rates of Kings fescue (*Hesperochloa kingii* [S. Wats.] Rydb.), smooth brome (*Bromus inermis* Leyss.), and intermediate wheatgrass (*Agropyron intermedium* [Host] Beauv.) were measured gravimetrically under natural harsh-site conditions at an elevation of 2,896 m in the Wasatch Mountains of northern Utah. The highest transpiration rates were attained by the two introduced species, smooth brome and intermediate wheatgrass, for the two different periods studied during the growing season. Maximum transpiration rates ranged from 9.8 to 7.3 g dm^{-2} hr^{-1} for smooth brome and intermediate wheatgrass respectively, to 6.8 g dm^{-2} hr^{-1} for Kings fescue, the native species. Midafternoon reductions in transpiration were evident for most species at both periods during the growing season. Smooth brome had the highest diurnal transpiration rates, and Kings fescue had the lowest. The transpiration response of Kings fescue closely followed the solar radiation flux in the afternoon, whereas the two introduced species maintained much higher transpiration rates even after the incident solar radiation had decreased to zero. Transpiration of the two introduced species increased rapidly with solar radiation in the morning, but the transpiration of Kings fescue increased much more slowly.

Diurnal changes in leaf temperature for the three species corresponded to their transpiration rates. Kings fescue maintained the highest leaf temperatures during the day, whereas smooth brome maintained cooler temperatures closer to air temperature. Leaf temperatures at night for all species closely approximated air temperature. Transpiration responses of plants to microenvironmental fluxes appear to be of importance in determining the adaptability of species to harsh-site conditions.

INTRODUCTION

One of the most important and complex environmental factors limiting plant growth and survival on harsh sites is the relationship of both soil-water availability and atmospheric-evaporative demand to the internal

30*

water status of the plant. The transfer of water, hence energy, through
the soil-plant-atmosphere continuum is not only subject to physical forces
of the environment, but is also influenced to a certain degree by physiological control. As such, transpiration is an important physiological
mechanism intimately linking the plant to the physical environment. Of
the three processes by which plants exchange energy with the environment,
namely radiation, convection, and latent heat transfer, the latter in the
form of transpiration represents the one mechanism over which the plant
can exert some degree of control. The primary significance of the environment to an organism is the dynamic exchange of energy between the organism
and its immediate environment. In terms of the most important limiting
factors therefore, the range of physiological adaptability of a plant can be
defined as the degree of efficiency with which the plant is capable of maintaining a balance between the sources and sinks of energy around it.

The assertion that certain physiological characteristics of plants have
some survival or adaptive value is justified when reference is made to
plants native to alpine and other severe or harsh environments (Bliss, 1962;
Ellison, 1949 and 1954; Mooney and Billings, 1961; Tranquillini, 1964).
Plants native to harsh environments normally show a very intimate relationship with microenvironmental fluxes; these plants are capable of closely
regulating their transpiration rates, particularly during periods of stress.
A comparison of the transpiration responses of introduced species with
native species under harsh environmental conditions should provide a
quantitative measure of relative adaptability of the introduced species.
The native plant would serve as a frame of reference against which quantitative evaluations could be made in terms of the physiological response and
environmental conditions being studied. The ability of the plant to exert
some degree of control over transpiration in close response to demands of
the physical environment would be a definite advantage on sites where
available soil water is limited.

The importance of transpiration regulation as a survival mechanism has
been thoroughly investigated (Idso and Baker, 1967; Gates, 1968; Tranquillini, 1964). However, detailed transpiration studies to determine the
relative efficiency of plants in regulating the rate of water loss under natural
conditions are scarce. Midafternoon reductions in transpirations rates
during periods of high evaporation demand have been reported for plants
from moist sites in alpine environments (Mooney, Billings and Hillier,
1965; Tranquillini, 1964). Plants growing on dry sites normally have much
lower transpiration rates than species on wet sites, and have single-peaked
diurnal transpiration curves. Mooney et al. (1965) and Bliss (1960) found

that transpiration rates of alpine species are particularly responsive to temperature, solar radiation, and vapor pressure deficit (VPD). Midday transpiration reductions for moist-site species occur when the environmental factors of temperature, solar radiation, and VPD are at the afternoon maximum (Mooney et al., 1965). Conversely, the transpiration rates of dry-site species increase concomitantly with temperature, radiation, and VPD, but do not show rate reductions during stress periods. Bliss (1960) found that diurnal water loss is directly related to windspeeds below 6 mph, and inversely related to windspeeds above 6 to 8 mph. Mooney et al. (1965) concluded that inherent differences in transpiration of different species are involved in determining the local distribution patterns and lower elevational limits of the alpine plants studied.

The major objective of the present study was to determine the magnitudes and daily pattern of transpiration for native and introduced species under natural harsh-site conditions. Measurements were also made of leaf temperatures to determine the effectiveness of transpiration as a leaf cooling mechanism under natural conditions. Finally, the transpiration responses of the introduced species were evaluated in terms of those of the native plant so that a quantitative comparison of relative adaptability could be made. Adaptability in this case would be in terms of the degree of physiological control over transpiration. Also, the influences of various microenvironmental factors on transpiration rates were investigated.

METHODS

Transpiration rates of three species of grass were measured under natural harsh-site conditions in the Wasatch Mountains of northern Utah. The three species selected for study were: Kings fescue (*Hesperochloa kingii* [S. Wats.] Rydb.), the dominant native plant on the study site; and smooth brome (*Bromus inermis* Leyss.) and intermediate wheatgrass (*Agropyron intermedium* [Host] Beazv.), both introduced from Europe and now widely used for revegetating rangelands in the West. The specific study area is located on a severely overgrazed exposed ridgetop at an elevation of 2896 m (9500 ft), on a SW slope just south of Logan Peak (41°43' N, 111°43' W). Ellison (1949) indicated that these exposed harsh ridgetops in the Wasatch Mountains represent very severe environments and that accelerated erosion from them is difficult to prevent. This study area is representative of the high elevation headwaters of many local watersheds above densely populated areas along the west face of the Wasatch mountain range.

Young plants of the three species were transplanted into plastic containers of 1-liter capacity and allowed to establish themselves for a period of about a month. Natural silt loam soil from the study area was used, and the plants were regularly supplied with a complete nutrient solution. The day prior to making transpiration measurements, all of the containers were brought to field capacity and sealed to prevent evaporation. Four replications of each species were used at each of two different times during the growing season (July 17–18 and August 7–8, 1968).

The plastic containers with the plants (phytometers) were placed in slightly larger plastic pots that were buried in the soil to their upper rim. This protected the phytometers and roots from direct solar radiation, whereas exposure of the leaves and stems of the plants was permitted. All transpiration measurements were made by the gravimetric method. The phytometers were weighed on a direct reading balance to ± 0.1 g every 2 hr during the day, and every 3 or 4 hr throughout the night. Transpiration was measured over a 24-hr period from noon of one day until noon of the next day for each of the two periods (July 17–18 and August 7–8) during the growing season. Total leaf surface area (cm^2, both surfaces) was determined by harvesting all the leaves of each plant and planimetering their outline. The total area of the upper and lower surfaces is reported in this study because the stomates occur on both surfaces in about equal densities.

During the study a number of microenvironmental factors were measured within the canopy of the experimental plants. Air temperature and relative humidity were continuously recorded with a calibrated hygrothermograph and the incident solar radiation flux was recorded with a pyrheliograph. Windspeed at plant height was measured with a hot-wire anemometer. Soil surface and leaf temperatures were measured with an infrared radiometer at hour and half-hour intervals respectively, during the day, and every 3 or 4 hr at night.

RESULTS AND DISCUSSION

Transpiration responses

The diurnal course of transpiration for the three species is illustrated in Figs. 1 and 2 for the July and August study periods respectively. Transpiration rates are expressed in grams per square decimeter per hour (g dm^{-2} hr^{-1}) and represent hourly averages ending at the time shown. The magnitude of solar radiation (cal cm^{-2} min^{-1}) for both study periods is also illustrated in Figs. 1 and 2, on a separate scale, to show the relationship between transpiration and radiation. The diurnal variations in vapor pressure deficit (VPD, mm Hg) and windspeed (mph) are illustrated in Figs. 3 and 4 respectively, for both study periods.

The two introduced species, smooth brome and intermediate wheatgrass, attained higher transpiration rates during both study periods than did the native species (Figs. 1 and 2). Maximum transpiration rates of smooth brome for both July and August were 9.8 and 7.7 g dm^{-2} hr^{-1} respectively;

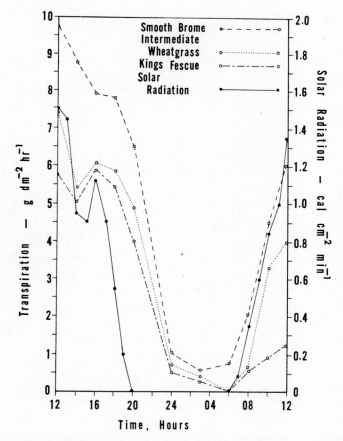

FIGURE 1 Transpiration of Kings fescue, intermediate wheatgrass, and smooth brome, and the diurnal variation of solar radiation during the July 17–18, 1968 study period.

for intermediate wheatgrass the maximum rates were 7.4 and 7.0 g dm^{-2} hr^{-1} respectively. Kings fescue, the native species, maintained the lowest transpiration rates; maximums were 5.9 and 6.8 g dm^{-2} hr^{-1} for July and August respectively. Smooth brome maintained the highest transpiration rates throughout the afternoon and following morning for both study periods, and Kings fescue almost always maintained the lowest rates.

During the July 17–18 study period, the relative day and night transpiration rates of the three species were similar, but during August, slight changes in the relationship occurred. Smooth brome had a slightly lower transpiration rate than the other two species at 2400 hours, but maintained

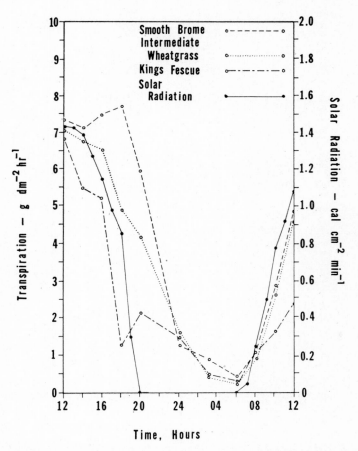

FIGURE 2 Transpiration of Kings fescue, intermediate wheatgrass, and smooth brome, and the diurnal variation of solar radiation during the August 7–8, 1968 study period.

a higher rate at all other times. Kings fescue had a higher transpiration rate than intermediate wheatgrass during the early morning hours of the August study period. However, after 0800 hours Kings fescue maintained a much lower rate than either of the two introduced species.

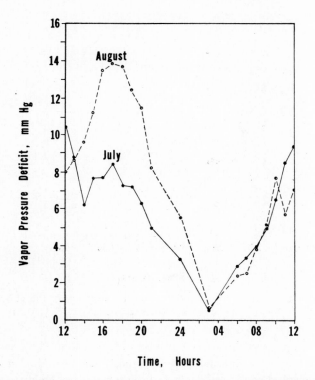

FIGURE 3   The diurnal variation of vapor pressure deficit (VPD) during the July and August study periods.

Midafternoon reductions in transpiration of Kings fescue occurred during both July and August. However, midafternoon reductions for intermediate wheatgrass occurred only in July, and for smooth brome only in August. Midafternoon reductions in transpiration were particularly evident for Kings fescue and intermediate wheatgrass in July in response to solar radiation flux (Fig. 1). An intermittent cloud cover between 1300 and 1500 hours caused a reduction in solar radiation from 1.45 to 0.90 cal cm^{-2} min^{-1}. During the same time period VPD decreased very rapidly (Fig. 3), and windspeed increased (Fig. 4). After 1500 hours the transpiration rates of

Kings fescue and intermediate wheatgrass increased in direct relationship
with an increase in solar radiation and VPD. Smooth brome, however,
had only a slight reduction in the rate of decreasing transpiration, with an
evident lag in response to radiation and VPD.

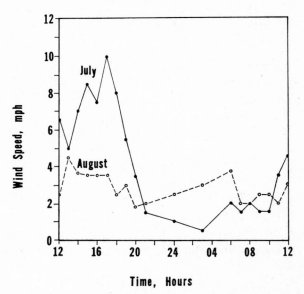

FIGURE 4   The diurnal variation of windspeed during the July and
August study periods.

In the August 7–8 period, midafternoon transpiration reductions occurred
for Kings fescue and smooth brome. The sky was clear during this study
period, and solar radiation decreased uniformly in the afternoon until
sunset. Transpiration of Kings fescue decreased rapidly between 1600 and
1800 hours, then increased until 2000 hours. Smooth brome showed a
decrease in transpiration at 1400 hours, then increased to its afternoon
maximum at 1800 hours, followed by a rapid decrease. During the afternoon, VPD increased rapidly to a maximum of 13.8 mm Hg at 1700 hours.
The transpiration rates of Kings fescue and intermdiate wheatgrass rapidly
decreased during the same time period, however.

A very striking relationship was found between the rapid increase in
incident solar radiation and the morning rise in transpiration (Figs. 1
and 2). In both study periods (July 17–18 and August 7–8), the morning
transpiration rates of smooth brome and intermediate wheatgrass increased
rapidly with increasing solar radiation, whereas Kings fescue increased at

a much slower rate. During both of these study periods, the transpiration rates of the three species at noon of the second day did not reach the maximum rates attained at noon of the preceding day. This appears to be a response to decreased soil water potential on the second day. All the phytometers were brought to field capacity before each study period, but as transpiration proceeded during the afternoon the soil water potential decreased. A comparison was made of the total water lost per unit area of leaf surface for the three species during the afternoon of both study periods. In July, Kings fescue lost 63 and 88% as much water as smooth brome and intermediate wheatgrass respectively, whereas in August the respective figures were 60 and 72%. It appears that smooth brome and intermediate wheatgrass, by virtue of their higher transpiration rates, reduced the soil water potential more than did Kings fescue. However, the transpiration response of Kings fescue in the morning indicates that the native species is more efficient in regulating transpiration under conditions of soil-water stress than are the two introduced species.

Some general observations concerning comparisons of transpiration rates of the three species can be made. It is instructive to note that the transpiration rate of smooth brome at 1800 hours for the July 17–18 and August 7–8 study periods was higher than the afternoon maximum of either of the other two species. In July, the smooth brome rate at 2000 hours was still higher than the diurnal maximum rate of Kings fescue, even though solar radiation had fallen to zero. An analysis of variance was made to test for the significance of difference between transpiration rates of the three species for both study periods. The times of the day for which the differences in transpiration rate between species were significant at the 0.05 level were:

July: 1200, 1400, 2000, 0800, 1200
August: 1600, 1800, 2000

Differences were not significant during other times of the day because of large within-species variation among the replicates.

Leaf temperature responses

The diurnal variation of leaf temperatures for the three species, together with air temperature and soil surface temperature for the July 17–18 and August 7–8 study periods, are shown in Figs. 5 and 6 respectively. Leaf temperatures of the three species tended to reflect their transpiration rates, and generally followed the course of air temperature and solar radiation. Leaf temperatures were usually higher than air temperatures during the day, but tended to remain rather close to air temperatures at night. During July and August, Kings fescue had the highest leaf temperatures during the day, reflecting its lower transpiration rate. Smooth brome, however, had the lowest leaf temperatures which followed air temperatures rather closely.

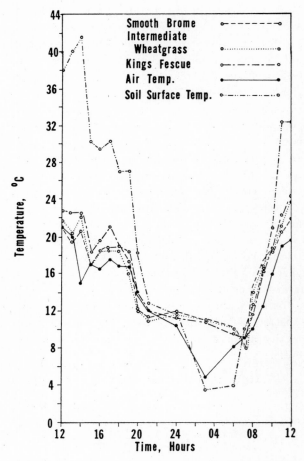

FIGURE 5 Leaf temperatures of Kings fescue, intermediate wheatgrass, and smooth brome, and the diurnal variation of air temperature and soil surface temperature during the July study period.

In July, fluxes in afternoon leaf temperature and air temperature reflected the intermittent cloud cover and consequent decrease in solar radiation. There was also a slight decrease in soil surface temperature and a rapid decrease in VPD (Fig. 3) during the afternoon in response to the reduced solar radiation. Air temperatures and soil surface temperatures decreased rather rapidly during the early morning of July 18, but leaf temperatures maintained a more moderate rate of decline and remained warmer than air temperature. The influence of rapidly increasing solar radiation on leaf temperature, air temperature, and soil surface temperature following sunrise is apparent in both Figs. 5 and 6.

A uniform decrease in afternoon temperatures occurred during the August 7–8 study period (Fig. 6), apparently in response to the rather uniform decrease in solar radiation. An interesting observation is the sharp

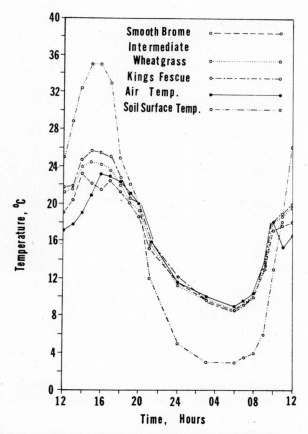

FIGURE 6   Leaf temperatures of Kings fescue, intermediate wheatgrass, and smooth brome, and the diurnal variation of air temperature and soil surface temperature during the August study period.

decrease in smooth brome leaf temperatures between 1400 and 1600 hours. This is a clear reflection of the rapid increase in smooth brome transpiration in response to increasing VPD during the same period on the afternoon of August 7. Following sunset and through the early morning hours, leaf temperatures followed air temperature rather closely. The extremely wide fluctuations in soil surface temperatures are illustrated in Figs. 5 and 6.

In the July 17–18 study period, following a decrease in solar radiation in the afternoon, windspeed increased and leaf temperatures decreased. However, at night windspeed was relatively constant (Fig. 4) and averaged about 1 mph. This reduction in convective cooling may explain why leaf temperatures during the night and early morning of July 18 were higher than air temperature. Windspeeds during the August study period, however, were not as variable as during July, ranging from 1.8 to 4.5 mph.

CONCLUSIONS

A direct relationship exists between both solar radiation and VPD and the transpiration rates of Kings fescue and intermediate wheatgrass. However, it appears that solar radiation is the most important environmental factor affecting transpiration of these species, at least when soil water potential is high. Raschke (1960) explained that under natural conditions it is not surprising that transpiration follows the diurnal march of radiation during the day. He cites evidence that 90% of the variation in transpiration is attributable to radiation, probably resulting from stomatal reactions and the necessity for energy budgeting. During the August 7–8 study period, transpiration rates of Kings fescue and intermediate wheatgrass decreased during the afternoon with decreasing solar radiation, even though VPD was increasing rapidly. Smooth brome, however, showed an increase in transpiration rate with increasing VPD, and transpiration began to decrease only when solar radiation fell to zero. This indicates that smooth brome is not as physiologically capable of restricting transpiration in response to VPD increases as are Kings fescue and intermediate wheatgrass. The transpiration data for smooth brome indicate that, under high elevation harsh-site conditions, this species is an absolute slave to momentary fluctuations in the physical environment.

Kings fescue shows a greater ability to restrict transpiration in response to decreasing soil water potential than do intermediate wheatgrass and smooth brome. The transpiration rates of the two introduced species increased rapidly in the morning in reponse to increasing solar radiation and VPD. However, transpiration of Kings fescue increased more slowly and by noon was only one-half or less the transpiration rates of the two introduced species. Even though the transpiration response of intermediate wheatgrass to radiation and VPD is similar to that of Kings fescue, its response to soil water availability is more similar to that of smooth brome.

On the basis of the data presented, it appears that Kings fescue is physiologically adapted to exert a greater degree of control over transpiration in response to environmental fluxes than the two introduced species. Intermediate wheatgrass is better adapted to this harsh site environment, in terms of its ability to regulate transpiration rate, than is smooth brome.

As a final note, Raschke (1960) felt that in environments where temperatures are below optimum, a gain in heat, reflected as higher leaf temperatures, may be beneficial for plant growth. Leaf temperatures will increase if the plant receives more heat than is dissipated by the various heat transfer mechanisms. If the plant is physiologically capable of efficiently restricting its transpiration response to physical environmental demands, this would reduce the cooling effect of transpiration and result in higher leaf temperatures. This same effect would be enhanced if leaf surface characteristics resulted in a low heat-transfer coefficient. The transpiration and leaf temperature data for Kings fescue suggest that this species is physiologically adapted to restrict transpiration through stomatal control, thus contributing to relatively high leaf temperatures. Also the irregular and ridged leaf surfaces of Kings fescue suggest that its heat-transfer coefficient would be lower than the relatively smooth leaves of the two introduced species. Certainly, the natural environment to which Kings fescue is adapted is characterized by low air temperatures with high solar radiation loads during the growing season. However, before a complete quantitative explanation of harsh-site adaptability can be made, more detailed studies will be required under both natural and controlled conditions.

LITERATURE CITED

Bliss, L. C. 1960. Transpiration rates of arctic and alpine shrubs. *Ecology* **41**, 386–389.

Bliss, L. C. 1962. Adaptations of arctic and alpine plants to environmental conditions. *Arctic* **15**, 117–147.

Ellison, Lincoln. 1949. Establishment of vegetation in depleted subalpine range as influenced by microenvironment. *Ecol. Monogr.* **19**, 95–121.

Ellison, Lincoln. 1954. Subalpine vegetation of the Wasatch Plateau, Utah. *Ecol. Monogr.* **24**, 89–184.

Gates, David M. 1968. Transpiration and leaf temperature. *Annu. Rev. Plant Physiol.* **19**, 211–238.

Idso, S. B., and D. G. Baker. 1967. Relative importance of reradiation, convection, and transpiration in heat transfer from plants. *Plant Physiol.* **42**, 631–640.

Mooney, H. A., and W. D. Billings. 1961. Comparative physiological ecology of arctic and alpine populations of *Oxyria digyna. Ecol. Monogr.* **31**, 1–29.

Mooney, H. A., W. D. Billings, and R. D. Hillier. 1965. Transpiration rates of alpine plants in the Sierra Nevada of California. *Amer. Midland Nat.* **74**, 374–386.

Raschke, K. 1960. Heat transfer between the plant and the environment. *Annu. Rev. Plant Physiol.* **11**, 111–126.

Tranquillini, W. 1964. The physiology of plants at high altitudes. *Annu. Rev. Plant Physiol.* **15**, 345–362.

DISCUSSION

KNABE: I would like to ask two questions. (1) Did you investigate whether there are any relationships between the organic-matter production and the higher transpiration of the introduced grasses? Did they produce more organic matter than the Kings fescue? (2) Did you start your experiments always from full field capacity, or did you make investigations with lower quantities of water in the soil? Did you find any decrease in transpiration after the soil had become drier?

BROWN: In answer to the first part of your question regarding organic-matter production, no specific measurements were made of this parameter. However, casual observations showed that the introduced species, particularly smooth brome, produced a greater quantity of leaf material than Kings fescue. The average leaf surface area of smooth brome was approximately 1200 to 1500 cm², whereas for Kings fescue, the native, it was 800 to 900 cm². These were all first-year plants just prior to setting flower primordia, and under natural harsh site conditions, I would have to say that smooth brome would be more likely to produce a greater abundance of organic material. With respect to the second part of your question, transpiration rates were investigated only under field-capacity conditions. However, transpiration studies are being continued in the laboratory, but are not reported in this paper. These studies are concerned with transpiration and other heat-transfer characteristics of these three species. Smooth brome is affected more severely by decreasing soil water potential than the native species. The native species is apparently able to prolong the point at which physiological wilting occurs. On the other hand, the introduced species wilts at relatively higher soil water potentials, and transpiration drops nearly to zero.

SCHMEHL: Where did you measure soil temperatures with the infrared thermometer?

BROWN: I measured the soil-surface temperatures next to the pot. There was one large plastic container buried in the soil inside of which was placed the other, smaller container. The measurements were made adjacent to the larger plastic container.

SCHMEHL: Would it be under leaf cover?

BROWN: Yes, in some cases. It depends on what time of the day it was, but I was only interested at this particular time in the soil-surface temperature of areas adjacent to the plant and not that under shade.

SCHMEHL: You would not then try to relate these soil temperatures to any kind of growth or transpiration?

BROWN: No. The only way to handle this would be to also measure net radiation. I didn't have the facilities to do this at that time. Consequently these data were not evaluated for heat-transfer characteristics.

GROWTH AND DEVELOPMENT
OF ALDER PLANTINGS ON
OHIO STRIP-MINE BANKS*

David T. Funk

Principal Geneticist, Forestry Sciences Laboratory,
North Central Forest Experiment Station, Forest Service,
U.S. Department of Agriculture, Carbondale, Ill.

Alnus glutinosa plantations containing several European seed sources have survived and grown well on strip-mined areas in southeastern Ohio with pH ranging from 4 to 5. After 7 years, trees from southern Germany were generally larger than those from northern Germany, Belgium, Denmark, or Sweden; the tallest 20% of the trees in the best seed source averaged 20.4 ft in height, and 2.7 in. in diameter at breast height (d.b.h.). Multiple stems were more common in trees from provenances showing slow height growth. Trees from all seed sources in the trial grew much better on lower slopes with adequate soil moisture than on well-drained upper slopes.

Other alder species and hybrids, such as *A. incana*, *A. inokumae*, and *A.* × *spuria* may also be useful for pulpwood production, and *A. cordata* and northern sources of *A. glutinosa* should be well suited for use as nitrogen-fixing nurse trees in situations where strong competition is undesirable.

INTRODUCTION

For many years alders have been used for afforestation of disturbed areas throughout much of the temperate world (Knabe, 1965; Kohnke, 1941; Wood and Thirgood, 1956). In the past dozen years, planting of European alder, *Alnus glutinosa* (L.) Gaertn., and a few other *Alnus* species has increased in the United States, especially on areas previously strip-mined for coal (Lowry, et al. 1962). State nurseries in five northeastern coal-

---

* The nursery stock was grown by the Ohio Division of Forestry; and the Ohio Power Company and the Wayne National Forest assisted in establishing the study plantations.

mining states produced 3.7 million European alder seedlings in 1968 (Sidney H. Hanks, personal communication), almost double the 1.8 million seedlings grown in 1964 (Abbott and Eliason, 1968). Alders are preferred for strip-mine reclamation because of their ready establishment, rapid growth, abundant leaf-litter production, and ability to fix atmospheric N and make it available to associated trees (Virtanen, 1957). The latter characteristic is especially important when choosing species for planting on spoil banks, which usually contain little available N (Limstrom. 1960).

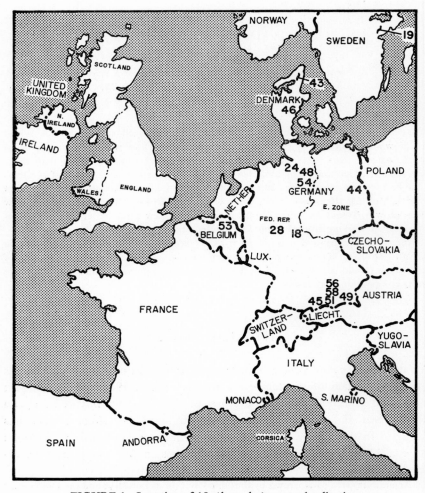

FIGURE 1   Location of 15 *Alnus glutinosa* seed collections.

In 1958, the Central States Forest Experiment Station (now North Central) began research on the performance of alder planted on strip-mined land. Early results were reported by Dale (1963) and Funk and Dale (1961). This paper describes growth and development of 6-year-old plantations containing trees from 15 *Alnus glutinosa* (Fig. 1) seed sources as well as a few other *Alnus* species.

The study plantations are located in southeastern Ohio on graded spoil derived from mining either Middle Kittanning or Lower and Middle Kittanning coal together. Surface pH throughout the plots was generally between 4 and 5 at the time of planting. One-year-old seedlings were bar-planted in April 1963. Average root-collar diameter of the *A. glutinosa* collections ranged from 0.18 to 0.24 in. The seedlings used in the *A. glutinosa* provenance trials were planted in three 25-tree replications, and those used in the alder species comparison trials were planted as 10-tree row plots. Additional replications of both studies were established on spoil with pH below 3.5, but survival was low and the plots were abandoned.

TABLE 1

Mean height of five tallest trees per plot in 6-year-old[1] Alnus glutinosa provenance study plantations

Seed source			Height[2]
No.	Location	Lat (°N.)	ft
56	Diessen, Germany	47°57′	20.4 a
51	Peiting, Germany	47°48′	19.1 a b
54	Uetze, Germany	52°28′	18.9 a b
18	Ysenburger Hedges, Germany	50°09′	17.9 a b c
44	Spreewald, Germany	52°00′	17.6 a b c
49	Wasserburg, Germany	48°03′	17.6 a b c
58	Kaufbeuren, Germany	47°52′	17.4 a b c
45	Sulzschneid, Germany	47°43′	17.2 a b c
28	Dietz, Germany	50°23′	16.8 a b c
48	Danndorf, Germany	52°31′	16.7 a b c
53	Antwerp, Belgium (plantation)	51°13′	16.7 a b c
24	Danndorf, Germany	52°31′	16.6 a b c
46	Graasten, Denmark	54°55′	16.6 a b c
43	Havno Lounkiaer, Denmark	56°43′	14.9 b c
19	Uppland, Sweden	59°30′	13.6 c
	Average		17.2

[1] Seven years from seed.

[2] Height values followed by the same letter are not significantly different according to Hartley's multiple range test (Snedecor, 1956).

After 6 years in the field, the tallest five trees in each of the 25-tree *A. glutinosa* study plots were measured. The provenances having the tallest trees are all from Germany, south of the 53rd parallel (Table 1 and Fig. 1). Four seed sources—56, 51, 49, and 58—are from the German seed collection Zone II/12, and all these have trees of above-average height; when compared statistically with the other 11 sources, the height advantage for the II/12 trees is highly significant. The ranking of the provenances has remained nearly constant since planting with the exception of source 46, from coastal southern Denmark, which had the second tallest trees after 2 years in the field, and the third tallest after 4 years. Some of the study trees from this source have been damaged, apparently during seed collection, which may partly explain the decline in height ranking.

Trees from the faster growing sources gain their superiority, at least in part, by growing longer into the summer. During their second year in the field, trees from all the *A. glutinosa* provenances grew at a similar rate from mid-April through mid-June, but the trees from the seven tallest sources

TABLE 2

Average number of stems per tree in Alnus glutinosa *provenance study plantations*

Seed source	Avg. no. of stems per tree[1,2]
45	1.11 a
56	1.12 a
46	1.16 a
51	1.22 a
18	1.24 a
53	1.24 a
48	1.32 a
28	1.38 a
43	1.39 a b
58	1.39 a b
49	1.44 a b
44	1.44 a b
24	1.51 a b
54	1.57 b c
19	2.44 c

[1] Only includes thrifty trees without sprouts.
[2] Values followed by the same letter are not significantly different according to Hartley's test.

required an average of 107 days to complete 90% of their total height growth, ranging up to 116 days for source 56. In contrast, the trees from the eight shortest sources completed 90% of their height growth in an average of only 100 days, with source 19 reaching that stage soonest of all—in 85 days.

European alders that grow fastest are more likely to be single-stemmed (Table 2). Two of the four provenances from Zone II/12 ranked among the "best four" (Fig. 2), while the shortest source, Uppland, Sweden, also had the poorest form, averaging 2.4 stems per tree. The correlation between height and number of stems per tree is −0.31.

Alders are often planted on poor sites because they will survive and provide vegetative cover where other species fail, but site selection is important.

FIGURE 2   European alder from Diessen, Germany, combines rapid
growth with good form.

where plantations are intended to yield timber products. European alder grows best on sites with adequate soil moisture (Funk, 1965; McVean, 1953) and yield may be sharply reduced on dry slopes. For instance, the following tabulation shows average 6-year growth of 16 *A. glutinosa* provenances planted in 10-tree row plots perpendicular to the slope contour. To avoid edge effect, the second, fifth, and ninth tree in each plot was measured.

Row	D.b.h.	Height
	in.	ft
2 (upper slope)	0.60	10.5
5 (midslope)	1.36	16.3
9 (lower slope)	1.96	21.0

Other *Alnus* species and hybrids may also be useful in reclaiming disturbed areas. Trees from most European *A. incana* (L.) Moench. provenances have grown very rapidly in our plantations as they did for Lowry et al. (1962), but they all tend to have multiple stems (Fig. 3). One of the *A. incana* collections, from 65° lat in central Sweden, produced attractive shrubby plants that might be useful as a nurse crop. *Alnus cordata* Desf. is another possible nurse-crop species, although it is not completely winter-hardy

FIGURE 3   These *Alnus incana* trees have many multiple stems.

in southeastern Ohio; the few seedlings included in our trials developed into attractive broad shrubs with glossy foliage. *Alnus inokumae* Murai & Kusaka has apparently not been planted in the United States before; it survived and grew much better than any of the other Japanese alders and deserves further testing. And one collection of *Alnus* × *spuria* Callier, the hybrid between *A. glutinosa* and *A. incana*, grew very well and may be a good timber prospect.

Alders have not been planted much for timber production in the eastern United States, but they are used for turnery, plywood, and other products in Europe (Anonymous, 1942; 1953). A few *Alnus* species were introduced into the United States as ornamentals more than two centuries ago, and *A. glutinosa* in particular has occasionally escaped from cultivation and become naturalized (Rehder, 1940). On good sites, pulpwood yields of 115 ft³/acre per year should be possible using a 20-year rotation (Schwappach, 1916), although only a small proportion of strip-mined land is good enough to support such rapid growth. About 50,000 acres per year are presently being mined in the central United States, and alder plantings could provide not only site protection and improvement but important wood fiber production as well in the future.

LITERATURE CITED

Anonymous. 1942. *Alnus glutinosa* (No. 81), Alder. *Wood* **7**, 143–144.

Anonymous. 1953. Alder, *Alnus glutinosa*. *Woodworking Digest* **55**, 279.

Abbott, H. G., and E. J. Eliason, 1968. Forestry tree nursery practices in the United States. *J. Forest.* **66**, 704–711.

Dale, Martin E. 1963. Interplant alder to increase growth in strip-mine plantations. U.S. Dep. Agr., Forest Service, Cent. States Forest Exp. Sta., Res. Note CS-14, 4 p.

Funk, David T. 1965. Silvics of European alder. U.S. Dep. Agr., Forest Service, Cent. States Forest Exp. Sta., 21 p.

Funk, David T., and Martin E. Dale. 1961. European alder: a promising tree for strip-mine planting. U.S. Dep. Agr., Forest Service, Cent. States Forest Exp. Sta. Note 151, 2 p.

Knabe, Wilhelm. 1965. Observations on world-wide efforts to reclaim industrial waste land. In *Ecology and the Industrial Society*. G. T. Goodman, R. W. Edwards, and J. M. Lambert (Ed.). Blackwell Sci. Publ., Oxford, p. 263–296.

Kohnke, Helmut. 1941. The black alder as a pioneer tree in sand dunes and eroded land. *J. Forest.* **39**, 333–334.

Limstrom, G. A. 1960. Forestation of strip-mined land in the Central States. U.S. Dep. Agr., Forest Service, *Agr. Handbook* No. 166, 74 p.

Lowry, G. L., F. C. Brokaw, and C. H. J. Breeding, 1962. Alder for reforesting coal spoils in Ohio. *J. Forest.* **30**, 196–199.

McVean, D. N. 1953. Biological flora of the British Isles: *Alnus glutinosa* (L.) Gaertn. (*A. rotundifolia* Stokes). *J. Ecol.* **41**, 447–466.

Rehder, Alfred. 1940. *Manual of cultivated trees and shrubs hardy in North America.* 2nd ed. The Macmillan Co., New York, 996 p.

Snedecor, George W. 1957. *Statistical methods applied to experiments in agriculture and biology.* 5th ed. The Iowa State College Press, Ames, Iowa, 534 p.

Schwappach, Doctor Professor. 1916. Unsere Erlen. *Mitt. der Deutsch. Dendrol. Ges.* **25**, 30–37.

Virtanen, Artturi I. 1957. Investigations on nitrogen fixation by the alder. II. Associated culture of spruce and inoculated alder without combined nitrogen. *Physiol. Plant* **10**, 164–169.

Wood, R. F., and J. V. Thirgood. 1956. Tree planting on colliery spoil heaps. *Colliery Eng.* **33**, 27–32.

DISCUSSION

SCHLATZER: Normally, in European forestry, we regard black alder, on soils other than those on which it naturally occurs, as an aid; short-lived, and susceptible to attacks from *Cryptospora suffusa*, it faces an even worse situation on strip-mine soils. Black alder trees deteriorate about 5 years after planting. We have had to cut many at about 10 years of age because they were dying. However, this species is still a very effective pioneer in the first years.

FUNK: We have tried to refrain from making big claims. We feel encouraged, but I am sure that on severe sites we cannot hope for too much. On some of our better spoil we are getting trees to pulpwood size, at least 5 in. d.b.h. by age 10. That is the best claim I can make at this time.

NEUMANN: How far were the sites in which you found earthworms from undisturbed forest sites?

FUNK: Not very far; 75 ft probably.

AHARRAH: How do you compare alder with black locust for withstanding insect attack or fungus?

FUNK: Of course, the locust has had a lot longer time to be exposed to pest buildup than alder. I find a few sawfly larvae, Japanese beetles, and assorted leaf chewing insects; wooly aphids are common, but I don't think cause much of a problem. Up to now we haven't had much trouble with either insects or diseases, but it is very early on that score.

DAVIS: The tops of some of the alders I received from Mr. Funk are dying. You mentioned that *Alnus inokumae* was doing so well in Ohio. We got some from a different seed source; and either because of seed source or the Pennsylvania climate, they all died from frost damage.

FUNK: Several other Japanese species didn't do so well; some of the *Alnus japonica* germinated poorly, and none of the *A. japonica*, *A. hirsuta*, or *A. firma* seedlings survived the first winter in the nursery.

KNABE: I was very much impressed by the growth of the alder here; I have seen some years after their establishment. The oldest stand is situated at Pomeroy, Ohio. The alder grew faster than the black locust there, but I don't think this is generally true. Unfortunately, we have found some of the insects you mentioned: aphids and some caterpillars eating the leaves; also insect larvae, perhaps *Cryptorhynchus lapathi*. This is a beetle which develops in the wood. In general, I would agree to what Mr. Schlatzer said. You can be sure you at least have a very good nurse crop, but it would be fine if it could be harvested for pulpwood or timber. The growth is much better than in Germany, in Denmark, or in the other European countries that I have visited.

PLASS: In a 7-year-old plantation of alder in eastern Kentucky, the wooly aphids made their appearance, and shortly after we recorded death of tops and branches. The stand was examined by the U.S. Forest Service Disease and Insect Laboratory in Ohio, and in their opinion, the wooly aphid contributed but did not cause death. The aphid created portals for entry of secondary organisms.

JACOBY: If you want to produce pulpwood, why do you not use a mixture of hybrid poplar and alder, since you have such substantial growth in the alder?

FUNK: Alder is easier to produce in the nursery, and in my experience, it is more tolerant to moderately low pH, say around 3.5 to 4, than are the hybrid poplars I am familiar with. I don't advocate pure alder planting. We usually recommend interplanting one or more hardwood species with alder, and on spoils with medium texture and pH above 5.5, an alder-hybrid poplar mixture might be a good proposition.

GENETIC VARIABILITY IN SURVIVAL AND GROWTH OF VIRGINIA PINE PLANTED ON ACID SURFACE-MINE SPOIL

William T. Plass

*Principal Plant Ecologist, Northeastern Forest Experiment Station,
Forest Service, U. S. Department of Agriculture,
Princeton, West Virginia*

Fifty-seven open-pollinated Virginia pine (*Pinus virginiana* Mill.) progeny from 10 natural stands scattered through Tennessee and Kentucky were evaluated under field and greenhouse conditions to determine if genetic variability would influence survival and growth on an extremely acid spoil. In the field after two growing seasons, survival, total height, and second-year growth were significantly better for some progeny. Large variations occurred between individuals from the same stand, and there were differences between stands. Greenhouse growth of 11 of the progeny did not correlate with growth under field conditions. This may relate to variability between progeny in their response to climatic conditions in the field, or to differences between the field and greenhouse spoils. Tissue analysis of needles from seedlings grown in essentially the same spoil in the greenhouse showed significant differences between progeny for Mg, B, Zn, and Mo. Growth was closely related to nutrient uptake.

INTRODUCTION

Intraspecific variation in wood properties and physiological processes have been conclusively demonstrated for many tree species. This knowledge has been used to select and breed individuals considered superior for specific tree-improvement objectives.

Intraspecific variations may also be expressed by the tolerance of some progeny of a species to chemical and physical site factors that may reduce survival and growth. This presents some interesting possibilities for improving growth and survival on drastically disturbed areas.

Many areas strip-mined for coal are plagued with one or more of the following: acidity, toxic concentrations of chemicals, nutrient deficiencies, and unfavorable microclimate. The success of each planted seedling may depend on its physiologic efficiency in coping with these adverse conditions. Thus it may be possible through selection and breeding to develop genotypes that are better adapted to the site conditions common to drastically disturbed areas.

The objective of my study was to make a preliminary evaluation of the variation in survival and growth of open-pollinated progeny of Virginia pine (*Pinus virginiana* Mill.) on a strongly acid strip-mine spoil. In this study, tree characteristics relating to site protection and an improvement in aesthetic appearance were considered more important than those relating to wood quality and production. Significant differences between progeny would indicate that, through selection and breeding programs, there may be a possibility of developing improved planting stock for strongly acid surface-mine spoil.

METHODS

In 1962 the members of the Kentucky-Tennessee Section of the Society of American Foresters sponsored a genetic study of Virginia pine. This consisted of two parts: first, to determine the natural variation in wood properties; and second, to document the variation in wood properties in open-pollinated progeny. This species was selected because of the lack of knowledge about variation in its wood properties, and because of its increasing importance for pulping.

Dr. Eyvind Thor, associate professor of forestry at the University of Tennessee, was responsible for both of these studies. He reported on the first part in the *Journal of Forestry* in April 1964.

Under Dr. Thor's direction, seed collections for the open-pollinated trials were made from the same stands, using many of the individual trees included in the first part of the study. Located in several important physiographic regions, these were typical of even-aged average or above-average stands for the species in Kentucky and Tennessee. The individual trees were healthy dominants and codominants. The stands varied in age from 28 to 53 years, and the site index ranged from 60 to 87 feet (Table 1 and Fig. 1).

One-year-old seedling stock was grown at a nursery in Tennessee. Seedlings from 57 open-pollinated progeny representing 10 stands were assigned to a planting on a strongly acid strip-mine spoil. Growth characteristics of individual seedlings for each progeny planted on this surface-mine site

TABLE 1

Sample plot location and average site index and age

Stand No.	Physiographic region	Location	Site index	Total age yr
2	Western Kentucky	Dawson Springs, Ky.	69	52
3	Cumberland Plateau	Sewanee, Tenn.	73	34
4	Eastern Rim	Rock Island, Tenn.	74	42
6	Cumberland Mountains	Wartburg, Tenn.	87	35
7	Eastern Ridge	Pineville, Ky.	82	42
8	Cumberland Plateau	London, Ky.	83	47
9	Cumberland Plateau	Morehead, Ky.	69	32
10	Great Valley	Etowah, Tenn.	81	53
11	Great Valley	Vonore, Tenn.	60	53
13	Great Valley	Elizabethtown, Tenn.	64	43

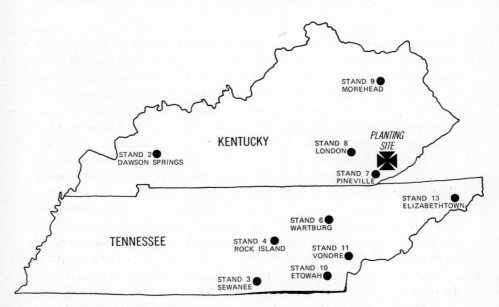

FIGURE 1   Locations of the strip-mine planting site and the parent stands in Kentucky and Tennessee.

may be compared later with seedlings of the same progeny planted by Dr. Thor on old fields and forest clearings.

The strip-mine site selected is located in southeastern Kentucky, in the extreme northeastern corner of Bell County. The spoil resulted from mining the Hindman coal seam. Overburden rock is predominantly sandstone, so the spoil is coarse-textured, with many large rock fragments. A majority of the samples collected on the site had a pH between 4.0 and 4.5. All blocks are located on a relatively level bench.

A randomized block design with nine replications and 10 tree plots was used; so 90 trees were used to evaluate the field response of each progeny.

The total height of each seedling was measured to the nearest 1/10 ft at the end of the first and second growing seasons. The difference between total heights at the end of the first and second growing seasons was considered net second-year growth. Survival was determined at the end of the second growing season.

A greenhouse study was also made to determine if results comparable to those in the field could be obtained under greenhouse conditions. Not only would this be a more efficient way of evaluating progeny, but also it would permit more detailed observations and measurements of each individual seedling.

Three seedlings of 11 progeny were planted singly in large pots filled with 30 lb of spoil collected at the field site. The spoil was carefully mixed before potting to minimize spoil differences between pots. Each pot was brought to field capacity or 20% moisture by weight with distilled water. Additional water was added when the spoil on the top of the pot became dry. Randomly selected pots were weighed periodically to confirm that soil moisture by weight remained between 15 and 20%.

The top length of each seedling was measured at the time of planting to the nearest 1/10 in. The potted seedlings were placed for one growing season in a lath house with a solid translucent roof. After being exposed to several days of below-freezing temperatures in the fall and early winter, the pots were brought into a greenhouse. Artificial light was used to increase day length and supplement natural light. The light source was a combination of fluorescent and incandescent bulbs. After 5 months in the greenhouse, the study was terminated. Thus in a 12-month period I observed two flushes of growth. This would approximate two growing seasons in the field.

When the study was terminated, all seedlings were removed from the pots by carefully washing away the soil from the roots. Top length was determined by the same methods and to the same degree of accuracy as before. The seedlings were then destroyed, and all needles were oven-dried and ground for tissue analysis. Foliar concentrations of 12 nutrients were determined spectrographically. Nitrogen was determined by the Kjeldahl method.

FIELD VARIATION

Field response was evaluated in terms of: total seedling height at the end of the second growing season; net growth during the second growing season; and survival. For each of these dependent variables, I found by analysis of variance highly significant differences between some of the progeny. A few progeny survived and grew very well on this site; other progeny had low survival and grew slowly. Significant differences between blocks for all three variables indicated that different growing conditions existed between blocks. This is not an uncommon occurrence in spoil-bank field trials.

Seedlings of the three tallest progeny had mean total heights of 21.6, 19.6, and 19.1 in. (Fig. 2). Statistically there was no significant difference

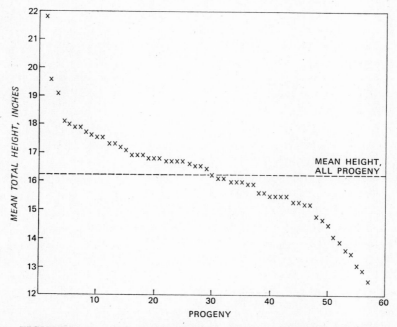

FIGURE 2 Array of mean total heights for the 57 progeny under field conditions.

between the heights of these three progeny. At the other extreme, the mean total heights of the three shortest progeny were 12.5, 12.9, and 13.1 in. Thus there was a difference of 9.1 in. in mean total height between the tallest and shortest progeny after two growing seasons.

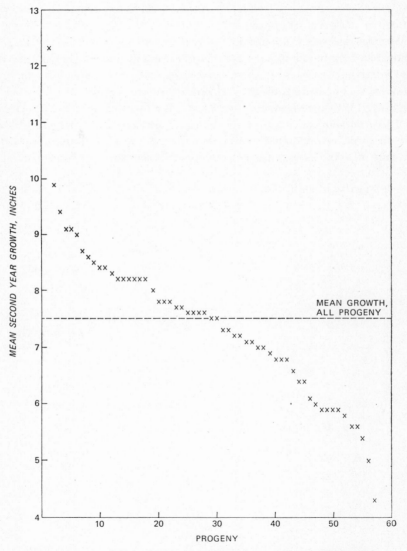

FIGURE 3   Array of mean second-year growth for the 57 progeny under field conditions.

The three progeny with the greatest mean annual growth averaged 12.3, 9.9, and 9.4 in. during the second growing season (Fig. 3). Duncan's multiple range test showed no significant difference between the top two progeny; the growth of the third was significantly less than that of the one with the best growth. The three progeny having the slowest mean annual growth averaged 4.3, 5.0, and 5.4 in. Thus there was a growth difference of 8.0 in. between the progeny having the fastest and slowest growth.

Highly significant differences in survival existed between progeny, as shown by an analysis of variance. Survival ranged from 91 percent to a low of 47% (Fig. 4). Two progeny ranked high in growth had survivals of 80 and 78%. Two other progeny making superior growth had survivals of 66 and 63%. Thus superior growth was not always related to high survival.

Progeny from one stand often responded similarly in growth and survival. To show this, I compared the means for 29 progeny representing stands 4, 7, and 10, which represented different physiographic regions. Basis for

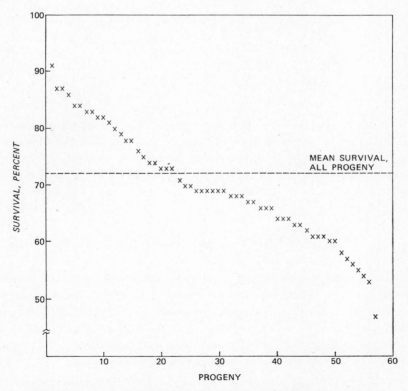

FIGURE 4 Array of survival for the 57 progeny under field conditions.

comparison was the percentage of progeny from each stand occurring among the 10 progeny ranked highest and lowest in terms of growth and survival. Forty percent of the progeny from Stand 7 were among the top 10 with respect to growth (Table 2). Survival for progeny from stand 7 was poor, with 60% occurring among the lowest 10. Forty percent of the progeny from Stand 10 were among those with high survival. Growth was mixed—30% in the highest group and 30% in the lowest. Progeny from the third stand, No. 4, were the poorest of the three. Ten percent were among the top 10 in survival, and 30% were ranked among those having the slowest growth.

TABLE 2

Percentage of progeny from stands 4, 7, and 10 occurring among the highest and lowest 10 progeny with respect to growth and survival in the field

	Description	Stand 4	Stand 7	Stand 10
Survival	Highest 10	10	0	40
	Lowest 10	0	60	0
Growth	Highest 10	0	40	30
	Lowest 10	30	0	30

So it would appear that collections of open-pollinated seed from Stands 7 and 10 would be preferred for plantings on this site. The choice between Stands 7 and 10 would be difficult until the cause of mortality for Stand 7 could be determined. If survival for Stand 7 could be improved, its superior growth would be an advantage.

GREENHOUSE VARIATION

In designing the greenhouse test, an attempt was made to minimize environmental and spoil differences between individual seedlings. The purpose was to accentuate response attributable to the complex chemistry of this strongly acid spoil. Comparisons of greenhouse results involved total height at the end of the study period, growth, and foliar nutrient levels.

Analyses showed significant differences in total height, and highly significant differences in growth between progeny. The mean height by progeny ranged from 11.6 to 15.0 in. (Table 3). Mean growth ranged from 2.9 to

TABLE 3

Mean total height and growth for 11 progeny grown under greenhouse conditions

Progeny		Total[a] height in.	Total[a] growth in.
Stand No.	Tree No.		
2	1	13.9	8.7
3	15	12.2	3.6
4	2	13.0	2.9
4	4	12.5	3.4
4	12	15.0	6.2
4	13	14.4	5.9
6	11	11.6	7.0
8	9	12.2	6.5
10	4	16.7	7.3
10	5	13.3	6.9
13	1	11.6	5.9

[a] Mean of three measurements.

TABLE 4

Mean foliar nutrient levels of Mg, Zn, B, and Mo by progeny grown under greenhouse conditions

Progeny		Mean foliar nutrient level (oven-dry weight basis)			
Stand No.	Tree No.	Mg %	Zn ppm	B ppm	Mo ppm
2	1	0.070	50.0	17.7	0.42
3	15	0.073	44.7	23.3	0.78
4	2	0.080	30.3	11.3	0.44
4	4	0.073	54.7	11.7	0.40
4	12	0.053	35.0	12.0	0.45
4	13	0.050	80.0	10.3	0.36
6	11	0.053	33.0	14.7	0.47
8	9	0.103	58.0	15.3	1.23
10	4	0.075	41.0	15.0	0.50
10	5	0.077	30.0	9.7	0.22
13	1	0.077	69.3	16.3	0.40

8.7 in. Since significant growth differences occurred in the greenhouse where environment was controlled and spoil differences between seedlings were minimized, one can assume that variations in growth in the greenhouse relate to the response of each seedling to the complex chemistry of this spoil.

The analysis of foliar nutrient content involved individual analysis of variance for 13 nutrients and 11 open-pollinated progeny. Foliage samples were collected from three seedlings of each of the progeny. Significant differences did occur between progeny for Mg, Zn, B, and Mo (Table 4). In many cases, there were wide variations among seedlings from the same parent tree. Much of this probably relates to variability introduced by open pollination.

These results support evidence from the field trials that significant differences in growth do occur between progeny. Furthermore, the foliar nutrient analyses confirm previous published evidence that the variance between open-pollinated progeny is due in part to individual seedling response to soil chemistry.

COMPARISON OF FIELD AND GREENHOUSE TRIALS

In the preceding analysis, it has been shown that the progeny included in this study differ in their rate of growth both in the field and in the greenhouse. Now it is necessary to determine if there is any similarity in growth response for progeny grown under these two growth regimes.

Tabular comparisons of growth and height for 11 progeny showed little similarity under field and greenhouse conditions (Table 5). Only one progeny exhibited a tendency toward slow growth under both types of growing conditions.

Since greenhouse height and growth do not appear to be reliable indicators of field response, the foliar nutrient data were examined. First the foliar nutrient levels of nine greenhouse-grown seedlings from three progeny making the best field growth were compared with nine greenhouse-grown seedlings from three progeny making the poorest field growth. Individual analysis of variance was made for each of 13 nutrients. For all nutrients except Zn, the higher growth rate was related to higher levels of foliar nutrients. These differences were significant for Ca, Fe, B, and Mo (Table 6).

Examination of the data for these nutrients indicates that foliar nutrient analyses may assist in identifying progeny that would grow well on the field

TABLE 5

Comparisons of mean total height and growth by progeny under field and greenhouse conditions

Progeny		Total height		Growth	
Stand No.	Tree No.	Field in.	Green-house in.	Field[a] in.	Green-house[b] in.
2	1	15.5	13.9	7.6	8.7
3	15	14.1	12.2	6.0	3.6
4	2	16.9	13.0	6.8	2.9
4	4	13.5	12.5	5.0	3.4
4	12	14.7	15.0	7.7	6.2
4	13	13.6	14.4	5.6	5.9
6	11	15.5	11.6	7.6	7.0
8	9	16.9	12.2	8.2	6.5
10	4	16.7	16.7	7.8	7.3
10	5	13.9	13.3	5.9	6.9
13	1	17.1	11.8	8.2	5.9

[a] Net growth during second growing season.
[b] Net growth during total growth period.

TABLE 6

Comparison of foliar nutrient levels of Ca, Fe, B, and Mo in greenhouse-grown seedlings for the three progeny making the highest and lowest growth under field conditions

Descriptions	Progeny		Foliar nutrient level (oven-dry weight basis)			
	Stand No.	Tree No.	Ca %	Fe ppm	B ppm	Mo ppm
Highest field growth	13	1	0.24	225	16	0.40
	8	9	0.30	144	15	1.23
	10	4	0.23	189	15	0.50
Mean	—	—	0.26	186	15	0.71
Lowest field growth	10	5	0.13	147	10	0.22
	4	13	0.14	145	10	0.36
	4	4	0.16	128	12	0.40
Mean	—	—	0.14	140	11	0.33

site. Calcium and B appear to be the best indicators. If this is a valid method, those progeny with foliar nutrient levels of 20% Ca or more and 15 ppm B or more in the greenhouse may make above-average growth in the field. Although the conclusions apply only to the conditions related to this study, the evidence suggests that it may be possible to develop methods for identifying superior individuals by foliar analysis.

SUMMARY

The objective of this study was to make a preliminary evaluation of the variation in growth of open-pollinated Virginia pine when grown on a strongly acid spoil. Results from field and greenhouse studies establish the fact that large differences in growth occurred between progeny. Some progeny are definitely superior for planting on this acid spoil, while others are considered inferior. There is evidence that this relates to the physiological efficiency of seedlings in their nutrient utilization. On this spoil, the foliar nutrients exhibiting the greatest correlation with growth were Ca, Mg, B, Mo, and Fe.

Differences in growth and survival were also related to the stand from which the seed for each progeny were collected. In this particular cace, considerable improvement in survival and growth could have been realized by using planting stock grown from seed collected from a particular stand.

Attempts to duplicate patterns of field growth by greenhouse methods met with little success. However, a relationship was found between field response and the foliar nutrient content of greenhouse-grown seedlings. This may provide a method for selecting the more promising progeny before field testing begins.

These results clearly indicate the importance that intraspecific variation has in the growth and survival of Virginia pine on strongly acid spoils. Opportunities for improving planting stock follow the traditional avenues of tree improvement. Use seed from stands producing progeny that will make better growth on strongly acid spoils, or begin a breeding program to produce genotypes specifically adapted to these adverse sites. It may be possible to have several select progeny, each adapted to a given set of site conditions.

I hope these results will encourage geneticists to give more consideration to the problems on drastically disturbed sites. If they do, we may see a dramatic improvement in revegetation success.

DISCUSSION

RUFFNER: Was there any correlation in the foliar nutrients from the stands where they were collected? Did you make any comparisons to see if you could predetermine by foliar nutrients the best place to collect seed?

PLASS: This was not done. I recognize the deficiency in the study, but I did not make collections from the field to compare them with the greenhouse tests.

CARUCCIO: It is possible that the survival rate for progeny from stand 10 was greater because its underlying geology was similar to that of the strip-mine planting site.

PLASS: I made no investigations of the soils in each of these stands. Dr. Thor made all the collections; I merely received the stock. This indicates that further study of soils would be valuable and should be made.

BENGTSON: In sampling the foliage, were all the needles stripped from the tree and then composited to make a single sample?

PLASS: This was done in the greenhouse trial. This procedure may differ from field collections in that many variables were controlled in the greenhouse, and we were dealing with very small plants, not mature individuals. We felt that these were representative values for each plant. I recognize that the nutrient contents of the older foliage would be different from those of the younger foliage. This is another sophistication that could be included in this particular type of evaluation.

BENGTSON: I just wanted to point out that for some purposes it is considered better to collect foliage samples from a specific location on the plant. This reduces differences in chemical composition of foliage due to stage of maturity of the foliage. If you want to measure differences in nutrient uptake among individuals or provenances, you would do well to composite the foliage or, even better, to analyze a sample representing the whole plant. But if you are concerned with characterizing differences in nutrient content of foliage associated with genetic entities (e.g. provenances), sampling from one or more specific locations on each plant would give more meaningful results.

PLASS: Under greenhouse conditions, you can use the whole plant. In fact, I did save the root tissues. Some of the previous discussions, however, indicated problems may be associated with evaluations of root tissue analyses.

MEDVICK: Leyton suggested using only the terminal foliage for an indication of need for fertilization. Now, you are relating this to genetics; is there a possibility of confounding?

PLASS: I am using it as a tool to identify a particular plant condition. You control as many things as you can in the plant environment. The differences in foliar nutrient level suggest genetic variance that is related to growth. In horticultural crops this is an accepted technique to determine fertilizer rates.

RICHTER: Are you far enough along to consider the creation of seed orchards, or are you going to be satisfied with seed collection areas?

PLASS: In Pennsylvania, West Virginia, Kentucky, Ohio, Indiana, and Illinois over 50% of the production of state-operated nurseries goes onto strip-mined land. Therefore, it behooves the states to use this information to improve their planting stock. I would assume they would go into a seed orchard program first and then get into a breeding program.

ZARGER: There is an old axiom among tree improvers that when you are in doubt about which of several sources is best, you always use the local source. Perhaps until you have delineated those stands which are best suited for spoil planting, you would not go wrong to collect seed from a source near to your planting site.

PLASS: The only comment I have on that is that this would apply only if you were planting on natural soils. When you are involved with disturbed conditions such as strip-mine spoils, this old axiom may or may not apply.

J. BROWN: You used "strongly" acid spoil material for your greenhouse work. What range of acid conditions are you referring to?

PLASS: The spoil we used in the greenhouse tested by laboratory methods ranged between 3.8 to 4.0.

BROWN: It is just at the breaking point for what is commonly classified as toxic?

PLASS: Yes. This same spoil was used in other greenhouse tests of herbaceous plant materials. These tests indicated that it is very low in basic nutrients and that toxic ions are present.

BROWN: Would you make any prediction as to whether these same plant materials might also be suitable on very toxic materials with pH of 3.0 to 3.5?

PLASS: No.

BROWN: It was not designed for testing under "toxic" conditions?

PLASS: No. It was just to point out that genetic variance does exist. We used only one species too but I would imagine the same would apply for many of the woody plants.

SEEDING OF PINE ON COAL SPOIL BANKS IN THE TENNESSEE VALLEY

T. G. Zarger, J. A. Curry, and J. C. Allen

Staff Forester, Supervisor, and Staff Forester, Strip Mine Reclamation Section, Tennessee Valley Authority Division of Forestry, Fisheries and Wildlife Development, Norris, Tennessee

The current rate of land disturbance by coal strip mining in the Tennessee Valley counties of Alabama, Tennessee, and Virginia is a little more than 5000 acres a year. Throughout the region, Tennessee Valley Authority surface mine coal suppliers are required by contract provisions to reclaim all disturbed areas. In addition, Alabama, Tennessee, and Virginia have reclamation laws which include the revegetation of spoils. Reforestation by the usual hand planting of seedlings is often difficult and expensive. Seeding of tree species, either by ground or aerial methods, may be an economic alternative to the usual reforestation methods.

In 1966, seeding tests were established at 38 sites on a total of 158 acres to evaluate time, rates, treatments, and other factors. Loblolly, shortleaf, Virginia, and white pine were seeded on both graded and ungraded spoils at rates varying from 1/3 to 3 lb/acre.

After two seasons, results show seeding during the period March to mid-April gave satisfactory seedling stands. Best results were obtained in Alabama and southeastern Tennessee and poorest in northeastern Tennessee. Stratified and repellent-treated loblolly pine seeded at 1-$\frac{1}{2}$ lb/acre or Virginia pine at 1 lb/acre produced stands of 1500 seedlings per acre. White pine stratified for 60 days and seeded at 1-$\frac{1}{2}$ lb. produced 1300 seedlings. Poorer results were obtained from seedings of shortleaf pine. In 1967, aerial seeding of 54 acres in northeastern Alabama produced from 1000 to 1600 seedlings per acre after 1 year with loblolly and loblolly-Virginia pine mixtures.

INTRODUCTION

In the Tennessee Valley, coal is produced by strip mining in parts of three states and 27 counties. The coal field extends from southwestern Virginia through Tennessee into northeastern Alabama (Fig. 1). The annual rate of land disturbance is a little more than 5000 acres, with over 58,000 disturbed so far. With passage of legislation this year by Alabama, all of the

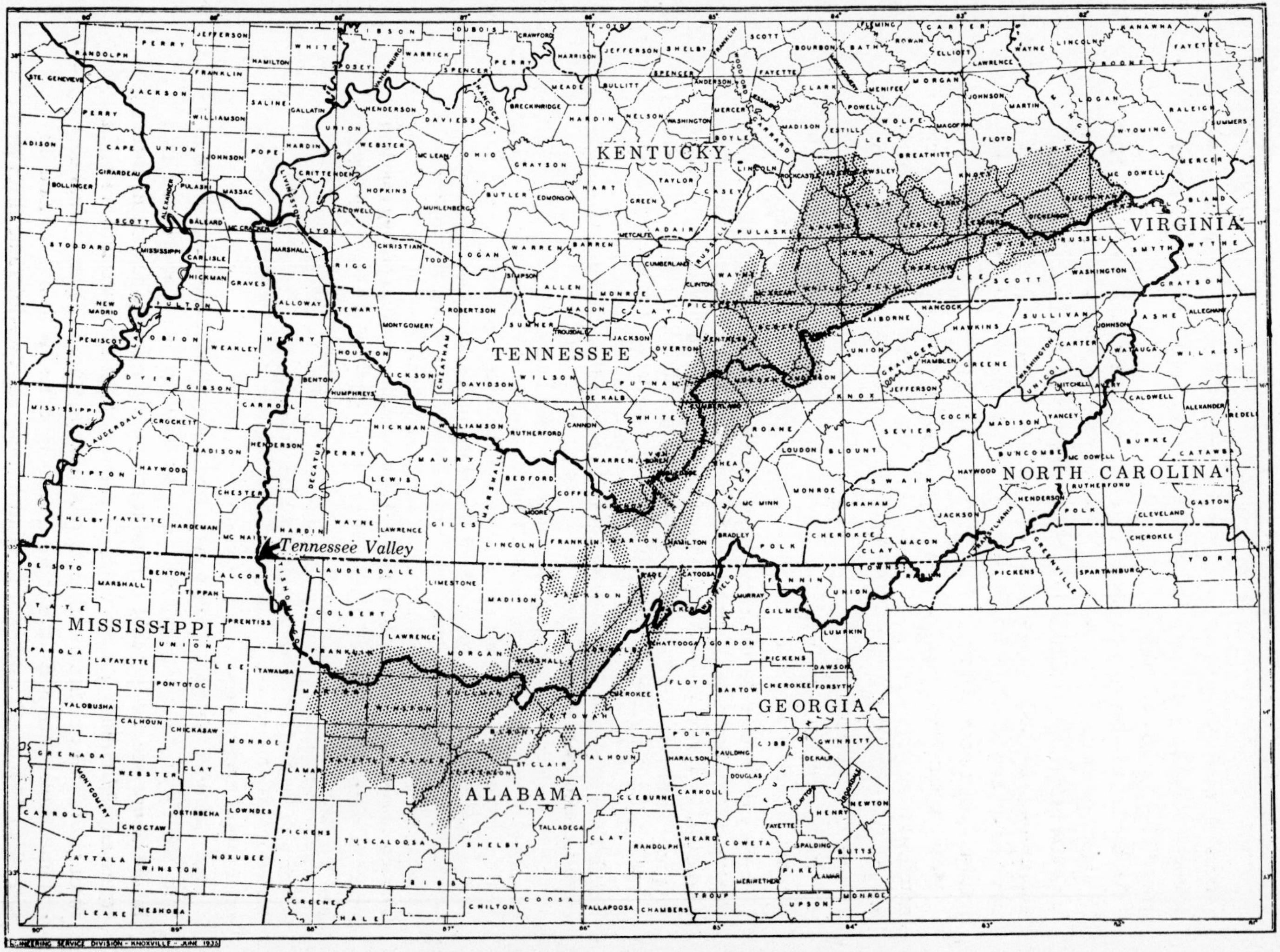

FIGURE 1   Appalachian coal field in Tennessee Valley region.

current mining is covered by state reclamation laws. In addition, the Tennessee Valley Authority includes reclamation provisions in its surface mined coal purchase contracts.

Mountain or contour stripping predominates, although some flat land or area-type stripping is found on the Cumberland Plateau. Spoil banks are extremely variable depending on the nature of the parent material and the mining method. Proportions of acid sandstone, shales, limestone, clay, sand, and soil are intermixed to form an agglomeration of varied texture and mineral content.

Most reclamation is aimed at forest and wildlife production, since practically all mining is in forest land. Yellow pines and black locust are the species planted, although other hardwoods and wildlife shrubs are gaining in popularity.

Planting seedlings by hand is often difficult and expensive. Seeding by ground or aerial methods may be an economic alternative. Seeding of pine has been a recognized reforestation practice in the South for 10 years (Mann, 1968), and it has shown promise in southern portions of the Tennessee Valley (Hinton, 1967) and in the Tennessee Highlands (Russell and Mignery, 1968).

This paper reports the results of tests in the Valley to determine the feasibility of establishing pine trees on coal spoil banks by seeding; that is, planting seed instead of nursery grown seedlings.

METHODS

During late winter and early spring 1966, a series of tests were established on coal strip mine spoils in 12 Valley counties in Alabama, Tennessee, and Virginia. TVA foresters used a general work plan as a guide to develop specific tests pertinent to conditions in their respective areas. They arranged for cooperation with landowners and coal producers and followed through on establishment and scheduled measurements.

Test variables included species, rates and dates of seeding, and combining pine seed with grass and legume seed and fertilizer. Basic block and plot layouts were in randomized block design with three to five replications per treatment. Minimum plot size was 0.1 acre. Since tests were modified to fit local needs and conditions, all variables were not tested at all locations.

The loblolly (*Pinus taeda* L.), shortleaf (*P. echinata* Mill.), Virginia (*P. virginiana* Mill.), and white (*P. strobus* L.) pine seed was of regional origin acquired for use in TVA nursery operations. Storage had been in airtight containers at 18 F. Number of viable seed/lb averaged 16,000 for loblolly, 40,000 for shortleaf, 44,000 for Virginia, and 21,000 for white. Unless otherwise noted, all test seed was stratified for 30 days and coated with bird and rodent repellents prior to use. Follow-up germination tests showed seed treatment did not reduce seed viability.

There was no special site preparation. The more recent mining or grading operations provided a better seeding chance. Weathering had improved the soil surface on some older spoils, but others were hard and compact. There was little or no natural vegetation on any of the sites.

The 37 test sites ranged from 0.9 to 8.4 acres in size and were located on a variety of spoil conditions. Sites varied in slope and aspect and elevations ranged from 1200 to 2800 ft. The range in pH was 3.4 to 5.5. Spoil age was 1 to 8 years. This is a breakdown of areas by location and acreage:

Area	Sites	Counties	Acres
NE Alabama	8	3	36.8
SE Tennessee	8	4	8.7
NE Tennessee	10	3	13.4
SW Virginia	11	2	19.1
Total	37	12	78.0

Seedlings were counted in late spring and fall 1966, and again in late spring 1967, on quarter-milacre sample plots spaced at half-chain intervals. Counts were also made in 1968, after 2 full years, on six tests in Alabama and seven in Virginia to obtain additional information on stand development.

Species comparisons

Eighteen tests totaling 26 acres were seeded by hand or cyclone seeder between March 8 and April 21. Two were in Alabama, 11 in Tennessee, and 5 in Virginia. Species and seeding rates are listed in Table 1 for Tennessee and Table 2 for Alabama and Virginia. In six Tennessee tests comparing loblolly, shortleaf, and Virginia pine, the shortleaf and Virginia rates were reduced so that number of seeds approached that for loblolly. In the other tests, rates were the same (often 1 lb), and number of seeds varied by species.

Rate and date

Rate of seeding usually involved three rates, with one lower and one higher than that recommended for normal reforestation. For loblolly pine on a good seeding chance this is 1 lb/acre. So the rates for loblolly were 1/2, 1, and 1-1/2 lb/acre. At one Alabama location, test rates for loblolly were 1, 2, and 3 lb, with the 1-lb rate serving as a control. Time of seeding covered three dates at about 3-week intervals between early March and late April. The intermediate date was the one judged to be optimum for the area—that is, the time most of the seed was expected to germinate. Thirteen rate and date tests were established.

Supplemental treatments

Various combinations of grass and legume seed and fertilizer were applied with the 1-lb rate of pine seed on 23 tests at 14 locations. Grasses included annual ryegrass (*Lolium multiflorum* Lam.), perennial ryegrass (*L. perenne* L.), and tall fescue, K-31—alta (*Festuca arundinacea*, var.). Lespedeza sericea (*Lespede zacuneata* [Dumont] G. Don) was the only legume. Fertilizers included ammonium nitrate (33.5% N) at 100 to 150 lb/acre and complete fertilizers (10-10-10 and 14-14-14) at 300 lb/acre.

Other tests and demonstrations

On March 24, 1966, 80 acres of 1-to 5-year-old unreclaimed spoils in southeastern Tennessee were seeded by helicopter. The acreage was divided into seven plots ranging from 6 to 14 acres. Loblolly pine seed, unstratified and stratified for 2, 3, and 4 weeks, was broadcast at 1 lb/acre on four plots. Shortleaf stratified for 2 weeks was sown on one plot at the same rate. One plot had a mixture of 1 lb of loblolly and 1/2 lb of Virginia pine. Seed counts in milacre traps scattered over the plots indicated excellent seed distribution. Stand conditions were evaluated in May and October 1966, and in October 1967.

In late March 1967, a 2.7-acre 1966 white pine test in Dickenson County, Va. was reseeded—half with 60-day stratified white pine and half with 30-day stratified loblolly. Seedling rates were 1/2, 1, and 1-1/2 lb/acre. Plots were evaluated in December 1967 and May 1968. The test was designed so second-year germination of white pine seed from 1966 plots could also be measured.

32a   Hutnik/D (1440)

Also in March 1967, pine was seeded on a pilot scale by helicopter on 105 acres of newly mined and graded spoils in northeastern Alabama. Species mixtures and rates were based on 1966 test findings. Stocking was evaluated after 1 year on 54 acres seeded to two loblolly-Virginia pine mixtures and to loblolly at 1-1/4 lb/acre.

TABLE 1

One-year stand development from seeding pine at nine locations in Tennessee

County	Acres No.	Soil pH	Species[a]	Seeding rate lb/acre	Average no. seedlings per acre			Stocking[b] %
					May 66	October 66	May 67	
Northeastern Tennessee								
Campbell	0.6	3.5	VP	1.0	5000	2332	0	0
			WP	1.0	0	0	0	0
Morgan	0.9	5.0	LP	1.0	1667	—	667	17
			VP	1.0	6000	—	3667	33
			WP	1.0	1667	—	667	17
Morgan	0.6	4.0	LP	1.0	3660	—	1665	25
			SP	1.0	8685	—	5328	25
Southeastern Tennessee								
Grundy	1.0	5.0	LP	1.2	4160	6560	1280	28
			VP	0.3	7260	8960	5600	52
Grundy	1.2	5.0	LP	1.2	6400	2800	800	20
			SP	0.3	8000	0	0	0
			VP	0.3	8400	8000	0	0
Hamilton	1.2	4.5	LP	1.2	3600	4000	2000	20
			SP	0.6	2900	2000	0	0
			VP	0.6	6600	4600	2400	35
Hamilton	1.2	5.0	LP	1.2	4000	3500	c	—
			SP	0.3	4000	1400	c	—
			VP	0.3	12600	8500	c	—
Hamilton	1.2	4.5	SP	0.6	800	800	533	13
			VP	0.6	1600	1800	800	13
Marion	1.0	5.0	LP	2.4	2240	1600	400	8
			VP	0.6	8160	10000	4000	24

[a] Species: loblolly (LP), shortleaf (SP), Virginia (VP), and white pine (WP).

[b] Proportion of sample quarter-milacres having one or more seedlings 1 year after seeding.

[c] Plot markers missing on May 1967 inspection.

RESULTS

Species comparisons

One-year results from 11 tests in Tennessee (two failed) showed more seedlings of Virginia pine than the other species (Table 1). This was true even when seeding was at one-half to one-fourth the loblolly and white pine rates and at a comparative shortleaf rate.

Virginia pine produced acceptable stands* in four of eight tests, loblolly in two of seven, and shortleaf in one of five. The average Virginia pine stand contained 2350 seedlings/acre and 22% stocking compared with 1135 seedlings and 20% for loblolly, and 1460 seedlings and 10% for shortleaf. All species suffered heavy first-winter mortality.

Two-year results with loblolly, shortleaf, and Virginia pine at two Alabama sites showed acceptable stands of all three species at one site (Table 2).

TABLE 2

Two-year stand development from seeding pine at 1 lb/acre

Pine species	Average number seedlings per acre on				Stocking[a] %
	May 66	October 66	May 67	May 68	
Etowah County, Alabama (1.8 acres)					
Loblolly	667	667	1000	778	25
Shortleaf	1333	667	1222	2333	42
Virginia	3111	2778	3222	2778	58
Jackson County, Alabama (5.0 acres)					
Loblolly	1333	1222	667	111	8
Shortleaf	1222	1000	222	333	25
Virginia	2667	1889	444	222	17
Wise County, Virginia (1.0 acres)					
Shortleaf	2600	6400	2600	1600	25
White	400	800	200	200	5
Wise County, Virginia (0.6 acres)					
Shortleaf	9667	12000	2333	1667	25
White	b	—	—	—	—

[a] Proportion of sample quarter-milacres having one or more seedlings 2 years after seeding.

[b] Negligible germination.

* Stands with 700 or more seedlings/acre and a quarter-milacre stocking of 25% or more

Only a moderate stand of shortleaf pine was obtained at the other. Second-year germination of shortleaf pine was evident in both tests. One of the better stocking successes was with Virginia pine in Etowah County, Ala.— 2778 seedlings/acre and a 58% stocking.

Two-year comparisons of shortleaf and white pine at two Wise County. Va., sites showed acceptable stands of shortleaf pine only (Table 2). In three other Wise County tests followed for only 1 year, shortleaf was the only species to produce an acceptable stand.

Rate and date

In 8 of 13 rate and date tests, the highest rate generally yielded the best 1-year stands (Table 3). Exceptions were a Morgan County, Tenn. site with a pH of 4.0 that was best at the intermediate 1-lb rate and a Jackson

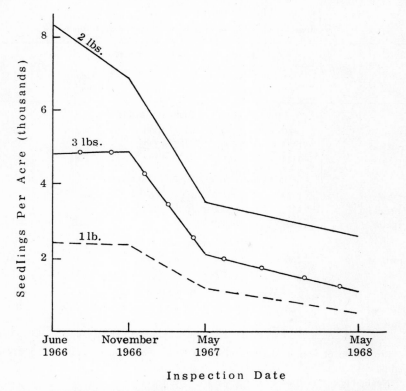

FIGURE 2   Average number of seedlings per acre from seeding loblolly pine at 1, 2, and 3 lb/acre.

TABLE 3

Number of seedlings and stocking percent after 1 year by rate and date of seeding

Location County and State	Acres No.	Soil pH	Test of		Best Treatment			
			Rates No.	Dates No.	Rate lb	Date Mo. & Day	Seedlings No./acre	Stocking[a] %
Loblolly Pine								
Etowah, Ala.	5.4	5.0	3	3	1.5	4/25	333	8
Jackson, Ala.	6.2	5.0	3	3	2.0	4/1	7333	42
Winston, Ala.	5.4	5.0	3	3	1.5	3/16	3000	42
Morgan, Tenn.	1.2	4.0	3	2	1.0	3/4	667	8
Morgan, Tenn.	1.6	3.4	4	1	2.0	3/31	500	6
Dickenson, Va.[b]	1.4	5.0	3	1	1.5	3/28	1333	25
Shortleaf Pine								
Morgan, Tenn.	1.6	3.4	4	1	2.0	3/31	3000	25
Sequatchie, Tenn.	0.9	5.5	3	3	0[c]	—	—	—
Wise, Va.	0.9	4.0	3	1	1.5	3/29	1000	25
White Pine								
Dickenson, Va.	2.7	5.0	3	3	1.5	4/14	333	8
Dickenson, Va.[b]	1.2	5.0	3	1	1.5	3/28	1333	25
Wise, Va.	0.9	4.0	3	1	0[c]	—	—	—
Wise, Va.	1.8	4.5	3	1	0[c]	—	—	—

[a] Proportion of sample quarter-milacres having one or more seedlings 1 year after seeding.

[b] 1967 tests; white pine seed stratified 60 days.

[c] Shortleaf seedlings lost by frost-heaving; white pine had negligible germination.

County, Ala., site where the intermediate rate was 2 lb. Germination was negligible at two sites. Another had excellent germination and 100% stocking, but all seedlings were frost-heaved during the winter. Best seeding dates were between March 15 and April 1, but the best rate and date treatment did not always provide an acceptable stand.

Two-year follow-up studies on four rate and date tests showed stocking increased on two, remained the same on one, and declined on the other. Increases were from second-year germination.

Rate and date effects on 2-year stand development are illustrated in Figs. 2 and 3 for the 7.2-acre Jackson County, Ala. test. The 3-lb rate yielded fewer seedlings than the 2-lb rate (Fig. 2). Unstratified seed sown on March 9 produced fewer seedlings than stratified seed sown on April 1 (Fig. 3). Heaviest mortality occurred during the first winter; some also occurred during the second.

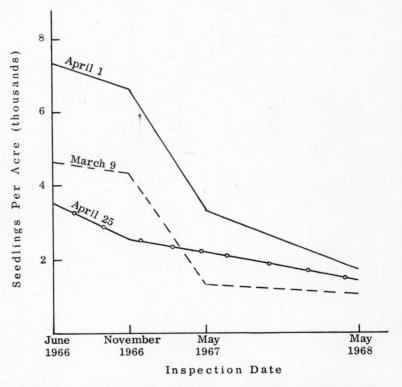

FIGURE 3   Average number of seedlings per acre from seeding loblolly pine at three seeding dates in 1966. March 9 seeding was with unstratified seed.

Supplemental treatments

Germination was negligible in 7 of the 23 tests involving grass seed and fertilizer. In 10 more tests, the supplemental treatment plots were no better than the control plots (Table 4). Ryegrass helped in two, ryegrass and fertilizer (14-14-14) in one, legume in one, and the legume and fertilizer (10-10-10) in one. In another, seeding with fescue or with the legume and fertilizer (10-10-10) was better than the control. This series of tests provided six acceptable stands—three with shortleaf and three with Virginia pine. Of these, the best shortleaf stand was in Wise County, Va., where the legume and fertilizer treatment resulted in 5667 seedlings and a 58% stocking. The best Virginia pine stand was in Etowah County, Ala., where seeding with ryegrass resulted in 2667 seedlings and a 75% stocking. Supplemental treatment promoted herbaceous cover when fertilizer was applied with grass or legume seed.

TABLE 4

Effect of seeding pine in combination with grass and legume seed and fertilizer

Location County and state	Acres No.	Treatments[a]	Pine species	Best treatment		
				Kind	Seedlings No./acre	Stocking[b] %
Etowah, Ala.	3.6	G, GF, C	Loblolly	GF	444	25
			Virginia	G	2667	75
Jackson, Ala.	8.4	G, GF, C	Loblolly	C	222	17
			Virginia	C	4000	42
Campbell, Tenn.	1.2	F, C	Shortleaf	C	1337	17
			Virginia	C	20000	42
Morgan, Tenn.	1.8	G, GF, C	Loblolly	G, C	667	17
			Virginia	G	333	8
Dickenson, Va.	1.8	G, LF, C	White	C	300	8
Wise, Va.	1.8	G, LF, C	Shortleaf	LF	5667	58
			White	G, LF	667	17
Wise, Va.	1.8	GL, GLF, C	Loblolly	GL, C	333	8
			White	C	667	17
Wise, Va.	0.9	G, C	Shortleaf	G, C	2000	25
Wise, Va.	2.0	G, C	Shortleaf	C	2600	40
		L, C	White	L	600	15

[a] Treatments: grass (G), grass and fertilizer (GF), grass and legume (GL), grass, legume, and fertilizer (GLF), legume (L), legume and fertilizer (LF), fertilizer (F), and control (C).

[b] Proportion of sample quarter-milacres having one or more seedlings 1 year after seeding.

Other tests and demonstrations

The 1966 helicopter seeding demonstration in southeastern Tennessee showed fair success with Virginia pine and mixed loblolly and Virginia but unsatisfactory results with shortleaf and lobolly alone. On one 13-acre plot, Virginia pine at 1-lb/acre produced 1500 trees/acre and a 43% stocking after 2 years. On a 14-acre plot, a mixture of 1-lb loblolly and 1/2-lb Virginia produced 1600 trees and a 32% stocking. Seedings on five other plots, mostly on older spoils, gave very poor stands—less than 200 trees/acre.

In the 1967 reseeding test, 60-day stratified white pine resulted in 1-year stands averaging 1000 trees/acre. This was almost seven times the number obtained with a 1966 seeding with 30-day stratified seed. The best stands of loblolly and white pine were from seeding at the 1-1/2 lb rate. Seedlings averaged 1333 trees/acre and stocking 25% for both species. Second-year germination of white pine on the 1966 plots averaged 340 trees/acre.

The 1967 pilot scale seeding of 54 acres in northeastern Alabama produced 1430 seedlings/acre after 1 year. Stocking of milacre sample plots averaged 62%. On 18 of the 54 acres, a mixture of 3/4-lb loblolly and 1/4-lb Virginia yielded 1625 seedlings/acre and 64% stocking. On 13 acres, a mixture of 1-lb loblolly and 0.2-lb Virginia yielded 1000 seedlings/acre and 56% stocking. On 23 acres, loblolly pine at 1-1/4 lb resulted in 1520 seedlings/acre and 65% stocking.

DISCUSSION

Much has been learned from this rather extensive series of tests. According to the results, seeding is most likely to be successful in northeastern Alabama and southeastern Tennessee. Some success is also likely in Virginia, where follow-up trials were conducted. But at a "standard" 1-lb seeding rate, the only acceptable stands from 1966 tests were with shortleaf and Virginia pine in Alabama and with Virginia pine in southeastern Tennessee. Obviously, these species have more seeds per lb than loblolly and white.

A stand of 700 trees/acre and a stocking of 25% after 1 year appears acceptable for revegating coal mine spoils. Based on quarter-milacre sampling, an average stocking of 25% provides at least one tree every 13.2 ft. The acceptable stands in these tests should compare favorably with stocking obtained by hand planting and also meet state reclamation requirements.

Weather conditions (Tennessee Valley Authority, 1966) were not favorable when the 1966 test plots were established. March was the fifth driest in 77 years of record. Although April was slightly above normal, very little rain fell early in the month. Also, June rainfall was less than half normal. To guard against seasons like this, partial (30-day) stratification of seed appears desirable. Some stocking is assured the first year and more later from delayed germination. If seed was fully stratified (45–60 days), all could sprout soon after seeding and be lost from an early season drought.

Rate tests indicate that loblolly and white pine should be seeded at 1-1/2 lb/acre. A 1-lb seeding rate appears adequate for Virginia and short-leaf pine. Why a 3-lb loblolly rate in one test did not yield more trees than a 2-lb rate cannot be explained (Fig. 2). Block and plot layouts were at random and site inspection did not reveal any between-plot differences in spoil conditions.

Loblolly is preferred for planting in Tennessee and Alabama. Erratic performance with this species indicates that sowing in a mixture with Virginia pine will help assure a stand.

Perhaps the biggest obstacle to seeding success is the loss of seedlings during the first winter from frost-heaving. Seeding at the proper rate and timing operations to get full seedling development the first growing season should help reduce losses. Tests being conducted by TVA at one mine are providing information on how fertilizer helps seedlings survive the first winter.

Improvements in methods and techniques are needed to assure more uniform stands. However, our experience does indicate some areas where seeding can successfully serve as an alternative to costly hand planting.

LITERATURE CITED

Hinton, J. H., Jr. 1967. Pine seeding in the Tennessee Valley. *Forest Farmer* 27 (3), 6–8, 22.

Mann, W. F., Jr. 1968. Ten years' experience with direct-seeding in the South. *J. Forest.* 66, 828–833.

Russell, T. E., and A. L. Mignery. 1968. Direct-seeding pine in Tennessee's Highlands. U. S. Dep. Agr., Forest Service Res. Paper SO–31, p. 22.

Tennessee Valley Authority. 1966. Precipitation in Tennessee River basin annual 1966. Tennessee Valley Authority Division of Water Control Planning Report No. 0-243.

DISCUSSION

CONWAY: Do you have any natural seeding on any of these spoil banks?

ZARGER: Very little. We do have some on long narrow contour strips. On the north Alabama site with its area-type stripping and broad expanses, there is none. A lot of the test sites were at least 5 years old, and there was little or no natural vegetation present. The pH of the spoil was still 4.0.

CORNWELL: Did you take any soil temperature measurements?

ZARGER: No.

CORNWELL: Did you have any appreciable seedling losses on any of these sites?

ZARGER: We had seedling losses for several reasons. The major one was from frost heaving in the winter.

BAUER: Was there any difference in germination according to the slope or aspect?

ZARGER: In one southeastern Tennessee area where we had rows of ungraded spoil banks, germination was better on the western and northern slopes than on the drier southern slopes.

BAUER: Do you think the difference was due to frost heaving?

ZARGER: Well, that could be a factor.

DeLONG: You stated that seeding may be an alternative to planting. Have you considered supplemental planting?

ZARGER: No, but that would be a good follow-up step. Some of the seeded areas have gaps in the stand, and it would be desirable to supplement by planting.

AHARRAH: When you mixed these seeds, were they pelleted with fertilizers or treated in any way?

ZARGER: The pine seed was prepared as you would prepare seed for sowing in a nursery. The seed was stratified for 30 days, then treated with a mixture of latex, bird and rodent repellents, and a little bit of Al powder to keep the seeds from sticking together on drying. Then the treated seed was put back in the cold room until ready for use. You can hold this seed for a year, and it will still be viable. Fertilizer and grass seed were applied separately.

RICHTER: Was any seeding ever done in the fall so that you would get natural stratification over the winter and spring germination at the earliest possible date for maximum growth?

ZARGER: No, that was not included in this test.

RICHTER: What was the method of distribution of this seed?

ZARGER: It varied. Some was applied with cyclone seeders; some was mixed with sand and spread over the plot by hand.

Paper IV-9

COMPARISON OF FALL AND SPRING PLANTING ON STRIP-MINE SPOILS IN THE BITUMINOUS REGION OF PENNSYLVANIA

Grant Davis

Project Leader, Northeastern Forest Experiment Station,
Forest Service, U. S. Department of Agriculture,
Berea, Kentucky

To evaluate fall versus spring planting of 10 coniferous tree species and 5 hardwood shrub species, experimental plantings were established over a 2-year period on 7 graded strip-mine spoils. In general, initial tree survival was better with spring planting than with fall planting, especially on the more acid sites. Shrubs survived well with both spring and fall planting on the better sites, but spring planting of shrubs was more successful on the more acid sites. Season of planting had no significant effect on fifth-year height of either trees or shrubs.

INTRODUCTION

The climate of Pennsylvania is such that trees and shrubs are usually planted on soils during two seasons: spring—April, May, and early June; and fall— late September, October, and early November. Most planting on strip-mine spoils is done in spring, but it would be desirable to be able to plant seedlings throughout both planting seasons. This would allow planting contractors to retain their experienced employees and distribute work loads over a longer period. The question arises as to whether both seasons can be utilized on these exposed and often acid sites. A study to determine which species of shrubs and trees perform best during each planting season was proposed by the Research Committee on Coal Mine Spoil Revegetation in Pennsylvania. The study was conducted by Forest Service personnel, and member agencies of the Research Committee provided funds, planting stock, field assistance, and guidance.

THE STUDY

In 1961, the study was initiated to evaluate the relative success of fall versus spring planting of 10 tree species and 5 shrub species on strip-mine spoils. Because spoil material is quite variable, experimental plantings were placed on seven graded strip-mine banks formed by stripping the coal seams most common in the Bituminous Region of Pennsylvania. Four sites were very acid, and three were less acid and were considered more favorable for vegetation. In order to assure that planting was done under a variety of weather conditions, the planting covered two years and included three planting dates each season. This paper summarizes the results of 5-year height growth and first-year survival.

Species tested in the study were restricted to those that previous studies had indicated were most likely to perform well on spoils. Tree species included in the test were: white pine (*Pinus strobus* L.), red pine (*P. resinosa* Ait.), jack pine (*P. banksiana* Lamb.), pitch pine (*P. rigida* Mill.), Scotch pine (*P. sylvestris* L.), Austrian pine (*P. nigra* Arnold), Norway spruce (*Picea abies* [L.] Karst.), white spruce (*P. glauca* [Moench] Voss), European larch (*Larix decidua* Mill.), and Japanese larch (*L. leptolepis* Gord.). Shrub species included were: autumn olive (*Elaeagnus umbellata* Thunb.), Asian crabapple (*Crataegus* L. sp.), Tatarian honeysuckle (*Lonicera tatarica* L.), silky dogwood (*Cornus amomum* Mill.), and multiflora rose (*Rosa multiflora* Thunb.).

Coniferous tree species were selected because previous success in establishing satisfactory stands has been inconsistent, especially when planted in the fall. Fall and spring planting of hardwood tree species has been generally reliable; and so they were not included in this experiment. Also, hardwoods represent only a small percentage of trees planted on spoils in Pennsylvania. Hardwood shrubs were included because little was known about the effect of season of planting on their performance on soils.

DESIGN

A modified random block with a split-split plot design was used. Two replicated blocks of trees and shrubs were placed on the graded portion of each of the seven banks. Species were assigned a plot at random within each block, but the trees were grouped separately from the shrubs. Each plot consisted of 12 rows of 35 trees or shrubs spaced 2 ft apart within the row. Rows were 6 ft apart and ran perpendicular to the highwall and parallel to the slope in order to equalize any effect of slope. The 12 rows were split randomly into 2 years, 2 seasons each year, and 3 planting dates each season. The planting dates were selected to represent early-, middle-, and late-season planting. Planting took place during the weeks beginning 2 October, 23 October, and 13 November 1961 and 9 April, 30 April, and 21 May 1962 and approximately the same dates in fall 1962 and spring 1963. Local contract planters supplied experienced crewmen and mattocks for planting. As far as possible, the same crew planted the same species throughout the experiment.

Spoil samples were collected from each plot, sieved, and the soil-size portion (<2 mm) was analyzed for acidity and texture. The results of the spoil analyses of 30 samples from each bank appear in Table 1. Spoils from the Clarion and Kittanning seams were quite acid, and the pH of the Freeport and Pittsburgh seams was considered favorable.

TABLE 1

Spoil characteristics of experimental planting sites

Coal-seam spoil	Spoil texture			Texture class	Spoil acidity
	Sand	Silt	Clay		
	%	%	%		pH
Clarion at Clearfield	59	21	20	Sandy loam	3.6
Clarion at Clarion	61	20	19	Sandy loam	2.9
Lower Kittanning	61	21	18	Sandy loam	3.3
Middle Kittanning	44	27	29	Sandy clay loam	3.6
Lower Freeport	55	21	24	Sandy clay loam	6.4
Upper Freeport	66	18	16	Sandy loam	5.9
Pittsburgh	56	21	23	Sandy clay loam	7.8

Survival was measured after the first, second, third, and fifth growing seasons. Percent survival data for three planting dates were averaged, transformed (arc-sine), and subjected to analysis of variance. All tests were conducted to the 5% level of significance.

Height was measured after the fifth growing season. The tree plots were then thinned to approximately 6- by 6-ft spacing, and height will be measured again at 10 years.

34*

WEATHER

Both fall 1961 and spring 1962 were extremely poor planting seasons. The dry fall 1961 was followed by a cold winter with little snow cover to protect the seedlings. Late spring and early summer 1962 was one of the driest seasons on record. Precipitation deficits started as early as March in some areas. By the end of August, the following accumulated deficits were compiled in the Bituminous Region of Pennsylvania: Central Mountains, 7.1 inches below normal; Northwest Plateau, 5.9 inches below normal; and Southwest Plateau, 6.1 inches below normal. In spite of the generally dry conditions, seedlings were planted in moist spoil, although it was necessary to postpone planting for a few days on several occasions. Rainfall during the second year also was below normal, but not quite as critical as the first year.

RESULTS

First-year survival was used to compare the relative success of fall vs. spring planting. After the first growing season, all trees are subject to the same weather stress regardless of time of planting; and subsequent survival data may reflect the influence of site and competition more than season of planting. Survival data are summarized in Table 2. More detailed data on survival of individual species appear in Tables 3 and 4. Percentages in the tables were computed directly from the untransformed data.

Overall survival was lower than was expected because of unfavorable weather during and after establishment of the study. Shrubs survived better than trees, especially on the three better sites where shrubs averaged over 70% survival.

Spring planting of trees was better in terms of survival than fall planting over all sites and both years. Differences between spring and fall plantings were significant within each site and year except for the second-year planting on the Upper Freeport spoil. The advantage of spring planting was greater on the more acid sites. Fall survival was 30% of spring survival on the two spoils where average pH was below 3.5; 65% of spring survival on the two spoils where pH averaged 3.6; and 73% of the spring survival in the three spoils above pH 6.

Season of planting had a significantly different effect depending on species. It had no detectable effect on the larches. Spring planting was some-

TABLE 2

Average first-year survival of fall- and spring-planted trees and shrubs (in percent)

Coal seam	Test year[a]	Trees			Shrubs		
		Average survival		Average	Average survival		Average
		Fall	Spring		Fall	Spring	
Clarion	I	20	39	30	44	55	50
at Clearfield	II	43	59	51	51	62	57
	Average	32	49	40	48	58	53
Clarion at Clarion	I	1	12	7	>1	1	1
	II	3	11	7	1	3	2
	Average	2	11	7	>1	2	1
Lower Kittanning	I	14	50	32	13	30	22
	II	30	46	38	21	38	30
	Average	22	48	35	17	34	26
Middle Kittanning	I	32	52	42	13	21	17
	II	36	54	45	7	14	10
	Average	34	53	43	10	17	14
Lower Freeport	I	39	52	45	70	80	75
	II	61	73	67	73	88	80
	Average	50	62	56	71	84	77
Upper Freeport	I	31	62	47	75	75	75
	II	51	52	51	70	65	68
	Average	41	57	48	72	70	71
Pittsburgh	I	44	66	55	86	79	83
	II	22	35	29	65	70	68
	Average	33	51	42	76	75	76
Totals	I	26	48	37	43	49	46
	II	35	47	41	41	49	45
	Average	30	47	39	42	49	45

[a] Test I planted fall 1961 and spring 1962; Test II planted fall 1962 and spring 1963.

TABLE 3

First-year survival of fall- and spring-planted trees on seven spoils (in percent)

Coal-seam spoil	Test year[a]	White pine		Red pine		Jack pine		Pitch pine		Scotch pine		Austrian pine		Norway spruce		White spruce		European larch		Japanese larch	
		F	S	F	S	F	S	F	S	F	S	F	S	F	S	F	S	F	S	F	S
Clarion at Clearfield	I	25	31	26	48	7	30	16	54	9	31	2	50	46	49	30	42	32	22	10	33
	II	41	64	60	78	54	50	36	73	37	76	8	33	63	66	43	36	45	64	46	52
	Average	33	48	43	63	30	40	26	63	23	53	5	41	55	58	37	39	38	42	28	42
Clarion at Clarion	I	2	3	1	22	2	9	1	17	4	17	>1	33	0	10	2	9	0	0	0	3
	II	3	13	2	11	9	19	1	22	3	22	>1	12	1	3	5	5	>1	0	1	0
	Average	3	8	1	17	5	14	1	19	4	20	>1	22	>1	6	3	7	>1	0	>1	1
Lower Kittaning	I	32	61	5	41	8	57	19	62	9	57	0	47	14	76	5	34	10	25	23	44
	II	43	51	44	80	47	67	13	36	15	60	4	28	34	35	29	20	31	32	37	55
	Average	37	56	25	60	28	62	16	49	12	58	2	37	24	56	17	27	20	29	30	50
Middle Kittaning	I	43	62	64	70	29	56	22	64	10	31	3	68	22	42	39	80	33	14	50	37
	II	71	71	43	74	46	81	15	47	22	55	15	36	20	34	49	45	22	39	61	60
	Average	57	66	53	72	38	68	18	56	16	43	9	52	21	38	44	62	28	27	55	48
Lower Freeport	I	35	35	72	72	28	50	15	42	14	41	7	53	71	89	43	67	58	38	43	32
	II	71	55	62	74	68	77	46	86	22	78	27	55	70	61	84	88	79	77	81	76
	Average	53	45	67	73	48	63	30	64	18	60	17	54	70	75	64	78	69	58	62	54

TABLE 3 (*cont.*)

Upper Freeport	I	32	75	45	72	26	49	6	52	29	72	10	75	63	85	28	68	49	26	27	44
	II	61	50	67	61	70	69	38	60	27	63	24	34	60	51	45	44	54	46	63	43
	Average	47	63	56	66	48	59	22	56	28	67	17	55	61	68	36	56	52	36	45	43
Pittsburgh	I	55	78	69	80	37	61	7	78	65	82	10	64	49	82	32	73	83	35	32	30
	II	19	41	48	34	30	39	19	28	23	44	10	32	13	25	16	31	41	60	5	21
	Average	37	59	59	57	33	50	13	53	44	63	10	48	31	53	24	52	62	47	18	25
Average all seams		38	49	43	58	33	51	18	51	20	52	9	44	37	50	32	46	38	34	34	38

[a] Test I planted fall 1961 and spring 1962; Test II planted fall 1962 and spring 1963.

what better than fall planting for the spruces and red and white pine. Spring planting was much better for jack, Scotch, pitch, and, especially, Austrian pine (Table 3).

Spring-planted shrubs survived better on the average than those planted in the fall. However, there was no significant difference between fall and

TABLE 4

First-year survival of fall- and spring-planted shrubs on seven spoils (in percent)

Coal-seam spoil	Test year[a]	Autumn olive		Asian crabapple		Tatarian honey-suckle		Silky dogwood		Multi-flora rose	
		F	S	F	S	F	S	F	S	F	S
Clarion at Clearfield	I	43	51	58	57	41	37	32	63	48	67
	II	51	62	60	72	53	50	38	48	56	77
	Average	47	57	59	65	47	43	35	55	52	72
Clarion at Clarion	I	0	0	1	6	0	0	0	0	0	0
	II	0	0	2	12	0	0	0	>1	2	1
	Average	0	0	2	9	0	0	0	>1	1	>1
Lower Kittanning	I	9	24	19	24	4	11	16	57	18	35
	II	16	35	35	51	11	34	26	52	14	21
	Average	13	29	27	37	7	23	21	54	16	28
Middle Kittanning	I	24	41	4	15	1	7	26	28	7	16
	II	10	30	2	4	4	12	15	20	3	3
	Average	17	36	3	10	3	9	20	24	5	10
Lower Freeport	I	67	92	72	88	70	43	74	98	67	78
	II	65	94	85	95	61	69	89	97	65	82
	Average	66	93	79	92	66	56	82	97	66	80
Upper Freeport	I	66	74	86	87	59	54	73	83	92	79
	II	36	73	90	82	58	45	77	67	88	60
	Average	51	73	88	85	58	50	75	75	90	69
Pittsburgh	I	93	80	88	92	67	48	89	91	96	82
	II	44	74	80	95	72	60	42	43	90	78
	Average	68	77	84	94	69	54	65	67	93	80
Average all seams		37	52	49	56	36	33	43	53	46	48

[a] Test I planted fall 1961 and spring 1962; Test II planted fall 1962 and spring 1963.

spring planting of shrubs on the three sites with pH above 6, as contrasted with the better survival of spring-planted trees. The average fall survival was only 52% of spring survival on the four acid sites.

Season of planting had no detectable effect on survival of Tatarian honeysuckle and multiflora rose; but spring planting was somewhat better for autumn olive, Asian crabapple, and silky dogwood (Table 4). On the three better sites, all shrub species had at least 50% survival for both seasons.

The spoil had a significant effect on overall survival as well as on the results of season of planting. Very few trees and shrubs survived on the most acid site. Initial survival on the other three acid spoils was quite good considering the unfavorable weather and sites, but additional trees and shrubs died throughout the second and third growing seasons.

The second-year planting was a little more successful than the first, especially for tree survival, except on the Pittsburgh spoil where severe competition from heavy herbaceous cover substantially reduced tree survival. After 5 years in this site, only red, Scotch, and Austrian pines had better than 25% survival. Survival of the second-year planting of silky dogwood and autumn olive was reduced some on the Pittsburgh spoil, but the other shrub species showed little effect of herbaceous competition.

Although the study was not specifically designed to determine the effects of planting dates, survival data of the three dates within each season over both years were subjected to Chi-square tests. No significant differences could be detected among planting dates for any species of trees or shrubs. Amount and pattern of rainfall after planting apparently have more effect on survival than early-, middle-, or late-season planting.

Fifth-year height of surviving trees and shrubs was not significantly affected by season of planting (Tables 5 and 6). Chapman (1944) reported that spring-planted shortleaf pines not only survived better, but were 11.0 ft tall compared to 8.6 ft for fall-planted trees after 7 years. Reduced height growth associated with poor survival after fall planting is not an uncommon phenomenon and may be attributed to over-winter damage to roots from frost heaving. Very little frost heaving of fall-planted seedlings was noted on the 7 spoils in this study, which may account for the small differences in height growth.

Fruiting of shrubs was observed during the study. Healthy autumn olive and multiflora rose produced heavy crops during the second growing season, honeysuckle during the third, and silky dogwood during the fourth. A few Asian crabapples produced fruit during the sixth year. No differences in fruiting were detected between fall- and spring-planted shrubs.

TABLE 5

Average five-year heights of fall- and spring-planted trees on spoils
(in ft)

Coal-seam spoil[a]	Test year[b]	White pine		Red pine		Jack pine		Pitch pine		Scotch pine		Austrian pine		Norway spruce		White spruce		European larch		Japanese larch	
		F	S	F	S	F	S	F	S	F	S	F	S	F	S	F	S	F	S	F	S
Lower Kittanning	I	1.4	1.0	1.0	1.1	3.2	2.8	2.8	2.0	2.4	2.2	—[c]	0.8	0.6	0.6	0.6	0.8	2.7	2.8	4.2	3.9
	II	1.0	1.2	1.4	1.7	2.7	3.2	3.0	2.2	2.7	2.8	1.8	1.3	0.9	1.0	1.0	0.6	2.6	3.1	4.6	5.2
	Average	1.2	1.1	1.2	1.4	3.0	3.0	2.9	2.1	2.6	3.0	1.8	1.0	0.8	0.8	0.8	0.7	2.6	3.4	4.4	4.0
Middle Kittanning	I	1.4	1.3	2.1	2.1	3.6	3.0	3.2	2.4	4.3	3.8	1.6	2.0	0.5	0.4	1.1	1.1	2.2	1.5	3.9	3.6
	II	1.6	1.4	2.4	2.0	3.0	2.8	3.4	3.0	4.4	2.6	2.6	1.6	0.9	0.9	1.1	0.9	1.6	2.0	3.8	3.9
	Average	1.5	1.4	2.2	2.0	3.3	2.9	3.3	2.7	4.4	3.2	2.1	1.8	0.7	0.6	1.1	1.0	1.9	1.8	3.8	r3.8
Lower Freeport	I	1.5	1.4	1.6	1.4	3.4	2.9	2.8	2.7	3.0	2.9	1.4	1.6	1.1	1.1	1.6	1.4	2.6	2.4	2.7	2.5
	II	1.4	1.4	1.4	1.2	3.6	2.6	1.6	1.8	2.4	2.4	1.6	1.2	1.0	1.0	1.4	1.4	1.8	2.1	3.0	3.0
	Average	1.4	1.4	1.5	1.3	3.5	2.8	2.2	2.2	2.7	2.6	1.5	1.4	1.0	1.0	1.5	1.4	2.2	2.2	2.8	2.8
Upper Freeport	I	1.5	1.4	2.4	1.8	3.6	3.0	3.0	2.8	3.0	2.9	1.6	1.8	1.2	1.2	1.2	1.0	2.0	2.0	3.1	2.8
	II	0.8	1.0	2.0	1.6	2.2	3.6	2.0	2.4	3.3	2.8	1.6	1.4	1.0	1.0	1.1	1.1	1.8	1.6	2.2	2.2
	Average	1.2	1.2	2.2	1.7	2.9	3.3	2.5	2.6	3.2	2.8	1.6	1.6	1.1	1.1	1.2	1.0	1.9	1.8	2.6	2.5

TABLE 5 (cont.)

Pittsburgh																				
I	1.6	0.8	1.5	1.2	1.8	2.2	1.3	1.5	2.4	2.2	1.4	1.2	0.8	1.0	1.1	1.0	1.5	1.6	1.6	3.4
II	1.0	1.0	0.9	1.2	1.4	1.6	1.4	1.6	2.3	1.8	1.0	1.0	0.6	—	1.2	1.4	1.3	1.2	—	4.0
Average	1.3	0.9	1.2	1.2	1.6	1.9	1.4	1.6	2.4	2.0	1.2	1.1	0.7	1.0	1.2	1.2	1.4	1.4	1.6	3.7
Average all seams	1.3	1.2	1.7	1.5	2.9	2.8	2.5	2.2	3.0	2.7	1.6	1.4	0.9	0.9	1.1	1.1	2.0	2.0	3.0	3.5

[a] There are no height data available for the Clarion at Clearfield seam. Planting has been destroyed by re-stripping. Data from Clarion at Clarion was omitted because of insufficient survival.

[b] Test I planted fall 1961 and spring 1962; Test II planted fall 1962 and spring 1963.

[c] Indicates zero survival, thus no height measurements.

TABLE 6

Average five-year heights of fall- and spring-planted shrubs on spoils (in ft)

Coal-seam spoil[a]	Test year[b]	Autumn olive		Asian crabapple		Tatarian honey-suckle		Silky dogwood		Multi-flora rose	
		F	S	F	S	F	S	F	S	F	S
Lower	I	7.0	5.2	2.0	2.1	2.0	1.6	3.0	2.2	2.0	1.2
Kittanning	II	3.7	4.3	1.8	1.2	2.0	2.3	1.8	1.8	1.9	1.5
	Average	5.4	4.8	1.9	1.6	2.0	2.0	2.4	2.0	2.0	1.4
Middle	I	3.0	3.4	2.6	2.6	1.0	2.6	2.5	3.0	3.0	2.7
Kittanning	II	3.2	4.2	2.1	1.4	1.4	2.2	2.2	1.8	2.8	3.0
	Average	3.1	3.8	2.4	2.0	1.2	2.4	2.4	2.4	2.9	2.8
Lower	I	7.1	5.5	1.9	1.9	1.5	1.8	2.2	2.0	3.0	2.3
Freeport	II	5.1	5.6	1.6	1.6	1.6	1.6	1.6	1.6	2.3	2.0
	Average	6.1	5.6	1.8	1.8	1.6	1.7	1.9	1.8	2.6	2.2
Upper	I	7.6	7.3	3.6	3.2	2.7	2.6	2.6	2.4	3.9	3.8
Freeport	II	7.2	6.8	2.7	2.5	2.4	1.8	2.0	2.1	3.0	2.5
	Average	7.4	7.0	3.2	2.8	2.6	2.2	2.3	2.2	3.4	3.2
Pittsburgh	I	4.4	4.0	2.2	2.3	2.8	2.6	1.1	1.4	N[c]	N
	II	2.4	2.7	1.8	2.0	2.0	2.0	1.4	1.6	N	N
	Average	3.4	3.4	2.0	2.2	2.4	2.3	1.2	1.5	N	N
Average all seams		5.1	4.9	2.2	2.1	1.9	2.1	2.0	2.0	2.7	2.4

[a] No data collected for the Clarion at Clearfield seam. Data from Clarion at Clarion were omitted because of insufficient survival.

[b] Test I planted fall 1961 and spring 1962; Test II planted fall 1962 and spring 1963.

[c] N indicates heights not measured on this planting.

RECOMMENDATIONS

The results of this study indicate that spring planting is better than fall planting, especially on acid spoils. Fall planting of trees and shrubs is generally unsatisfactory on highly acid spoils. However, on favorable spoils, some fall-planted conifers—such as the larches, spruces, red and white pines—and some hardwood trees and shrubs may survive adequately.

On exceptionally good sites, competition to trees and some shrubs from herbaceous vegetation may be severe. If tree cover is desired on such sites, seedlings should be established as soon as possible after mining; and the slower growing conifers should be avoided.

The good performance of shrubs indicates that their wider use is warranted, especially on good sites where wildlife food and cover are desired. Autumn olive produced the best cover and yielded heavy crops of berries, but the other four shrub species also grew well enough to be considered for multiple-use plantings.

LITERATURE CITED

Chapman, A. G. 1944. Forest planting on strip-mined coal lands with special reference to Ohio. U. S. Dep. Agr., Forest Service, Central States Forest Exp. Sta. Tech. Paper 104. 25 p.

DISCUSSION

SHEETS: Have you done any work with grasses and legumes?

VOGEL: We made some comparisons of fall vs. spring seeding in 1963 and 64. Those early seedings, in general, were failures which we learned later were due more to infertility of spoil than time of seeding.

DAVIS: Many operators are trying to regrade all the operations close behind the actual removal of coal. It works much better to seed the spoils immediately after grading, before they get several rains on them and get crusted over. We would like to determine what seed mixtures can be seeded throughout the spring, summer, and fall.

RUFFNER: Seedling survival on spoils of low pH's seemed high. Did this continue throughout the growing season or did mortality set in?

DAVIS: You remember that this test was followed by several dry years. Except for one of the acid areas where almost everything died by the end of 5 years, survival stayed just about the same. The one exception was the Pittsburgh seam which has such heavy vegetation, and anything that didn't get growing fast in the beginning passed out of the picture due to competition. The same thing was true on two of the other sites where the spruces suffered from competition.

PRETO: Was the planting and the seed source the same for spring and fall?

DAVIS: The trees and shrubs were from the same seed sources both years and grown in the same nursery.

MEDVICK: A friend of mine in Indiana has actually planted trees in every month of the year. Although it was not a research study, he points out that his best success for fall work was where there was very little clay. Would you comment on that?

DAVIS: It may be possible to plant some species all through the summer, but you run into supply problems; the nurseries can keep the material only so long because of limited cold storage space. On the heavier spoils frost heaving may be an important factor in fall plantings. We didn't get any damage from frost heaving, probably because our Pennsylvania spoils are quite porous.

BENGTSON: Were your seedlings that were planted in the spring lifted in the fall and stored over winter, or were they lifted in the spring just prior to planting?

DAVIS: They were lifted in the spring and those that were planted in the fall were lifted in the fall. In the spring they were all lifted at the same time and stored to be planted on the three dates.

KRAUSE: Did you experience any difficulty with hardening of the plants before fall planting; and second, did you experience any heating in the bundles?

DAVIS: We didn't experience much trouble with this in the fall planting because we used mostly conifers which had already finished growing. We did have trouble with larch heating in the spring, and we lost the late planting in the first year because of heating. The next year the nursery had a cold storage building, so we didn't have that problem. However, you might have difficulty using alder for fall planting. Pennsylvania nurseries report that sometimes alders grow too late into the fall for fall lifting.

DARMER: Do you mean that testing the plants over a 2-year-period is good enough to characterized the growing of the plants?

DAVIS: No, I don't think it is long enough, but we had to set some sort of limit on this study. We hoped to get good weather conditions through at least one of the years or at least get about the same relative conditions in the fall and spring planting. As it turned out, we had four poor seasons, but the relative success should be fairly indicative.

RENEWALS: 691-4574

DATE DUE

DEC 3			

GAYLORD

PRINTED IN U.S.A